*"Annual income twenty pounds.
Annual expenditure nineteen, nineteen and six,
result happiness. Annual expenditure twenty
pounds nought and six, result misery."*

Mr. Micawber
(David Copperfield by Charles Dickens)

Launch Day
August 4th 2003
Dave Thomas

IT'S BURNLEY NOT BARCELONA

The Search for Champagne with Beer Money

DAVE THOMAS

With a Foreword by Tony Livesey

The Parrs Wood Press
MANCHESTER

First Published 2003

THE PARRS WOOD PRESS
St Wilfrid's Enterprise Centre
Royce Road, Manchester, M15 5BJ
www.parrswoodpress.com

ISBN: 1 903158 42 7

Printed and bound by Biddles Ltd of Guildford

CONTENTS

ACKNOWLEDGEMENTS AND GRATEFUL THANKS TO:

Everybody at Burnley FC who has been so helpful:
Andrew Watson, Edoardo Abis, Nick Veevers, Dean Williams,
Anthony Fairclough, Alison Loftus, Chris Gibson and Dean West.

Stan Ternent and Tony Livesey, whose book Stan The Man
solved the problem of what to call this one.

Everybody whose words I have used throughout the book.

Tony Scholes. For permission to use material from Claretsmad.com.

London Clarets, and in particular Firmo, for permission
to use their website material.

Martin Barnes for permission to use When The Ball Moves material.

The Official Burnley Website, Phil Bird and
Burnley FC Official Programme.

Watford Website. Blind, Stupid and Desperate.

Grimsby Website. Electronicfishcake.

The Burnley Express and The Lancashire Evening Telegraph.

Friend and neighbour Bradford John Barker for the loan of his books, his
humour and his insights into the complicated world
that is Bradford City FC.

All photographs were taken by Phill Heywood
and kindly supplied by BFC.

FOREWORD

ON LAZY DAYS when I lie back and think of Burnley, my mind plays tricks. Were we humiliated at Wigan - 'you're the *** of Lancashire!' in 1980 or 81? Which flag post did Phil Cavener kick into the Cricket Field Stand when he tried to take a corner for us live on Granada TV? Did we really sign Joe Gallagher?

The problem for most Longsiders like me, born in the sixties, is that we have seen too much bad football at Turf Moor to be able to make much sense of it all. Like shell-shocked veterans of the First World War, we have developed glassy-eyed stares and short-term memories in a desperate bid to forget. As a result, my recollection of life with BFC consists of a fog of images lost in time and space.

Burnley scarves hanging above the Longside… boards on the Cricket Field Stand announcing half time scores around the country… trying to identify Bob Lord by his pork pie hat during a game… 'Bring on the Champions'… the scoreboard that lasted a full season before the bulbs went… open air toilets… pints in wobbly glasses… an unsegregated Longside… the rugby kit with a giant 'V' on the front… 4-1 at Spurs… Bob Lord out… Teasdale out… Gazza and Ian Wright Wright Wright in claret and blue… Taffy taking off… John Bond dressed as a steward… last minute win at York to finally escape the Fourth Division… scoring seven against East Fife or was I on drugs?… dogs wearing flat caps… Glen Little's nose on a giant screen… George Oghani and an ironing board… it goes on, and on, and on…

Thankfully there are people like Dave Thomas among us. I'm supposed to be a professional journalist but when Burnley score I'm so busy laughing at the away fans that I am lucky to be able to remember which end we were facing. Dave, however, is a chronicler. No detail however small escapes his eye. From the number of litterbins in Stoke to the flavour of the Guest Pie served at Huddersfield, Dave collects details like Ulrika collects men. And here is the result.

There is too little about Burnley for this book to be anything other than required reading. It is not just an account of last season. Plenty of stories about players, matches and fans from the past find their way onto the pages of It's Burnley Not Barcelona. The book I wrote with Stan Ternent which was published at Christmas, Stan The Man, was described by the Sunday Times as 'Wonderful'. I hope Dave's work receives similar recognition. It is fitting that he chose last season to begin his encyclopaedic work. We have in Stan Ternent one of Burnley's greatest ever managers. We are finally enjoying some of the best seasons at Turf Moor for almost 30 years. Let's pray that Dave has charted the beginning of something big…

Tony Livesey, Editor, Daily Sport.
May 16th, 2003.

INTRODUCTION

NORWICH AIRPORT. Supporters have funded the plane journey. It's early evening in the departure lounge. Burnley have lost again 2-0. Wins these days are few and far between. Player's faces look subdued, drawn and worn out in their club grey suits. Some of them stand around talking quietly. Others sit, outstretched legs bruised and scarred, ankles swollen and red, lost in their own private world. No one likes to lose, especially in a game where they have given everything. They've run, chased, tackled, equalled Norwich in every department except the one that matters, putting the ball in the net and scoring; 12 attempts at goal and just 3 on target tells its own story. They've had their chances and missed them. Norwich had theirs and didn't. It's been a routine home win in a game that could have gone either way but which sod's law decrees inevitably and predictably goes to the home team. Burnley have given everything but today, in the great universal scheme of things, they've been the team chosen to lose and Norwich get the points.

They look drained and pale. It's been a hot day. Sitting close to the pitch we have seen the sweat pour off them, the stained shirts, felt the bone-jarring fierceness of a 50:50 challenge, seen the pain when a foot goes in high, seen the grimaces when a ball hits them hard and seen the agony when an elbow goes in the face. We've seen Robbie Blake whacked so hard he's sent spinning head over heels and lands yards away. All of them have had seven bells knocked out of them. Brisser is lucky not to have had his leg broken by a late tackle unspotted by the referee. As it is he has recovered, though he won't play in the next game. Deano sits quietly. Lost in his own thoughts, with one foot in a slipper. Blisters. He has run half a marathon. Steve Davis stares blankly ahead with a kind of faraway look in his eyes. What's he thinking? Losing hurts and losing when you've got a plane full of supporters is the last thing you want. Stan is there with the coaching staff but says little. His face too is impassive, resigned, and almost weary. What's he thinking? Missed chances maybe, the run of the ball, endless injuries, selection problems, who to retain, who to release? No luck at all today. No referee's decisions going Burnley's way, no little stroke of luck that makes all the difference between winning and losing, the luck that turns a game. Just another defeat and another injury to cap the day: Who'd be a manager?

The run of results since early March has seen their world turned upside down. Knocked out of the cup ignominiously by Watford, some of them are maybe thinking of what might have been. Tomorrow is semi-final day against Southampton. Newspapers are full of it. The headlines could have read Burnley not Watford. For some of them these are uncertain, anxious, nervous times when a new contract may or not be offered. They have families, mortgages, and bills to pay. It is a fragile, fleeting life. Today some of them will be wondering what tomorrow will bring. None of them know, or do they? Maybe some of them have had the hint already. For those who are released the world will suddenly be full of footballers seeking new clubs. Only a few will succeed and if you're 34 or 35 what chance have you got? For some, it's the end of the line.

If a football season is a journey then this last part has been one long, rough ride. Since the win at Stoke in early March there has been just one more against Preston a few days ago to lighten the gloom and clinch another season in Division 1. For that we are grateful. That is success. Survival is all.

The supporters on the plane have no complaints. They've played well today and given everything but saying 'hard luck' or 'well done' to someone who has run himself into the ground to the point of exhaustion for no reward is inadequate. They deserved something today but as ever the gods of football gave us a referee called, of all things, Conn. Yet again the gods have been unkind as they so often are to Burnley. A win would have been the icing on the cake today and I don't doubt for one minute that every player is disappointed that we can't all of us go back smiling and celebrating.

I'm looking at these tired faces around me, some of them beginning to thaw out a little, to cheer up, to smile and chat and I'm wondering where's all the glamour in this then? There are no Beckhams or Vieras here. This is Division 1 and it's hard and relentless and bruising and painful. Where's the glamour in the punishment of pre-season training, or training in the cold, the rain, fog, sleet and mud? Where's the glamour in an injury and the solitary road back to fitness? Where's the glamour in a game when it's freezing at Grimsby, or pouring down at Rotherham?

Football: The Beautiful Game. But where's the beautiful game when you're stretchered off at Norwich wondering if your leg is broken, your career ended? Where's the beauty being sent off at Gillingham, being stung by hailstones at Stoke? Where's the glamour being abused by supporters, unable to show your face in the town after you've lost at home 6-2 or 7-4? And where's the glitter when the end of a career is in sight and the fag end of the season approaching?

I'm looking into these player's eyes trying to see what's behind. Maybe they're thinking that next it's the long six or seven hour haul down to Portsmouth by coach and then back the same night until they arrive back in Burnley in the early hours feeling like zombies. Portsmouth are going up. For Burnley the season is over. We're expected to be the patsies, the fall guys, and the sacrificial lambs on the altar of Pompey success. They are the re-arranged fixture list's gift to Portsmouth, and a packed baying stadium. They don't want to lose but they probably will. The script is written. They have to turn up.

The bottom line is, I've come to realise, is that there is very little glamour when at the season's end you're just a middle table team from a small, deprived town in Lancashire. But, at least we have another season in Division 1 and some kind of financial stability. That's no mean achievement. Let's not forget that.

The other bottom line is simply this. We are Burnley, not Barcelona. Let's not forget that either.

David Thomas. April 12th, 2003.

AUGUST

THE TWO CLARETS

As at their work two Clarets sat,
Beguiling time with friendly chat,
They touched upon the price of meat,
So high, a Claret scarce could eat.

"What with my brats and sickly wife,"
Quoth Dick, "I'm almost tired of life
So hard my work, so poor my fare,
'Tis more than mortal man can bear.

How glorious is the Premiership!
His house so fine! His wealth so great!
Heaven is unjust, you must agree,
Why all to him? Why none to me?"

(Hannah Moore 1796)

****

ONCE UPON A TIME there was no football in July and Burnley FC were a great power in the land. Then one year, long before flat back fours, diamond shapes and Christmas tree formations were ever even heard of, they won the championship and their reward was to be sent to New York to stay in a hotel so bad they had to move out, and to play Glenavon and Kilmarnock. The latter immediately kicked them all over the park. Not for nothing is their nickname the Killies.

In that distant era there were steam trains and the world, according to nostalgia, was a sane sensible place where the rich man stood in his castle and the poor man at his gate. Children said please and thank you and teachers were respected. Just thinking about it almost makes you want to sigh. There were no such things as social workers. It always snowed at Christmas. Crowds of over 50,000 crammed into Turf Moor in cloth caps and good humour and other teams feared a visit to this Northern outpost which Southern teams, and much later Ian Wright Wright Wright, thought was way beyond the outer regions of civilization.

In that far-off time you didn't wear long trousers till you were fourteen, and lads like me used to kick a ball against the backyard wall all day long. There was a clear divide between one season and the next whereas today, football never ends. There's the European Championship and the World Cup. There's the InterToto Cup, friendlies, pre-season tournaments, transfer sagas and endless media speculation about this and that and who's going where.

Even Burnley go to an international tournament. But while Leeds go to China and Australia and Man Utd go to Scandinavia, the Clarets take the short hop and go to the Isle of Man.

This season, 2002/2003, the Club has decided that every first team player is available for sale because of financial problems that now exist. Meanwhile back in the Isle of Man we drew with Wrexham and lost to Luton.

The club finances are approximately £4.5million short over the next two seasons thanks to ITV Digital and its collapse. So Burnley, along with all other league clubs lulled by promises of riches and worthless contracts with ITV, now find themselves with players they can't afford. Dean West, last season's player of the year, is on a month-to-month contract. There are others on high salaries to pay. Marlon Broomes was with the club in the Isles De Manne. Stan it is said would like to have signed him but he was beyond our now stretched resources.

It is the same too with goalkeeper Marlon Beresford. In a loan spell with the club last season he was outstanding but the loan spell was cut short. Nikos Michopoulos returned in goal. It is quite possible that Beresford's return to Middlesbrough, when called back by Steve McClaren, cost us a play-off place in 2002 at the very least. Beresford too was in the Isle of Man with the Clarets, guesting whilst out of contract.

You support a club through thick and thin, in times of trouble, through trial and tribulation, and there have been plenty over the years, as any supporter will testify. Oh to be a follower of a team that wins and wins and wins. But no, Burnley is our team for better or for worse. We all develop our allegiance in different ways. I inherited mine from my father, who also left me a pair of pyjamas and a watch that didn't work when he cast off his mortal shackles many years ago sitting in an armchair by the gas fire reading a travel brochure, a fitting end for a man who loved his holidays in Portugal or Knott End. We grumble and we groan, we criticise and we complain, but underlying all of this is endless loyalty and devotion, passed down from father to son, just like season tickets at Liverpool.

In these pages, you won't be faced with team sheets, times of goals, masses of statistics, or endless lengthy full reports of games. It's not for me on these pages to continually question team selections, criticise or constantly complain. This is no journalistic investigative hatchet job pulling skeletons out of cupboards or lifting the lid on simmering tensions. This is just a record of the feelings and emotions of supporters, the ups and downs, the highs and lows, and the triumphs and humiliations during one particular season. As I start to write I have no idea what they will be but they'll surely appear round every corner.

Wherever you are or whatever you are doing there is that tiny corner of the mind that dwells on the last result and what the next one might be. The football fan is the eternal optimist one minute and the next feels like a doormat. We exist on humour, of the gallows variety 'tis true. But humour keeps us going, saves our sanity and acts as a cushion against the next calamity.

The last two decades have been rollercoaster years at Burnley but the 2001/2002 season encapsulated all the emotions and ups and downs you could ever experience over 20 years in just one season. We had it all. And at the end of the day it ended in bitter heartache when the play-offs were missed by just one goal. Up until Christmas we seemed destined for the Premiership. The football was delightful and here was a team scoring goals for fun with confidence sky high. After Christmas, unfathomably, it was relegation form, but the on-loan

David Johnson and an odd win here and there kept us up with the leaders until the very last day.

Troughs and humiliations are all part of a Burnley supporter's lot. You might argue that they are part of any football supporter's lot but any Burnley fan will insist that Burnley have had more than their fair share over the years. Not for us a sugar daddy who can pump endless millions into the club and buy success. Any success here is fought for and hard won. It is therefore cherished all the more. We have inched our way back from the edge of the abyss of non-league football and probable oblivion in 1987. For that, the football world - well, most of it - has a soft spot for us and the pundits and football writers applaud our efforts.

"We gathered like predatory undertakers and professional mourners lured by the death throes of a stricken giant," wrote Ian Wooldridge all those years ago. "Reporters who'd forgotten where Burnley was spilled out over the press seats, which had gathered the dust of disinterest. Some had their obituaries already written."

I still have this old newspaper cutting of which these few words are just the beginning and regard it as one of the best pieces of football writing I have ever read.

For years it's always been three steps forward and two steps back yet here we are surviving and without the ITV fiasco might even have been prospering.

Nobody at the beginning of season 2000/2001 could have foretold that the play-offs for the Premiership would have been so tantalisingly close. Promotion the previous season from Division Two was amazing enough, the signing of Ian Wright a masterstroke, and Stan Ternent demonstrated his canny knowledge of the game, finding bargains, wheeling, dealing and getting free transfer players. All of that has continued and on a shoestring we have reached where we are now.

Nobody could have foretold that during season 2001/2002, we would be top and seven points clear at one stage, and in the play-off places for such a lengthy spell, in fact for most of the season. Nobody could have foretold that Burnley would sign the legendary Gazza near the season's end but that's what we did and the town went wild - not that it ultimately did much good. Poor Gazza too often seemed lost and bewildered by all that went on around him. Two exquisite free kicks miraculously kept out by Hedman of Coventry on the last day and that was about it. If one of those free kicks against Coventry had gone in we'd be saying it was the best money the club ever spent. Sadly it was not to be.

Football is emotive. Can a supporter be objective? Some players have a couple of poor games, miss a couple of chances, misplace a couple of passes and become immediate targets for the boo boys; others can have poor games yet still remain a crowd favourite. The chemistry of this is unfathomable but at the end of the day nobody chooses deliberately to play badly. Garry Nelson, in his excellent book 'Left Foot Forward', says that not everybody can be a Shearer or a Sosa and it's understanding that's needed, not derision.

Of course it all looks so easy from where we are in the safe, dry James Hargreaves Stand clutching a Bovril and eating pie and peas. All of us imagine we can manage a football team better than any manager, in just the same way we think we know better than the doctor what's wrong with us, or why a teacher isn't doing their job. All of us want to spend more money to see the team strengthened and think we can afford a million every now and then. All of us in our dreams would wish to be out there on that field if we had the talent, but that talent is granted to just a chosen few. For ninety minutes we are supporters but we are not supporters. In our fantasy we are the footballers we wanted to be as boys and we are out there on the pitch, kicking every ball, crunching into every tackle, never missing a chance… and then we remember who and where we really are… and we sit back in the reality of our seat.

The psychology of being a supporter is beyond me. Desmond Morris tried to explain it all those years ago in *The Soccer Tribe*. Maybe it's to do with seeing players as extensions of ourselves. They represent our town, our hopes and us, and when they lose we're as disappointed with ourselves as them.

****

Burnley as a town is a place you might not want to visit for any particular reason. It isn't the biggest or wealthiest of places and certainly has its collection of problems. When Burnley is featured in the media and makes national front-page headlines it is often for the wrong reasons.

It isn't a pretty picture-postcard place. But the people are resilient, warm, friendly and open. The surrounding areas, hills and uplands have a beauty of their own. There are plenty of fine attractive tourist areas around, tiny villages, hamlets and narrow valleys filled with woodland and streams. The Trough of Bowland, Pendle witch country, quaint villages, acres of green meadows, heather-clad landscapes, wild and wonderful moorlands… none of them are that far away, some of them not much more than a short walk. But, sadly, if a TV documentary team were to do a piece on the town they'd look at derelict housing, empty properties and the shabbier streets with the Hovis bread advert brass band music for the soundtrack.

It is a town whose growth was centred around the cotton industry and cotton mills, and as a result of cotton workers needing cheap housing there are now rows and rows of small terraced houses which once upon a time had an outside loo and a small back yard. Acres of them surround Turf Moor. Estate Agents call them Town Houses today. Anyone who has read William Woodruff's *The Road To Nab End* will get an inkling of what life in Burnley must have been like years ago. It's set in Blackburn just up the road but Burnley was not much different. And yet within minutes you can be out in open country under a huge clean sky and hear the calls of lapwings and curlews.

Even with modernisation empty rows of these little houses fetch some of the lowest prices in England. Others have been made into palaces, especially those near the football ground whose windows you can peer into and see trendy lounges and IKEA kitchens.

But decades ago when cotton was king and the town flourished economically, this was a grim place where life was hard, arduous and repetitive for those who were mill workers. Although new industry has moved in, the name Burnley belongs to a long list of decline, along with countless other small town places. In 1921, when Burnley were Champions and went thirty games without defeat, the town then wove more cotton than anywhere else. There were 100,000 people and 100,000 looms. Burnley cloth went round the world. The town thrived. In 1960 they were champions again and the town's strengths were still cotton along with coal, the Burnley Building Society and Bob Lord. There were 18 Burnley pits in 1946. The last one went in the seventies. The Burnley Building Society has gone, now swallowed up by another bigger one. In the seventies the mortality rate was 21% higher than the national average and it wasn't too long ago that people could still remember and describe the conditions of mills where the noise was deafening, the sheds were gas-lit, people were treated like cattle and women like my grandmother had to lip read their conversations because the noise of looms had deafened them.

It is sometimes said by experts that of all the teams that have declined, Burnley's was the most dramatic. The maximum wage was abolished in the sixties. Burnley and Bob Lord were accused of putting too much money into a new stand, which at the time was simply seen as a grandiose piece of indulgence by Lord. The club lost the knack of home-growing outstanding young players. Managers came in after the Lord era and some spent money like they had somebody else's bank account - which I suppose in fact they did.

Yet, the football team has survived and remains the one real claim to fame that makes the town known nationally. Had The Orient Game ended differently all those years ago, there would now be few mentions of the town's existence.

"We noted that the sun shone down on the old dying cotton town with ironic brilliance. We recalled that for years it had the highest suicide rate in Britain. We looked at the beautifully appointed ground with a pitch barely scarred at the end of the season and agreed how sad it was," Ian Wooldridge wrote of the Orient day.

"As near to a religious experience as you could imagine," one fan said.

"The most emotional experience of my life," said another.

I too was there and the lump in my throat that day and the wet eyes around me are memories as clear now as they were then.

The football team today, perhaps, is almost the town's raison d'etre. When the ground is near full it has a following out of all proportion to the size of its hometown. It has a Claret and Blue away following which is the envy of bigger clubs.

Following Burnley is a mixture of heartache and hope, agony and, yes, sometimes joy. But on the very final day of 2001/2002 our hopes ended in despair. Until just minutes from the end of the game we were in the play-offs, but then another team, far away in Norfolk, where people torks funny and the mangel worzels and turkeys grow, scored just one more goal before the end of their game, and the effect was catastrophic. The morbid mood afterwards lasted for days. The electric David Johnson vanished back to Notts Forest from where he had come on loan during the final few games, lighting up Turf Moor briefly with his goals, rekindling the dream of Premiership football. Burnley did indeed think big with just a few weeks to go and the signing of Gazza could have had a similar impact to that of Ian Wright when he inspired the late and successful bid for promotion from Division 2. It was not to be. The gamble failed. But we applauded the attempt.

This coming season, now beset by financial problems, probably just staying up will be a success. The signs are not good. From Christmas 2001 onwards and in the early months of 2002, the team struggled to win a handful of games. Week in and week out the form was described as relegation bound. Only the bank of points accumulated before Christmas kept the club at the top end as other top clubs continually took points off each other.

This season's journey, which began with the tournament grandiosely titled The Isle of Man Steam Packet International Football Festival, you would hope to be rich in promise. Instead we worry about lack of resources, lack of money and lack of players. Those of us who are realistic will settle for bottom half survival this season. The signs and portents suggest that it might be even worse than that. No new players have been signed, either on free transfers or loans. The squad is small. The cash box on the boardroom mantelpiece is empty.

****

By the end of August 2002 there was despondency. I read and heard of Turf Moor doom and gloom, of growing demoralisation, of website and supporter's clubs criticism and dissatisfaction. There had been a month of poor games and individual below par performances resulting in public criticisms.

The Isles de Manne event appeared to be uninspiring though it may be argued that it was only an opportunity to ease the way gently into a new season and test fitness. Friendlies against Bolton and Bury ended as tame draws and the club continued to protest about the loss of ITV revenue. Marlon Broomes went to Preston for two years instead of Burnley, who it is said offered him two months. Marlon Beresford went to York.

After three games we were pointless, had scored one goal and the reports I read in the English papers, so easily obtainable on the Greek Islands, of defeats against Wolves and Brighton made for depressing reading even lazing under a hot, cloudless blue sky. Even sitting on an idyllic Greek beach there seemed good reason to feel real apprehension.

Back at home I switched on the London Clarets website. Wolves 3 Sheep 0 it said. Nuff said. We lost the opening home game of the season against Brighton and then away to Wolves who always score at least three against Burnley. It's a tradition of theirs. Backs against the wall already and the impatient knives of the critics already flashing. Then it was another home defeat, this time by Sheffield United. There were muttered mumblings on the website pages I clicked onto.

****

So, this diary of 2002/2003 starts a month late, not in August but in September with fans aspirations at a low point and supporters struggling to be optimistic. To summarise, we have so far lost four consecutive games, to Brighton, Wolves, Sheffield United and Reading. We have scored just one goal. We sit at the bottom of Division One. We are £4.5 million out of pocket and don't and never have had the kind of money to buy players at random when we feel like it. We have signed no new players and couldn't manage to attract Marlon Beresford or Marlon Broomes, two definite targets. In a nutshell, what we have is what we got.

The second half of last season, 2001/2002, from New Year onwards was essentially relegation form. It has emphatically continued into August of this season. There is barely a Burnley supporter who is calm or confident, happy or buoyant.

On Claretsmad, Steve Cummings wrote his Reading match report on the coach after the game as he and other miserable supporters journeyed back north, eventually getting back to Burnley at 3.00 in the morning and after it had cost him the best part of £50 and a day's leave from work:

The mood following tonight's defeat at the hands of Reading is bordering on despondency... Even at this early stage, deep concern is being expressed. Concern that we have conceded 10 goals in four games. Concern that we have only found the back of the opposition net once in six hours of football. And concern that we find ourselves utterly pointless and bottom of the league after our fourth consecutive loss... the Royals were full value for their win over a Burnley side whom Ternent dubbed an embarrassment... Reading wrapped up the points in farcical fashion.... Pushing forward, Burnley were caught with their pants down. Jamie Cureton found himself all alone on the left flank and from fully 30 yards lobbed Nick the Greek who was so far off his line... the ball sailed over him and nestled into the empty net... You can whinge all you want about the collapse of ITV Digital and Burnley Football Club have, but the start to this season has little to do with cash. By Ternent's own admission this is by and large the same squad of players who finished seventh last time out. Truth be told... this has been going on since the middle of last season. It was put to me this evening that the Clarets had won just six games since November... The bottom line is we need to improve dramatically...

"Where next for sorry Clarets," began Tony Scholes in another piece. His passionate report criticises the club for intrusive telephone calls that basically ask for money, he worries about rumours of unsettled players, the financial problems and suggestions the club is for sale. He asks that the club takes a long hard look at itself and begins to put things right. He suggests there is a lack of motivation and the club is at a low ebb. "We are hurting very badly," he says.

Of this game, even Stan said it was awful and a blind man on a galloping horse could see that. Embarrassed, he said he would consider his future and speak to the Chairman. We may all of us have our differing opinions, but nevertheless at this moment we all fear the worst, that after this terrible start the season will be one almighty struggle. On current form, relegation looms.

David Thomas. August 31st 2002.

SEPTEMBER

Monday, September 2

BURNLEY 0 PALACE 0

And so it began this weekend. If a football season is a journey, then at the moment we're having trouble getting started. The first trip to see them was on Saturday against Crystal Palace. As we drive over, there are nagging doubts about the season ahead. We are bottom and things look dreadful. For us it's an eighty mile round trip each time. But it's a warm dry day; we drive round the suburbs of Leeds and then around Bradford. On to Halifax, Mytholmroyd and then Hebden Bridge, a small picturesque place, where mills have been replaced by tearooms, book and antique shops. It nestles amongst steep wooded hillsides on all sides, and roads from here lead on to Haworth, the Brontes and steam railways. Sometimes it's called Little Switzerland. Other roads lead on over the hilltops and moorlands, one of which takes us up through Heptonstall Slack and then Colden, a place surrounded by wild treeless landscapes and the ghosts of the Brontes, and Heathcliffe.

From Colden the moorland road takes us along to Blackshawhead where there in full swing is a traditional village fête in a large windswept field with nothing above but sky and cloud. The spirit of village England is thriving. There's a line of parked Range Rovers, battered Land Rovers, Freelanders, and other sundry 4 x 4s in the £20,000+ class. Merrye Englande seemed alive and well on these desolate Wuthering Height Moors. Would that it were so at Turfe Moore.

From this point on however, the afternoon was all downhill. The undulating road leads on downwards into Burnley passing by one of those huge wind farms that scar the landscape in upland areas. The roofs of the two newest stands of Turf Moor eventually become visible as you approach the outlying urban areas. They rise high above the lines of terraced rows around. It was 2.20 and our first thought was, where is everybody? We spotted a lone supporter making his way along in a Burnley shirt. It had Gascoigne on the back. Sad.

The pitch was green and immaculate. 12,000 regulars braved the pessimism. Burnley huffed and puffed and looked like they probably wouldn't ever score again. It's not so much a question of when will we win, but when will we score?

Briscoe was at left back and Branch was omitted. Claret purse strings are such that there isn't even a spare goalkeeper on the bench now that Beresford has gone to York. York has a new wealthy chairman who is something to do with motor racing. The York strip now has black and white chequered sleeves. When a York player waves his arms the rest of them all slow down and think they've finished. Johnrose was back from the wilderness of being released last season and was back on a months contract. Gnohere was suspended for being sent off in the first game of the season for a head butt. Cook was suspended for being sent off against Wolves. Davis was injured. Our cup runneth over. Papadopoulos was in for his first ever full game. Stan bought him 18 months or more ago and keeps saying he is one for the future. The future is here. Blake sat on the bench. Moore sat on the bench. Two million pounds sat on the bench.

Papadopoulos ran and chased endlessly with more optimism than success, and was proclaimed man of the match. Man of the match in reality was Cox at the back who kept Palace at bay single-handed. We had a couple of shots and that was about it. But in fairness there was a clear penalty when Papadopopopoulos had his shirt nearly pulledoffoulos in the box. Everyone bar referee and linesman saw it. On such decisions relegation issues are eventually decided and at the moment relegation is a stark possibility. Michopoulos was sound and confident.

Around us were the usual selections of pundits and experts. The ones in front were alternately laughing or shaking heads at the attempts on goal, the poor passes, the struggling midfield. The foulmouthed yobs behind us bombarded Stan and team with every obscenity imaginable, in the loudest voices possible without let up from start to finish. Tell them to shut up and the tirade is then directed at you. I came home with earache. Who'd be a footballer? Where's the beauty in this then?

Thursday, September 5

I looked up the piece I sent to the London Website back in January. It brought back all the thoughts and feelings of how it was then in that month that things went pear-shaped and it re-affirmed my view that the Sheffield Wednesday game early in 2002 was the clear turning point. The stuffing at Man City in December was bad enough but strangely it's always a result that we resignedly expect and shrug off cheerfully in just the same way that any Wolves result, however bad, is consigned to the dustbin of memory.

But this coming Saturday it's Derby away. Who'd be in their position, millions in debt, facing administration, big name players on mammoth wages and struggling in the First Division? Apparently their players haven't been paid for several weeks and there's some small print somewhere that says a player can walk away from a club to any other which wants him, after fourteen days of not being paid. Derby players allegedly are queuing up to leave. This pre-supposes of course that anyone else wants to buy them.

This Saturday: A 0-0 draw would be priceless but a 3-0 defeat more realistic. We're missing Gareth Taylor and Dimitri Papadopoulos, both away on international duty. Taylor is in the Welsh squad. Gnohere should be back and Stan might well revert to his favoured 4-5-1 formation, which usually means we sit back and soak up the opposition and then rely on breakaways. At least that's the theory. In reality at the moment we give away sloppy goals and get beat. Surely there is no way he can leave out Cox, who was my man of the match on Saturday. Perhaps Blake will start a game. Bradford fans who are my neighbours keep telling me what a class act he was for them and for a long time their best player.

Friday, September 6

There's a fair chance we'll get all three points at Derby tomorrow. Derby players haven't been paid for weeks and are threatening a strike. That's our only hope - that they walk out. There's not much pretiumque at Derby at the moment. If they do actually play they'll be without ace striker Fabulousizio Ravioli, who has returned to Italy. Officially he is there for treatment to a leg but unofficial sources say he has an injured wallet, which is allegedly owed £300,000. Derby are said to be losing thousands a day and takeover talks with other groups are coming to nothing. Star defender Danny Higginbotham has already invoked the fourteen-day rule whereby he can walk out on a free transfer if he is not paid. At the moment after what we have seen so far, we think there are a few folk here who shouldn't be paid for fourteen days.

Goalkeeper Marlon Beresford has come back for a month from York City saying he wants to continue playing at the highest possible level, which currently at Burnley is bottom of Division One. Current goalkeeper Michopoulos is presumably about to revert to the benchoulos.

Derby is not a place I've been to. I understand it was once a centre of the railway industry. Didn't Rolls Royce have factories there? There is a street named after Frank Whittle, the inventor of the jet engine - not a lot of people know that. This is Bess of Hardwick country. Brian Clough first made his name here with the great side that was cheated out of the European Cup (well according to him anyway). Then he fell out with them, went to Notts Forest and the rest is history, as they say. Derby describes itself as the Real Ale capital of England. It was once famous for its porcelain. It was the most southerly point reached by Bonnie Prince Charlie in the Jacobite rebellion of 1745. He turned back as soon as he saw the state of the Derby pitch and decided that it would be of little use to his ball-playing wing wizards. Dr. Samuel Johnson who wrote the first English dictionary got married here. One wonders what he would now make of current Oxford English if he came to Turf Moor where the elegance of our language was admirably expressed by the tossers behind me on Saturday. Derby's once huge railway works in recent times produced the legendary Advanced Passenger Train. That's the one that wobbled and leaned so much going round corners everybody fell out of their seats. It was the Millennium Dome of the railways and was abandoned after millions of pounds had been wasted. The Derby Museum and Art Gallery has works by Joseph Wright, one of the greatest of all English painters, "a master of exaggerated light and shadow and chronicler of English Scientific Enlightenment." If that's your scene, there you are then. If not, do as the London Supporters website suggests; just have another pint.

Derby's Pride Park is one of those new post-Taylor Report grounds built miles from anywhere in the suburbs in a barren wilderness. It's all black seats and breeze blocks and looks like a clone of many other new purpose-built characterless grounds. It replaced The Baseball Ground, which was famous for its mud and hardmen like Dave Mackay and Bruce Rioch. Those were the days and in this respect Derby County is much like Burnley, a once great club now fallen on lean, hard times.

Monday, September 9

DERBY 1 ROLLS ROYCES 2

"Will the real Burnley please stand up", said a website reporter after this totally unexpected win on Saturday. The omens and entrails for this game were not good other than one little thing - something about a cup win in 1999, the last time we were there, but nobody thought for a moment that a win could be repeated. Having subscribed an extra £34 to the Claretsworld bit of the Burnley FC web page (we now pay for what last season was free) I switched it on half-heartedly and even reluctantly at 3.00.

True to form we are a goal down after just eight minutes after the usual slack defending. Pundit (?) Lou Macari on Sky Soccer Saturday depresses me further by saying that Christie and Strupar are running riot, Burnley are woeful, and more goals look definite. I listen to him saying this on three separate occasions and think that's enough. The dog looks at me and I look at him and I think well that's that, we might as well go for a walk round the fields and come back to get the final humiliating score. The dog looks mournful at the best of times and as we left the house my face matched his.

We return home, the dog with tongue hanging out and me morose expecting the worst. My jaw hits the floor as I look at the screen back in the house. Derby 1 Burnley 2.

This is truly the last thing I expected to see. From that point on it's sit in anguish listening to Phil Bird getting himself into a lather and a frenzy on the website commentary as Burnley could have had at least two more with better finishing, As excitement increases with each goal chance, e.g. Moore bearing down on goal having outpaced all markers, Bird's voice goes up three octaves so that he sounds like he is being throttled and nobody can tell a word he is saying. This is commentating at its very best.

We dominate the rest of the game. There are good things in all the reports: "... introduction of Glen Little at half-time galvanised Burnley and with Robbie Blake in inspirational form they turned the match on its head... Burnley hardly had a shot on goal in the first half but they were rampant after the break... the introduction of Glen Little at the break was the key as he orchestrated events... on the evidence of Burnley's second half display do not write off Ternent's team from making another sustained challenge for the play-offs..." (What, are we really talking Burnley here?).

The secret of our success though (as well as an alleged half-time Stantrum in the dressing room) is clear the London Clarets website reported:

Forget all that rubbish about lucky underpants. We know why we won. Before the match London Clarets Phil and Lee were approached by a nun, who asked them to help carry her bags. Naturally they were only too pleased to assist (despite being en route to the pub). Afterwards the nun said, "bless you," to each of them in turn. It doesn't take a genius to work out that carrying a nun's bags before a match can result in a win. Obviously you have to receive a blessing as well, one blessing equals one goal.

But this morning in the cold light of day reality returns. One swallow doesn't make a summer says the gaffer. There is a newspaper report in *The Mail on Sunday* that suggests Stan might be leaving. The paper says that having had his team-building plans scuppered due to the financial position at the club Stan has been asked to take a pay cut and refused. Rumour or fact, is *The Mail on Sunday* trustworthy? It crystallizes my thoughts. Stan must stay. This is no time for change.

"It makes you wonder just how bad the financial situation is at Turf Moor..." says Tony Scholes, the man behind the Claretsmad website.

Nothing can be as bad as the dire financial situation at Derby though. Just how they feel after losing at home and having been given the runaround by the club that WAS bottom must be unprintable.

Tuesday, September 10

Stan says this about the alleged going to quit article: "I can't comment about it because I know nothing about it."

But Blackpool tonight and we're home to this lower division outfit in the Worthington Cup. This competition for us has been a slippery banana skin for many a year. Last year it was out in the first round to Rushden and Diamonds. The FA Cup is also a slippery banana skin. Last year it was out at the second hurdle to Cheltenham. In years gone by we have lost to all manner of piddling teams including Telford who weren't even in the league.

Blackpool are a constant reminder of the fate that awaits us. They have hung around the lower divisions for years in a half-decrepit ground which is only half redeveloped. Is it really true that one of the new stands is called The Pricebusters Matthews Stand? And which Matthews is it, the one who played football in long baggy shorts or the one who reared turkeys in Norfolk? In greater years than these the Blackpool Burnley fixture almost ranked on the Man Utd v Man City level. Now, whilst Blackpool scrape around for crumbs, Burnley are on the breadline.

Bill Bryson summed Blackpool up all right. He described it as ugly and dirty with the largest number of public toilets anywhere in the world. Everywhere else they call them doorways. I get the impression Blackpool pissed him off but he doesn't go into too much detail about being there late on a Saturday night. Did he go in The Star, the big pub at the top end of the Golden Mile? Did he queue up and visit the Funny Girls Night Club, have a Chinese at 1.00 in the morning, trudge round the Pleasure Beach for three hours? Did he experience the culinary delights of a Holland's Pie and Fries café, get in a Yates's Wine Lodge and actually reach the bar? Did he dodge police SWAT teams down Talbot Road? If he did he might well have stood there thinking the same as me. What in God's name am I doing here?

There is a tide of people in Blackpool at all hours wherever you go that you force your way through. There are great gangs of women, hen parties, all dolled up in fancy dress as nuns, schoolgirls, schoolteachers; short skirts, skimpy tops, low tops, see-through tops… and they're just the pensioners. Groups of lads all tanked up on lager and chips block the pavements. Of the world's commercially produced tat, 90% of it is sold in Blackpool. If you put the chips produced in Blackpool end to end they'd circle the globe. The trams clank up and down the prom with steamed-up windows, which is a blessing for the people inside because they can't see what's outside. Nobody can possibly know in these trams where they're going or when they actually get there. Horses gasping for air and mercy pull carriages full of fat giggling women between the crawling traffic.

Here's an interesting statistic Bryson missed. Of the world's horse manure, 50% is on the road in Blackpool. Cars filled with gawping passengers drive along in a trance clearly bewildered by the shuffling blocks of human flotsam before them.

Here's some more interesting stats. Of the world's shab, 99.9% is in Blackpool. It has the shabbiest streets, the shabbiest shops in Europe. Above ground floor level everything is decaying, dilapidated and dissipated. And we haven't even mentioned Bloomfield Road. This is not the place to look for Europe's finest architecture. The Imperial Hotel is about the best of what there is. Just walk a bit further on, passing the porn shops on your right, and you're there. Traces of elegance remain but at £75 a night so it should. For £95 a night you get a few extras like a bowl of fruit, an executive tea tray, exclusive toiletries and a magic duck fun sponge for your late night bath. Magic duck sponges are big in Blackpool along with inflatable dolls, sex shops, false busts, and giant plastic penises.

In spite of drunks in doorways, scuffles and punchups, marauding women, club bouncers so big they block the pavement, racing fire engines, the gentle smell of late night urine wafting down the promenade, couples who've only just met having it off behind bus shelters, inch-deep puddles of lager, music in pubs that's only marginally less than deafening, spotty youths dressed up as Vikings... Blackpool draws you back.

I brought back fond memories and a silly jesters hat. The point of me having written all this in case you're wondering is that the hat is in Claret and Blue and hangs in pride of place behind me. It's two seasons ago now and I remember it because Burnley had played Notts Forest, losing 1-0 in the land of Robin Hood.

Tonight Blackpool have every reason to be confident. They are unbeaten in six and haven't given away a goal in four. Superclarets meanwhile have won one in six and haven't been beyond round two for the last twenty years.

On top of all that the *Daily Mail* have followed up their Sunday Stan is going story with another one. This one says that Burnley Football Club will run out of money in three weeks time. This is no speculation, they maintain, but is a fact given out by the club at a meeting in Walsall last week attended by Burnley's Andrew Watson. Are we the next Bradford City? The club website is silent for the moment.

Wednesday, September 11

BURNLEY 3 SEASIDERS 0

Some people have fun looking at O.S. maps and AA books picking out all the wonderful sounding English names like Mankinholes, Chipping Sodbury, Pilling On Sludge, and Little Wittling on the Dearne. Football fans looks at team lists on a Saturday morning or in the Sunday results. We look at footballers' names like Sithole, Zamperini (which I always thought was the cheapest lambrusco), Quashie, Chippo (a personal favourite of mine), Agyemang, Wanchope, Lua Lua, Doig and Fish. Just imagine having Fish and Chippo in the same team, or Wanchope and Rice. Charlton used to have Costa and Fortune. There are managers with exotic names like Arsene and Gerard. Ours is called Stan. Crewe came last year with Ademole Bankole and Kenny Lunt, which I defy anyone to say after eight pints of lager. We ourselves have Michopoulos and Papadopoulos and Gnohere. Even our media manager goes by the name of Edoardo. Teams in the English leagues used to be populated with Smiths, Joneses, Hartles and Banks.

After the minute's silence last night though, the seasiders were swept aside by tides of Burnley attacks. The Tangerines were well and truly tangoed. Burnley played the same eleven who trounced Derby and they carried on where they left off with Little and Blake again outstanding. Grant too had his best game ever; Gnohere and Cox were impeccable. Clarets oozed confidence (honestly). It was a night of firsts. Dean West scored his first Burnley goal from a free kick. Papadopoulos scored his first for the club and followed it up with a second from a penalty missed by Gareth Taylor but Papaquickaslightning followed up and put the rebound in. Stan has headaches now. Which of the strikers will start on Saturday? My money is on Blake and Little being in the starting eleven again. but who else? Stan took a risk taking them off early in the second half with the score at only 1-0. By the end, two and a half thousand visitors were leaving early well and truly silenced. The upstarts must have thought this was a game they could win. "A tremendous all round performance," said the Claretsmad website, "... crisp passing... neat interplay... good runs." One swallow may not make a summer said canny Stan on Saturday, but this was the second swallow in just a few days. There are two home league games to come now. Consolidation and continued improvement, or will it be after the Lord Mayor's show and disappointment?

With money so tight the real bucks don't start until the third and fourth rounds when the big clubs come in. After twenty years surely we are due to do more than take an early exit. Seven and a half thousand in total last night will hardly pay the gas bill or petrol for Bendyman's limo. Now there's a sign of the times - we're back to singing Super Glen's praises.

Thursday, September 12

The dog and I enjoyed our middle-aged stroll today. It puts a different complexion on things when the team has won. The sky seems bluer, the grass seems greener, the normally litter-filled canal looks beautiful and even the abattoir and the tram sheds look picturesque. The system is always the same. The dog lies under the desk where I type. Then he gets restless. Then he moans a bit. Then he asks can we go. No, I tell him, this is a good bit I'm doing. The muse has descended; the pen won't stop.

We move into the field. There's a crow there as usual just within taunting distance. As ever the dog would like to rip it apart. They go through the usual routine of chasing, landing, squawking and taunting until the dog is haggard with exhaustion and the bird sits on the post grinning triumphantly. One day this cocky thing will seriously mistime things and the dog will have it. It's just a matter of time.

"One day, one day," I hear the dog wheezing, "one day you bastard..."

If the dog, poor thing, had the speed of Papadopoulos then perhaps he'd have a chance. On seizing the penalty save and ramming it home in the flash of an eye, Papawingsonhisboots earned the ultimate accolade from a cloth-capped elder brought up on Jimmy Mac and John Connelly.

"By thi 'eck, e's like a bloody whippet yon lad."

No fairer word was ever spoke, ee by gum.

Saturday, September 14

BURNLEY 2 POTTERS 1

Match day. You can't beat the feeling. Every football fan be they from Scunthorpe or Exeter, Carlisle or one of the giants, knows the feeling of mounting anticipation and nerves. The nerves in our case come from the poor start but then the promise over the last two games of better things to come. This is Burnley though, a club where being kicked in the teeth by the sheer inconsistency and ups and downs of the team over the years has made us permanent pessimists and gloomists, always wary of being cheerfully optimistic or confident. Then there's this bloke called Bald Eagle Mooney coming with Stoke. There are players you dread seeing the name on the team sheet because you know they always score against you. Tommy Mooney is one of these names and Stoke have him on loan from Birmingham, for whom he scored last year at the Turf during that long post-Christmas run of ours which saw us slide from genuine Premiership contenders to relegation form hasbeens.

Leeds is blanketed by grey skies and murk but across the Pennines there's brilliant warm sunshine which makes driving across the moors between Hebden Bridge and Burnley an absolute delight. If we lose today I think at least there's been the pleasure of this great landscape and vast blue sky. It's where I grew up.

But we don't lose, although with ten minutes to go it looked like another 1-0 defeat was on the cards. We start with Blake and Moore (Ian) up front and for the first half they and Little work well but can't find a way through. Stan prefers the muscle and brawn of Johnrose to the guile and craft of Cook. Johnrose is game and brave, Bury fans say he was once awesome. Intricacy meanwhile does not break Stoke down so on comes Taylor. Taylor was a boo boy victim last year in spite of being top scorer. This year his play is appreciated more. Moore (Alan) comes on with immediate impact and more than once he skates down the wing. On other occasions he dances down the flanks beating his man and men several times. This is how he was a year ago. It's an open game and Stoke could easily have scored with better finishing and against a poorer goalkeeper than Beresford, who is preferred to the Greek Michopoulos. The latter seems to have lost his marbles of late. But damn, damn, Stoke score in a breakaway and we groan as the Stoke end erupts - and there's a lot of them. They're almost as voluble as West Brom, who came last year and were outstanding as away supporters go.

Stoke think they've done the job and so do we. But ey up, 'ang on, within two minutes King Arthur has powered in a header from a Moore corner.

Jubilation, bedlam erupts. And then ey up, 'ang on some more, a Little cross is glanced home by the diving Dimitri Papacandonowtwrong for his first league goal. One for the future Stan keeps saying. The future is Papa. Apparently Papa speaks no English but then neither does Geordie Stan some folk say. My Uncle was a Geordie and I could never understand him. They all call each other pet up there, which seems strange because that's what we call our cat.

Anyway, all this in the last ten minutes at the end of what has been a decent game of which you might have said this was a thoroughly entertaining 0-0 if it had stayed that way. Exit 12,000 jubilant Clarets. Exit 2,000 morose and fuming Potters, probably hell bent on smashing a few windows and lamps in the town centre. And Tommy Mooney, did I need to worry? He was sent off for stamping on Tony Grant who I have to report played well.

The nice thing now is that we seem to have options. If two good little 'uns don't score in the first half, then two good big 'uns can come on in the second after Stan has had his half-time fag. We are out of the bottom three and up to the heady heights of 20th with seven points.

Monday, September 16

So on Saturday it is Bradford and Valley Parade. No, sorry, it's now called The Pulse Stadium. The smarmy Geoffrey Richards resigned as chairman in the summer. Bradford survived their financial troubles by the skin of their teeth. Benito Carbuncle, paid some ridiculous salary and owed thousands, departed for Italy and returned to the land of spaghetti and shapely bottoms.

Bradford City are just round the corner from here. They aren't doing too badly either, occupying a respectable mid-table position. The day is set up for a decent game between two currently winning teams. Better than that, my pal John, who is a Bradford supporter and does silly things like buy players signed shirts and other assorted expensive memorabilia, knows a very nice man who knows another very nice man who has an executive box which then gives us access to a pre-match meal in the banqueting suite. John is treating me and Mrs. T. to the full Monty as it were.

My loyalties are torn. For the sake of friendship I'll settle for a barnstorming 3-3 draw. For the sake of Claret blood I'll settle for a dull boring 1-0 win. Last year Burnley were none too popular here after their 3-2 win, being described as the ugliest, dirtiest team ever to visit Bradford.

We know Bradford for two reasons. Firstly, we go to The Alhambra theatre every year to the pantomime, and the second is that we skirt the city on our drive from home to Burnley on a match day. Ah, and sometimes we visit The Cocina Mexican restaurant up Manningham Lane. The quaintness of this place is that you wait for your table in a pub across the road. Then when it is ready someone hotfoots it across from the restaurant, dodging the buses and taxis to fetch you over. From the windows of The Cocina you can watch the race riots in safety and have a meal at the same time. Now I call that value for money.

There's life, bustle and colour along the last Yorkshire Golden Mile of the Leeds/Bradford Road. When you reach at last the city centre it's a sad drab mixture of concrete jungle, empty shops and vacant offices. It's all dull architecture replacing Victorian splendour. There's the relentless spread of dual carriageways, and six lane highways that are impossible to cross, roundabouts where you take your life in your hands and pedestrian underpasses where even in broad daylight the wise and wary steer well clear and no sane person would go anywhere near late at night.

Bryson visited Bradford, his target being some cinema or other but at some stage he ended up in The Museum of Photography and Sundry Other Things, wherein lives some huge wraparound cinema screen, which is apparently quite famous. He arrived three hours early and asked the not unreasonable question just what does one do in Bradford when one has three spare hours other than look at peeling posters covering up vacant shop windows and have a drink in a pub that once served The Yorkshire Ripper but now serves chilli to people who, inevitably, ask did The Yorkshire Ripper come here and which stool did he sit on?

Little Germany is all that is left of what was once this vast stock of imposing buildings and woollen prosperity. A drive to Valley Parade, (oops sorry, The Pulse), takes the driver from Leeds right by it. A cluster of tall buildings stand unbulldozed, with modern Bradford, tarmac and traffic lights all around them.

In short, Bradford is a mess, steeped in decay and decline, gutted, demolished and taken apart in the name of progress with everything replaced by inner ring roads. It long ago ceased being a rival to Leeds, which left it behind in the commercial stakes a decade ago. All it has to offer, other than the house wherein lived The Yorkshire Ripper and dozens of curry houses, is the annual Billy Pearce Christmas Pantomime, a statue of J.B. Priestley and The House of Islamic Treasures.

I thought a bit more about Saturday and the euphoria you feel when a game is turned on its head and victory replaces defeat in a matter of minutes. There we were, two middle aged old dears in our fifties, perfectly respectable, me a retired Head and Mrs. T. still teaching and a Deputy Headmistress to boot. And there we were when the second goal goes in against all expectations, arms raised to the skies, heads laid back, yelling into the heavens, PAPA… PAPA… PAPA… in fluent Greek of course. We still have no voices left even two days later, after all the shouting we did throughout the game, not just the last ten minutes. Yes, there we were joining in even that most crude and boorish of chants you abuse the opposition fans with, OO ARE YER… OO ARE YER… OO ARE YER…

Before Bradford on Saturday though and the promised slap up meal, comes Millwall at home tomorrow night. The games come thick and fast now. Soon there's the next round of the Worthington Cup to fit in where it's an away banana skin tie at Huddersfield (tricky). We can't get to the Millwall game but it's on Sky for some reason. If you're a neutral what on earth would possess you to watch Burnley v Millwall especially as on ITV there are Champions League games to watch. But Mrs. T and me will sit glued to it. Last season it was the first of the games after Christmas where decline set in. It was a 0-0 draw and the lingering memory (along with Steve Claridge trying to referee as well as play) is Alan Moore hitting the crossbar. One goal kept us out of the play-offs. That's why you remember a shot hitting the bar against Millwall.

Rumours however of administration and liquidation continue, fuelled by the *Daily Mail*. Again this last weekend on Saturday morning, there was a piece saying that Barry Kilby is now desperately trying to sort out a rescue package. Sky a few days ago reported he had put a million of his own money into the club. Our man in the know, Tony Scholes, on the Claretsmad website has friends here, friends there, contacts everywhere it seems, who all seem to substantiate the rumours. Three different articles over the last week however, smacks of somebody somewhere knowing something nasty.

Tuesday, September 17

Burnley fans have been banned from attending the away game at Millwall this season by the powers that be. Accordingly Burnley have banned Millwo' supporters from Turf Moor. This is not such a bad idea. Millwo' supporters have the unfortunate habit of rearranging the furniture and being generally unpleasant when they visit other grounds. Being a Tuesday night game, attendance won't be hit too much anyway. Accordingly the club have had the brainwave idea of reducing entrance prices as it's on Sky and opening up the away supporters to Burnley fans.

There's a choice of games tonight. On ITV there's Liverpool Valencia in the Champions League. On ITV2 there's Arsenal. Sky are countering this with Burnley v Millwo'. On a scale of ten with Liverpool Valencia at nine, where would you rate the Burnley game? To a neutral it must rate alongside Walsall v Watford, or Grimsby v Wimbledon in the wow area. Even I am sorely tempted to turn to another channel - actually the National Geographic channel where live probe cameras are going to unlock secrets that have lain hush-hush for thousands of years, behind a door at the end of a tunnel, deep in the bowels of The Great Pyramid of Cheops. Such a camera might be useful behind the closed doors of the boardroom at The Turf or in the halftime dressing room during games like the ones at Reading, or at home against Brighton.

Andrew Watson today did at last comment on the clubs supposedly perilous financial state: "The financial situation has been made clear," he said. "We almost broke even last year and this year we will be facing a loss that has to be paid for somehow. We are having meetings with the creditors to buy ourselves time and we are looking for investment in the club. We are not an unusual case because at a recent First Division meeting, 21 of the 24 clubs are in the same position as us, living off loans from the directors. In fact the creditors have told us we are in a better situation than most other clubs, as we don't have as many debts as others."

Commenting on stories in circulation, he went on, "I suspect that the stories of these meetings with creditors have got out and people have put two and two together but the situation is no different from the past few months. It is a concern, of that there is no doubt, but we are doing all we can. The chairman, directors and staff are making great efforts to try and bring things together, but we are certainly no different to a lot of First Division clubs. The 12,000 or so supporters who turn up every week are different class and they have been fantastic. It's a concern financially when people don't turn up, because we lose money, but we are now four games unbeaten, so crowds should start to pick up."

Wednesday, September 18

PUSSYCATS 2 LIONS 2

Well, crowds certainly didn't pick up for last night's game in spite of reduced prices to try and lure them in. Just over 11,000 ensured that the club continue to lose money and that the ground looked and sounded like a morgue. We watched the game on TV unable to make the trip over from Leeds. We sat with a kind of resigned detached indifference as what came over on the box was a seemingly colourless, drab, dour affair with little or no atmosphere, punctuated occasionally by good play from Millwo' and several shots on goal from Burnley. To be frank, the Millwo' wide men Kinet and Ifill ran Burnley ragged. Their goalkeeper kept out most of what we had to offer.

In spite of the dross, the lasting feeling is one of disappointment that we didn't win. We could have. A tame header from a yard out after the goalkeeper had parried a shot from Papa, which on a luckier day would have gone in. A shot straight at the goalkeeper when three feet either side the goal gaped wide open. Other shots just missed or were saved but by the same token Beresford kept Millwo' at bay more than once. Put it this way, the football was played by Millwo' but Burnley had most of the shots. Strange that in a game where there were 32 shots on goal in total and some of them good ones at that, the over riding verdict on this game was that it was dull and lifeless.

And the Millwo' goals: When they went in there was utter silence, quite eerie really. Both of them were the result of Burnley players waiting for the pies to be delivered, instead of cutting out danger or getting a body in the way.

Any neutral watching this game in the silent ground must surely have switched over to something else by the end. Gnohere tangled repeatedly with the lippy Claridge until the latter went off. Papadopoulos flung himself about and got the penalty, my ex pupil West smacked it home, just. Somehow we contrived to score the equalizing goal 5 minutes from the end with our one footballing move of our night whereupon King Arthur ran across to gesticulate to the Millwo' bench in general and the moaning Claridge, football's best known pensioner, in particular.

"Bang out of order," said Stan, "But he's only 21 and French."

You knew that the second half would be a repeat of the dire first as soon as Burnley kicked off. Straight from the kickoff there was a magnificent 60-yard crossfield diagonal ball but sadly it went straight over the touchline like a missile. Eventually with four strikers now up front, Blake, Papa, Taylor and Moore (Ian), the image was one of the proverbial headless chickens. A better side than Millwo might have had a field day. Out of sorts Little and Moore (Alan) were replaced which meant that ineffective though they had been, there now seemed no focus or plan other than kick and chase stuff. Cox and Beresford distinguished themselves tonight. The latter preferred to Michopoulos who is now Greek History.

Meanwhile, back on the National Geographic channel as things reached their climax towards 11 o clock, the robot did indeed drill a hole in the mysterious door and the camera in the end of the probe revealed not the bones of King Khufu as hoped but (wait for it) another empty space and another closed door. This was deemed to be a terrific discovery. The assembled commentators and pundits tried hard to whip up some excitement out of nothing. Much the same thing happened at Burnley.

Thursday, September 19

Scamper and me wandered around the fields this morning. Whilst he was engrossed, sniffing in the brambles and nettles, and all I could see of him was a stiff upright tail sticking up out of the grass, my mind drifted back to Tuesday's game and then further back than that. The hour of highlights on Sky yesterday afternoon leaving out all the dross actually made it into something reasonably entertaining. Perhaps there is a case for shortening all games to one hour. Then you could reduce player's wages (memo to club accountant). My brain however pondered on the endless list of great Burnley players who would have got a place in last night's team standing on one leg, not that I'm being critical; they're decent, honest lads who have good days and bad just like the rest of us.

I was thinking of great players? Les Latcham and Freddie Smith were the first ever attacking wing backs long before the term was ever invented and Graham Le Saux hadn't even been thought of. The half back line of Blant, Merrington and Waldron was legendary. Any one of them would have made Roy Keane look like a Sunday School teacher and we had all three in the same team. Funnily enough Dave Merrington (still around in the game somewhere) was a Sunday School teacher. Colin Blant allegedly was kept chained up in a cage until match days. Colin Waldron, it is said, used to practise his sliding tackles against the garage door. The list goes on. It begins I suppose with Jimmy McIlroy and goes on with Ray Pointer, Brian Pilkington, John Connelly, Jimmy Adamson, Ralph Coates, Brian O'Neil, Leighton James, Willie Irvine, Andy Lochhead, Dave Thomas, and Steve Kindon.

Steve Kindon was a big six-foot winger with the speed of lightning. With his size and bulk stopping was a problem and the gate had to be opened at the end of the pitch for him to run through after he had whipped in a cross. Then there were Willie Morgan, Martin Dobson, Brian Laws, Ray Hankin, Brian Flynn and Trevor Steven. The list is endless and there are countless more.

Our manager Stan was in fact a Burnley player but left for Carlisle, released by Harry Potts. A Stan tongue-lashing is known as a Stantrum. I wish I was clever and could invent words like that.

Somewhere along the line many years ago, this endless stream of players stopped and now we exist on bargains, an occasional million pound buy, free transfers and loan players. Through good luck King Arthur was unearthed at the beginning of last season. Rumour has it that as part of current cost cutting exercises some of the scouting network has been paid off. Not one player in the current first team other than Paul Weller is a youth system product. Very little seems to be coming through the lower ranks. And in any case Stan's policy seems to be that it is better to pick an experienced old 'un than a maybe good young 'un. There is little if any incentive therefore for any outstanding youth prospect to select Burnley as his club. There is no Academy. Once upon a time it was the first place outstanding kids came to.

The London Clarets website today contains an impassioned plea 'LET'S HAVE THE FACTS' relating to the *Daily Mail* stories and the rumours of impending administration.

> *Andrew Watson did say a few words on the official website recently, but while acknowledging that financial problems are serious, that the club is meeting creditors and looking for new investors, it was notable for avoiding the details. It did not address or deny the specific stories that have appeared. There are many questions a concerned supporter would like to see answered. The club may well be taking the principled stance that they do not comment on rumour. But these stories are appearing in a major national newspaper, and as a series. This stuff is now in the public domain. These are serious allegations and if they are not true the club must rebut them, point by point. Even if they are not true, there is still a danger that negative PR can damage the club, and hurt the morale of the team at a time when there are signs we are getting our act together on the pitch.*
>
> *Supporters too cannot help but be alarmed when they read stories like these. At the same time there has been a mushrooming of rumours about the club in recent days. When we read these stories, while also hearing that the club is allegedly trying to re-negotiate player and staff contracts, that takeover bids may be mounted, and that the club may soon go into administration, how can people not be concerned? And then when you read we've just laid off our scouts...*
>
> *People are bound to ask why the club have not made a statement to rebut these stories, and this can only fuel rumours. Unless they're denied, people are bound to think they are true... the key question we need to an answer to is: are we in danger of going into administration or not... if administration is a possibility we need to know now... Burnley FC must be honest with supporters...* (Firmo, September 2002)

Friday, September 20

Valley Parade tomorrow, or is it The Pulse? Or is it The Bradford and Bingley Stadium? Does anyone know? Bradford's record attendance is against us. The away end used to be called The Charlie Brown, now it is called The Symphony. Whatever happened to good old names like The Shed? What else can you say about Bradford other than it is a way of getting to nicer places like Skipton, Bolton Abbey and The Dales or even Leeds? Of course there's the world-renowned Mumtaz Indian restaurant, which has excellent Kashmiri food.

There used to be an advertising hoarding at the ground for a Bradford solicitor, Kama Sutra: We'll defend you in any difficult positions. But in spite of that, Bradford City in The ValleyParadePulseBradfordandBingley Stadium to their credit have shown that it is possible to have once had a chairman like Geoffrey Richmond, be over thirty million in debt, employ Benito Carbonio, almost go out of business, and still survive.

But first there's the small matter of the visit to the doctors.

A visit to the doctor has nothing to do at all with a football diary about Burnley... except my doctor is a Leeds supporter and there might be the chance of the odd bit of banter. Today I can say well done for beating Man. U but that watching Leeds versus Metalurg Zaporizhya on TV last night in the UEFA Cup was even more excruciating than watching Burnley versus Millwall.

My appointment this morning is 10.00 a.m. Behind the glass partition in the office area are receptionists and secretaries who busy themselves and bury their heads in files and cabinets. Occasionally one of them sallies reluctantly to the window to see a patient who is reporting in. One of them greets a friend and then whispers something but we can still all hear what she says; "Good morning Betty, I thought the doc had cured those piles..."

The first time I ever had piles myself I didn't know what they were and thought I was dying of something horrible. One of our early medieval kings was murdered when he had a red-hot poker thrust up his b**. Mystery surrounds the death of Edward II and his red-hot skewering was reputedly ordered by his wife Queen Isabella on account of he was never in on a Saturday afternoon. They used to do things with red-hot pokers a lot in those days and don't forget they had no anaesthetics. The feeling I had was much the same. The threat of a red-hot poker up the a*** was apparently a great medieval motivator. Football managers and Stan should take note.

There's a coloured card system and a flashing light to say when it's your turn. It's mine now. I'm number 9, Ray Pointer. I'm here because I have fungal nail infection. All I want is a prescription for some Lamisil because my chiropodist says it does the business. Till now I thought Lamisil was one of Keegan's second-rate buys at City.

He looks nonplussed and I decide that this is not the best time to chide him about how pathetic Leeds were last night.

"Yes it's fungal nail infection alright," he decides. "Yes I'll do you a prescription for Lamisil. Now about these pills, some people have a reaction. They could make you sick, change your colour and bring you out in spots."

Watching Blackburn sometimes has the same effect.

Back down the corridor I went and through into the waiting area. It was still silent even though there were still a dozen people in there. A yob with a shaven head, earrings and Leeds Utd tattoos was sat in the corner. He looked so awful it would have been a kindness to put him to sleep.

Monday, September 23

BRADFORD CITY 2 STRUTTING PEACOCKS 2

The facts are these. On Saturday the sun is shining, the sky is blue; the ground is colourful and bright. The drive from home takes just twenty minutes and we park within two minutes of the stadium. Two sets of bedecked supporters are in good voice and there is a fine spectacle in prospect. We draw 2-2, which on the surface seems a good away result at BradfordValleyParadePulseBradfordandBingley Stadium and we watch the game from the privileged comfort of a warm, food laden, drink filled Bradford City supporter's corporate box.

Non-playing spectators Padiham Predator, Graham Branch, Gordon Armstrong and Paul Weller sit in front of us, close enough to speak to.

Bradford score first. First half did we have a shot? Two Bradford players are sent off. The crowd is incensed. We score two and lead 2-1, and then Bradford with nine men equalize in the very last minute. Mrs. T and I eventually think of something to say to our four idols, one of them scoffing chips, along the lines of 'aren't you playing today?', which has to be the dumbest question of all time bearing in mind they're all wearing smart grey suits and injured. Courage plucked, we chat to the four Burnley musketeers Aramis Branch, Porthos Weller, D'Artagnan Armstrong and The Padiham Predator. I take her picture with them and she tells them that I once taught Dean West.

"Tight bugger from Yorkshire?" says one of them.

One of them tells me that yes, Burnley a little while ago were indeed two days away from administration. The Padiham Predator tells me they need to sell a player but nobody is buying. They all look hungry and I feel I should ask them into the box to finish the food in there.

Back in the warm corporate box we (not them) eat heartily, slurp several glasses of Chardonnay and settle in our excellent view seats. But…

If those are the facts though, the story behind them is this. Bradford had two players deservedly (the view of a totally unbiased Burnley supporter) sent off by a brave referee who could never be called a Homer. Our young Greek God Papadopoudiveandfalloveralot could easily have been red carded himself by any other referee for his antics. The Bradfordites are incensed because he isn't sent off. Stan takes him off for his own protection. The Clarets are already remembered from the game last year when my corporate host assures me that we kicked Bradford all over the park and *The Argus* said words to the effect that we were physical, ugly and brutal. You may deduce from this that Burnley are not well loved in Bradford and that Greek restaurants will not do well in this city.

We began with our traditional hoofer style and got nowhere giving away the by now customary generous sloppy goal to give ourselves a challenge. The second half changes saw the artists come on a la Moore (Alan) and Robbie Blake and we played football. Blake transformed us and once the game became more evenly balanced (with Bradford handily reduced to nine men), it became a game we were on the way to winning 2-1 until…

Disgrace, embarrassment and torrents of Bradford derision set in roughly with about fifteen minutes to go. Every Burnley supporter left that ground baffled by what we did at the end. We threw away the chance of a gift three points by spurning the chance to play the ball in the Bradford half and going for a third goal when Bradford were on their knees. Burnley elected to play showboat keepball in their own half with the inevitable slip up which then gave the ball away and off Bradford go and score with 5 seconds left on the clock. My mouth dropped open wide enough to swallow Vince Overson.

"A third goal would have killed it, but we didn't get one," said Stan.

Clarets preference to showboat, play ridiculous keepball patterns and try to run the clock down through downright arrogance led to their downfall, snatching a draw from the jaws of victory... Totally unprofessional over the last 15 minutes in their conduct and preference for playing keepball rather than put the game well and truly beyond a depleted and dead on its feet Bradford side left many Clarets in moods ranging from disappointment to downright anger as they left the stadium in states of bewilderment and embarrassment... Amateurish tactics allowed Bradford to equalize in the dying seconds. How long it will take the Clarets to recover and where it leaves relationships with supporters, players and management only time will tell... A horrid final 15 minutes of utter contempt shown in particular by showboating Clarets defenders...(David Clark, Claretsmad website)

The London Supporters website has a mixed bag of reactions...

What the hell was that? I don't know what to think. Why were we messing about like that? The most unprofessional, amateurish, non-league, pathetic display in the second half I have ever seen. I walked away from the ground feeling like we'd lost... I can't believe what I just saw... dock all their wages until they play with more conviction... I just hope that conceding that goal doesn't have disastrous consequences for the campaign ahead... This was a team playing without brains or heart... It was just more embarrassing than anything else; we should have put them away but just showed our limitations... Today was one of the strangest games I've seen in a long time. It was a contest between two hopeless sides. It's now three hours after the game and I still can't believe we didn't win. The reason why we didn't win is down to sheer unprofessionalism on the part of players and the management. The team should feel ashamed of themselves. They have let us all down today. I was sickened when Bradford scored their equalizer. It's going to take a long time to forgive Burnley.

You don't need to ask what the Bradford websites say. Their boysfrombrazil site says everything damning that you would expect about nasty, physical, cheating Burnley. Apparently it was the ball not an elbow that gave West a fat lip and their man sent off. But their web report ends with 'And what of Burnley? You, Burnley supporter, deserve better than that'.

When the final whistle went you'd have thought Bradford had won the Premiership. It must have been just like that in the boardroom when they got shut of Benito Carbootsale. Burnley fans slunk away including me and the Mrs. At least though we were full of top-notch chicken, salad and moussaka.

Put any two Burnley supporters in a room a thousand miles from home and if one of them says The Orient Game, the other will know which game he means, and recall it with pride. From now on I should imagine if any two Bradford supporters meet a thousand miles away from home they will talk about the day Bradford drew 2-2 with Burnley.

Monday, September 23

The controversy rages on. The Bradford Yul Brynner look-alike, Nicky Law, not somebody I'd like to meet down a dark alley on a Saturday night on Manningham Lane, vented his spleen on the website and in *The Argus*, saying that the three scout's reports they had on Papafalloveralot said nobody should go near him because he dives about all over the place. Law laid the blame entirely on Papaguiltyofcourse for the sending off of his player Bower, adding that he wouldn't condone it from any of his own players. What Mr Brynner of course doesn't realise is that Papa just can't keep on his feet anyway a la Emile Heskey. Some players are just prone to falling over. Gravity seems to exert an extra pull. They don't dive; they just naturally by some mysterious process forever end up on the floor in an undignified heap. Papa just naturally fits into this category.

Tuesday, September 24

Stan responded to Mr. Law. No dull moments or tame dull draws on our travels and peace and quiet afterwards; it's war after a Bradford Burnley game.

> *Nicky Law's comments were absolutely disgraceful, they were slanderous and he should apologise. His comments were those of a young, inexperienced manager, talking about other teams when he should be talking about his own. He must be a very good manager if he has time to talk about others. He should concentrate on his own. Dimi is not a diver; their manager was totally unprofessional and ridiculous. Dimi had a rough time with their defenders; they were like a flock of locusts around him. I took him off in case he got sent off. The crowd was roaring and bawling and the way that Law and his assistant behaved during the game was nothing short of disgraceful. I should imagine that the fourth official will report them and if they carry on like that they will end up sitting in the stand.*

"I would like to say sorry for the comments I made about Dimitrios Papadopoulos," said the former Chesterfield chief. "They were said in the heat of the moment immediately after the match. Unfortunately I made comments about another team's player and I shouldn't have done. I intended no harm towards Stan or to Burnley."

Apology accepted.

The controversy thus dies away, the ground has been swept and the litter cleared. For us it's Milton Keynes at home on Saturday. A crowd of fewer than 11,000 or maybe just over, more than likely I should think. With that level of support the club will continue to lose money on a weekly basis.

Wednesday, September 25

I read recently that there are something like 600 professional footballers without clubs thanks largely to cost cutting, staff trimming and the Digital fiasco. Add to that the large number of young players at Premier clubs who are probably available on loan. We think about signing Lennie Johnrose for another month. He has done well for Burnley. He's had a great career, played over 400 games and scored a few goals. In his prime at Bury he was excellent they say. Now, he does his best, puts his head and feet where the likes of you and me would keep well clear, gets up off the ground when the likes of the average supporter would be poleaxed for a fortnight and is still a useful tidy getstuckin, get it and give it kind of player.

Clearly we can't quite be in the dire position that Watford find themselves in. News has broken that apparently Watford need to find £9.5million pretty damned quick and have asked playing staff to take a 12% pay cut. They sold their ground some time ago for £6million and in the summer managed to get rid of several highly paid stars although the word stars might be a bit strong. There but for the grace of God go we.

Last night at the launch of the latest Burnley FC book, Andrew Watson told the audience that Burnley were not going bust in the next three weeks.

> *We will not be asking any of our players to take a pay cut and don't feel we can... the players at this club have signed contracts and as a club it is up to us to honour them... the players have been doing a terrific job on the pitch in the last few weeks, being unbeaten in the last six games and at the same time we are trying to get things right off it.*

Thursday, September 26

Mutt and me wandered down along the canal again this morning first thing, after the routine search of papers for Burnley snippets and then the trawl through the websites for Claret gossip updates. There must be a dozen Burnley sites and that's not counting *The Burnley Express* or *The Lancashire Evening Post*.

The walk as ever starts with the path of a thousand piddles and the advantage of an early start is that we don't meet many other dogs. He and other dogs do not get on and sadly he has few if any friends: A bit like Roy Keane I suppose.

The builders/fishermen across the other side fall about laughing at the sight of a small Scottie setting about a dog twice his size. I used to watch Brian O'Neil knocking seven bells out of players twice his size in a similar sort of manner, which was always very satisfying if they were from Manchester United.

There wasn't much on the webs this morning. There's rivalry not just between teams, but also between websites like Burnley and Watford. Last season's account of Watford 1 Burnley 2 by Igor Wowk should be required A level English Literature reading.

It's at moments like this when I wonder what it must be like to be an Arsenal supporter. They thumped PSV Eindhoven 4-0 in Holland last night. They did the Double last season. They remain unbeaten for God knows how many games and play a brand of football that is a delight to watch. How boring.

Friday, September 27

Nope, we have not signed Lennie Johnrose for another month. Does this mean we are at the bottom of the financial barrel or is it a common sense decision now that Gordon Armstrong is back to fitness, Paul Weller is nearly fit and Paul Cook seems to be back in favour? Or, are we saving our money to enable us to keep Marlon Beresford for another month? You do feel a sense of sorrow and sympathy for a lad with a wife and family. He joins the 600 or so fellow professionals on the scrapheap and has only known football as a job. This is the other side of the so-called glamour game. Yes, Digital has a lot to answer for. The human side is a disappointed Lennie Johnrose. Two or three days ago he must have thought he was being kept on. Reality today is otherwise. I really do hope he can find something somewhere.

Tomorrow sees the arrival of Wimbledon or is it Milton Keynes? How can they possibly call themselves Wimbledon, when they upstick themselves 70 miles northwards? In articles so far about the move to MK I've read that it's 70 miles from Plough Lane, or 83 or even 110. The move is cloaked in controversy. How would a Burnley supporter feel if Burnley FC suddenly decamped to Morecambe? How would anybody feel if they had to go to Morecambe? My understanding of this controversy is limited to say the least but seems to go like this:

Once upon a time there was a non-league club called Wimbledon who became very good and eventually played their way into the Football League. In 1975, as a non-league club they put Burnley out of the FA Cup (we were actually quite mighty in 1975) and held the great Leeds Utd when they really were giants, 0-0 at Plough Lane in a game memorable for Dickie Guy saving a Peter Lorimer penalty. 13 years later they had won the FA Cup and become a legendary club in the world of football.

Over the years they have produced a string of great players and great characters, not necessarily the same thing, people like Dennis Thumper Wise, Vinnie The Terminator Jones, and Harry The Gob Bassett. It is even said that bandleader Billy Cotton played centre forward for them in the 1930s. For years they were propped up by Lebanese Chairman Sam The Man who used to say things like: "We have to remain the English bulldog SAS club. We have to sustain ourselves by power and the attitude that we kick ass.," and "Before we go down we will leave a stream of blood from here to Timbuktu."

Well anyway, having sold the ground to Safeway for £8million, then later on 80% of his stake to two Norwegians for £25million, and then three years later the last 20% for £3 million, he eventually took off to Cardiff City. He never quite made it to Timbuktu, which is a pity, as I understand that Timbuktu is a much nicer place than Cardiff. Play It Again Sam, in his early days at Nincompoop Park, used to wind up the Cardiff supporters by parading round the pitch and make them even worse than they really were until the FA had a quiet word with him after a Leeds cup game.

With the exit and demise of Plough Lane, Wimbledon have since been playing their games at Selhurst Park. Enter Mr. Koppel, businessman and entrepreneur, who wants, and in fact is about to move Wimbledon to Milton Keynes against the wishes of all real Womble fans. An FA panel consisting of the Three Stooges finally sanctioned the move after it was twice turned down.

So, the plan is that Wimbledon will play at the Milton Keynes Bowl and the move is linked to a leisure/retail development allegedly involving IKEA, ASDA and other sundry big names. Enter Wimbledon, but not the Wimbledon we know. This is the WimbledonMiltonKeynesFranchise. And hey presto!Milton Keynes have a Division One football team without having to work its way up the football league pyramid. Can Milton Keynes sustain a Division One team? Is Milton Keynes interested in Division One football?

They will play in The Bowl for the second half of the season, or at least that's the plan. All roads in the paradise that is MK are apparently identical and The Bowl is in the middle of scruffy parkland, knee high in weeds. Even by modern standards it is a concrete monstrosity. It is a former rock music venue which, according to *The Mirror* yesterday, will be converted to have a 12,000 capacity set of temporary stands until they can build the 28,000 seat stadium which is proposed but for which there is as yet no planning permission.

> *This whole thing isn't about building a football ground to rehouse a famous club. It's about constructing a retail and leisure development with a football ground attached. It's about making money out of doing so. It's about people who bought a Premier League football club for a whole heap of money, didn't realise they might get relegated and are now looking for ways to make money out of the investment... do you honestly think that there's no patch of brown land in West London where Wimbledon couldn't build a new ground?* (Firmo, London Clarets website).

No real Wimbledon fans will set foot in the place or even watch the team at Selhurst Park now. They prefer to support the new club they have set up, AFC Wimbledon, which plays in the Combined Counties League at level 8 in the football pyramid. For their first game, played at the Kingston Ground, there was a crowd of 4,000 and 1,000 were turned away.

Some team called WimbledonMiltonKeynesFranchise or whatever their name is are at The Turf on Saturday. The real Wimbledon will be playing Frimley Green in the Combined Southern Counties League and here's wishing them all the best. Even the most neutral, disinterested football minded person could not say the whole thing isn't bizarre

Saturday, September 28

What perceptions have other fans of Burnley? No doubt what they are in Bradford. They don't like us. I got an e-mail from a Bradford bloke I know. It was brutal and to the point:

> *The same fixture last season left us with 5 or 6 injured players. Ward was out for 8 weeks after the shoeing that he got. I was flabbergasted that Burnley ended with 11 men in that game too.*

'Physical play has always been the Clarets trademark… a team of gamesmen, a team of cheats…' said the boysfrombrazil Bradford website.

What, us?

Tim Shaw, Watford's Chief Executive, talking about current financial problems, told *The Observer*:

It is not just the headline loss of £4.3 million from ITV Digital, but the decimation of the transfer market and the loss of faith from banks and other investors. We've had informal conversations with 5 or 6 clubs in our position and the PFA have met with around 10 in significant financial difficulties.

Graham Simpson, who took over as Watford Chairman, recently said:

Survival rather than promotion is now the priority for all but a handful of clubs in the First Division.

Monday September 30

PROPER FOOTBALL TEAM 1 SHAMPRETEND 0

FRIMLEY GREEN 0 REAL WIMBLEDON 5

Never mind that. The big news is John Major and Edwina Currie. The Prime Minister who said we must return to basics and family values, we now discover was having it away with the egg lady and steamy novel writer Edwina Currie way back years ago. How the course of history might have been changed if the affair had been outed in the newspapers and he had never become Prime Minister. Her newly published diaries reveal the four-year affair, which took place in the late eighties.

What were Burnley doing then? The Orient Game was 87. Had that been lost we wouldn't be here today. There was a Wembley appearance the year after when we lost to Wolves but after that we just scrabbled about until 91/92 when Jimmy Mullen came and made us fourth division champions. Jimmy Mullen transformed the fortunes of Burnley FC. But people have short memories and seasons later he was hounded out of the club. It's not often that I read the front page first on a Sunday but yesterday was one.

When I did eventually get to Burnley matters, (a game we couldn't get to for reasons various) yes they had won, yes Little had scored, yes they had played well most of the time, yes, they deserved the win, was the overwhelming opinion, and the attendance was a reasonable 12,000 plus. Shambledon apparently, according to which report you read, brought 60 or 71 supporters with them in a fleet of cars. The real Wimbledon beat Frimley Green 5-0.

Worryingly however, more snippets emerge from the meeting of Division One chairmen. These latest revelations suggest that several clubs in the division are in danger of being unable to fulfil their fixtures by the end of the season. Our man with his ear trumpet to the boardroom door, Tony Scholes, says that Burnley are a club that can offer no guarantees that they will reach the season's end. Only Norwich, Portsmouth and Wolves could give assurances that they could definitely complete their fixtures. Watford executive Tim Shaw says he has spoken to six other clubs in the same precarious position as Watford. The PFA have had talks with ten clubs who have expressed significant financial difficulties. It's not just the ITV Digital loss. It's lack of player sales. When was the last time a Premiership club paid a big fee to a Division One club? Movement to any other clubs in fact has stopped and then there's the horrendous and ridiculous wages paid to average players. Crystal Palace chairman Simon Jordan says that the average player salary there is £297,000 a year and must be cut.

To save money at the Turf, Michopoulos was offloaded ironically to Palace for a month to cover their goalkeeper injuries. That presumably means Beresford is safe at Burnley for another month but left us without cover on the bench on Saturday.

****

So, after the debacle that was August, with 4 defeats and embryonic calls for Stan's resignation, we creep and splutter, counting every penny, towards mid-table respectability with 12 points from 6 games.

You start to think. Ambling with the dog round the field, silly thoughts emerge. Twelve points from the last 6 games, this is promotion form. Don't be ridiculous, but it's true; maintain this and we'll end up with over 80 points. Take 12 points every month and that's play-offs at least.

The clacking of a wren, funny how such a tiny bird produces such a din, disturbed this fantasy train of thought. September has been excellent in terms of points and results. Forget the Bradford mess up and we should be pleased. But this is Burnley we're talking about here. Good month, bad month, lurch along and stutter. No, don't be silly. Play-offs, you're joking. Just two or three weeks ago you were thinking relegation is a certainty. Now you think we're on the up. This is how a football supporter's mind works if you follow a club like Burnley, one minute downcast, and the next upbeat and optimistic. Imagine being a Portsmouth fan at the moment. All those years of misery and now top of Division One and well clear of the third spot: echoes of ourselves at the beginning of last season.

And, if you want to read about the paradise that is Milton Keynes, then look no further than Chapter 14 in Bryson's *Notes From A Small Island.* Like me you will close the chapter having determined never ever to visit the place.

OCTOBER

Tuesday, October 1

Tonight in the Worthington Cup there is Huddersfield to dispose of, a team who haven't won or scored in five games, have all their first choice strikers injured, are without their two first choice centre backs and are second bottom of Division Two. Cakewalk? Don't be silly, this is Burnley we follow. With Huddersfield being so close to Leeds, it's well less than an hour from home, so we shall be there.

Huddersfield apparently has claims to be, or would like to claim to be, an Arts Centre Of The North. My limited experience of the place is that it is a dump and the wool and cloth industry upon which it was founded has gone very much the same way as everything has gone in Bradford. The names Harold Wilson and Denis Law spring to mind but not many more. What Huddersfield can claim is that in the surrounding areas there is wonderful wild countryside and there are places like Marsden and Holmfirth which are much more worth a visit: the one for its Jazz Festival and the other for *Last Of The Summer Wine*. Holmfirth a hundred years ago was part of the great Yorkshire woollen workshop with hundreds of clattering looms. Now it is a sleepy postcard village where evidence of the past can be seen in the old weaver's and mill worker's cottages. Ginnels, narrow alleyways, wind up behind them towards the hillsides. Old loading doors and winching beams still decorate many a shop front.

The best you can probably say about Huddersfield itself is that it is a traditional Northern Yorkshire town, with names like Gasworks Street (honest), and that the McAlpine Stadium is a visually superb stadium. This Arts Centre stuff is based, I am informed, on the work of poet Simon Armitage who has apparently written about the strains of supporting Huddersfield Town, of which there must be many, and the modern art of the stadium with its curves and wonderful symmetry. It's a stunningly attractive ground especially at a night game when it is lit and illuminated. It's just a pity about the rest of the surrounding area and the struggling team that plays in it that looks destined for yet further decline.

Wednesday, October 2

TERRIERS 0 HUFFERS AND PUFFERS EVENTUALLY 1

Accrington Stanley are alive and well. Accrington Who? You might well ask but any football fan should know off by heart that Accrington FC were one of the founder members of the Football League in 1888. Then five years later they resigned. Another team, Stanley Villa, whose players largely lived in and around Stanley Street, changed their name to Accrington Stanley. In 1921 they were then one of the founder members of the Third Division North. In 1962 they bowed out of the Football League Division Four. At that point Burnley FC ruled supreme, one of the giants of English football, and there was talk of them taking over Accrington as some kind of reserve team. Since then both clubs have faded into obscurity, the one into near oblivion, and the other very nearly if it hadn't beaten Leyton Orient 2-1. More than just a few Burnley supporters have a soft spot for Accrington and Stanley, which acts as a sort of buffer between Burnley and Blackburn.

Accrington Stanley now find themselves top of the Unibond Premier Division by five points, unbeaten in eleven games. The Vauxhall Conference beckons and after that the Football League. Now hey up, 'owld on, some realism is called for. Isn't this the club whose very name was a music hall joke, the name being used for a laugh in a TV advert for milk some years ago?

But enough of this illuminating digression: somehow we ground out a win last night. The away end was crammed with probably three thousand Burnley supporters, a phalanx of claret and blue, 1,000 of them consuming pies and downing pints. There was the usual list of pies on offer including a Guest Pie. It deserved enquiry as to what it might be. It turned out to be Cornish Pasty. Of course, they were sold out. A couple of thousand Huddersfield fans were dotted about the rest of the stadium. The seats are in claret and blue, which seems a strange choice for a team that plays in blue and white. A dire first half passed tediously. Little and West were rested with the result that down the right hand side there was nothing eventful or dangerous. The midfield was largely bypassed with overhead balls for the runners Moore (Ian) and Blake to chase. The Terriers were sharp and incisive but demonstrated in the box why they can't score. They should take lessons from John Major. He had no trouble.

And then the second half livened up somewhat. Any noise came from the Burnley end. Chances came and went. Both goalkeepers made stunning saves. Excitement eventually appeared but so did extra time. Branch by then had replaced Alan Moore. Please explain to me why Branch is moaned at and Taylor too, although the latter not as much as he was. Branch then demonstrated that as a wide left attacking player he is terrific. Taylor is like good wine and gets better with age. Papafallalot replaced the fitful Blake. And in extra time, mercifully sparing us penalties, Papascoreagain got the winner finishing off a slide rule through ball (on the ground, please note) made for him to run onto and slot home. Beresford kept us in the game after a Bradfordesque giveaway by Cox. The whistle blew. Cue delirium but mainly relief that we could now go home. Five and a half thousand fans in total turned up, probably enough to just about cover the McAlpine Stadium electricity bill.

Friday, October 4

Sheffield. Once upon a time you could smell it as you drove up the M1 from the South towards it. A haze of smoke, grime and pollution used to hang over the place like a shroud. Not so any more although heavy industry remains visible from the great concrete viaduct that carries you by. To the left, if you are heading north, is Meadowhall, acres and acres of parked cars, shopping malls, and a specially built station. It's awesome and frankly not for the faint hearted. There are stories of people who went into Meadowhell and it took them a month to find their way out. If you find the Metro at Gateshead too much, then Meadowhall is Hell. To the left, if you are going south, oh God, lies Rotherham. We shall leave any further mention of that northern paradise till later.

Today though, the air round Sheffield is clean and the image of a smoke-belching town is gone. Modern art and architecture mix with the old. The derelict areas are being filled with retail areas, and many factory buildings have been or are being restored. In the surrounding wooded hillsides, streams tumble down that once provided the power for the making of knives and tools as early as the thirteenth century. In Victorian times the immense iron, steel, silver plate and cutlery industries were world famous. It might be said that Sheffield was the archetypal grim northern industrial city in the Victorian age. Leeds, Manchester and Bradford might argue with that. But its history goes way before the Victorian era and amongst the possessions of Edward III, a Sheffield-made knife was found. History does not recall whether it was inscribed with Up The Blades.

Maybe of more interest to the football supporter is that it was once a brewing centre as well. Ward's is an example and many a factory man quenched his thirst at the end of a day's work slaving in the heat of a steel works. Now, much like steel in the city, it is gone, shut down by its owners Vaux. Stones had a brewery here as well but not today. If you want to see a fine collection of Ward's memorabilia, then a pint in the Red Lion on Charles Street is a must.

If Sheffield is known for one thing (other than Joe Cocker), then it must be the World Snooker Championships held at The Crucible Theatre. The world seems to be divided into two camps, those who sit enthralled at the sight of little coloured balls being propelled into a string thing by men in fancy waistcoats poking a long stick about, and those who find it a great cure for insomnia.

And so to the game, Wednesday not United. Probably there is a history of the club somewhere that kindly explains why they are called Wednesday. Actually there is, you can find out in the wonderful Simon Inglis Book, *The Football Grounds of Great Britain*. I am pleased that I have found out the reason but I am feeling mischievous, shan't tell you, and you can find out for yourselves. But I will share my knowledge that the nickname Owls comes from the time they used to play at Owlerton.

I have told you why Accrington are called Stanley. The latter won again by the way, 4-2 on Wednesday and want to sign Kevin Ball. There's a bloke playing for Wednesday who always scores against us, Shefki Kuqi. Wednesday won the competition to sign him at the beginning of the year. It wasn't much of a competition really. Burnley gave Wednesday an unfair advantage: they wouldn't pay as much. So, bless him, he took his boots to Sheffield and his goals kept them in Division One and us out of the play-offs. He'll score against us tomorrow. These things are in the stars. We've a mixed history against this team, now a faded struggling club in a renowned stadium.

Sunday, October 6

CHUPA CHUPS 1 CHAMPS 3

There are two reasons why it is good to beat Wednesday. Firstly, any team which is daft enough to parade around with shirts adorned by the words Chupa Chups deserves to be beaten. And secondly any team that allows itself to play in front of the cacophony that calls itself a band deserves to plummet down to Vauxhall Conference ignominy. It is excruciating.

There's a sadness about Wednesday these days. A poor team play in a superb but half empty stadium. You still sense the ghosts and memories of the tragedy of '89, and dwindling numbers of supporters barely fill the stands. Yesterday the sun shone and what would otherwise be gloomy and shabby surrounding streets of terraced housing looked brighter and cleaner. There's a plethora of chip shops and fast food takeaways on the approaches and fans mill around with plastic plates laden with pies, fish, kebabs and chips. The smell of vinegar is everywhere.

This band at Sheffield defies description. Apparently there are supporter's movements and campaigns to have it banned such is the racket it drums up - literally. The drum thudding is incessant, intrusive and loud to the point of pain. As the chief anti-band campaigner says, who wants to listen to that racket when you're 4-0 down. Well, it was 3-0 down in the case of the currently all-conquering Clarets although Wednesday pulled a goal back after that.

Something strange has happened at Burnley. We are winning. And now it is three wins in a row and suddenly we lift up to twelfth place in the table with fifteen points. At the end of August there was gloom and now there is delight.

There's nothing like the sensation when a goal goes in right under your noses and you're sitting behind the goal. The second, scored by Little, was a delight, involving intricate little one-twos, and then a ball played through to him by Blake, now being called a genius, which enabled him to beat a man and slide it home from a difficult angle. There's a sort of slow motion silence that takes place as the ball rolls in and you actually hear it rippling the netting before bedlam erupts and we all go wild. The sound of the ball rolling down the back of the netting was even louder still as Moore (Ian) hit an unstoppable shot from 16 yards (some say 20, it makes it sound better), and then again the Burnley fan noise filled the ground.

In the Worthington Cup, it's Totteringham next. The news was passed along like pass the parcel, eyes opened wide, hands were rubbed and excitement swelled. Tottenham, memories of great games in the Sixties and a 4-1 win there in the Eighties, and when they come to Burnley again in November, they'll know they've been in a game. Burnley fans have a soft spot for Tottenham: it goes back years.

Most of us are amazed and puzzled that Stan Ternent was not named manager of the month for September following the great results and the recovery from the debacle that was August.

Monday, October 7

Groups of Wednesday fans, I won't say hordes, there weren't enough of them, left the ground looking morose and miserable on Saturday. Why are they called Wednesday:? Because it wouldn't sound the same if they were called Sheffield Tuesday. They're allegedly £23million in debt. Spotting a smiling Wednesday supporter was harder than finding an accurately graded A level paper. It's just a pity we declared at 3-0 giving us that ridiculously nail biting last 20 minutes. Only Burnley can be 3-0 up and still leave your nerves in shreds and give the clear impression that we're just hanging on. We can thank their centre forward Owusu, who was rank, for them not scoring more. Out went Okoku in the summer, in comes Owusu. He's even oworser. That goalkeeper Beresford was our man of the match tells you something. His month here is almost up and we need to sell the family silver to keep him, that's how important he has been. But up come the tables on all the Sports Channels and yes there we are on screen, up to twelfth and are in the top half. Who'd have thought that four games into August? Play-off place only six points away and with a game in hand.

Stan gets lots of plaudits in the Sundays and the Mondays and rightly so at the moment. I saw him close up at Bradford as he passed by me just a couple of feet away, half an hour after the game. He has a warm; lived-in kind of face but one which gives away nothing and which is impossible to read other than the eyes saying 'I don't suffer fools gladly'. Nobody is better at wheeling and dealing and fashioning a team, wherever he is manager and yet... why do we lose at places like Walsall and Grimsby, or at home to Brighton who haven't won a game since, when we win at places like Derby and Wednesday? Why was August so rank? It's the same players.

Tuesday, October 8

Talks open this week to keep Beresford at the Turf. If he doesn't re-sign for another month or season or whatever, then the club has somehow got itself into a silly situation. Nikos Michopoulos is absentos at Crystal Palos on loanos, and the third goalkeeper we have, James Salisbury, is injured. Michopoulos was allowed to play for Palace in their recent Worthington Cup tie so he is therefore cup-tied should he return to Burnley if Supermarl is injured. Nikos can come backos immediately if required but would be unavailable for the Tottingham game. Marlon could leave at the end of his current one month spell should any club come for him with more money than the cash-strapped Clarets.

The good news though is that cash is on its way. The Football League in spite of being left in the mire by ITV in the summer has ,believe it or not, signed a new deal with them to allow them to show Nationwide highlights. Apparently Burnley's share will be £88,000. That plus something similar for some website deal, plus Sky money for the Tottingham game which is to be shown live, means that presumably creditors can be fobbed off a little longer. I imagine too Beresford's eyes will have spotted this good news. When Stan and Chairman Kilby sit down to talk about him staying at the Turf and what to offer him, the conversation will presumably go something along the lines of:

"Na then Mr. Chairman, we've got ter keep 'im. He won us the game at Huddersfield and he won us the game at Sheffield."

"Right Stan ah know, but we can't offer 'im the moon. We can offer 'im a fair wage for a fair day's work but yer musn't fer god's sake mention the Sky cup game money, the website money or the ITV money... anyway we've banned ITV from the Turf so ah don't quite know what'll 'appen abart that. Right then, ask 'im to come in an' leave all the talkin' ter me."

Thursday, October 10

Barnsley are in administration with perhaps ten more to follow by the end of next month. (Telegraph Sport)

There have been rumours that Burnley will sell the ground and the training ground at Gawthorpe but these have been denied by the club. Gawthorpe is a place they have owned since the Bob Lord days but is a soggy, badly drained, permanent flood area when it rains. Who would buy a place like that, and why then could we not beat Birmingham at home last season in the rain on a waterlogged pitch, if that's what we train on?

Stan started a touchline ban this week because of his cussedness way back last season during the controversial Wolves game when a referee of dubious parentage, competency and eyesight awarded Wolves goals that weren't, and disallowed a goal that was, for us. On such decisions are play-off places decided. A perfectly good Gareth Taylor goal was disallowed at one end only for Wolves to break away and score a clearly offside goal at the other. To say the ground and management was incensed is the understatement of all time. Result - missed play-off place.

They found me guilty and fined me two and a half grand and warned me about my future conduct and banned me from the touchline, which comes into being sometime in October. But I'll get the thing through. I had a fair hearing with them but I think they made the wrong decision, which I told them. But we're all big boys now so I have to accept it. They accused me of confronting the referee and saying some things. But I've defended myself and told them that I didn't do that. But they rule in all probability, how you would in a court of law. We are governed by the Football Association, and the Football Association have won, so that's where I am up to.

Watching Burnley, I sometimes worry about my blood pressure but it is fine. This is good and quite a relief because I thought I had really high BP. I can bandy words like hypertension, elevated, systolic and diastolic with anybody. I had mine checked at the Well Man Clinic this morning. I sat in the waiting room listening to the usual coughs, sneezes, groans and wheezes, and that was just the doctor. Anyway, eventually I get to see the nurse who prods and pokes and tests this and that and I am pronounced fine, which surprises me because watching Burnley at the moment is enough to produce no end of blood pressure.

"And do you have any exercise, relaxation or hobbies?" she asks.

"I watch Burnley as often as possible," I said.

She looked nonplussed and puzzled.

Bombshell news today is the appointment of Howard Wilkinson as new Sunderland manager. I have a pal who is a Sunderland supporter and he is tearing his hair out. I have it on good authority that fans are wandering around the town bereft of speech, open mouthed in a state of amazed bemusement and perplexity. Howard Wilkinson is dour, boring, anonymous, unexciting, schoolmasterly, and largely uninspirational, and that's on a good day: the football equivalent of Ian Duncan Smith. I should imagine the whole football world is stunned. A cheerful Sunderland supporter is harder to find today than a happy Tory at this weeks Bournemouth Conference. Stan has invited the sacked Peter Reid to visit Burnley anytime he wishes. Apparently they are big pals. Stan always embraces jobless managers, Brian Flynn when Wrexham sacked him, and now Peter Reid.

Friday, October 11

Marvellous Marlon has signed for another month. Presumably that will use up any money coming in from the newly announced sponsorship deal with local Ford car dealer CD

Bramall. The Jimmy Mac stand will be The Jimmy Mac Stand Sponsored by CD Bramall. These names get longer and longer.

How will they fit them on a ticket?

I'm doing some more teaching today. It used to be a job where you could have lots of laughs. Not any more. It's one reason why I abandoned being a Head. It's a shame. Studies by The University of Maryland Medical Centre, Baltimore, show that people with a well developed sense of humour are less prone to cardiac problems and mental stress. That's why it's essential I suppose to have a sense of humour not just to be a teacher but a Burnley supporter as well. And when you're both…

In some mysterious way laughter protects the heart. The research team tested the sense of humour of 300 people and said that people should set aside some time every day to have a laugh. Teachers should seriously consider this though deciding which part of the day might be a bit difficult. Bursting out giggling in the middle of an OFSTED Inspection or one of the Head's more serious assemblies might not be advisable. Nor would it be appropriate I suppose for a Burnley first teamer in the middle of a Stan ear bashing at half time, after you've just let the third goal in and had a stinker.

"What's that gaffer?"

"It's your f*****g P45."

"Ha ha ha ha ha…"

It is thought that mental stress is associated with impairment of the endothelium, the protective barrier lining our blood vessels. This can then cause inflammatory reactions that lead to fat and cholesterol build up in the coronary arteries - and then bang, heart attack. Laughter counteracts this mental stress and people who see the funny side of things (a Papa dive, Little's gangly legs, Gnohere kissing Stan, a Blackburn defeat), are less likely to have a heart attack. The message seems to be when the doctor tells you one day you have a heart problem and you're a teacher, or Stan tells you you're finished at Burnley because you couldn't score a goal from one yard, just laugh.

"What's that gaffer?"

"It's my f*****g fist."

"Ha ha ha ha…"

Not funny if you're a Leicester supporter, the latest club to be on the rocks. Trading in their shares has been suspended and players have been asked to take a 20% wage cut. Bradford, Barnsley, now Leicester, who will be next? Their goalkeeper Ian Walker pointed out that they play in a full stadium, have sold several players, have got rid of Dennis (let me hit you) Wise and his £30,000 a week wage and then he asked the reasonable question, 'how come we are in financial trouble?', as he laughed all the way to his bank probably. Then there's Fabrizio Ravioli at Derby, a club millions in debt. What's he on? Another one allegedly on £30,000 a week and hasn't played for weeks with his ankle injury. He must be malato comme un parrot.

I have heard we have had an offer of £10 million for Turf Moor. If this is the case, whoever is offering it had better hold on. I'm coming. There is very little we can do with Gawthorpe because although we own 59 acres it is classed as agricultural land and is protected. Currently it is valued at around £300,000. (Barry Kilby. Lancashire Evening Telegraph)

Saturday, October 12

Two England supporters are shot/knifed in Bratislava. Alex Ferguson is accused of indecently assaulting a young woman during a trip to South Africa. George Burley is sacked as Ipswich manager. Coventry ask their players to take a wage cut. Ulrika Jonsson is about to publish her kiss and tell book about her affair with Sven Goran Eriksson, and the world (and England team) wait with bated breath for her to spill the beans. But enough of trivia, there are weightier matters. Burnley are at home to Walsall today.

There are a lot of press stories circulating in the media plotting the club's demise. We can only repeat that we are doing everything we can to ensure its survival, which we will do. The Directors and staff on the financial side have probably done more for the club in the last couple of months than in the previous three or four years. Unfortunately it is not the glamorous side of football. We are asking people who we have debts with to hold off and hope to make announcements shortly... the latest media rumours of the club selling Gawthorpe and Turf Moor are not on our agenda... (Chief Executive Andrew Watson, Match Programme today).

The Football League have negotiated a highlights package with ITV which is expected to be signed in the next few days. You may well ask have we no morals in accepting a deal with ITV? The situation is that Division One clubs will receive a cheque for over £100,000 in the next couple of weeks. There is no club in the Football League that can turn down that amount of money at this time of crisis. (Andrew Watson. Match programme today)

Phil Gray, ex-Claret and Northern Ireland international striker, has signed for Chelmsford City having been out of contract with his last club Oxford United. His new manager said, Phil is a class act and has a proven record with top clubs. His vast experience and ability round the box will really help our promotion push this season. In the pub the other night a Chelmsford fan (there are some) asked me whether Gray was the big fat donkey who used to play for your lot? I told him he must be mistaken. No fat donkey has ever played for the Clarets. (Burnley fanzine, number 19, When The Ball Moves issued today)

Aranalde, Zdrilic, Rodrigues, Leitao, Corica, Herivelto, Martinez, Matias... Impressed? Real Madrid? Juventus? Deportivo? Inter Milan? No... Walsall.

BURNLEY 2 (only just), WALSALL ALL STAR CONTINENTALS 1

And yet again we came away wondering quite how we won that, quite how we now extend the unbeaten run to ten and quite how we are now in ninth place only three points away from the play-offs. Some team, somewhere, sometime, is going to give us the mother of all clatterings.

As ever the final quarter of an hour was nail-biting stuff as we hung on after AC Inter Walsall La Coruna scored following a rare Beresford misjudgement. There was no large target man today so we had the two small forwards (Moore Ian and Blake Robbie).

Together they have a height between them of not much more than 5 feet. Nevertheless they were more than a handful for the large, physically strong Walsall defence when the ball was on the floor. Blake's goal was a classic, a little dink over the defence; there he was running onto it and then a lob over the too far advanced goalkeeper. Steve Davis scored the second after the pass of the season from Tony Grant to Little who then got the cross over. Davis had a reasonably good midfield game again. The Sunday *Sport First* then placed him surprisingly in the team of the week at centre back. Perhaps they went to a different game than the rest of us.

The club made an extra £561 in a novel enough way. With Stan banned to the front row of the stand his place in the dugout was auctioned to the highest bidder on the Internet site. Quite where the odd pound comes from is not clear. Someone has suggested that each week one place in the team could be auctioned.

"It was crap," said manager Stan from the front row of the Directors' box immediately behind the dugout, though whether he was referring to his new seat, or the game, or something the dog left behind is not clear.

Monday, October 14

I've been reading *Blue Moon*, an account of the season Man City spent in Division Two. Chapter Three brought back some memories of the nightmare time we had when managed by John Bond, (is it really nearly twenty years ago?), who when last heard of was Director of Football at some obscure Unibond club somewhere.

Nobody can forget John Bond. He arrived at Burnley when things were bad. By general agreement he left them no better. He was a big time flash manager before anybody even knew what a big time flash manager was. He invented them, with his coiffured mane, big car, Rolex watch, designer suits, charisma and celebrity status. When he smiled his teeth glinted and sparkled in the sunshine. He was the original Mr Suave, Mr. Cool, all glamour, image, lustre and enormous overcoats. He was the very opposite of all that Turf Moor had sunk to. He arrived at a time of Boardroom upheaval and near 14% unemployment in the town. Burnley, you may not know, at one time had one of the highest suicide rates in the country though whether this was linked to the club's results, economic decline or the pies was never clear. This then was not a time for a Flash Harry. But nevertheless Flash Harry came.

In hindsight after he left, he said words to the effect that he should never have come to Burnley. Maybe it was the climate or the food that upset him but he allegedly said similar stuff about his tenure at Man City.

Bond cleared out players from the team who were firm favourites, none more so than Brian Laws who went on to great things at Nottingham Forest with Brian Clough. He cleared out Lee Dixon who he thought should work harder on his defensive skills. He eventually went to Arsenal and… we all know the rest. He belittled the legendary Martin Dobson and stripped him of the captaincy, which was baffling to rank and file supporters. If Steve Davis is currently the legend, then Martin Dobson was a God in claret and blue.

He sold the wonderful Trevor Steven for what was then big money. Spent wisely that money might have done wonders but… Eventually even Billy Hamilton was sold for a paltry £80,000. A very young schoolboy, Andy Payton, was released. Just think, had he been kept, the whole history of Burnley FC would have changed and been re-written by the probable 3,000 goals he would have scored by now. Andy P. (a man who went on to play for Glasgow Celtic) maintains that Bond never even bothered to check out what was on offer in the youth ranks. The mud at soggy Gawthorpe would have spoiled the expensive shoes.

In came Gerry Gow, (for whom the word turkey might specially have been invented), and Joe Gallagher (he of the alleged one leg shorter than the other). Bond blamed the club doctor for failing to identify the full extent of Gallagher's injuries when he was signed. The clue might have been the limp. But Gallagher came back eventually to play in The Orient Game and thus assumes automatic hero status. Then there was a player called Mal Waldron who came from Southampton. Mal interestingly is French for bad. Nuff said. He lasted all of six months. Steve Daley came; he had once been one of the first ever million pound footballers. At Burnley if we'd had the money we'd have paid a million to get rid of him.

His two good signings were Tommy Hutchison and Kevin Reeves. The latter was injured at Oxford and retired prematurely. That was a shame. His goals were frequent and if he had not been injured… who knows? Tommy Hutchison must have already been 40 when he arrived. He played for Man City in the 1920s. But it didn't stop him from eventually becoming a crowd favourite and a consistent performer.

By and large under Bond, it seemed that Burnley were becoming the new Man City reserves and there were allegations of there being two cliques in the camp, the ex-Man City and the rest.

Nevertheless, Bond at one point said, "I'm really happy here, I love it… It would take something really exceptional to remove us from this football club now."

By the end he couldn't wait to get away with team spirit at rock bottom and friction between himself and the chairman. I used to watch this man on the touchlines at away games and always thought there was something totally incongruous, incompatible and even bizarre about the image of this immaculately groomed golden man with not a single strand of hair out of place, at god forsaken dreadful places like Rotherham and the old Wigan. The look on his face seemed to say 'what on earth am I doing here?'. In those far off days when dreadful really was dreadful, the ladies toilet at places like Doncaster was a painted bucket in the corner of a brick shed (Mrs. Thomas discovered).

Tuesday, October 15

A while ago it was uncertain as to whether we would play Derby with their financial troubles. Now it's Leicester on Saturday and there's the same uncertainty, although as Mr Micawber used to say, "something will turn up."

Clubs have a habit of lurching on, a la Bradford, paying ludicrous salaries to players like Benito Carbootsale, pursuing financially barmy policies backed by starry-eyed Directors divorced from reality sitting in oak panelled boardrooms. Such policies wouldn't be tolerated in any other business.

Whilst little Walsall showed a profit for the eleventh season running, Leicester, relegated last season, are on the edge of administration. With debts of around £30 million and an immediate need of £5 million, they are currently meeting creditors and bankers. Massive loans were taken out to pay for their new ground. An administrator has already been lined up and the club can only avoid him walking through the door with his brief case and calculator if the players cooperate. Guess what - they won't, surprise, surprise. Player's wages at Leicester are around £15 million a year. Some individual players are on a million a year (Muzzy Izzet, Ian Walker, Brian Deane and Matt Elliot, according to *The Daily Telegraph* today). The mind just boggles. Hardly household names are they? For the moment the players have agreed to leave payment of things like bonuses and signing on fees till the end of the season, very good of them I'm sure. A proposed 20% pay cut was not surprisingly kicked out. They'd only have £800,000 a year left - that's £15,000 a week, give or take a few bob, to us ordinary folk.

Gordon Taylor helpfully explained. "They're prepared to defer some of their contract payments, but they can't take a cut in their wages."

Wednesday, October 16

The Lancashire Evening Telegraph (15.10.02) reports that Burnley FC's board have considered selling Turf Moor for £4 million in their struggle to come to terms with the loss of TV money. The move would still be an option if a buyer came forward and offered the Clarets a long-term lease on the ground. West Sussex development company Grimleys valued the ground. The news caused concern in fans who have been worried about the club's future.

Chairman Kilby said:

We looked at a number of different ways of dealing with the financial crisis but we have absolutely no plans to sell the ground at the moment. It is just one of the options that we have looked at, along with the sale of players and taking out loans... I repeat that it is not on the agenda although if someone did come along and offer to buy the ground for around £4 million and give us a 25 year lease, we would have to consider it... You have to look at what it is worth as a flat piece of land and as an investment opportunity. So yes it is something we have looked at, but it is not something we are actively pursuing at this moment. It was just one of the many options...

Mr. Kilby spoke after rumours that Turf Moor was for sale surfaced at neighbours Preston North End's annual meeting last night. Owen McLaughlin, chairman of Enterprise PLC, claimed that he had heard about the publication of a document that proved Turf Moor was on the property market. He added that he had been told that the proposal being put forward was that Burnley Football Club would sell the ground and then have it leased back to them.

****

Season of mists and mellow fruitfulness,
Close bosom friend of the maturing sun;
Conspiring with him how to load and bless
With fruit the vines that round the thatch eves run.

wrote John Keats about the glories of autumn. 'Clearly', wrote Peter Heywood on the Claretsmad site, 'Keats had never been to Oldham in October where the reserves won 1 -

0 last night'. 'Reserves' is a bit of a misnomer. Not a lad in the side had any first team experience, not one was over 19.

Oldham FC. on a good day is a bad enough place. On a bad day it is dreadful, a windswept, gale-ridden, rain-sodden, god-forsaken place where no sane person would set foot without a lining of weather proof Damart and several blankets. When God invented Siberia he must have been to Boundary Park first. I went to this ground one Boxing Day years ago, turned slowly blue and took a week to recover and thaw out. Apparently in the reserve game centre half Earl Davis was a colossus. One day in years to come he might be the backbone of an all-conquering Claret side unless he gets pneumonia first. But what do I know? I once predicted that Neil Kinnock would beat the Tories by a landslide.

Friday, October 18

The wretched, bloody and usurping boar,
That spoiled your summer fields and fruitful vines,
Swills your warm blood like wash, and makes his trough
In your embowell'd bosoms, this foul swine,
Lies now even in the centre of this isle,
Near to the town of Leicester, as we learn
From Turf Moor thither is but one half days drive...
(Shakespeare, Richard III)

Leicester play in the aptly named Walkers Stadium. It was to be called the Walkers Bowl, but somehow it was decided that lacked crispness. As well as Walkers Crisps and a certain Gary Lineker's ears there are one or two other things that Leicester is half famous for. The city's most famous son other than the above mentioned, is probably Simon de Montfort who forced Henry III to set up the first English parliament in 1265. He later went on to play outside left for Boston United. Cardinal Wolsey died here too, after hearing the news that Leicester were about to sign Dennis Wise. Dennis Wise is now commencing civil proceedings against Leicester for £2.3 million of lost earnings after they terminated his contract for breaking the jaw of a teammate in a row over a game of cards: just what Leicester need. In what other job might I ask could you clock a fellow worker and not expect to be dismissed? Who says Football is part of the real world?

However, of greater importance than any of these is undoubtedly Saint Martin of O'Neil, and after his departure Leicester plummeted to the First Division faster than this year's FTSE index and hence our current interest in them.

Of other historical curiosity is the old Filbert Street ground where Burnley qualified for the 1961/62 cup final beating Fulham 2-1 in a replay, goals from Jimmy Robson (2) now on the current coaching staff at Burnley. It was an odd ground with one great big enormous stand looking like a sore thumb amongst distinctly Division Four surroundings.

The city of Leicester is significant for its ethnically diverse population. There is an inevitably named Nelson Mandela Park. Is there a city in the UK that doesn't have one? I seem to remember in school geography lessons several decades ago learning that Leicester was an important shoemaking centre. Nobody seems to make anything in the UK any more.

The history of the place goes back to Roman times. There are bits of the Saxons dotted about, then the Normans, then the Tudors and the Georgians. There are Victorian arcades, streets of shops with bow windowed upper storeys and an imposing Corn Exchange that stands in the centre of one of Europe's largest markets. So who needs to go to Bruges? All in all it's a place by the River Soar where old and new go side by side. In Roman times it was called Ratae Coritanorum. So an occasional very old Leicester supporter will shout 'comeon you ratties'.

Richard III, last of the Plantaganets, stayed here at the Blue Boar Inn before riding out to his death on Bosworth Field. He returned as a mangled corpse on the back of a horse. Then he was put on display for a few days for the amusement of the peasants of Leicester. Today, they support Leicester City. Stan Collymore stayed here for a few weeks before riding out to the fields of Spain and his eventual disappearance from any football field.

In the Guildhall is an amazing old chair made from the shattered stump of an ancient oak and it is decorated with golden balls. The Lord of the Manor of Beaumanor sat on this when receiving his tenants' rents. It would today make a very fine chair for Becks and Posh. Castle Hall, built in about 1150, faces the Green to which condemned prisoners were brought to face the executioner and his block. Today Leicester City players are brought here to face the club accountants.

Well I never knew all that. Just goes to show how educational it is being a Burnley supporter. You find out all sorts.

Saturday, October 19

Marlon will have to be on top form today against Leicester in the Walkers Crisp Bowl. Suddenly against a top team, or at least a team more topper than us, even though you could say we are the in form team, we look vulnerable and the midfield as ever looks weakish. Truth is in this unbeaten run of ten games we haven't played any team significantly above us in the tables. It's a game today between two teams hoovering, sorry hovering, on the brink of administration, one desperate to be back in the Premiership at the first attempt, and the other just happy to be currently mid-table. I have a horrible feeling that today we shall lose by 3-0.

FOXES 0 HOUNDS 1

Oh we of little faith. Could any of us imagine that the impregnable Walkers Stadium would be breached by as crisp a goal as you could wish to see? A Little corner, headed back into the area by the head of Davis from the far post area, flicked forward into the six-yard box by Gnohere, and flicked in by Moore from a couple of yards. There could have easily been two more but for world class saves from millionaire Walker, and Taylor hitting the foot of the post. Up we go to eighth, only two points behind the top six with this fourth consecutive win.

This was not some ordinary performance against a disappointing Leicester, but a magnificent performance against probably the best side we have played all season... this was our best performance so far in 2002 and a million miles away from the appalling shambles we witnessed at Reading less than eight weeks ago... Robbie Blake turned in a second half performance of sheer class as he made runs at the heart of the home defence... everyone played well and nobody played badly. We played as a team with great endeavour and commitment... Arthur Gnohere was simply awesome in defence; nothing was going to get past him... they were all simply magnificent... The Leicester fans thought we had done well too and on four separate occasions after the match I had a Leicester fan come up to me and shake my hand and tell me that we are the best team they have played all season and offer congratulations for an excellent performance. It's not often you get the opportunity to witness that sort of true sportsmanship... (Tony Scholes, Claretsmad match report)

'Good defence... fast attacking forwards... one of the better sides we have played this season...' said forfoxsake.com, a Leicester fans' website. Leicester sites were all complimentary and acknowledged the victory by a better team.

Yes, absolutely right: but who on earth would have thought these things possible at the end of August? Robbie The Hernia Blake is now Robbie the Genius. Ian Moore is currently on fire. Arthur Gnohere and Ian Cox unbeatable. Gareth wins everything. Dean West last season's player of the year, remains rock solid, Marlon Beresford is truly inspired, Steve Davis majestic in midfield, and Glen Little back to his tantalising best.

Monday, October 21

Some Burnley fans would be more at home at a BNP rally than a football match...(Leicester fans' website)

But we try to give a balanced view in these diaries.

Here is another morgue like stadium, hushed by people having to sit in a single tiered library like atmosphere, Leicester's plod only too willing to over zealously clamp down on anyone wishing to generate an atmosphere, or worse having the audacity to stand up. So as Marlon collected Dickov's low shot with ease, the unnecessary first bout that saw the Lancastrians versus the plod took over at the rear of the stand, the plod managing to find at least two visiting supporters measuring less than five feet six...(David Clark, Claretsmad website)

But from Eddie Lea, London Clarets website, yet another view -

It was my great joy and privilege to be seated with two of my kids about ten rows below the Burberry baseball caps. These scum with their chants of 'town full of pakis', and 'no surrender to the IRA', no more than about thirty in number spent the first half looking for an excuse to start trouble. Ten minutes before half time, the Leicester constabulary moved in and took a couple of teenagers away. The police drew batons and hit a few. Good, it's about time somebody did... they aren't Burnley fans and have no interest in football...

It was the sort of afternoon it makes you feel proud to be a Claret. We are on the march again. All we need now is to rid ourselves of the fascist dregs... whatever was wrong in August is not wrong any more...

Is financial help on the way? In The Observer there are reports that the FA and the Premier League are about to inject £10-£15 million in emergency funding into the ailing Nationwide Leagues in a massive rescue plan. All parties say substantial agreement has been made and it is now not a question of if but rather how much. The 24 First Division clubs will get about 70% of whatever sum eventually is decided. If it is £15 million that would mean each of them receiving almost half a million. That may be nothing to clubs like Derby, saddled with the ridiculous wages of Mr. Ravioli who hasn't kicked a ball all season with his mystery ankle injury or Leicester who we totally outfoxed on Saturday. Leicester's debts are self-inflicted being the result of the brand new Walkers Stadium, which cost a packet. But to a club like Burnley hovering on the borderline, nearly half a million could be the lifeline that makes all the difference. One condition however is that the Nationwide gets some sort of wage restraint in place. League chairman say they are willing to take that step' probably starting next season. Bradford I understand already have a wage ceiling of £80,000 a year in place other than for players like the injured Wetherall and Ashley Ward, relics of their loftier, sillier days.

Tuesday, October 22

"In Ipswich ma'am! A football match in Ipswich!"
said the magistrate perfectly aghast at the notion.
(The Pickwick Papers. Charles Dickens)

Ipswich is another town steeped in history. The Danes pillaged it several times. The Danes enjoyed that sort of thing. King John gave it a charter in 1199. It was a wool port in the middle ages. There are twelve medieval churches and several sixteenth century buildings. Cardinal Wolsey was born here and Thomas Gainsborough lived here. Mr. Pickwick had several of his misfortunes here. Alf Ramsey pioneered 4-4-2 here in the early Sixties. Bobby Robson learned his trade here. Charles II hid in the chapel of The Ancient House built in 1567. George Burley hid there early this season when he knew the axe was imminent.

Alf Ramsey brought his revolutionary Ipswich 4-4-2 to Burnley on August 22 1961. I know. I was there. Even now I can remember seeing a slight thin-legged chap called Jimmy Leadbeater wearing number eleven. It was rumoured no one knew how old he really was and he looked an old man then. In those days a number eleven meant outside left and it was expected that an outside left was a player who would be sharp, fast and tricky, who would take on the full back and get to the byline and sling the ball over. In those far off days don't forget tactics were little sweets you sucked. They came in a tiny tin you then kept your threepenny bits in. People like Venables, Wenger, Wilkinson, and managers who made notes on clipboards during a game, hadn't been invented yet.

Anyway, Leadbeater was a fragile little twig of a man who looked like the gentlest breeze and certainly John Angus, just looking at him, would knock him over. John Angus never got near him for one simple reason. To hoots of derision Leadbeater never came further than the half way line, but from there he proceeded to put long crosses into the box or precision passes just to the edge of the box for two big chaps called Ray Crawford and Ted Phillips (the latter looking more like a giant farmer) to latch onto. You can tell that a match has left a powerful imprint when you remember the names forty years later. From there these two powered shot after thunderous shot on goal with one of the finest displays of shooting I can remember. Burnley won 4-3 that night - just, but had been given a warning. They were in their prime but a week later down they went to Ipswich and were murdered 6-2 with Crawford and Phillips amongst the goals, naturally. The town of Burnley and football in general was quite simply stunned: England's finest had been humiliated by people we had never even heard of from a rustic place a five day journey away by ox and cart. How could this possibly happen with a player who was supposed to be an outside left but never came across his own halfway line?

1961/62 was a season when Burnley finished second and drilled in some mammoth scores, sixes, sevens and fives were commonplace. I do believe we scored 101 goals that season in just the league alone. Ray Pointer scored 25 of them. But a tame end to the season, one win in ten games cost them dear: Different era, same story?

I tell you; Burnley's history is one long story of disappointment and might-have-beens. In 1961/62 as runners up in the league and beaten finalists in the FA Cup, Ipswich cost us the title. Tottenham, soon coming to the Turf on November 6, cost us the Cup. We have debts to settle. The BBC is currently running a series and a poll on the 100 Greatest Britons. Win at Ipswich tomorrow night and Stan could well come in at 101.

Tuesday, October 22

Leicester go into administration. A consortium headed by Gary Lineker will attempt a rescue package. In gratitude there are moves to make the Lineker Fruit and Veg stall in Leicester market into a national monument. Half the administrative staff look set to lose their jobs but the fat cat footballers with their sacred untouchable salaries will continue to feed on the double cream. By avoiding paying debts Leicester can continue their push for an immediate return to the Premiership. Is that right? If the takeover fails there are plans for the new ground to be made into an enormous crisp factory.

As part of the support package coming from the FA and Premier League, it is proposed that one reform should be that players' wages are reduced when their club is relegated and that there is a national structure for this and any other wage reform. More than one Prima Donna at the bottom end of the Premiership must be looking with bated breath at this morning's newspaper having a near heart attack as he eats his breakfast of poached salmon and scrambled eggs, washed down with a Bucks Fizz.

A great player who never benefited from these obscene wages came onto the pitch at half time at Leicester on Saturday and received an ovation from all supporters. Andy Lochhead played for both clubs but had his best years at Burnley where he arrived in 1958 and stayed until 1968. He played 265 games and scored 128 goals. He still lives in the Burnley area. What a player he was and he was generally reckoned to be the hardest centre forward to play against who ever lived. He was six feet tall, made of indestructible lean muscle and had a forehead made of granite. His face overall looked like a boxer who had done ten rounds too many and then for good measure been hit repeatedly with a well-used frying pan. Even in his prime he was no oil painting, having lost his hair at an early age. Just the appearance of his name on a team sheet made many an opposing goalkeeper hapless. When challenging for any high ball he reduced many a centre half to dithering gibberishness. He scored five goals twice, four goals twice and then three hat tricks for good measure. On one occasion at Turf Moor, when he enjoyed one of his four goal performances, he nutted himself on a post diving for a fifth. He was carried away on a stretcher and legend says that it was eventually discovered the post was split from top to bottom. It's interesting how Burnley have always been innovative. Harry Potts and his captain Jimmy Adamson in the Sixties were thinking of things way ahead of their time. Lochhead was the first ever 'target man' before the name was even thought of.

Andrew Watson of Burnley is part of a three-man panel, including Millwall's Theo Paphitis and Watford's Graham Simpson, devising possible solutions to the financial problems being endured by the entire Football League, reports *Something To Write Home About,* the London Clarets magazine.

Andrew Watson said:

We will be bringing forward recommendations in December and all options are being considered. Every rumour or story you have heard has been considered, from regionalising the lower leagues to bringing in the big Scottish clubs. We are exploring every single thing and there are 15 to 20 proposals. I am on the committee with the chairmen of Millwall and Watford because all the clubs have been unhappy with the way the Football League has run the game, not just over the ITV Digital and Internet fiascos. That means that we at Burnley are right at the heart of the debate on how football should be in the future, which has to be a good thing. KPMG have been brought in as experts and they have spoken to every First Division club before drawing up a comprehensive document. The discussions have now been extended to Second and Third Division clubs and after they have been consulted we will produce our recommendations.

Wednesday, October 23

TRACTOR BOYS 2 TRACTOR DRIVERS 2

Frantic, breathtaking, pulsating, thrilling, end-to-end; just some of the descriptions of last night's game. Stan apparently was not there having stayed at home with a mouth full of ulcers, unable to speak and in excruciating pain.

A goal down after a minute, the result of some sloppy Beresford goalkeeping coming out too far to a cross he couldn't reach, Gnohere then equalized minutes later from a corner. Ipswich went ahead again around the fifteen minute mark and you thought, listening to the website, this is it; we're in for a thumping. Not so. Beresford twice made amends for his clanger. The second half was very much Burnley but the signs were not good. Little did not come back out. Chances came, shots were saved, a clearance off the line, near misses, Steve Davis everywhere, Moore (Ian) running amok, flashes of Blake brilliance, Cox and Gnohere firm and strong, Branch's name mentioned over and over again in the thick of everything. Beresford with little to do - but still no equalizer.

Papadopoulos came on for Moore with just ten minutes to go, Moore apparently looking displeased on the bench. His reasoning is that he wants to stay on for the whole of the match to take advantage of tiring defenders. But one minute to go and West slings the ball across from the byline. Up goes Papa in a crowd but he gets highest and thunders a header into the roof of the net. Then there's bedlam, ecstasy, sheer wild uncontrolled joy and 750 dancing Claret travelling supporters. For a full minute all you can hear from the commentary team Phil Bird and his assistant is shouting, laughing, screaming, a sort of manic gurgling and total wild unrestrained delirium. 22,000 Ipswich fans stand mute and disbelieving - just like we did at Bradford. Three minutes injury time and the score stands at 2-2. Just listening to the commentary I am drained.

How can these be the same players who were so abysmal in August? The test is Portsmouth on this Saturday coming. Don't say it too loud but we seem to have a team now that we expect to win.

Thursday, October 24

I need to see my Leeds Utd doctor friend. The pills for my fungal feet are used up. I am number 7 in the queue (Willie Morgan). At last I went in.

His Leeds Utd team picture hung on the wall at an odd angle. I looked at it and mentioned it to him.

"Venables fault," he said. "Everything's his fault."

"You should come to Burnley on Saturday," I said.

"God forbid," he replied, a little brusquely I thought.

"Your feet again?" he asked.

"Yes, I've brought them with me. Time for more pills I think. Distal Subungal Onychomicosis isn't it?"

I could see by his expression he was either genuinely impressed or baffled, or maybe thought it was the name of another African signed by Keegan for Man City.

"So they're going to be OK?" I asked about my feet as I put the sock back on.

"Not while Venables is there," he replied, his mind still down at Elland Road. "Come back O' Leary."

Newspaper reports now suggest that the FA and Premier League are to provide £30 million for Nationwide League teams and this would mean approximately £800,000 for Division One clubs. Portsmouth have signed Steve Stone from Aston Villa on loan just in time for the Burnley game on Saturday and what do you bet he has a blinder?

Monday, October 28

I will start by giving an update on the club's financial side. We realise it is boring to some but others want to know and we have taken on a policy of being open to supporters. I think everyone is aware now of what we needed to achieve to secure the club's future. We have asked our main creditors for a 'holiday' on our repayments and we now hopefully have an agreement. The contracts are with our lawyers and if we could get that tied up in the next few days it will be a major step forward. It by no means makes everything wonderful but it would ensure that the club does not have to go down the Leicester, Bradford, Barnsley route.(Andrew Watson, Chief Executive, Programme notes. 26.10.02)

I like the idea of a 'holiday' from paying the bills. I should try it with the Gas Board and BT. Steve Stone of course had a blinder on Saturday and with him playing superbly well and making a huge contribution, it was…

STAN'S BARGAIN TEAM 0 'ARRY'S WHEELER DEALER TEAM 3

Harry Redknapp by golly knows his footballers. Portsmouth simply purred and were deserved winners in a truly excellent game. Burnley played well and for sure could have had a couple on a better day. A shot cleared off the line, a penalty miss, other near misses and many instances of good play in a second half they just about controlled overall. But it was Porstmouth who took the chances, one of them a gift from Beresford though to be fair the shot bobbled just in front of him and totally deceived his outstretched hands. Merson and Stone were class. Merson, the same age as Gazza, our last season's might-have-been, had time, room, space, and was an education to watch. Merson was for Portsmouth what we wanted Gazza to be for us. This was the same Merson who once said to his psychiatrist, "I want to be Dennis Bergkamp because my life is sh**."

The Portsmouth front two were fast and mobile, all over the width of the pitch. The whole Portsmouth team looked like a Premier outfit. We weren't that bad either, just up against a much better team. Gareth Taylor won just about everything in the air. Dean West's penalty miss was a wild blast; too high and sailing over after it had clipped the bar directly above Shaka Hislop's head.

Stan says he doesn't mind losing to a much better team and a crowd of over 15,000 unanimously agreed. It was not all one-way traffic, by any means and even having lost, the Clarets were given a standing ovation as they left, although it was possibly as much for Pompey as well. A Burnley crowd, though partisan, will always appreciate a class team.

Two cruel moments dictated the eventual result, one being the ball kicking up in front of Beresford's hands and looping over into the net, and Dean West's penalty miss. Supporters always think every penalty should go in but then even a Bergkamp can miss a penalty. All this was in a long spell of Burnley dominance and unceasing attacking play, with a good Taylor header tipped over the bar, a Little shot which would have gone on any other day, a Blake miss again destined to not go in, and other good attempts.

It's been said before, but we can't expect perfection from our players. I expect commitment, hard work and attacking intent, and certainly during the second half I think we got that. But I don't expect some magic blend between Brazil and Real Madrid. I know our players aren't the best. If they were, they wouldn't be here. If Little was a complete player someone would have signed him by now. If Gnohere didn't have flaws in his game, ditto. If Taylor was the best centre forward in the division, he wouldn't have come to Burnley on a free transfer. This is our reality. What we have is a decent bunch of players, some with talent, who try hard and are managed well. They're better than a lot of teams, but sometimes they get turned over. They do many good things, but they cock things up too… It was a defeat to take some heart from. We'll play like that again and beat teams less good than Portsmouth. If we continue to play like that we'll certainly achieve our aim of staying in the division and that will do. Don't forget that success will be measured by staying up and avoiding administration and on both fronts things are much more encouraging than they were in August. If only though, our miserable home supporters would start bucking their ideas up. (Firmo, London Clarets website)

Full credit to our 'arry, he claims his team will not have a better chance of going up and with yet more wheeler dealering (a la Steve Stone) feels there are even better chances now of picking up bargains in a market where impoverished clubs are desperate to offload high earners. What he has clearly done is bring in quality players and make the players already there into better ones.

"I took over a side that had struggled for two or three seasons and in the process I got rid of 18 players and brought in new players while balancing the books. People who talk about moneybags Portsmouth have got it completely wrong. The chairman has not given me any money."

We left the Turf feeling we had been given a lesson but not feeling despondent. The result was by no means a foregone conclusion and 'arry was well pleased with what he called his team's best display this season. Isn't that Sod's Law as well? The best team in the division has its best day when they come here. So, in the battle of the wheeler dealers and the player on loan experts, Stan versus 'arry, it was 'arry the winner. We have no complaints. It was a game Clarets dominated for long spells yet such is football, could easily have lost five or six nil by the end.

Decent referee too, Mike Clattenburg (I thought they were cakes), from Northumberland.

'Pompey Simply Breathtaking' said *The Times* report headline.

It was a fantastic performance, our best of the season...Burnley's shell-shocked manager could only concur, Portsmouth are easily the best side we have faced this season, he said, probably before going for a lie down...

For a long time Portsmouth have been a joke club with a massive squad of poor players lead by poor managers. Now that's all different and the difference between the two clubs is this: While Portsmouth take in players like Merson and Stone on high wages, we take players by the month. Burnley have their limits and I stick to my forecast; somebody, somewhere, someday will give us a clattering.

Tuesday, October 29

Surely not Grimsby though, in spite of it being a team we haven't beaten at Blundell Park since 1947. For us it's more of a Blunder Park.

Well yes, it's hard to talk about Grimsby without mentioning fish and chips so we may as well get that out of the way at the start, even if these days, what with Euro fishing quotas and the fact that cod's an endangered species there aren't too many opportunities to sing when you're fishing. As eating North Sea cod now seems to be the equivalent of tucking into a nice juicy panda steak, you may just have to stick to drinking beer...(Firmo, London Clarets Website pub guide)

The coming of the railway in 1848 transformed this sleepy medieval fishing port into a great trading centre. At its peak sometime in between then and now it had 3000 fishermen supplying a market where there were 350 fish merchants. One factory alone handled 200,000 lbs of whole fish a day. It was here, it is said, that Eric Cantona found the inspiration for his epic observation… when the fishermen throw the fish into the sea the seagulls are sure to follow. Literature experts and doctors of philosophy have been pondering on its profound meaning ever since. Arrogant violent French sod that he might have been, he could sure play football.

A sunny Saturday at Grimsby, (a swift easy drive from Leeds via M62) or to be precise Cleethorpes, makes a nice day out but it is now the end of October and a wild and wet one at that as gales batter Britain, rain lashes down and power lines and trees are felled by the dozen.

Grimsby don't play in Grimsby, they play in Cleethorpes. In Cleethorpes you don't get the smell of fish. Mind you with the slow death of the fishing industry there isn't much of a fish smell in Grimsby any more either. The whole area is a place of smells if you include the aroma of Scunthorpe foundries and smelters, and the petrochemicals of Immingham. They make fish smells infinitely enjoyable. God created the world in seven days, then Bridget Bardot, and then after that cod created Grimsby.

Cleethorpes is a fine bracing place full of good pubs and fish and chip shops. In its day it was like other coastal resorts such as Skegness and Morecambe. Train after train packed to the roof with factory workers from Leeds or Sheffield headed east to sample the brown muddy waters of the Humber and the North Sea. Now these places are sad lingering remains of busier days, battling against cheap flights to Majorca, the Costa Mucha, Corfu, Magaduff and Disneyland.

Grimsby, like Fleetwood on the opposite coast, is a fraction of what it was when boat after boat came back loaded to the gunnels with prime fat fish. Now this dwindling industry is a sad spectacle in an almost fishless North Sea protected by EU fishing quotas and limits. It's always seemed a miracle to me anyway that there are any fish left at all in any sea.

If the North Sea is a fishing graveyard then Blunder Park is a burial ground for Burnley. Grimsby are currently one off the bottom of the division. This means nothing if Burnley are in town. Grimsby have been habitual strugglers and relegation flirters ever since they came up to Division One a few years ago. This means zilch when Burnley are here. The three goals they put past us last year near the season's end effectively killed off our play-off hopes. Experts agree that the Burnley display that day was one of the worst 5 of all time and believe me there have been some stinkers. There were reports of dressing room altercations at half time at which point we were three down after Michopoulos had experienced one of his nightmare days. A player called Boulding, an ex-tennis player who had lightning pace, destroyed us. He has never been heard of since. It is sad teams like Grimsby and Walsall and other assorted mediocre dross who always somehow manage to put the skids under Burnley (ah, and the dreaded Warnock). There is no reason to suppose that tonight will be any different.

The truth is, the only good thing Burnley has ever had from Grimsby is Doug Collins. This was in the early Seventies when after a cup game there, he was bought from Grimsby for whom he had an outstanding game. It took him a while to establish himself at Burnley but he eventually became a key player in the team that won the second division title in

72/73 and then nearly became the team of the Seventies that Jimmy Adamson had predicted. He was skilled, cultured, neat and provided pinpoint passes and crosses. One of his rare goals, the result of a delicate chipped lob from the edge of the penalty box in the Leeds 1 Burnley 4 game, the season after promotion, will live in the memory of all those who saw it, and I was one. It was a game where Burnley played the then invincible Leeds off the park but then just a week later lost an FA Cup semi-final thanks to a bow legged centre forward called Malcolm Macdonald.

After Burnley, Collins wandered round the lower divisions for a while before leaving for Sydney and today he has a McDonald's franchise somewhere in Australia, which is, I suppose, a long way from Grimsby and a bloody sight warmer.

Wednesday, October 30

Finding a good Burnley defender last night at Cleethorpes was about as easy as it is to find the now vanished John Leslie and about as easy as it will be to find a fire engine if the fireman strike. I have to pinch myself still to take in, to make sense, to accept, to believe, a scoreline that reads

MARINERS 6 LOST AT SEA 5
YES, GRIMSBY 6 BURNLEY 5!!!

We found a new way to lose last night, by scoring five quite good quality goals (although one was a penalty thankfully this time entrusted to Robbie Blake, not put off by the Grimsby goalkeeper's fine impersonation of an ape), but then just letting the opposition score when they felt like it with grotesque defending. Absenteeism was worse than any old British Leyland factory.

It would be an insult to kids to say this was schoolboy defending. If ever a game summed up the letdowns, heartaches, perils, trials and tribulations of being a Burnley supporter this was it. Michael Boulding skinned us alive last year. Thus it was the same again this year as their on loan player Steve Kabba tore us to pieces time and time again and ripped us apart.

> *Some team somewhere is going to give us the mother of all clatterings...* (Me, Saturday October 12th after we beat Walsall 2-1)

And yes you've guessed it, it was Grimsby, second bottom before the game, scorers of just 4 goals at home so far, only one win at Blunder Park, the perennial strugglers in the division, who found every frailty and gave us the predicted clattering. We listened to the website commentary just open mouthed with disbelief.

Stan's elected to play the slightly built McGregor, who has rarely started a game in the two seasons he has been here, at centre back in place of injured Cox; Davis was in midfield; Branch at full back and Briscoe in midfield. With Arthur having an off night and taken off five minutes before half time, Grimsby had a field day in the first half.

If a game maybe called out for the embryonic Earl Davis to be given a debut at centre back (if Steve Davis was to be left in midfield), this might have been it. Little sat on the bench until the second half. After Gnohere was taken off the assumption was that Steve Davis would move back into the back line and shore up the others. But instead Stan put Branch into the centre of the defence. The Dutch called this moving around of players Total Football. They invented it. At Grimsby it was just Total Disaster. Amazingly, frantic Burnley pressure for the last fifteen minutes resulted in chances to have won 7 or even 8-6 believe it or not. But in what is a graveyard for Burnley the Grim Reapers hung on, and all in a stadium where the tannoy played the theme tune for The Addams Family as the teams came out and the game was advertised as Fright Night SPOOKTACULAR. The supporters who made the trip must have driven home in an absolute daze.

"It's the first time in my career that anything like this has happened and I'm gobsmacked and I really don't know what to say… I am lost for words to be quite honest with you…" said Stan afterwards.

"I took him off because he cost us three goals," said Stan about Arthur and added, "the only place he is injured is between the ears."

The only good news today is that the ITV highlights deal is sealed. The League will receive £2 million cash and a £3 million advance on the liquidation of ITV Digital. The League will not have to pay Carlton and Granada's estimated £1 million costs from the failed action against the ITV owners. 72 clubs will receive immediate cash payments. Division One clubs will receive £111,000 and Richard Masters, Football League commercial director, said it was possible there would be further payments.

NOVEMBER

Friday November 1

At Wimbledon in midweek for the game against Rotherham there was a crowd of just 849. Twelve of those had just gone for a pie. Club scouts were told to find new supporters instead of new players. Arsenal have now lost four in a row. So much for Wenger's claim they could go through the season unbeaten: a clear case of *Moi et ma grande bouche.*

At cash strapped Burnley somehow they found the money to give supporter's best player of last season, Dean West, a new contract to take him up to summer 2004. I'm pleased for him. I used to teach the lad and here he is at Burnley. I keep saying to myself I must try and contact him on account of the schoolwork he never finished.

I'm still in shock re the 6-5 game at Grimsby. It really is surreal. Two years ago it was a Grimsby Chinaman who sank us and then vanished into obscurity, last year it was a failed tennis player. The game this year was Stan's 200th in charge since taking over. He and assistant Sam Ellis have signed extensions for another season to their contracts. Rumours say that they are determined to stay until they can say that they have at last beaten the crap out of Grimsby. It may take some time.

I wandered round the field with the dog this morning trying to make sense of this mad result and life in general. Him and me ambled round watching goldfinches rising up in little flocks from the long grass as we disturbed them feeding. The hairy one has a friend called Buster who is short and portly, in fact bearing a sneaky resemblance to Robbie Blake. Buster is not of recognisable pedigree stock whereas the shaggy one is thoroughbred Scottie with the certificates to prove it. Buster comes with a nice old lady who always carries biscuits and speaks kindly to him as she doles them out. Sometimes Buster comes with the nice old lady's husband who is a Bradford supporter so we always have a chat about how we are doing. Today thank goodness he is not here. I do not want to talk about Grimsby 6 Burnley 5. After the Bradford 2 Burnley 2 game he could barely contain his glee and what could I say other than quickly change the subject and ask him had he found any mushrooms yet?

Saturday, November 2

Preston is on the River Ribble and used to have a thriving dock area. There were cotton-spinning factories by the dozen and sundry engineering industries. Now it just seems to have hundreds of pubs and a prison. Perhaps the two are connected. Apparently it is a very good drinking town.

Both the Old Pretender and the Young Pretender were proclaimed King in the market place in 1715 and 1745 respectively. On both days Preston were playing away so there was a reasonable crowd watching with nothing much else to do. Preston is synonymous with Tom Finney and there were moves to crown him in the market place too, but with typical modesty he declined and went back to his plumbing business. Sir Richard Arkwright, the inventor who revolutionised the cotton industry with new machinery, was born here. The mill owners were delighted; the factory floor workers less so. In the town museum there are prehistoric timbers. They came from the old Deepdale ground. This must be the only ground in the country where you can sit on Bill Shankly's face. Let me explain. The single tiered stands with steeply rising seats are decorated in such a way as to resemble faces of past legends. Apparently Quakers owned the land around the ground, which accounts for the distinct lack of hostelries in contrast to the town centre.

In the town centre if it's serious drinking you need before a game then Friar Gate is the street to be. This, I am told, is a wonderful drinker's street stretching from the centre of the town up towards student land. Without a game it would be possible to spend a whole day in this area if this is your inclination, drinking in every pub and partaking of the variety of takeaway food shops. On match days however many pubs are closed, the result of Man City, Wigan and Blackpool fans sacking the town and trashing the pubs in previous years.

Like all Lancashire towns that were once prosperous centres of civic pride and thriving industry, today Preston focuses on leisure. There are 160 miles of public footpaths and from Beacon Fell you can see as far as… er… Turf Moor and, believe it or not, Llandudno.

The Preston game is now the only Lancashire derby game we have. Last season was excellent; we beat them twice: The first during our vintage first half of the season, and the second during the mini revival after the long slump. Unlike Burnley they are not short of a bob or two. With money from a couple of big sales and compensation for manager Moyes moving to Everton, they have a happy and contented bank manager. We will begrudgingly admit that Moyes did a good job for Preston and is now successfully reviving Everton.

Sunday, November 3

PRESTON 3 PANSIES 1

(Stan's word, not mine)

Oh fortuna, velut luna, statu variabilis, semper crescis aut decrescis.
Oh fortune you are like the moon, ever waxing and waning.
(Carl Orff, Carmina Burina)

I think we can safely say that normal service has been resumed as soon as possible, fortune has indeed deserted us, and we had our third defeat in a row at Quakerland last night. Preston are now managed by Craig Brown. He never did much for Scotland when he managed them and until last night had only won three games this season with Preston. Naturally we made it easy for him to win a fourth.

In the first half the Clarets were content to pass the ball around nicely, but unfortunately this was mostly to Preston and we went behind in the customary third minute, a feature of our play which has now become as routine as losing to Wolves 3-0. And where was the defence? It was doing a Perry Mason… resting, and was about at as organised as the prosecution case against Diana's butler. The Royals are currently the nation's most dysfunctional family, followed closely of course by the Spencers and then in third place Leeds United.

Stan signs a new extension to his contract to keep him at Turf Moor until Summer 2004 and might now be wondering should he go and get the Tippex.

I am delighted to have signed an extension and I see it as a big vote of confidence from the chairman and one in the right manner. Normally when a manager gets a vote of confidence it means he is going out but the new deal shows that we are staying. As far as I am concerned that is brilliant. Burnley has been good for me and I hope that I have been good for Burnley. I feel I have made progress all the way down the line and we have to keep to that... the new deal will take me to the end of next season.But I hope that I will be in the same situation at this time next year because that will show we have been successful.

It was at Sunderland coaching the youth team that Stan started his long coaching/managerial career after a playing time cut short by injury. He has coached at Crystal Palace, Chelsea and Bradford as well as managing Hull, Blackpool, and Bury, the latter with great success. It's interesting that his success with Burnley mirrors that at Bury, winning promotion for both clubs to Division One but then finding further progress difficult, the stumbling block being money for further development.

A while back Stan had some comments to make on the selling front. Our entire first team was, and still is, on the open to offers list.

I've had a few offers for players, but it's a buyers market at the moment and who do you sell them to? Who has the money to buy them? You're looking at Premiership clubs and maybe one or two clubs at our level with a benefactor. The sort of money they offer for them would be far removed from their true valuation. But what is their true valuation now? If somebody's skint - and we're not skint -we have to make some adjustments. If somebody is in need then if they want ten bob for something, you can bet your bottom dollar they'll offer five for it. Then you have to decide whether you accept that. But that isn't my side. My recommendation to the chairman and the board is that I would like to keep the players. But they know the financial side of the club. I've a fair grasp of it, and we're the best part of three million the wrong side. In defence of the chairman and the board they've been brilliant all the way down the line.

He'll argue that yesterday could have been a very different scoreline if Blake, who had a good game, had taken one or two of the chances he had, if Moore had scored instead of blazing over from close range after a brilliant run, and Lucas had not kept out a couple of others. It might also have been different if Burnley had started with Little on his best side, the right side, instead of the left where he is less effective. In the second half Burnley's best spell coincided with Little's switch to the right.

Burnley had a prolonged purple spell in the second half but purple spells are no good with the defence in current 'stand and watch, lookout it's Christmas next month, let's give away presents' mode. Two goals were gifts, and the third a flash of individual brilliance where Fuller just ghosted past our defenders. The charitable might say it took a wicked deflection. The rock solid Cox and Gnohere partnership is a thing of the past with Cox suffering yet another injury. Weller, maybe not fully fit, is still a shadow of the lad who was once player of the year.

At the moment we're just pansies. Either some of the players have taken their foot off the accelerator or I have picked the wrong team.(Stan. The Times. 3.11.02)

Added to all this, crowd trouble at the Burnley end was the icing on the crumbling cake.

Monday, November 3

These are not then the best days to be playing Tottingham. The chances of a bank-account-saving full house of 20,000+ begin to look remote. Mention the name Tottenham though and memories of great games in the early Sixties come flooding back. The clubs then were the big two of the old First Division with names like McIlroy, Blanchflower, Mackay, Pointer, Connelly, and Greaves on the teamsheets.

On March 1 1960 Burnley beat Tottenham 2-0 at Turf Moor in front of 33,000 people. I can see a Ray Pointer bullet header hitting the back of the net from a John Connelly missile-like cross as clear as yesterday. Adam Faith was top of the charts with Poor Me. It was poor Spurs when they left Burnley. Tottenham had recently bought Dave Mackay, Cliff Jones and a gem of a player called John White who was eventually killed by lightning whilst standing under a tree. In those days coming to a northern town like Burnley from sophisticated London was like going back in time. The north south divide was alive and well and northern towns were still dark and satanic where southerners thought people wore clogs and shawls.

On December 3rd 1960 Burnley were 4-0 down at White Hart Lane and came back to draw 4-4. It has since been recognised as one of Burnley's all-time great celebrated performances. Don Smith in the Burnley Express wrote,

> *If there were a roll of honour whereon could be inscribed in golden letters the most meritorious deeds of any club... then the performance of Burnley at White Hart Lane would be given most careful and special recognition...*

Away from home and losing 4-0 before half time to the mighty Spurs, you could have forgiven any team for lying down. Spurs were then the reigning champions. But before half time John Connelly pulled one back and then one by one further goals levelled the score in the second half. In addition to all that, both sides hit the woodwork. It was the match of the season on a mudbath of a pitch and Burnley came off covered in mud, pride and glory.

You don't see mudbath pitches these days like you did then. If mud existed today like it did forty years ago players would refuse to come out on account of it dirtying their hair and white designer boots. The last such pitch was probably at Derby County but new grounds and scientific treatments and pitch protection, with all manner of drainage and covers, has spoiled the spectacle of twenty-two players caked in mud from head to foot serving up a football treat. Of all the games in all the mud one Burnley player revelled time and time again. His name was Brian O'Neill. He and mud were made for each other.

On 5 May at Wembley, Burnley lost to Spurs 3-1 in the Cup Final. I was there. A pal and me played hooky from school on the Friday and went down to London by train. Ed had a brother who was a doctor there at the time so we stayed in his flat. I remember wearing a pair of nearly claret and blue pyjamas on top of normal clothes and singing Abide With Me. I remember Burnley going behind to a Jimmy Greaves goal in the third minute (so what's new... this tradition goes back forty years). Jimmy Robson equalized from a Gordon Harris cross. But Spurs took the lead again within a minute. And then in the 82nd minute they scored the third. Arguments rage today about that goal. Cummings handled on the line but before that the linesman had flagged for a Cliff Jones foul on Adam Blacklaw. For some reason he then stopped flagging and Blanchflower went on to score the penalty. In the evening Ed's brother took us to a plush restaurant called Simpsons in the city centre and we ate Roast Beef and Yorkshire pudding served by plummy voiced waiters in white aprons calling us sir. For two young lads aged fifteen from the distant cobbled streets of the north, this was a new world.

Revenge on Wednesday night even four decades on would be sweet. In case you don't know, Blanchflower by the way was the first person ever to refuse to appear on *This Is Your Life*.

In the last game of the season on April 21 1964, Burnley hammered Spurs 7-2 at Turf Moor. It had been a fairly mediocre season for Burnley so a win like this was a nice way to end the season.

On October 5 1974 we won 3-2 at Tottenham when a half back line (that's what they were called in those days) of Doug Collins, Brian Flynn and Billy Ingham were just peerless. Doug Collins is in Australia. Brian Flynn is managing Swansea and Billy Ingham when last heard of was a bus driver in Burnley. In some old programme notes he said he liked travelling and meeting people. He got his wish. He was known as the Ginger Pele in his early days, though a less likely comparison can hardly be imagined; the one black and muscular and the other ginger and short. Today Pele does an advert for men with erection problems. Billy drives a bus. Which one is happier?

A year later though on January 19 1983, there was an unforgettable Tottenham 1 Burnley 4. This was the one of the most improbable and unbelievable scorelines of all time. Burnley were struggling to win any league games but had beaten First Division Coventry and Birmingham City in what was then called the Milk Cup, later renamed the Worthington and now by general acknowledgement The Worthless. On the morning of the game Burnley had replaced Manager Miller with Frank Casper, which hardly seemed the best preparation for the game. No one in his or her right mind dreamed of a win. The first half was goalless and after the restart Spurs took a 1-0 lead. It seemed a matter of how many Spurs would score. But by the final whistle Burnley had put four past a team that included Ray Clemence, Ossie Ardiles, Ricky Villa, Steve Perryman, Steve Archibald and the blessed Hoddle. Two were own goals and two came from Billy Hamilton, the second of those being a stunning twenty yarder in the final minute.

And that's about it. In between these occasional highspots when we clobbered the strutting cockerels, alas Tottenham hammered us on a more regular and frequent basis… but of that we will say nothing.

Burnley were relegated that same season having had magnificent runs in both Milk and FA Cup. Such is life at Burnley and has been for a long time.

I told you being a Burnley supporter is a labour of love, devotion and tolerance, a case of optimism over reality and heart over logic. To that we then add forbearance and forgiveness. Only the chosen few reach the pinnacles of true success, Arsenal, Liverpool, and Man Utd. Others touch it fleetingly, Leeds and Blackburn. Others only touch the hems of the chosen few. Others just dream and hang on in there in the middle regions or the lower end. And for a bunch of others like us, success is just surviving in Division One with maybe a decent cup run to lighten the struggle.

Tuesday, November 5

I had the strangest dream last night. I dreamed I was given a telling off by the Mrs for not cleaning the bedrooms. What I had been doing instead was practising my swerving free kicks with Jimmy McIlroy of all people. I wasn't using a ball though; I was using the best plates and china. Tell me what that means.

Ask who Jimmy McIlroy is and people of my generation will know immediately. His name and that of Burnley go together. He still lives in Burnley and a more modest, self-effacing man you could not wish to meet. When the Beehole End stand was named after him recently he announced it would have been better named the Champions Stand in memory of the 1959/60 team.

To look at, even in his prime, this dark haired Irishman looked just like you and me… distinctly average. He wasn't the tall, lean muscular type like an Anelka. He wasn't a huge powerful giant like a Heskey. McIlroy was just average size, average appearance, average shape, not too big and not too small, average build though perhaps just leaning slightly towards the stocky side, and average speed, not for him a hundred yards in ten seconds. But how he ghosted by opponents effortlessly is simple to explain. He just mesmerised them with a shake, a twist, a shimmy and a sleight of foot that was so subtle, so deft but beyond the realms of the average footballer. In those days a player like him was known as the schemer. Every team had one. For Spurs it was Tommy Harmer and then John White. For Fulham it was Johnny Haynes. They were the thinkers and the plotters. All the play went through them. When McIlroy played well, which was just about every game, then the team played well though no one should overlook the partnership with Jimmy Adamson. He was the second bedrock of the side that dominated the early Sixties.

When he was put on the transfer list on 21 February 1963 I recall my father being just open-mouthed with disbelief and shock, and for those of us just 17 and 18 in the sixth form at Todmorden Grammar School, and in the school football team, we talked of nothing else for days. We were Burnley mad and never missed a home game. Saturday morning was a school game (your genial scribbler was a dashing centre forward), and the afternoon was Burnley, either the first team or the reserves. In those days even the reserves pulled in 10,000 crowds.

Just who will take his place, was all we could ask? How can anyone wear that shirt again? The man was still at his peak and Bob Lord's decision to do this was inexplicable. Even to this day no one really knows why and Jimmy McIlroy himself has only been able to guess at the reasons. He eventually went to Stoke for just £25,000 and the heart went out of Burnley Football Club. First Arthur Bellamy, then Peter Simpson, and then Jimmy Robson tried valiantly to do the impossible and replace him as schemer. For modern fans who cannot grasp the significance of the transfer one can only suggest that the effect was much the same when years later Martin Dobson was sold to Everton. Just every so often a sale is made that deeply hurts both club and fan alike. There's an emptiness and nobody feels the same for a long, long time.

"I could scarcely take it in," said McIlroy later. "I cannot remember a day in my life when I felt so shattered."

Was it McIlroy's friendship with another Burnley director, Reg Cooke, whom Bob Lord detested, that prompted the sale? Years later McIlroy said he was convinced that was the reason. At one time Cooke was vice chairman of the club and his son would give McIlroy a lift home after some of the away games.

I can remember Jimmy Adamson saying to me one day that Bob Lord won't like this, being so friendly with the Cookes. But I thought I'm not going to let Bob Lord choose my friends for me. But I'm convinced that's the sole reason why Bob Lord put me on the transfer list. I feel sure that my friendship with the Cookes ended my career here.

Bob Lord's book *My Fight For Football* was published in 1963 but makes no mention of the McIlroy transfer. It looks like nobody will ever know for certain why he did what he did and it remains a mystery to this day. Lord took the reason to the grave with him.

Wednesday, November 6

It occurs to me it's probably true to say that two thirds or more of any crowd attending a game at Turf Moor will only have a faint, if any notion, as to who Bob Lord actually was even though one of the stands is named after him. Personally (cue nostalgia), I can picture him as though it were yesterday, a bulky, stern looking man, what hair he had left with a centre parting, who always looked as though he was about to pick a fight with someone.

His book starts with these words:

They say I'm the John Bull of football. They are nearer the mark than they know. I am not only an outspoken man: I am a John Bull because I have risen from a butcher's boy, a barrow boy crying his meat for sale as he went round the town. I have risen from the bottom to the top. I was brought up in a working class home and family and I'm proud of it. They call me Lord Bob, and Burnley Football Club 'The House Of Lords'.

As a youngster he stood in the crowd near the Town Hall and cheered home the Cup winners of 1914. He was six years old. Forty-six years later he was chairman of the League Champions.

At nineteen with a horse and cart he was hawking meat round the streets of Burnley. Next he bought the business off the butcher he once worked for and who refused to pay him more. Years later at the Cup Final of 1962, he was lunching with Viscount Montgomery and then sat with the Queen. His rags to riches story is what fiction is made of. But in his case it was reality. On that day he introduced himself to the Duke of Edinburgh as 'Lord of Burnley.' The Duke smiled in appreciation.

His legacy is immense. For years and years he WAS Burnley and made it into a nationally known club. The name Burnley was never out of the news because of his opinions and pronouncements. He was the man behind the purchase of the Gawthorpe training area and he continuously improved the ground. His love for the club started when…

To wear a flat cap, a white muffler and a navy blue suit announced to the world that you were a manual worker. As such you paid your shilling and stood to watch the game. Substitute a trilby for the cloth cap, a collar and tie for the muffler and wear a raincoat and everyone knew you to be a clerk or a teacher. If your wife or girlfriend came along, it was seemly to pay 1s. 6d. and go in the enclosure. In the stand were the businessmen, the manufacturers, the mill owners and the directors. Here was opulence, heavy belted overcoats, gloves and scarves kept out the biting winds, and bowler hats or homburgs were de rigeur. Woodbine, Park Drive and Robin cigarettes in the ground: Capstan, Gold Flake and Players in the enclosure, and Three Castles and cigars in the stand were the norm. Almost everybody smoked, and in the late afternoon when the gloom descended and the stand at the cricket field darkened, twinkling lights like glow worms would suddenly appear and die away as cigarettes were lit...(and sorry, I've no idea where this quote comes from. I found it in a fanzine)

It was still just about a time of people knowing their place and accepting their lot, although the rumblings of discontent would grow and then accelerate rapidly after the Second World War.

That Bob Lord ensured there was a continual stream of good players coming to Burnley was well illustrated by the signing of Mike Summerbee in 1975. It's said that Bob Lord made an enemy or upset somebody for every day of the year. Summerbee had a different view.

He said that on signing for Burnley he was a bit concerned because Bob Lord had the reputation of being a tough guy. When they met to sign a contract there was a huge desk in the room and nothing on it except the contract. Summerbee sat down and looked at it, thinking 'what a fantastic contract'. It was inflation proof and at that time inflation was going berserk. He said so to Bob Lord who told him he deserved it. Summerbee asked him why. 'You've met Jimmy Adamson and Brian Miller four times now and never mentioned money,' Lord replied, 'that's your reward.' Summerbee signed immediately and thought Lord was a superb man...

An obituary written by John Roberts in the *Daily Mail* does Bob Lord few favours. You can almost taste the vitriol. Remember, the *Daily Mail* had been a paper banned from Turf Moor.

Popularity was not Lord's strong suit. In fact his choicest insults almost merit a league table of their own. The Jews who run television he said were trying to obtain soccer on the cheap. Manchester people had too much sentiment about Manchester United after Munich. Manchester United played like Teddy Boys. Most players he knew couldn't run a chip shop and no more than 10% of them knew the laws of the game... The slam of a boardroom door was a sound familiar to him, signalling as it did a guest's premature departure, or his own, and the smattering of Latin he knew applied to journalists; Persona non grata... he advanced his business with contracts to supply the town's 59 schools and survived several court actions, including charges of selling mutton dressed as lamb. He ran his football club like a sausage factory. Players arrived young, many of them almost inevitably sold to the highest bidder... wages and transfer fees continued to escalate and in 1974 impressive ground improvements reached the point where the £300,000 Bob Lord stand was opened amid cries of anguish and derision. Burnley were all dressed up with nowhere to go but down... suddenly the man who fought for ten years for a seat of power on the League management Committee found his personal soccer empire crumbling until all that remained was a glossy empty shell. Some would argue that it was what he deserved, this arrogant butcher who told those who displeased him they were muck under his nose...(John Roberts, Daily Mail, 12/12/81)

Roberts makes a brief begrudging reference to the 'admirable gains Lord achieved for football in this country during his rebellious period of the 1950s and 1960s but the piece is largely characterised by scorn and dislike.

In his book Bob Lord refutes the suggestion that he labelled Man. Utd players as Teddy Boys. John Connelly presumably chuckles every time he reads the chip shop bit... he now (or did when last I heard), runs a chip shop in Nelson.

The words 'by the eck' and 'ee by gum' could have been invented for Bob Lord, a Lancastrian through and through. Put him in a darkened room with Vinnie Jones or Brian Clough or even both of them and it would be Bob Lord who came out alone having sorted the pair of them out. He was the epitome of the working class man who wanted to better himself and rise to prosperity and success. This he did, both in his personal and business life and in the life of Burnley Football Club.

The Tottenham game tonight is a reminder to us oldies of the better times we once enjoyed. If we win, I hope someone lets Bob Lord know.

Thursday, November 7

HMS HODDLE SUNK BY SUB

Shout for a mighty victory is won!
On Burnley ground the invaders are laid low;
The breath of heaven has drifted them like snow,
And left them lying in the silent night,
Never to rise again... the work is done,
Come forth ye old men, now in peaceful show
And greet your Clarets! Drums beat and trumpets blow!
(With apologies to William Wordsworth, Anticipation, October 1803)

FIRST HALF HOUR: CLARETS 0 TOTTINGHAM 1

VINTAGE CLARETS 2 NOT SO COCK A DOODLE SPURS 1

My God, we won on a magnificent, magnificent, glorious night. How did William Wordsworth know nearly two hundred years ago that such a night as last would occur, and a feeble first half hour Burnley would be transformed when sub Glen Little came on in an early reshuffle and totally transform the game. If this wasn't Glen Little's best ever game in a Burnley shirt, or in his lifetime, then I haven't seen it. His impact was immediate, electric, mesmeric and quite simply stunning.

Stan began with the defence that started at Grimsby with little McGregor up against the towering Les Ferdinand. Davis was in midfield again. Not a single Burnley supporter couldn't have been baffled. All we can suppose is that starting this way, playing as badly, gifting Spurs an early goal, lulling them into a sense of complacency and then bringing secret weapon Little on, was all part of some master plan.

Changes were made, Davis back into defence instead of McGregor and Little to his rightful place on the right. And from then on it was Burnerlee... Burnerlee... Burnerlee...

I swear a black cat from somewhere streaked down the far touchline at half time and disappeared out of the end of the ground. Maybe I was the only one who saw it but a black cat there definitely was. It was there for just seconds. God knows where it came from but from now on anyone who saw it will believe in the luck that black cats bring with them. The second half was then the Little and Large show as Blakey and Blake ran amok and totally destroyed Spurs. There were giant performances from them plus Davis and Taylor. Weller was transformed as soon as Bendyman came on. Yes Spurs had chances in the last ten minutes but to even that out we hit the post and Taylor missed a sitter.

But the man last night was Glen Little. In just a handful of games in a career a player rises to sublime heights and is untouchable and unplayable. For him this was one of those nights. The man gave a masterclass in wingplay from the moment he came on. Those who watched on Sky must have marvelled at his skill. Time and time again he ran past Spurs players, weaved his way through tight clusters, or jinked his way out of impossible situations. His legs go one way, his body the other. He ties himself in seemingly uncoordinated clumsy knots, all waving arms, long legs, large nose and knobbly knees, but still emerges on the other side with the ball glued to his feet. Blake's link play with him was a joy to watch.

"We couldn't handle him," said Glum Hoddle, "it's as simple as that."

It was a night of magic, emotion and deserved victory, leaving the blessed Hoddle initially almost speechless and wondering just where it went wrong after they had been one up and coasting. OK, for Tottenham there was no Sheringham or Redknapp but Robbie Keane and Sick Note Anderton did come on for the second half, not that either did much good. For the record Blake scored with a rasping shot from 18 yards and Davis with a thumping header from a corner. 'Caught like rabbits in headlights as the Burnley juggernaut gave them a battering' said *The Sun.*

All that plus 1970s legend Ralph Coates at half time, looking now a little like one of the Roly Polys but at least minus the trademark hairstyle wherein a few long strands of hair were carefully arranged over the empty scalp from left to right (a la Bobby Charlton) and which on a windy day trailed behind him several feet.

We drove home the 40 or so miles back to Leeds exultant, euphoric, voiceless and drained, but thoroughly enjoying distraught and angry Leeds fans venting their spleen on the radio phone in after their defeat at Sheffield United.

Who next? A home game please if you can arrange it and for some reason I fancy Everton... but just what if... what if it were Man U at home...

Friday, November 8

This week... Wigan beat man City 1-0... Sheffield Utd beat Leeds 2-1... Arsenal lose 5 out of 6... Mick McCarthy resigned as Ireland manager... Posh Spice won't let

Peterborough United trademark their nickname 'Posh'. Somebody should tell her it existed before she was even born... Howard Wilkinson announced that not even Jesus Christ could do much with Sunderland… Peter Reid didn't want anything to do with Sheffield Wednesday… who knows, maybe for the same reasons… 664 spectators watched Wimbledon v Rotherham on Tuesday…

And tomorrow is Coventry.

Images of Coventry last year in the final game of 2001/2002 are as vivid as they were then. The situation then was simple. Burnley could make the play-offs if they won their game by a bigger margin than Norwich winning theirs. Five teams were in with a shout of filling the vacant places. It seemed reasonable to assume that one of them might lose. For the first time in weeks none of them were playing each other. That's how Burnley had remained, in with a shout as top teams kept taking points off each other while we lurched along. I looked at my diary for the game…

The day after, I wrote…

I feel like I have a hangover, but that isn't because of any wild celebrations or a few bottles of wine. We did win 1 - 0 yesterday but it wasn't enough as all other teams in contention won, and Norwich scored more than us. Norwich scored one more goal than us. I can't stop saying it in disbelief. For the first time in months, on the very last day of the season, we slipped out of the top six by just one goal. That's how crucial yesterday was when Norwich scored two and we scored just one. Words like heartbreaking and anguish just don't seem enough. There's sixteen weeks to the next game in August and it's going to be a long sixteen weeks as we wonder if this will be the closest we ever get to further success. For the second consecutive season we are seventh but this time with 75 points. There's an irony. In any other season 75 points would have been enough for a play-off place...It was hard to swallow that Burnley played as well as they have done for weeks and hammered and pressured the Coventry goal. Then Gazza came on for the last ten minutes in the hope that chances of free kicks would occur. Yes they did. Twice he had magnificent accurate free kicks from outside the box heading like arrows for the bottom corner. On any other day one would have gone in but this was a day when fate decreed that goalkeeper Hedman would make wonder saves and keep them out. On any other day against any other keeper we would have scored three or more. Today their man was unbelievable. Gazza and the rest of us hung our heads in despair.

But meanwhile at Norwich the gods had decided that this was to be their day, not ours. After just 40 seconds Stockport had their goalkeeper sent off. In what other game, all season, has any team had their goalkeeper sent off after just forty seconds? When we heard that on people's pocket radios you just knew this was not our day. But even then, until the 75th minute, it was us in that golden final play-off place. The scores were 1-0 at both grounds, and then Norwich scored again.

If this was Melchester Rovers then somehow we would have nicked a 90th minute goal with one of those Gazza specials. There might have been a bit of magic or some stroke of fortune. But no, this was reality. This is Burnley... So near, so far, so close, so faraway.

The Burnley slump last year from December to March pointed to this current season 2002/2003, as being just a struggle against relegation and a fight for survival. At the end of August that's exactly what it looked like after four straight defeats and a bottom of the table position. Incredibly we now sit just three points away from a play-off place again and have dumped Tottenham out of the Worthington Cup with a truly magnificent display of football. Optimism reigns again.

Sunday, November 10

It is a goodly sight through the clean air,
From Hampstead's heathy height to see at once
England's vast capital in fair expanse,
Towers, belfries, lengthened streets, and structures fair...
(Joanna Baillie c.1790)

And thus to London (and there ain't much clean air now) on Friday. We went for the weekend (sadly missing the Coventry game), which, don't forget for us provincial folk living in a house on a hill with distant views of green fields and rolling moorland, and room to breathe and spaces and gardens between our little detached houses, is one giant adventure - and that's just driving down the motorway on a Friday afternoon.

It's an annual pilgrimage to Islington that we make to meet friends, he a Chelsea supporter, and see the sights and wonder how far it is to Highbury because I'd like in my life to see a game there just once with Henry and Kanu and Bergkamp and Pires and all the rest. Do these Arsenal fans brought up over the last decade on success, seeing the big names week in week out, ever stop to think what it is like to follow a small team where survival is the game and play-offs and Premiership places are just dreams for the likes of us from little Burnley. Of course, I remember the days when we could go to Highbury and win 5-2 but they were years and years ago and say that to an Arsenal fan today and they'd look at you as if you were a few saucers short of a tea set. Last year when we made this trip we were flying high and I promised Mrs. Thomas that if we got to the Premiership we'd have a slap-up London weekend when Burnley came down to Arsenal. It never happened.

Goodness me but isn't London big, says Bill Bryson and goodness me isn't he right. To me it seems to start forty miles away while you're still way out on the M1 and you just go on and on heading, you suppose, into the heart of a city that as each mile goes by you never think you're going to reach the middle of. It's a miracle that any football supporter coming from outside the city ever finds the ground he wants and reaches it in time for whatever time kick off is.

To us from the north, London is just a neverending, enormous place and we can only wonder at how people survive here, get from one end of the city to the other in less than a day, find their way anywhere by car, understand the tube system, catch a taxi, or just get their shopping home. There must be people here who never see the sky or children who have never seen a cow. It's a place where every cardboard box is someone's home, many accents are foreign, every bus comes along except the one you want - and that's just in Islington.

Bryson thinks it's a vast and exhilarating mystery. I can't decide whether it's marvellously magical or just a sprawling mess and a disastrous muddle, which somehow in spite of chaos, disorganisation, and frequent full stops, somehow keeps on righting itself and determinedly against all the odds keeps on going… a bit like the Royal Family at the moment I suppose or Manchester City.

The Strand in the evening where we went to The Vaudeville Theatre was just beginning to fill up with drunks and the incapable. Most of them were from Birmingham, thrashed by Chelsea earlier in the afternoon. By 10.30 the Tubes were cordoned off presumably to stop them filling up with refugees and the homeless. The second taxi we hailed miraculously stopped and we met an ecstatic Arsenal supporter at the wheel.

"Well I'm from Burnley," I said. He seemed unimpressed but proceeded to tell us as he drove along how well Arsenal had played, how they could have scored a hatful, how useless Shearer is and the 1-0 win in no way reflected the game and Gunners superiority. He simultaneously drove one handed with the other hand holding his mobile to his ear, having a conversation with some other Gunner fan who hadn't been to the game. He set off down The Strand, weaved in and out of hold-ups, dodged pedestrians, negotiated corners, and sped along the late night streets and never shut up the whole way.

"We once beat you 5-2," I said at the journey's end as we got out. But by that time he was off and halfway down the street.

CLARET AND BLUES 3 SKY BLUES 1

Between the reams and reams and endless newspaper pages of Palace and Burrell Butler stuff you can still find the odd space left for a bit of football. Thankfully the back pages are still devoted to things that matter - like our washouts in white crashing to a massive defeat in Australia by a million runs and Man. City beating, nay thrashing Man. Utd.

At The Turf by all accounts this was a definite after the Lord Mayor's Show kind of game, which somehow we contrived to win, leaving Coventry with a journey home wondering just what they had done to upset the fates that decree who shall win and who shall lose. Nothing could have matched the passion and atmosphere of Wednesday night. In this game though it was the sending off of Craig Hignett, he of Blackburn Rovers but on loan to Coventry, which delighted the Burnley crowd most, even more than the three goals and the three welcome points.

Any former Blackburn player is sure of one thing at Turf Moor, and that is the unceasing derision of a mercilessly unkind crowd. So it was with Hignett who during the week had been making unacceptable remarks about the coming game. But for a couple of saves from Marlon, one of them a definite super save, Hignett could have put Coventry two up. Instead, presumably frustrated and upset by constant baying and insults, plus referee decisions not to his liking, he took the long walk from the Bee Hole End to the players tunnel at the far opposite end, for gestures to a linesman and foul and abusive language. It was quite unexpected and the crowd was in raptures. The length of his walk from one end of the field to the other made it all the more pleasurable to Claret fans… poetry in slow motion.

The less said about this game the better is the general opinion. It is by and large accepted that to play badly and win is the mark of a good side. Hmmm… Blake, Grant and

Taylor scored, the latter with a wicked deflection carrying it over the keeper. Grant's goal was his first league goal for over four years.

Impressive though, was that grand old man of football Gary McOldAgePensioner. Nearly forty he may be but he wasn't that far short of man of the match by all accounts. The grand old man of Division One was rewarded with a penalty goal after Branch brought someone down - shades of Ron Chopper Harris. And Branch got man of the match and gets better every game.

Hignett sent off, Branch man of the match, Grant first goal in four years... and all in the same game... did you ever think you'd read that in the tea leaves?

AND on top of that comes the news that it will be MANCHESTER UNITED at Burnley in the next round of the Worthington. Could we wish for anything better? The gods smiled on us this weekend.

Tuesday, November 12

The Football Association and the Premier League have devised a secret plan to use money earmarked for stadium improvements in the professional and semi professional game to help fund a £20million rescue package for the poverty stricken football league. They are so secret they were in the papers this morning. The Sunday Telegraph revealed that, far from dipping into their pockets, they want to divert money from the Football Stadia Improvement Fund (FSIF), which provides funds for grass roots and Community Football Projects (CFP).

Football League Spokesman John Nagle (FLSJN) said, "as the season goes on it is going to get harder as Season Ticket Money (STM) starts to run out. Things will build up, the truth is noone knows what will happen."

The 24 First Division clubs would receive the bulk of the £20million over the next two years, about £580,000 a club. In truth this money is supposed to be spent on projects such as park pitches and school playing fields, in addition to grants for stadium work such as Improving Safety Standards (ISS), and better access for the disabled. A Football League Insider (FLI) said, "the point is that using this money for Football League clubs is the best thing to do with it at this time. There is no point having a pot of money allocated to improving stadiums if the clubs are staring bankruptcy in the face." Opposition comes from those who feel that diverting money from community projects to pay the wages of already overpaid footballers would be totally wrong. Assurances have been given though the Grass Roots Projects (GRP) will be unaffected. Proposals will be presented to Football League Chairmen (FLC) at a meeting in Oxford on November 21st. It will hinge on conditions being met such as player salary restraints.

"It's all about getting clubs organised over the next two years," said an insider. "This money will buy them time in order to get them into a Better Position (BP)." The whole thing comes under the heading of a Coordinated Rescue Assistance Package (CRAP).

But Burnley should be more than happy at the moment. Another £100,000 will come their way from Sky televising the Man Utd game and surely there will be a full house for this one. 21,000 spectators paying an average price of around £15 could bring in well over another desperately needed £200,000 after Man U have had their cut. Buggers... they don't really need it like we do. But the Directors have a dilemma. Do they put prices up? I couldn't blame them if they did if it was just another couple of quid on a ticket.

1955/56, September 24. Burnley 0 Manchester United 0 and that was my first ever dim and distant recollection of a game at Turf Moor. I have a hazy memory that Man U played in blue that day. I remember being bored silly and wondering if this is football, just what is all the fuss about? I didn't see another game for a couple of years and then got hooked the season the championship was won. And just look at me now. Fifty-seven and keeping a Burnley scrapbook like a big kid. Doesn't matter what team you support does it? Arsenal, Newcastle, Doncaster or Accrington Stanley, if you're hooked, you're hooked for life and bound forever to the colour and shirt you follow.

Unlike Burnley/Spurs games there is no great history of memorable games, either cup or league, between the two clubs. John Connelly and later Willie Morgan were both transferred there. Today, one is a world soccer superpower, the other relieved to be mid-table in Division One and looking as though administration will be avoided. Poles apart, but daft as it sounds never will Burnley have a better chance to beat them.

The treble winners of yesteryear are seemingly at this moment in time a team in decline. How much do they miss McClaren now at Middlesbrough? Veron is still a misfit. Blanc is a spent force. Forlan, the new hope (or was), can barely score. Barthez averages a clanger a game. Have they become a one-man Keane show and is he now in any case just a moody, violent liability? Replacements for absent first team players are distinctly average, in fact it could be argued that some of the first team squad are not much better than average. The magic has gone. There are questions over their desire to win. The Treble they achieved seems ten years ago. On Saturday a pale lacklustre side looked in need of an injection of new blood. Questions are being asked. Has Ferguson at 60 the ability to create a new side? Has he the time? How soon will their supporters become disgruntled and dissatisfied? The writing was on the wall last season when they won nothing. The Theatre of Dreams is in danger of becoming The Theatre of Has Beens. On MUTV, their own Sky channel, ex player Pancho Pearson who was one of the Tommy Docherty Utd team of the Seventies was stinging in his criticism announcing that Fergie has the team and the tactics all wrong; Veron is just embarrassing and should be sold; players lacked the passion of old; Blanc needs a rest and van Nistelrooy is struggling and close to burnout. The newspapers pick fault on every page.

We presume it will be a weakened team that comes to Burnley. The game is sandwiched between their league games at Liverpool two days earlier and Arsenal four days later. Burnley at their best with Little and Blake repeating their Tottenham form can win this, they really can.

"It is a dream draw and if we can get the ball off them we will have a go," said Stan. "I have come up against them before and my record is not that good... this is the draw that everyone would have wanted and we have been fortunate to get it..."

And the club will not raise prices said the website: Full credit to the club. I can't think of many who would have begrudged them a few extra quid if they had raised them just a little.

Thursday, November 14

Rotherham on Saturday; not a place where we do particularly well other than a draw every now and then. Rotherham is six miles from Sheffield and was a busy industrial town famed for its steel, coal and iron foundries. You can guess what's happened to those.

In the town centre is the magnificent Parish Church of All Saints, which is claimed to be one the finest examples of Perpendicular architecture in Yorkshire. Ronnie Moore is the other. On Rotherham Bridge is the Chantry Chapel of Our Lady and the bridge itself in 1643 was the site of battle between Royalist troops and the people of Rotherham, who had nothing much else to do because Rotherham weren't playing that day. Not surprisingly the Earl of Newcastle with 8000 troops at his disposal won hands down. In ancient times the Brigantes, not a particularly pleasant group, inhabited the area. Today on matchdays the few remaining members of this tribe can be seen at the Tivoli End of the ground.

Today Rotherham is striving to become modern, chic and European. Apparently last year there were all kinds of special events to mark the introduction of the Euro. Believe it or not you can (or could) actually spend Euros in Rotherham. Spend £10 in some shops and you got a Euro given back. This all sounds widely exciting and was, and maybe still is, part of the desperate attempt to shake off the image of ancient industrial grime. Rotherham seems to be campaigning to be a Brussels or a Milan. Last year there were delegations, press releases and special Euro events in the Town Hall Piazza.

Well, that's what they call it in Rotherham - The Piazza. Somebody obviously thought 'ah splendissimo, let's call this grotty bit of our town The Piazza del Town Hall, or if we go the whole way, the Piazza del Municipio'. Rotherham United now play at il Stadio di Millmoor and are managed by Ronnie di Mooro.

The other claim to fame of this fine industrial town, which straddles the River Don (Il Fiume Don) is that it is home to Stepwise, the Fungal Nail people, freephone 0800 056 50 10, or at least that was it when I phoned up.

It will be a trip down memory lane on Saturday, it being the days of John Bond since last I was there. I have no recollection of the score but seem to recall walking to il Stadio, down a narrow lane, this lane surrounded by enormous scrap yards, wherein lay old rusting locos waiting to be chopped up. Today, in keeping with its European dreams these yards have been renamed - Il Yardo Rottamo di Ferro.

You could say that last year's game at Rotherham cost us a play-off place when a referee who had awarded a penalty to Burnley (despatched by Taylor) decided later that he'd better award one to Rotherham for no apparent reason. Goodbye three points for a win. It was also an occasion when we decided to listen to the game not on the stress-inducing Phil Bird, Burnley website, but on Five Live with Peter Lorimer and Alan Parry. The difference is enormous.

On Five Live the game is much ignored but you do catch up on gossip, news, asides, what the weather is like, how high the gantry is, how they won't make it down the ladder at half time for a pie, how old the stands are, where the two clubs are in the league tables (which is fine until you hear it for the twentieth time), and how terrific the atmosphere is at the Stadio di Millmoor. You are treated to comments such as 'football at places like Rotherham is what the game is all about' (which translated means this ground is crap, I wish I was at Old Trafford) and 'this is football at grass roots level' (this is a bloody awful game what am I doing here?). Occasional commentary on the actual game itself comes in between all these snippets and leaves you sitting fuming and thinking just tell us who's got the f***ing ball will yer.

Il Stadio di Millmoor is a strange collection and conglomeration of bits and pieces. The Main Stand (Il Stando Grande) is only two thirds the length of one side of the ground and opposite this is The Family Stand (il Stando di Familia), which is sponsored by McDonalds

(Il Burgerissimo). At one end of the ground is a collection of what look like Portakabins piled on top of each other and the ground boasts some of the oldest floodlight stands in the country. Beyond one corner of the ground is a railway bridge upon which stand the poor of Rotherham trying to get a free view of the game. It is only this season for the first time in years that Rotherham have played anything worth paying to see. The Home supporters end is named the Tivoli End, which is a bit of a poofter type name I've never come across before at a football ground (il Stadio Calcio). Apparently there used to be a cinema of the same name across the road.

300,000 people a year are said to visit Rotherham, which is quite splendissimo. Like most former industrial centres now declined it has made a virtue of that same decline and developed a huge visitor centre called The Magna Centre which consists of four pavilions devoted to the elements of the steel industry, Earth, Air, Fire and Water, which up until now I thought was an American Soul group. Hands-on experiments make up much of what's on offer and in the Fire pavilion you can 'see how hot your bum is' (honest), not something I have ever wanted to do.

Also associated with Rotherham are David Seaman, Paul Hi de Hi Shane, The Chuckle Brothers (no not the Nevilles), Jive Bunny, William Hague and Frank Casper.

Friday, November 15

Frank Casper, slightly built and deft of foot, was a prince among footballers. Burnley bought him from Rotherham in June 1967, a move that shocked the football world because Burnley didn't buy players - they grew them at home, having first found them usually down a coal mine in the North East. The signing of Casper was a sad admission though that there was nothing coming through the ranks at that time. He had starred in an FA Cup Tie against the Clarets, scored, and was snapped up for £30,000, which was a tidy sum in those days. His career was virtually ended by Norman Hunter in a game at Elland Road against Leeds United. It was a game Burnley won 4-1 when they gave Leeds a footballing lesson. With Don Revie allegedly screaming 'break his ******* legs' from the touchline, Hunter clattered into Casper with an horrendous tackle just off the field of play by the goal where I was standing. Casper was clearly over the touchline when Hunter caught him with the ball nowhere near either of them. All this was nearly thirty years ago but I can still see it clearly, that's how bad it was. We were literally five yards away. Miraculously a patched up Casper managed to play in the next game, the cup semi-final against Newcastle, which we lost. Then it was eighteen months before he played again. After that there were just a handful of appearances where he always struggled, and in his very last game he scored his hundredth goal. His best season was 1972/73 when he scored some peachy goals - a twenty yard screamer in a 2-0 win at Wolves sticks in the mind on a roasting hot day in August. He went on to manage the club for a spell. Sadly it is the Hunter tackle that always comes to mind when you hear the name Frank Casper.

Saturday, November 16

The Firemen's strike (sorry Fire-fighters) has replaced Burrell's butling and Palace peccadilloes as newspaper headlines and this week saw the coroner's report that said former West Brom and England striker Jeff Astle died because of repeated heading of a football. It was the heavy leather footballs of his era that were to blame for his brain disease, the coroner ruled in a landmark judgement. Dr. Derek Robson, a consultant neurological pathologist told the inquest there was evidence of brain injury consistent with repeated minor trauma.

Debates have taken place for a while now regarding the dangers to players' health caused by repeated heading of a ball, which must be similar to being whacked by Mike Tyson over and over again. Today the view is that modern lightweight balls do not carry the same risk and are water repellent. In the old days leather balls absorbed moisture like a sponge whilst today the weight remains the same throughout a game. But in the olden days… fifteen years or more of heading a football… no wonder Bob Lord said he wouldn't trust footballers to run a fish and chip shop. Brain damage is also what what happened when you watched Burnley in the Eighties.

Marlon has signed only for another month at Burnley… efforts to tie him to a longer contract are wobbling… We await with bated breathe for Stan's imminent book.

Saturday, November 16

ROTHERHAM 0 BURNLEY 0

Full many a dreary hour have I past,
My brain bewildered and my mind o'ercast,
With heaviness…
(John Keats. August 1816)

My mind is more than bewildered. It is blank, numbed by this brain deadening experience. The less said the better. I'm home safe from the grubby and murky depths of South Yorkshire, that's all that counts.

Sunday, November 17

All I can say is I can't imagine why 300,000 people a year allegedly visit Rotherham.

Yesterday was dank, thoroughly wet and miserable. The motorway was awash with water and spray. But cheerfulness reigned; in my pocket were two tickets for the Man U game in a couple of weeks. Devotion is driving forty miles west from Leeds to Burnley first thing in the morning yesterday without even a slice of toast first to queue for tickets, and then driving the forty miles back… only then gulping down a couple of sausage sandwiches… before half an hour later driving east the forty miles to Rotherham, the new Milan of the North, and then the forty miles back.

The drive to Burnley was in fog. The drive to Rotherham was in torrential rain. Rain does nothing to enhance the appearance of Rotherham.

"Not even blue sky and brilliant sunshine could improve this throwback to the 1930s," said a steward queuing at the refreshment kiosk for his free cup of coffee as rain dripped down the back of his neck.

"Don't you get a free pie?" I asked, eyeing the Pukka Chicken Balti pies.

"Yer jokin', what with our skinflint chairman, 'e won't spend a penny," he replied, "them 'r 'is scrapyards there."

He pointed outside to the bottom end of the ground where the skyline was filled with rusting locos and cranes. This same scrapyard seems to extend inside the ground where the rust theme is continued with acres of corrugated metal roofing. Once inside the stand we looked for our seats in the gloom. The policy here is clearly one of why use a 100 watt bulb when a 40 will do? In fact no, the policy seems to be why put any bulbs in?

Millmoor and the grimness of the surrounding area appears to have changed little since I was last there, other than having had seats bolted onto the terraces, the knee room between them though being insufficient to avoid the immediate onset of DVT. And yes, there was the dark tunnel like lane away fans must walk down wondering where in God's name they are going if it is their first ever visit. It's like walking into a black and white Lowry factory painting.

This long, dark, narrow alleyway, which runs the full length of the ground, down which visiting supporters must file to get to the away end, is bordered along one edge by the 12 foot high perimeter stadium brick wall and along the other edge by unsightly derelict, dilapidated Victorian industrial buildings which look as though they have stepped off the pages of Charles Dickens' novels. Water pours from the cracked guttering above. Puddles of rainwater ankle deep gather along the alley, at the bottom end of which stand the scrapyards full of rusting diesels and electric locos. When last I came they were old steam locos. Now they are the hulks of diesels. I suppose this represents progress of some kind.

What we saw was dire, dreadful, and unpretty, with the ball in the air most of the time, hoofed and punted mercilessly by both teams. And that was just the warm up. After that it got worse. I asked my companion, John, a Bradford City supporter and neighbour who had come along for the ride, for his opinion of the Pukka Chicken Balti pie he was consuming.

"Hmmm... delicious," he muttered, "firm on the outside, flaky and soft on the top, and well filled inside... (For the minute there I thought he was talking about my Mrs... but no...) Delicious... a pie to treat with respect... one of these a day would keep a poor man from round these parts and his family fed quite happily."

I was pleased he had found something to cheer him up. Alas Bradford lost 3-0 and they slide slowly down into the bottom end and Burnley certainly did nothing to make him think the trip was worthwhile. With Davis, Little, Cox and Grant all missing from the line-up and then Taylor off injured concussed by an elbow in his ear after just fifteen seconds, (for which he somehow managed to be booked), our makeshift team with little McGregor in the back four again, kicked, lumped, hoofed, punted, scrapped, scraped, lurched, muscled, pushed, shoved and muddled their way along to the mother of all ugly 0-0 draws. Rotherham are big, tall, square shouldered, physical, robust, muscular and hard... and that's just the women. The ball is hammered up for the likes of the enormous Barker and Lee to power their way into the opposition box and batter away any opposition that is feeble enough. But, ah ha... but they hadn't met our King Arthur. We could even have pinched the unlikeliest of wins when Weller, taking a brief nap, appeared mesmerised by the ball arcing towards him at waist level, as he stood unmarked by the far past after a jinking run by Blake, and could only let it bounce tamely off his leg for a goal kick with the empty goal at his mercy.

I made Branchiera my personal man of the match, followed closely by Cook who lunged and parried, wellied and clattered into the nearest opponents manfully. Moore ran around to no avail. Papa came on for a cameo and reminded us all of what he used to be like before he improved and scored a few goals. Beresford made a few smart saves. The one highlight of the game was the final whistle.

Brain dead, I shuffled back up the sodden alleyway thinking 'God it must be awful being a Rotherham supporter watching this stuff week in week out'. At least at The Turf once in a flood we occasionally play brilliantly, and have Little and Blake to lighten the gloom.

The journey back up the ten feet wide ginnel after the game was even more wet, dismal and depressing than the walk down it. Two thousand Claret fans or thereabouts en masse funnelled, inched and stumbled their way up it shoulder to shoulder, water pouring on their heads from the leaky guttering above, which dangled precariously from the ancient buildings circa 1830. Feet were soaked as we stepped in rivulets of water rushing down the slope, and all wondering the obvious - how on earth would two thousand away supporters ever get away from this God-awful ground safely if there was ever any kind of emergency evacuation, or if at half time we all thought enough's enough and suddenly the lot of us decided to go home? One wonders if anyone from Health and Safety has ever had the privilege of barging and trudging up this alleyway in the dark after a game.

But in the cold light of day, you get to think a bit more. It's soggy days and ghastly games and cart horse performances and excruciating experiences like this that confirm what we know, that we're proud to be a Claret, and we'd follow them anywhere... even to Rotherham.

Monday, November 18

Most 0-0 draws are instantly forgettable, fit only to be left behind in the dustbin part of the brain. Some become folklore and live on forever. Napoli 0 Burnley 0 in the Inter Cities Fairs Cup was one such occasion.

It happened like this.

Burnley had already disposed of Stuttgart and Lausanne. For a 1960s northern mill town where going to Morecambe was a big adventure, these were exotic faraway names in an atlas. And Naples… well, it was a dream draw.

It was February 8 1967… Bob Lord was still alive and well… I was in the embryonic stages of my teaching career… marriage was just around the corner… you could fill a car with petrol for under a pound… 1967 was the death of Che Guevera… the building of Concorde… it was when the USA was bombing the hell out of Vietnam… it was a time of hippies and flower power… Engelbert Humperdinck's Release Me stopped the Beatles getting to Number One… Sandie Shaw won the Eurovision Song Contest with Puppet On A String… the big film of the year was Dustin Hoffman in The Graduate… Burnley had already beaten Napoli 3-0 in the first leg of the old Inter Cities Fairs Cup… then they went to Naples for the return… And Harry Thomson gave the greatest display of goalkeeping ever seen in a Burnley jersey.

In the first leg the millionaire Italians had believed they could stroll into Burnley, which at that time must have seemed like the back of beyond to them. This was a time when if you stood on the hills above the town all you saw were mill chimneys poking up out of the pall of smoke and fog. Even the moorland sheep were grey. When Danny Blanchflower came to Burnley on one occasion in the mist and drizzle with Spurs he asked his great friend Jimmy McIlroy, "How the hell do you live in a place like this?"

The Italian manager had done his homework to the extent that he thought Turf Moor was one of our players. When they went back to Naples with their tails between their legs they had found their fleeting visit to what was than a grimy wintertime Burnley (almost as bad as Rotherham), a chastening experience.

National pride had been hurt and the world-class Italians wanted revenge as local newspapers threatened to roast the Clarets on a spit. Napoli had already had their ground closed and been fined in the past for crowd disturbances in spite of the six foot moat around the ground. As soon as Burnley walked onto the pitch down came the showers of shoes (an odd choice), eggs, rotten fruit and abuse.

From the kick off it was one-way traffic in front of 60,000 screaming people who if they could would have lynched the whole Burnley team such was the hate and fury. In the next ninety minutes Harry Thomson made thirteen breathtaking world-class saves, as well as the routine stuff, and saved a penalty from Altafini. During all this, cushions rained down onto the pitch and coins rained onto Thomson. Fires were lit on the terraces in frustration and Burnley players were hacked, punched, savaged and elbowed,all working up into a climax in the closing minutes. Barely a Burnley move got into the Napoli half as the Italians attacked incessantly and in the end it simply became a contest between eleven Napoli players, desperate Burnley defending, and Harry Thomson. At the end of the game Burnley players made the not unrealistic assumption that that was that and the game was safely over.

But no: Thomson was punched and spat at. Reserve goalkeeper Adam Blacklaw raced to his rescue but was himself flattened by several Italians. Thomson, Blacklaw and the rest of the team managed to get to the safety of the dressing room but Italian police followed them in and demanded the removal of Blacklaw, who was then held for an hour in an adjoining room. The hostile crowd gathering outside was only dispersed by the threat of police gunfire. Six English reporters were taken into custody for their own protection. The team coach was eventually escorted away from the ground accompanied by an armoured lorry and nine military jeeps. There has never been another game like it and it has been known as The Battle of Naples ever since.

Burnley's Harry Thomson was then described in the following day's newspapers as a god in a green jersey. One awe struck journalist asked Harry was this his proudest day and his best ever performance.

"Not at all," replied Thomson. "This is how I always play."

Wednesday, November 19

PLAYED 19… W7… D5… L7… 26Pts

Which, with injuries, interruptions and suspensions and the atrocious August start of four straight defeats, is not bad and we should be happy just to be three points behind the play-off places.

Stan maintains that free from injuries and suspensions his squad can match anyone in the division. But we only have one goalkeeper with Nick the Greek still at Crystal Palace… where, by the way, he has been man of the match in two of his appearances there. At Rotherham he maintained he was down to just sixteen fit senior pros.

As things stand at the moment Dean West has had to play with injections to help cope with a rib injury. Steve Davis missed six games early in the season with calf problems and now has a groin strain. Gordon Armstrong has had hamstring problems all season. Glen Little has played though laid low with a virus for a long spell and now has a calf strain. Paul Cook has missed games because of suspensions. Gareth Taylor has missed games because of international call-ups and now has a head injury. Tony Grant has missed games through injuries and suspensions. Ian Cox missed the start of the season, came back and has twice had further absences with hamstring problems. Paul Weller has had foot problems and missed several games. Lee Briscoe now misses games because of a suspension. Brad Maylett has had hamstring problems. Arthur Gnohere has had a three match suspension. Robbie Blake has taken till the last month to recover fully from a hernia operation and lack of fitness. Marlon Beresford got a bad kick on the head in the Preston game but recovered to continue.

Stan says today that he only has sixteen senior players in contention for Saturday's game against Norwich. In season 59/60 Burnley only used eighteen players all season when they won the championship and three of those only played four games between them. Burnley essentially won that championship with just fifteen players.

Meanwhile, other than tickets waiting to be collected by season ticket holders, all seats are now gone for the Man. U game. Debates go on about whether the club was fair in its allocation and distribution but what else could they have done other than give priority to season ticket holders, Foundation members, shareholders and people who bought a ticket for the Norwich game. In some ways it is a bizarre situation. Glamour club they may be but Man U are currently a team out of sorts and it is odds-on they will field a semi-reserve team anyway. The mere name is the pull. The betting now seems to be will it be Ferguson or O'Neil in place as manager next season. If there is a God he will send us a fit Blake and Little at their unstoppable best for the game.

Thursday, November 20

There are suggestions that First Division clubs could be set to resign from the Football League. First Division Gillingham chairman Mr Paul Scallywag is apparently touting the idea. I mean no disrespect to the man. I wish there was a bit more of the wag in me. I admire any man who has the nous to buy up lots of the old fittings from The Millenium Dome dead cheap. Last year it was Bradford's Mr Pompous Richmond who supported the idea of the breakaway Phoenix League.

> *Scally, who is usually far too busy banning supporters from his Stadium for running websites, said that a new structure is desperately needed that will give the First Division more control over its affairs.* (Claretsmad site)

Claret's Chief Executive Andrew Watson has been involved in the discussions but has remained silent on the issue.

Salary capping will be on the agenda at today's meeting of League Chairmen. It's not long since that a secret plan (so secret it was in all the papers) was being put forward by the FA to impose salary capping in exchange for financial help to desperately in debt league clubs.

To be fair, Mr Wag, oops Scally, rightly points to the difference between Nationwide and Premier finances. Obscene is the word that springs to mind. It seems absurd that the Burnley v Man U gate should be split equally between the two clubs, the one in the millionaire bracket and the other wondering how to make ends meet.

Friday, November 21

This week Princess Anne is the first Royal to be given a criminal record because one of her more unpleasant dogs bit a child… the last senior Royal to stand in the dock was Charles I, and he was beheaded… President Bush has asked Blair for military help and to provide troops against Iraq… this may be difficult while they all man the Green Goddesses now that the Firemen's strike goes ahead for the next 8 days… the public have been warned that the 1950s Green Goddesses are very slow and are therefore requested to put more wood on the fire till they get there…

I pondered on these things while I walked the dog this morning. I also pondered on seeing an even worse game than the one at Rotherham. I never thought that could happen so soon, but it did, at the Greece v Rep of Ireland game on Sky on Wednesday, which I watched out of a sense of duty because our lad Papadopoulous got his first full cap. No wonder the Greeks prefer watching basketball.

The League chairmen had their meeting and the breakaway was squashed. No vote was taken on the salary capping issue said one report, because some chairmen felt all it would do would be to favour the bigger clubs with their bigger gates. Other reports said that yes they had agreed to a salary cap and to get a system in place which will have clubs reducing wage bills to 60% of income and then eventually down to 50%. The working party chairman David Davies said:

This show of support for our work should be seen as a considerable leap forward by the Football League and its clubs in terms of ensuring the ongoing sustainability of professional football in Divisions One, Two and Three. Our aim is to ensure that clubs are limited to spending only what they can afford. It is essential that we take action before it is too late, as spiralling player costs should not be allowed to threaten the viability of our clubs.

Apparently £25m is available from the Premier League, FA and the Government to share out. It would be available in two lots of £10m and one of £5m. Each Division One club would receive a grant of £330,000 and then a loan of £495,000. But to get this money each club will have to be audited to show they have enough money to last the season.

But this is daft, said one perceptive insider. If a club has enough money to get to the end of the season why then would they want to borrow the money? Nevertheless it was the prospect of available money that ended any breakaway proposals. The insider (same one or different this time?) said,

The First Division Clubs have been seduced by the idea they can get this money, and we are back in limboland.

Back at Burnley, chairman Barry Kilby announced that in extreme circumstances there could be loan signings but that basically Stan must make do with what he's got. However, it might be that Tony Grant may be on his way to Hull. Hull must have some money floating around. He who knows everything, Peter Taylor (don't mention him in Leicester), now manages them. Burnley paid £250,000 for Grant just over a year ago. He is a player of immense skill on his day. Nothing official has been announced but sources say (Our claretsmad website wizard Tony Scholes again) that he could be on his way. It would be a surprising move. Hull, along with Hell and Halifax is one of three places best avoided. Doing this would release some funds for a more robust ball winner. What we desperately need is a player who is Kevin Ball, Alan Moore and Tony Grant all rolled into one.

Sunday, November 24

Well actually no. Tony Grant is still a Burnley player and in fact came on yesterday and played as well as anybody in a thoroughly deserved win over the Norfolk turkey farmers.

BURNLEY 2 NAARCH 0

We came away glowing at the lovely football we played in spite of being without big Steve Davis, Ian Cox and big Gareth Taylor. The absence of these three did not bode well. Basically Naarch are a Rotherham who play football. They are big (very), direct, strong and classy with some excellent individual players. They have only conceded fifteen goals. They have the rough and toothless man/giant Iwan Roberts at centre forward who towered over little McGregor, hanging on to his central defender spot. I doubt McGregor won a ball in the air all afternoon - but Arthur more than made up for that.

Naarch are not third in the table for nothing. In all honesty a draw would have been more than acceptable and as the second half progressed I sat there thinking that this looked destined to be as classy and entertaining a 0-0 draw as last week's was abysmal.

But tell me how a team who performed so abjectly in August culminating in the dreadful display at Reading can now be so transformed. Is it the genius of Robbie Blake who was unstoppable again yesterday? Is it a fit Glen Little back to his best of a year ago? Is it the excellence of Beresford in goal who was outstanding? Is it Arthur who is back to his best and not making the basic errors as at the Grimsby farce? Is it to do with confidence, crowd backing, a willingness to run, work, chase and keep going a full ninety minutes? Or is it just the fact that in games like yesterday we played the ball on the ground, passed to feet, and everyone played well in front of the best crowd of the season so far of just over 16,000. And is it Stan pushing, nudging, roaring, and now getting the best out of players who were performing so woefully two months ago?

Can you beat the drive back home after a game you have won well, then a Saturday night meal out with friends? Can you beat a Sunday with the newspapers when your team have won? It's a Sunday when you go out and buy extra papers to read again of how well the team played. There's a sense of satisfaction seeing us well into the top half, just a couple of wins away from a clear top six place. The magic target is still 50 points says Stan.

I couldn't fault a single player yesterday and Robbie Blake was outstanding, now fully justifying the million pounds paid for him, contributing to both the goals that came from

McGregor and Little in the second half. Little's goal was the result of him sticking out his long gangly leg as the ball came over and somehow against all the laws of gravity it ended up in the net. The look of pleasurable surprise on his face was similar to that of a schoolboy seeing a cleavage for the first time.

It was as good a performance as we have seen all season and in it there was another perfectly good goal by Moore disallowed from a squared ball from Little. Tell me, linesman, how is it possible be offside from a squared pass?

"We played some good football," said Stan, "but we should have had a penalty in the first half and we had a goal disallowed for offside when there were two of their men on the line... I spoke to the referee at half time and he said he didn't give a penalty to play the advantage, so we score and it's then disallowed. That's some advantage... Marlon Beresford has had to make some good saves... The sponsors gave him man of the match, but I thought anyone of them could have had it because there were some good performances..."

All that plus Peter Noble, who once scored all four goals in a 4-4 draw against Norwich, came on at half time. He didn't look much different than he did thirty years ago. He looked sixty then, but what a player he was. He might only have been 5' 9" but nobody could get up and head a ball like he could. In one memorable game he scored a hat trick of headers in a 4-1 win over Newcastle in 1974. He could pass, tackle, score goals and was always in there where it hurt. Wherever he played he gave 110% - full back, midfield or striker made no difference. It has been said that if Peter Noble had been blessed with more hair he would have played for England. Only a perm was the difference between him and Keegan. For £30,000 at the beginning of the 73/74 season he was an absolute bargain.

Monday, November 25

I enjoyed the walk down the canal with mutt all the more this morning, still enjoying the warm glow that a good game leaves. The walk is drier, and there are one or two resident dogs for him to chat to unless he bites them first. At the old bridgeminder's cottage there's a large elderly hairy thing, which looks like a cross between a donkey and a yak. It always plods over for a sniff.

The owners of this particular canal-side house are an elderly couple who potter about on zimmers and yet still manage to produce an immaculate garden. They must be 80 if they're a day. The old bloke and I usually have a chat if he's out and about. He doesn't get to Leeds any more but he knows his football and remembers the good old Revie days as if they were yesterday. Today he was leaning on his gatepost taking a bit of fresh air and was none too happy with yet another defeat at Tottenham yesterday. His newspaper, he said, had a photo of Venables tossing the ball to Carr, the Tottenham full back. From the throw Tottenham went straight up the field and scored.

"What sort of a bloody manager's that?" he moaned.

"But hang on," I consoled him before he had an apoplexy, "look what he's got to contend with... the O'Leary inheritance, enforced selling of two of his best players, massive debts, a disinterested Tubby Viduka, a Bowyer who needs his head sorting, angry shareholders, an injury crisis as long as my wife's M&S shopping list..."

I got no pleasure seeing my friend's dismay, but I did feel massive satisfaction at Leeds' turmoil.

The sun has shone this week and there are still the remains of autumn colours. A carpet of fallen leaves still floats on the water's surface. Coots and moorhens dabble about. Wrens and Robins flit in and out of the hedgerows. Herons occasionally flap overhead. There are open fields on both sides of the water. On one side farmland and pasture rises up to the distant farm and church tower at the top. There's an old wooden bridge. At one point by the bridge all you can see are fields and woods teeming with birdlife foxes and rabbits, with the church and farm the only buildings in sight up on the skyline. It's a beautiful spot with an ancient wooden bench, which is where we usually sit a while pondering on the meaning of life and Burnley FC. Eventually when there seem to be no solutions we turn round and head home.

Beast and I wandered along, me thinking about McGregor's headed goal (ironic one of the smallest players heads a goal) and wondering if we can sustain this level of play, and beast presumably thinking about sniffs and what would happen if he gave the heifers we came across a good chasing. I grabbed him just in time and made our way back to read the papers again and phone the club to see if they're selling Boxing Day tickets yet for the Wolves game. The broad Burnley accents on the end of the phone are like a breath of fresh air. There must come a game when we will beat Wolves. This could be the one.

Wednesday, November 27

T minus 6. I really want to beat them. I think we can. I really do. They won last night in Basle but it was more the result of van Nistelrooy genius than the team as a whole. Take him out and United are decidedly ordinary. Veron was as ever elegant but peripheral. Giggs contributed little. Barthez was clownish as usual. Fortune is decidedly average. Neville (Phil) ditto. A less lenient referee would have sent Scholes and Fortune off. I am not worried. We can do this.

But first is Watford who disposed of the expensive Gianluca Vialli and his shiny headed assistant Ray Wilkins before the season started. In a word he, they, were a disaster and the club is now staging a kind of recovery and in fact, unusually, are above us in the table. Droves of players were brought in on ridiculous salaries and when the season finally went pear shaped Gianluca had to go.

Watford appears to have very little to recommend it other than one of the best supporter's websites around, Blind Stupid and Desperate. It contains all that is good about fans writing about their club, gallows humour and the sad but still chirpy despondency that comes from following lost causes. Football fans everywhere whatever their club come back for more, whatever the result, whatever the weather, however long the slump, however bad the football and however long the journey is to God's last football outpost - which Watford fans think is a place called Burnley faraway in the gloomy north. Trouble is, they've never been to Rochdale.

Watford seems to be the place where Southerners think the north begins immediately after you leave it. It is a place I see signposted when I career down the M1 and swerve onto the M25 and vice versa. I have seen it signposted so often I feel my car veering over towards it on its own. One day I have promised myself I will visit Watford.

Watford, Hertfordshire's own Xanadu, cultural oasis of the south, with their fantastic one way system, the outstanding curves of the Inner Ring Road, the place that gave the world the immense cultural talents of Elton John and Geri Halliwell, big shops like B&Q and the redundant power station next to Vicarage Road. It's hard for a down to earth place like Burnley to match the architectural majesty of the jewel of the M25 and the Parisian style sophistication of downtown Watford. It would be nice to think that with the brilliant Vialli at the helm Watford would have headed back to where they truly belong but unfortunately the Elysium fields of Division Three South don't exist any more. (Igor Wowk, London Clarets)

Watford people aren't exactly enamoured with Burnley either.

Can I give you a piece of advice? Always avoid a trip to Burnley if humanly possible, because, quite frankly, when God created a waiting room for all the evils bound for hell, he twinned that place with Burnley. Furthermore if you ever feel hungry in Burnley, try to resist all temptation of food... Burnley is a God-awful, pus-filled hole of a place. It has no redeeming features whatsoever. It is as much home to all the grossly generalised stereotypes of the north held by southerners as Essex to the north's equally blinkered picture of the south. Narrow minded, coarse and hostile are three descriptions that come to mind. Snakebite is another... A trip to Burnley is amongst the least pleasant of the football calendar... four trips there should be enough for anybody. Avoid a trip there if humanly possible... We have no real history of consequential or heated encounters with Burnley to base any vendetta on but the fact is that on each of my previous four visits the welcome has been something between hostility and open aggression from a large proportion of the local populace. Only Luton and Birmingham are comparable in terms of unpleasantness... so apologies to Burnley fans to whom the stereotype of a narrow minded knuckledragger doesn't apply, but until I see some real evidence that you may exist my view will be unchanged... witty, well maintained websites don't count... there are after all... an infinite number of chimps with typewriters. In fairness though, since the closure of Pie City, Watford is hardly much to write home about... (Watford Fans website Blind Stupid and Desperate)

Sadly Burnley fans disgraced themselves a couple of years ago when Watford was the last game of the season. Graham (do I not like that?) Taylor was the Watford manager and the game was his final swansong before retirement. The gurning (a Lancashire face-pulling pastime requiring both intelligence and rubber lips, with competitions and trophies) that went on behind him as he was presented by Burnley FC with a commemorative gift to mark this historic occasion has since become legend. Anyway, having received his present to mark his final retirement from football, Taylor promptly unretired himself, buggered off to manage Aston Villa, and to the best of my knowledge the cheeky sod has kept the present.

So, Watford seems to have little on offer, it is said that even Luton is better, although there's the flint, restored Perpendicular Church of St. Mary's and The Essex Chapel dating back to 1895. At St Mary's there are monuments by Nicholas Stone with reclining effigies and big architectural surrounds in the style of Elton John. There's the Elizabeth Fuller Free School of 1704. The Bedford Almshouses where Gianluca Vialli had a penthouse were founded in 1580.

Now managed by Ray Lewington and trying to come to terms with financial difficulties and near-administration brought about by the ITV Digital mess and absurd player salaries, they are in the same survival game as Burnley et al. Earlier in the season players and staff agreed to defer a percentage of their wages and must somehow raise £9.5million over the next two seasons. They are just above us, currently having a bit of a wobble after a bright start. Their website calls them The Golden Boys which rather makes you cringe. Inside the ground the décor is all garish red and yellow. Outside it stands the Watford General Hospital, which may or not be significant, and assorted allotments of all shapes and sizes. It's where instead of watching the paint dry, you can turn to watch the chrysanthemums, cabbages and cauliflowers grow if the football is dire.

Thursday, November 28

Whilst Cox, Davis and Taylor may well all be fit for Tuesday or even Saturday, Payton is now absent for 6 weeks following a hernia operation. I used to be Head of the little school where Ernie Wise went as a kid. He came to make a documentary about his old school. After he left one of the kids wrote about it: "A funny man came to visit us today and his name is Hernia..." Paul Cook went off before half time on Saturday after a bad fall and a shoulder injury. Earl Davis, our giant central defender, has been sent to Stalybridge Celtic for a month.

Chief Executive Andrew Watson stated this week that the club's annual turnover is now down to around £8 million following the collapse of ITV Digital. To my knowledge it's the first time this season he has put a figure on this year's incoming money. Before this season began and before the loss of TV money, I read somewhere it was £11 million with a wages bill of around £6 million. Isn't that what Roy Keane or David Beckham make in a year (each) with all their deals and bits and pieces added on? In such heavenly times just months ago we entertained the notion of signing David Johnson permanently.

> *"We've only got twenty players," said Stan after the Coventry game, "twenty-one if you count Nik, who's at Palace. And if you get a few injuries, the sixteen we had today, that's all we've got... We're still twenty one points away from fifty, and that's the first target, without trying to put a dampener on anything"* (Burnley Express)

Friday, November 29

Marlon Beresford has been offered a long-term deal to stay at Turf Moor, writes Tony Scholes on Claretsmad. Chairman Barry Kilby at the Foundation Forum confirmed this. The Chairman told the meeting that Marlon had been offered a deal until the end of the 2004/05 season. In a disappointing and very poorly attended forum he did say that any other new signings were unlikely with the best scenario likely to be a loan signing. Needless to say, finances were the top subject in the short, rushed forum and Barry Kilby said that the club had put together a four year plan where the club would use both director and commercial loans during the first two years and pay them back over the following two. So there is no doubt the next four years will be difficult. He said that he had personally loaned the club £1.2 million and the other directors were loaning a further £1 million...

Turf Moor is not for sale, that was the answer to one concerned supporter although they did admit the possibility had been investigated. It is not an option, said Kilby, much to the relief of those present. He did tell the meeting that the money raised from the Spurs game has only pulled back losses from the projected attendances at league games with the average gate this season more than 2000 per game less than last season.

We're the same everywhere aren't we: football fans, that is. No matter who we support, unless you're one of the big three up there at the top of the Premier and unaccustomed to losing, we can never take a thing for granted. And some games you just know you're going to lose. It's traditional, like any Wolves v Burnley game. We lose. We accept it. We know. It's a law. It's the same with Watford fans. They think exactly the same as us. They expect to lose to Burnley.

If there's one sure way to avoid disappointment in life, it's not to go into things with any expectation of success or enjoyment. Let's face it, it's going to rain whatever the forecast... if you're travelling by train there'll be delays... don't even think about buying a lottery ticket...
...We are after all playing Burnley, and the general way of things at the moment is that when we play Burnley we lose, it's the law. We have in fact lost our last five games against the Clarets scoring one goal and shipping eight in the process. It really doesn't seem to matter how we play or how the game goes...
...Our fate is compounded by the presence in the Claret's squad of a whole host of individuals who have scored goals or won penalties over us over the past five years...
(Watford website Blind Stupid and Desperate)

There are distinct similarities between Watford and Burnley; small towns, small teams, struggling to survive with money problems, lots of ups and downs, highly unpredictable, peaks and troughs.

Watford and Burnley fans clearly have a lot in common and share similar philosophies, that for every two steps forward you take there is one to be taken back, that for every night of elation there will be half a dozen of dross, and that if there is a Sod's Law it was invented specially for little teams like Burnley and Watford.

Watford fans glumly chant that Burnley always beat them but at the same time there is the accompanying silent unspoken conviction that these things, these jinxes, come to an end and that today might just be the day. That thought keeps alive the eternal hope and optimism that makes football fans what they are, wherever they are from. Watford one day will manage to beat us as Burnley one day will beat Wolves. This too is a law; that all laws one day come to an end.

And this one duly did.

GOLDEN BOYS 2 CLARET BOYS 1

DECEMBER

Sunday, December 1

There are few occasions more dismal than waking on a Sunday morning to see rain hammering down the windows and grey skies spreading as far as the horizon. One is when your team have lost the day before. When your team have lost a game they could, nay should have won comfortably, it makes it all the more miserable. The Sunday papers hold no interest. You mooch around the park with the dog and in the afternoon watch the telly with glazed disinterested eyes. Losing to a team like Watford is like losing at places like Grimsby and Walsall. It just shouldn't happen.

All the back-to-fitness stars were left on the bench - Cox, Davis and Taylor, leaving Blake and Moore (Ian) to play up front. Moore (Alan) came into midfield in the absence of the suspended Briscoe. Today Man U won at Liverpool. Unfortunately, since their clobbering at Man City they have not looked back.

Leaving our top threesome on the bench initially made sense. By the game's end opinions are reversed of course and we fickle fans then grumble they weren't on from the start.

London Claret Fan's opinions were unanimous:

We dominated the first half without really creating any clear-cut chances. Watford's first goal came after they got a free kick; our marking was poor and the guy who scored got a free header. Their second goal came when Tommy Smith was miles offside, but the fat useless linesman - who was around ten yards behind play - didn't give it... (Paddy)

*I'm a bit disappointed about today. I hate losing at Watford - it's a joke town, and they're a joke football club with joke supporters. We were so much on top in the first half and we utterly dominated the game - but we didn't have enough shots. When we were on top we didn't make it count and we paid for it... In the second half the officials decided to kick us while we were down and Watford were awarded a penalty for nothing when their player was offside. The linesman who was never anywhere near play decided that McGregor should be sent off. What for? That linesman gave so many bad decisions today. It would help if he was f***ing fit.* (Firmo)

I'm bemused how we lost the game. We seemed to control large portions of it... Weller got clattered early on. Papa was hauled down and even the Watford players stopped, awaiting the free kick. At the moment we seem to be the victims of double standards. I'm just waiting for us to get some of these biased decisions. I've been waiting for five years for someone to be sent off for clattering Little, and I'm still waiting. (Woody)

The first half was just incredible with us having probably 80% of the play. Watford were carved open time and time again. Grant, both Moores and McGregor all had good chances and Watford full back Cox made one miraculous clearance off the line. The lack of a consistent natural goalscorer was fully evident as low crosses fizzed across on at least three occasions with no one on the end of them. Oh for a fit Andy Payton of a couple of years ago. Stan was understandably livid about the penalty that never was. Watford attacks were few and far between with them hardly ever able to keep the ball for long.

All the top six clubs won leaving Burnley now six points away from a play-off place and Portsmouth seemingly unbeatable with a massive 51 points. This was a truly disappointing day.

Monday, December 2

There are always consolations in defeat. If Blackburn lose, the world always assumes a rosier hue. Sadly, they actually won this weekend, but then their victories are hollow to us anyway on account of them being the result of the Walker millions. With perverse logic we therefore regard them as all being shallow and unmerited whereas any Burnley victory is the result of graft, effort, and the will to survive. How much better and sweeter is the success of a team in Division One which has clawed its way there on a shoestring, than the moneybuysresults position of Blackburn Rovers in the Premiership. In all honesty I look at people like Cole and Yorke in a Blackburn shirt and think how absurd and I can't take it seriously. Apparently now they're after Hakan Sukur. They buy players like you and me go out and buy a newspaper. Chairman Barry Kilby is not short of a bob or two but he certainly isn't in the Walker bracket. Yes, we tolerate their existence above us but it's with a sort of disdain that is reserved for people for whom there can be no esteem. How can you respect someone who sees money as the answer to everything and faced with adversity simply nips out and buys a new player off the nearest continental shelf? True enmity no longer exists because we are no longer on a level playing field. That's not to say there wasn't real delight some years ago when Dalglish's millionaires were knocked out of the first round of the UEFA Cup by the part timers of Trelleborgs, a team of clerks, carpet layers and brickies.

Tuesday, December 3

A couple of weeks ago with Man U in mid-bad spell and Fergie being criticised from all quarters and with Little and Blake unstoppable, all seemed set for tonight. We can beat them, I remember saying. Now that the day has come I'm not so sure. And it's on Sky and I don't want to see a public humiliation.

They beat Liverpool at Anfield on Sunday against all predictions, they won last week in the Champions League and Forlan, he who never scores, actually scored twice on Sunday. It would be supreme irony if Forlan is about to embark on a hot streak and we become victim number two. But that's just the kind of thing that happens in football - and to us. Fergie is now saying he will field a strong team, not far short of the one that played at Liverpool. OK, Blanc, Ferdinand, Keane, Butt, Beckham are all out and probably Veron. But even without them they were more than a match for Liverpool. Suddenly I just want to know that van Nistelrooy, Giggs, Scholes, Solskjaer, Silvestre, Forlan and Co will not trounce us tonight.

Fergie is upbeat, positive, as he would be after a good couple of weeks. He thinks the breaks are going their way at the moment. They are hanging on in there without all their injured stars and even some of the ones playing are carrying gashes and knocks. It'll be an experienced side he'll put out with a sprinkling of one or two reserve players, he says.

Stan meanwhile has an almost full complement of players to choose from though Blake was suffering from sickness on Saturday and Davis has had five stitches in an eye cut. But Briscoe is back from suspension. The press conference yesterday was busier than normal. Stan says it's the most prestigious game he has been involved in here, a big occasion, a fantastic night, important financially, a cup game with just one go at it. He'll pick what he thinks is the best team for the job (eleven goalkeepers maybe?).

Steve Davis can't wait and wants van Nistelrooy to play. He wants to play against the best. But if he keeps him quiet there's still the small problem of Solskjaer, he adds. Davis has been described as the best English player never to play in the Premiership. Only a lack of pace has stopped him getting to the very top. Having beaten Spurs they have no fear about playing United, he says.

Mrs Thomas (a saintly woman, she feeds stray cats and puts food out for the birds) and I are excited but apprehensive. The sandwiches are packed, not prawns this time, and the coffee made. The ground will open earlier than usual. The team sheet will not be pinned up till 6.30. Can you imagine the feeling if we win?

Wednesday, December 4

BURNLEY 0 MANCHESTER UNITED 2

The team last night (just for once):
Burnley: Beresford, West, Davis, Gnohere, Branch, Little, Weller, Cook, Briscoe, Blake, Taylor. Subs: McGregor, Grant, Papadopoulos, Moore (Ian), Moore (Alan).
Attendance, 22,034, Full house.

No, it just wasn't to be. Big sigh. At the end of the day this was indeed a case of the little people eventually despatched by the masters of the universe. This was certainly not United reserves and by God we made them work for it. They began with eight internationals on the field and four more on the bench. They say everyone can be famous for fifteen minutes. Our fifteen minutes are sadly over. It was great while it lasted.

We were there early and effortlessly parked very close by. A good sign we thought. Listening in the car to the Radio Lancashire build-up, excitement and anticipation mounted. With all the crowds and mayhem at the other end of town, we at the calm civilised end ambled along, unruffled, into the ground at a leisurely pace and found our seats. Several of the terraced houses by the ground were festooned with Christmas decorations, Santas, Snowmen and yards and yards of bulbs and lights. The mood was set.

Curiously, once inside, I felt a slight detachment and a distance, in spite of this being a real occasion and a red-letter night. Maybe it was to do with where we were sitting - up with the pigeons at the back of the upper tier, far removed from the pitch, far away from the raw emotions, the sounds of crunching tackles and the close-ups of player's faces. From way up at the back they look like little Subbuteo models. Maybe it was to do with more omens and portents yesterday - seeing two hearses for example, in hindsight I now realise; one for each goal that United eventually scored.

Yes there was passion and atmosphere, the songs and noise from what became the Stretford End extension incessant and deafening. Not since West Brom's visit last year has Turf Moor reverberated to such constant wit and entertainment with songs about Cantona still the main event along with *You Are My Solskjaer* sung to the tune of *You Are My Sunshine* and *Diego* sung to the tune of *Volare*. Even hardened Burnley supporters had to smile. A Premier League team with Premier League supporters. Quite where Keane got his images of Man U fans being part-timers and prawn sandwich eaters I fail to see.

The start of the game was inevitably delayed because so many Manchester fans were still outside the ground or only halfway down the motorway. Apparently it's to do with a lot of people from Manchester still don't know how to tell the time.

Burnley fans roared and shouted themselves hoarse especially as we created three clear chances in the first half, one a Taylor header bringing a super save from Carroll, the Man U goalkeeper making a rare appearance. Two little bits of Blake genius sent crosses fizzing low down across into the six yard box. Taylor's toe pokes went agonisingly close but wide. On another day they might have gone in. Or let's say a van Nistelrooy or a Solskjaer would have had at least one of them in.

While Carroll just had the one super save to make, Beresford at the other end made a string of them, especially in one-on-one situations when at least four times he marvellously kept shots out and a one-on-one duel in the closing minutes with Giggs was alone worth the entrance money (Giggs lost). He had no chance with the Solskjaer goal, a shot of such venom and accuracy from just inside the box that without a net it would have travelled as far as Blackpool beach. Even by Solskjaer standards it was stupendous, the kind you score once a season.

Forlan scored the first goal and you knew that was it, game over. It was in fact against the run of play at that stage and a draw at half time would have been a fair reflection after all the pulsating end to end stuff. Burnley played delightful one touch football and made constant progress. Little was mesmeric. Blake was excellent. Davis was in emperor mode. A disinterested van Nistelrooy hardly got a kick. There wasn't a Burnley weakness - except we couldn't do it where it mattered, in the box. It either just didn't fall right, or there was backs to the wall last ditch defending. There were eighteen shots from us during the game which is not a bad total but the abiding memory is of too many of them sailing serenely over the bar in true Nationwide style. Solskjaer had one shot and put it straight in like an Exocet. There's the difference.

Bit by bit Stan changed things round in the second half, presumably to freshen things up a little and introduce some new ideas, bringing on Moore (Alan), Grant and Paparunaboutalot. None made a scrap of difference as we slowly tailed off, getting more and more ragged at the back as Man U eventually took complete control. Fergie must have quailed with pale-faced worry when we brought on our secret weapon Grant. Lord Stretford brought on Scholes to counteract this newly unleashed threat. Rodders made not the slightest difference. On came Moore (Alan) bringing fresh dread to the Dukes of Old Trafford. On came Giggs just in case Moore (Alan) scored a hat trick. He didn't. Papa came on in chase around in puppy mode; all windmill arms and legs, all going in different directions simultaneously. The crowd love him; just as you would a mad Labrador pup as it careers round the garden destroying the delphiniums.

So, while we bring on Moore (Alan), Grant and Papa, for Man U on come Solskjaer, Scholes and Giggs. It isn't fair.

For me Forlan was man of the match. Maybe he has gone 156 games without scoring and has been more forlorn than Forlan, but last night he continued his newly-started scoring spree and if you shut your eyes you could have been watching Denis Law - well, you know what I mean.

The newspapers today described Turf Moor as less than salubrious, full of spite, cold, unforgiving and hostile. Maybe it was our perch up at 1,800 feet but I'm not sure where those descriptions fit in. I think you could sense a respect, even if it was begrudging, that we Clarets had for the visitors, and maybe even just a little awe. Fergie and our Stan seem to have some sort of mutual admiration society thing, going off arm in arm afterwards. Stan presented his chum with a bottle of fine red wine, an investment maybe in case one day we want to take some of his young players on loan.

Burnley were described as enthusiastic, brave, spirited and plucky. Yes, they were all of those but it was more than that. They played so well, but just that final rub of the green was missing. We are so proud of them. We can have no grumbles - save one or two if we are picky - that every 50:50 decision seemed to go to United given by an occasional red eyed referee; that Carroll might just have been sent off an another day by a more eagle eyed linesman when he appeared to handle the ball outside the area; that in true Sod's Law style, Uruguayan Forlan chooses now to start scoring, to come of age and look like an outstanding £7.5million player; and that the more Stan brought on our subs, the three musketeers, the more we faded as the game died.

If we want to pick a bit more we could say that yes the United fans are wonderfully noisy and witty and sing endlessly and fabulously, but where were the seas of red and white at the away end? What a drab colourless lot they are. And if tonight we saw some of the pick of the up and coming United young 'uns I am not that impressed. The game was won by their big names.

But let's not be churlish, this was a great night. Think back to where we were three years ago and prior to that, the Orient Game all those dreadful years ago. Think of the Bond days and the Waddle season if you can force yourself. More than matching United for much of the game, and certainly bossing the first half is a measure of where we are now.

Ah well, the big red Man U juggernaut rolls on and last night we had the chance to see world-class players in the flesh. Yes it was a great night and the best summary is maybe this from the *Daily Mail*:

> *On another day glory could have been Burnley's. The only tangible difference between the two teams on the night was United's ability to take their chances. This was a gripping contest played in a feverish atmosphere in North Lancashire... with wonderful Turf Moor filled to capacity.*

Clarets, we salute you.

Thursday, December 5

So we lost, but the cash windfall resulting from Tuesday night's game is a lifeline in a league dominated by financial problems and near-bankruptcy.

Barnsley have been saved at the last minute only because The Mayor, Peter Doyle, has stepped in and made an offer to buy the club. "It's an investment in the town that I love," said Doyle, a self-made man now retired who has more than a touch of the Bob Lords about him. And don't mock. Barnsley is a loveable town with some of God's finest Yorkshire scenery and landscapes around it. The deal is scheduled to be formally approved in the next few days but there are rumours of another last minute bid from a rival group. But Barnsley, once everybody's favourite club when they spent a season battling to stay in the Premiership seem to be saved. Their debts may be small compared to others (around £3.5million) but £750,000 is owed urgently. Two relegations and four managers in quick succession haven't helped. It's interesting that their Academy boys played our boys off the park a couple of weeks ago at Turf Moor. At Burnley we can't afford one.

Gary Lineker and his consortium are almost there with the bid to raise £5million to save Leicester whose players have deferred part of their wages... York players won't get paid this month - just in time for Christmas... Derby millions in debt plan to unload more players as soon as possible, Craig Burley and others, and are looking at ways to pay off Ravishingelli, now sidelined for weeks with more injuries... Huddersfield's chairman has told manager Mick Wadsworth to use his substitutes less to save appearances money... Huddersfield are £6million in debt and on the brink of administration.

If anyone thought Bradford's problems, they're still in administration, were solved in the summer by the appointment of a new chairman and creditors being placated, then that is far from the case with news emerging on Friday last of City players being unpaid for November and one of the main creditors - understood to be finance company Lombards, unhappy with repayment plans - currently making very large waves. One Bradford player at the weekend before the Millwall game was stunned by the news, saying it had come right out of the blue. Further rumour points to possible liquidation by the end of this week. City players have apparently been considering new contract offers aimed at spreading out their wages over a longer period with David Wetherall, the club's PFA representative, saying that it was generally understood that if players agreed to do this then the major creditor involved would rearrange their repayment terms as well. It doesn't seem to have worked out that way.

And at Burnley who knows what state we are in. I can still hear the Burnley player telling me at Bradford that earlier in the season Burnley were two days away from administration. If that is the case then it does look as if we are slowly clawing and inching our way out of the mess and Tuesday night's money was priceless. Bradford's slow descent down into the bottom end of the table is as much the result of a squad hugely decimated by injuries as anything else. Burnley having their small squad similarly afflicted would undoubtedly have the same effect. It's a very fine tightrope that we walk at the moment. Other than Payton the squad is OK.

What is emerging is that an increasing number of clubs are entering the dangerous practice of selling off their players to companies on a lease and sell back basis just as they do with their grounds. It works on a kind of mortgage system just as in buying a house. Trouble is though that whereas the value of a house goes up, the value of a player goes down eventually. A company will give a club the value of a player's transfer, effectively leaving the company owning the player. Then they sell him back to the club charging high interest. It's the same with a ground. Companies buy the ground, lease it back and charge anything up to 24% interest. In the case of a player, when the club discovers the player is no longer worth the money they are paying plus all the interest, all they are left with is debt.

Help may be on the way by Christmas. Reports indicate that the Government-backed Football Foundation are poised to dish out a £25million package of grants and loans to patch up the damage done by the ITV Digital collapse. First Division clubs who were hardest hit will collect around 80% of that money. That could be an initial £800,000 and a later £300,000. There must be clubs up and down the land whose anxious Chairmen are waiting by the club letterbox every morning.

Friday, December 6

Two illustrious names were at the Turf on Tuesday, one from the '60s and one from the '80s. Both received a standing ovation. The latter, Mike Phelan, just happens to be one of first team coaches at Old Trafford now but that didn't stop those who saw him play for Burnley applaud him warmly. The first one though, Willie Morgan, was a spice boy and style icon, up there along with George Best, before David Beckham was even born and sarongs had been invented.

For a Burnley player of the '60s to be a glamour boy and clothes guru might almost beggar belief bearing in mind this was still the town of Bob Lord, clogs, mill chimneys, palls of smoke, and cobbled streets between the terraced rows of back to backs with their outside loos. But golden boy he was. It is alleged that as Jimmy Greaves used to ride down Manchester Road in the Tottenham bus for a game at The Turf his knees used to knock with dread, making a sound not unlike the two halves of a coconut, as he surveyed the murkiness and grime of 1960s Burnley. Yet here, like a beacon of light, was our very own Willie Boy with his dark swarthy looks, Beatle hair, trendy clothes boutique and one of the very first footballers to have a proper fan club.

He appeared at half time on Tuesday, striding nimbly onto the pitch and looking like he hadn't added more than a pound or two in weight. The style was still there, the fashionable black jacket with sleeves rolled up to below the elbow (Don Johnson, Miami Vice style) and black round-necked casual shirt. The shock however was what looked like a brilliant white tea cosy on his head made even more dazzling by the stadium lights. But no, this was his still Beatle style hair turned nearer white than grey.

Willie Morgan was a fifteen year old when he used to sweep the stands with Stan Ternent. Morgan eventually left Turf Moor for a then record transfer fee of £117,000. He would have been happy to stay but for falling out with Bob Lord. Shucks, everybody fell out with Bob Lord. He made his debut in a front line that included Bobby Charlton and George Best. Ironically he was part of the Burnley team that trounced Man U on Boxing Day in 1963, beating them 6-1. Morgan scored twice and Andy Lochhead scored four. His last goal came for Man U in a League Cup game at Old Trafford twenty-eight years ago when Man U beat Burnley 3-2.

For a while though it looked as though it would be Leeds United not Man U that he would join. By the end of the 1967/68 season he had played 183 games and scored nineteen goals. He had received his first full Scottish cap. But there were rumours that he was unsettled. That however was not the case it was the club seeking to cash him in. Leeds were just a year away from winning the title and Revie wanted him. Bob Lord would not countenance the idea of a move to Leeds and instead the deal was with Man United against

Morgan's wishes. But in those days the clubs owned the players and could very much do as they pleased with them and the idea of a player moving because it was he who wanted to move, was years away. Lord didn't like Man U either but £117,000 was very persuasive.

Morgan eventually came back to Burnley for a short spell in the Seventies but it was short lived. Having fallen out with Tommy Docherty, there was real aggravation between the two involving a court case that collapsed when Docherty admitted lying under oath. He came back to Turf Moor but, living in Altrincham, travelling was a problem in pre-motorway days. Like many players he had a stint in the USA playing for Chicago Sting and Minnesota Kick before ending up at Blackpool and retirement in 1981/82. Altrincham is still his home where he runs a marketing business with golf tournament connections and interests.

Before the game Morgan's deep affection for Burnley was still evident when he described it as still being a special ground in a special town. Before kick-off he expressed the hope it would be a special game with his feelings certainly leaning towards the Clarets in spite of his spell at Old Trafford. Special night it certainly was - with that mop of white hair part of it.

Local boy Phelan belongs to that small select group that we call Natural Born Clarets. Andy Payton is another and Martin Dobson, if you can count Clitheroe as Burnley. Then there was Andy Wharton and the inimitable Colin Blant who could cause a punch up in a monastery just by being there.

Phelan might not have had the glamour image of Willie Morgan but he was certainly one of the classiest players ever to emerge from the Turf Moor production line. Sadly his emergence coincided with a time of decline at the club (which was nothing to do with him) and he was sold to Norwich City.

He was part of the 1981/82 team that won the Division Three title. I still vividly remember a trip to Doncaster on a freezing but thankfully dry February night. Billy Bremner was their manager and Terry Cooper in the team. I still have the programme, which tipped us for promotion, tucked away in a box. It cost 30p. Whether we are from Burnley, Bury or Bognor Regis, we go glassy eyed when we lovingly take out these treasured items from our younger days. There was a 1-0 win with the goal coming from local boy Andy Wharton, a pint sized bundle of fury and aggression, who had BFC tattooed on his knuckles. We were stood out in the open at the away end behind the goal and I remember it well because of the look on Mrs. T's face when she emerged from the Ladies, which consisted of a whitewashed bucket in the corner of a little brick outhouse. South Yorkshire in the early Eighties had few frills. The mining industry was being destroyed and along with it came vast social and economic turmoil and huge unemployment. Flush toilets at Doncaster Rovers was on nobody's social or political agenda.

From Norwich, where he played in the Second Division championship side, he moved to Man U for £750,000, 194 games later. With them he won various medals including an FA Cup medal and his first England cap. He was a truly stylish and elegant player and for Alex Ferguson to rate him highly enough to make him one of the first team coaches at Old Trafford speaks volumes for a local Burnley boy.

My brain is still lingering back to Tuesday night. It was a real occasion and the memories will long remain; images of those two Taylor snapshots from the Blake crosses; the header Carroll somehow tipped over; Little's first half magic; Davis's power and command; the stunning saves by Beresford; the sights and sounds of a packed, heaving ground; the Man U singing and the Solskjaer goal. For a couple of hours the years had rolled back to remind us of what we used to be decades ago when we were a team that was on equal terms with all the other great names, when we were able to beat them and send them packing. Those of us who are old enough go just a little misty eyed at the rekindled memories of yesteryear. In one game we sent Tottenham home with their tails between their legs… and if one of those Taylor toe pokes had been just a foot this way… who knows?.. we gave Man U one hell of a game, didn't we?

But the reality of now looms. Back to earth tomorrow, Nottingham Forest and David Johnson, bread and butter stuff and we need three points. It won't be easy.

Saturday, December 7

Now we worry that Marlon is on his way. The long-term contract on offer to him remains on the table unsigned. His current month was due to expire before the Rotherham game next Saturday but he has now signed just another one month extension which takes him into the beginning of January and the transfer window. His form at the moment is stunning and with managers up and down the land on Tuesday no doubt seeing this on Sky, some of them must surely be sitting up and taking notice. There is speculation that yet again this could be another Burnley player on the way to Preston.

If Tuesday or Saturday at Watford revealed anything, it showed our lack of a natural goal poacher who can get 20+ goals a season. There was widespread dismay that David Johnson could not be retained after his loan spell here at the end of last season. Johnson is just such a player in the Andy Payton mould, the latter sadly now way over the 30 years barrier. Might Johnson or Payton have put away one of those Blake crosses?

These rare natural goalscorers are generally razor sharp, nimble and athletic, though Jimmy Greaves might not agree with the latter. Training for Jimmy Greaves was apparently having a quick smoke behind the bushes. But they are players who by instinct and movement, speed of thought, quick feet and some sixth sense more often than not are in the right place at the right time. Such players (Greaves, Law, Wright, Owen, van Nistelrooy, et al) over the course of a season will score at every third or fourth attempt.

Natural predators don't come along that often. Without the ITV debacle, Johnson, who has scored a stunning eighteen league goals already this season, might just have been doing it for Burnley. It was Stan who nurtured him at Bury after Man U released him. From there he had a big move to Ipswich and then a bigger money move to Forest. Then it was Stan again who got him back on track last season when he was having a bad time at Nottingham. Johnson hasn't looked back since.

I'm reading *Life Sentence*, about a season at Rochdale (yes, Rochdale) FC. It's a collection of Times essays with snapshots of life at Rochdale in between. The chapter I'm on now is about how much Rochdale fans hate Burnley.

By the end of it (*Supporters Brought Together In The Name Of Enmity, The Times*, Saturday 9 September 2000) I was bemused at how anyone from a team as insignificant and piddling as Rochdale can have the boldness to have opinions about a team like Burnley with its history, heritage and stature. Let's face it, just a few days ago we ran Man U ragged for 55 minutes until Solskjaer rescued them.

I have no antagonism whatsoever towards the fine town of Rochdale. I lived in nearby Todmorden for eighteen years. A Saturday morning ritual of my youth for several of those years was to catch the train to Rochdale with a crowd of pals and spend the morning in the swimming baths always finishing with a plate of beans on toast in the café. But Rochdale is... well... just Rochdale. I know it has a football team and a few thousand supporters. I know they flirted for years with re-election when the bottom four of Division Four were more or less always voted back into the league. I know they have a nice new ground now and are currently doing OK-ish. I also know it's a place where lots of Burnley players go when we've finished with them. What I didn't know was that their supporters had any feelings towards Burnley either one way or the other.

Oldham Athletic and Bury are Rochdale' other neighbours, but it is Turf Moor that Rochdale fans (surely not all of them) choose to dislike. One of the greatest moments in Rochdale's history was in September '91 when they played Burnley at Turf Moor and won even with two players sent off. Burnley pounded the Rochdale goal that night yet somehow they hung on. Unbelievably, Rochdale held out and some of their fans it is said cried at the final whistle.

Yes, I remember that result. That score was the pits and I felt life at the Turf couldn't get much lower than this as we visited places like Halifax, Lincoln, Aldershot, Doncaster, Hereford, Torquay, Carlisle, Maidstone... and often as not struggled. My God, Rochdale; how can you lose at home to Rochdale I thought?

It would indeed seem then that any Burnley defeat is greeted with cheers in parts of Rochdale and any half time score that says Burnley are losing at Grimsby is especially welcomed. If ever a remark is below the belt it is this final one. If there is one place we hate it is the graveyard of Grimsby. If there is a nerve to touch he has found it. If there is one comment he writes that makes me hope for an FA Cup draw against these Rochdale minnows (whom up until now I had never even given a minute of my attention, Rochdale being just a name at the end of the football results) it is this one. Then perhaps we can wallop them good and proper, as a Headmaster would thwack his scruffy Fourth Years.

Sunday, December 8

BURNLEY 1 NOTTINGHAM'S NOT SO MERRY MEN 0

Played 22. Points 32. Won 9. Drawn 5 Lost 8
Only four points behind a play-off place.

But just where were the missing people? Why were there only just fewer than 14,000 there yesterday? A couple of thousand were from Forest which means that Burnley's paying public, who came out for the night in their droves on Tuesday, stayed away for this one leaving just the 12,000 hardcore. What does the club have to do to get them back? Gates have gone down on last year's. The club deserves better than this. I felt a sense of anger that this was all that turned out for what in fact was a top game against one of the top clubs in the Division. Forest are third and had only lost one game in fourteen. And there was the added spice of the return of prodigal son Johnson, who in just a handful of games last season became such a favourite.

Today though The King had him firmly in his pocket and Johnson barely had a kick other than ballooning the ball over the bar on a couple of occasions. Des Walker, taken out of mothballs, (yes, *the* Des Walker) was in the Forest back four. Apparently, after twenty years with Forest, then twenty years with Sheffield Wednesday from where he was released, he was rescued from a building site and given a red shirt again. Just occasionally there were flashes of his once impressive talent. He was once one of the very best.

All in all this was much like the Norwich game, a deserved win, the result of delightful one-touch, sometimes quite sublime, football with every player a candidate for man of the match until the last twenty minutes maybe when as usual we fade and tire. Again the lack of a natural goalscorer was fully evident. Taylor grows in stature but will never be a twenty every season man. The scoreline should have been far more emphatic and three or four nil would not have been an unfair reflection. Forest for all their possession barely created a chance save for one where Del Branche made a miraculous goal line clearance. Beresford had his quietest game for weeks. A game where we caught up a couple of points on the crowd above and now lie four points away from a play-off place.

King Arthur has now been signed to give French lessons in our excellent fanzine, *When The Ball Moves*. The Introduction was in yesterday's new issue, number 21. This should prove most useful.

"Allo c'est le roi Arthur ici. Bienvenue aux traductions speciales des phrases de football a Burnley - partie numero un. J'espere qu'ils sont tres utiles pour vous en vacances etc".

("Hello it's King Arthur here. Welcome to the special translations of Burnley footballing phrases, part one. I hope they are useful to you on your travels etc".)

1. "Qui est le promeneur en noir???" ("Who's the walker in the black???".)

2. "Tu seras toujours sans pere". ("You will always be without a dad".)

3. "Oh la la, oh la la, oh la la, nous sommes les personnes gentiles habilles en Bordeaux et bleu!" ("Chim chimney chim chim chimney chim chim cheroo, we are the nice people in Claret and Blue".)

4. "Non Non jamais, non, n'en plus, quand en joue contre des cousins de Blackburn, non, non, jamais, n'en plus..." ("No nay never, no nay never no more, till we play our cousins from Blackburn, no nay never no more".)

The draw for the third round of The FA Cup was made today and we play... can you believe it... Grimsby. And it's away. I just groaned. My heart sank. Rochdale supporters will be cock-a-hoop: Grimsby at Blunder Park. Surely we can't lose again... can we? If we lose how can I ever set foot in Rochdale again?

Monday, December 9

So now we know why groups of police were videoing every row of spectators at the game on Saturday, including ourselves. Evidence Gatherers, or something like that, it said on the back of their jackets. Never seen that here before, I thought to myself. On the radio on the way home there were brief references to some kind of incident, but nothing to intimate the severity of whatever had happened. Then I felt deep shock and shame when I saw the news, that a Nottingham Forest supporter had been attacked before the game on Saturday and had died later in hospital. I saw the latest news yesterday and still feel today the same sense of disbelief and numbness. 'Forest Fan Dies', said the website heading with a bleak terseness, but added few details.

This is a family club but disgrace is now attached to the name Burnley FC. The lad in question was just seventeen and was attacked near the Yates's Wine Lodge in the town. It's just horrible, dreadful and becomes a blot that will fasten like a stain on the club forever. It follows on from trouble at Leicester and Preston, all reported and written about by rank and file supporters in the fanzine. There have been misgivings and suspicions for some while now that there is a group of thugs who have attached themselves to the club.

Where do we go from here? Are we to be the new Millwall? At any away game we visit will we be looked at with revulsion and loathing? The ignominy attaches itself to all of us. How will people look at us when we say our team is Burnley… ah, that's the place where a Forest fan was…

All the great things that have happened this week: A wonderful game against Man U which brought us national praise; a win on Saturday, we slowly claw our way to financial safety. But it all becomes insignificant and meaningless against this background where people everywhere who hear the name Burnley will listen with horror and disdain. The whole town is disgraced and we hang our heads in shame. Christmas approaches; some Christmas it will be for the boy's family.

Help for desperate Nationwide clubs moves closer. The League is to get a £20million boost, yet another announcement says. But how many times have we heard this? It never seems to actually materialise. Football League boss Peter Heard has welcomed the package:

I believe that football supporters should take great encouragement from the way that football's governing bodies have joined together in this way to help alleviate the financial problems of a number of clubs.

The Football Stadia Improvement Fund, the Football Association and FA Premier League are to set up a slush fund which League clubs can tap into to ease their plight. A grant of £10million will be made available immediately with another £10million released in August 2003. It comes at a time when Ipswich becomes the latest club to announce plans to offload expensive players to reduce their £30million debt. Bradford meanwhile are still in existence but lost their seventh consecutive game.

And what were we saying about Man U a couple of weeks ago? Was that the fifth game on the trot they won on Saturday, beating Arsenal 2-0 to move just three points away from the top? What were we saying about them and Fergie?

Tuesday, December 10

My mind is still thinking about the poor lad from Nottingham. His name was Nathan Blake and when you see a name, you see a real person and the family behind that person. There is still a sense of disbelief. On the London Clarets Website, Chairman Andrew Firmin wrote these words on Sunday. They speak for all of us:

I sit at the keyboard in a state of shock. Before yesterday's game a 17-year-old Forest supporter was attacked in Burnley. This morning he is dead.

Yesterday afternoon I sat in the stand and enjoyed Burnley's 1 - 0 win against Forest, oblivious to what had happened in the town centre. I woke up this morning with a smile on my face, preparing to write a match report that would describe our win. It now seems meaningless. Clearly, facts are scarce, and a murder enquiry is now under way. I couldn't comment on the details of the incident that led to this tragedy, but I know, fundamentally, this: no one ought to go to a football match and not come back alive.

People have refused to admit that Burnley has a growing hooligan problem. The club has been quiet, but so have the supporters. We have done nothing about the increasingly large number of yobs who have attached themselves to Burnley FC. Anyone who was in the away end at Preston could see the potential for serious unrest was there. Now, it seems, that awful potential has been realised.

I can't imagine what the solutions are. I can only hope that those who committed the crime are brought to swift and swinging justice and that if anyone has information that can assist the murder investigation they come forward. I'm too numb to think beyond this, but let us now admit that we have a problem and start taking that problem seriously. Let both club and supporters resolve to banish the yobs and turn around our reputation before we become pariahs of football. There must never be a chance of this happening again.

I am sure I speak on behalf of all members of our club when I say that our thoughts are with the victim's family at this terrible time. Football today is irrelevant.

The latest news is that the police have arrested a Burnley youth for the incident that took place near the Yates's Wine Lodge on St. James Street about a mile from the ground. My personal hope is that the club on Saturday is brave enough to ask for a minute's silence. It is the least we can do to show our heartfelt sorrow, penitence and remorse.

Wednesday, December 11

FINANCIAL REPORT

The annual club financial report was released earlier this week for the year ending May 31, 2002. It revealed that Burnley FC were close to balancing the books for season 2001/2002. Losses were down to £159,000, as opposed to £2.1million the season before. The tragedy now though is that the fallout from the loss of ITV revenue means that all the good work of the last financial year is undone and the next report for year ending May 2003 promises to be sorry reading. The next two years will continue to be difficult say the club following the loss of promised revenue. Up until now the club has managed not to sell leading players but that may have to change, said Chairman Kilby:

"The report shows that everything was going well and then we had a hand grenade thrown in our lap," he said. "We have been knocked off the ladder but we now just have to get back on and start climbing again. We have been team building but if any serious offer comes along that is halfway decent we have to look at it as we have a deficit to make up."

The report shows that by far the greatest costs were in connection with wages. Staff costs were up 23% to £7.5million, which represents 67% of annual turnover. The accounts are for the period ending May 31, 2002 and turnover for the year was a record £11.1million. This was a staggering 54% rise on the previous year. Purely football income was up an enormous 95% to £7.6million (league, season tickets, cup games, friendlies, Football League pool and TV revenue), and the rest was from commercial activities, £3.56million. The push for promotion towards the season's end was a major factor.

It is commercial activities that now take on a new significance. The ITV revenue is lost, £2.5million for this current year and gates are down at the moment by an average of 2,000. No one needs to be super intelligent to be aware of the consequences of this and the resultant struggle to make ends meet.

The report states that over the last four years transfer fee spending has amounted to £5.5million with incoming fees amounting to only £700,000. It adds that the club's key goal for 2002/03 is to first and foremost cement its place in Division One and remain a top thirty English football club. The club's strategy has up until now allowed it to resist selling players, which most clubs have to do to balance the books. It has been made clear by the chairman that this policy may need to change, as the club has a need for cash.

But within a day of this report being published came the news that at last clubs had received cash boosts from the Football Stadia Improvement Fund. It is reported that Burnley have received or will receive £664.000.

Football League spokesman Ian Christon said, "The initial £20million deal will see clubs like Burnley receive £332,000 immediately with the same amount at the start of the next season, August 2003. The fund is made up of money put in by the Premiership and the FA."

This is indeed welcome news though the extent to which it will repair damage already done is unclear. Burnley have already admitted to the possibility of selling players though Barry Kilby did say, "With the transfer window open in three weeks time I have not had one single approach from anyone for any of our players at Turf Moor."

Speculation and rumour, worry and anxiety about player sales abound at spectator level. Little and Blake gave tremendous displays in the televised games against Spurs and Man Utd. Other managers must have noticed. Southampton and Portsmouth are names linked with bids for Little. But even in the current economic climate at Turf Moor fans would be horrified to see anyone of Little's stature sold. Beresford on a one month contract can leave in January if he wishes. That would be a blow enough. But to see any of Little, Blake or Gnohere sold would make fans wonder just what is the point of continuing to provide support. We are in a Catch 22 situation. Sell the best players, support disappears, relegation beckons and income dwindles even more. The club must resist selling and must hang on in there. The money from the two cup ties and the FSIF cash handout helps enormously and it must be used as the foundation on which to hold onto the good players. Imagine a Burnley team minus Little, Blake and Taylor from January onwards. We'd be where Bradford are now, heading inexorably down towards Division Two.

Thursday, December 12

The Burnley teenager arrested was named as Andrew McNee from Haslingden. He appeared at Burnley Magistrates Court at 10. a.m. yesterday and was charged with murder.

All true fans are delighted, if that is the right word, and relieved that the culprit has been found so swiftly. Nottingham Forest, indeed all the football world, needs to know that thousands of Burnley people and supporters are sane, normal, civilised human beings and that we continue to feel the pain of what happened. Nathan Blake wasn't stabbed; he was clubbed with a bottle.

Burnley MP Peter Pike, who has long supported the club, said, "It is an appalling event which has further damaged the image of Burnley as a town and as a football club."

Firmo of London Clarets website added:

Remember that this is ultimately only a game we talk about. Football is a brilliant waste of time, and an enjoyable thing to do with your Saturday. It's also a great way of meeting other supporters, both of your team and of others, and one of the things I love about football is the fellowship and comradeship it offers with other people addicted to their weekend fix. It is at times like this that it is tempting to take the Ceefax and B&Q route. How can any game be worth this?

I know of course really this game belongs to us, to the kind of people who visit this site, and the kind of people who write for it: the decent supporters who want to see their team win, who are passionate and sometimes unreasonable, but who don't see the need to assert their identity through confrontation, or prove their masculinity through violence. We'll have to keep going, because otherwise the yobs win. And we'll have to keep writing, because we need to prove to other football fans that there's more to Burnley than our current debased reputation.

People have started to lay flowers at the scene in Burnley town centre.

The sentiments expressed below are typical and come from the heart of a Burnley person whose sadness and feelings are shared by hundreds more.

We are very sorry to hear about the tragic event.
Thinking of You.
From all true Burnley fans
9 December 2002.

Friday, December 13

A name from the past appeared a couple of days ago… Jimmy Mullen. The announcement was brief and stark. Mullen will become manager and take charge of Midland Alliance League team, Bridgenorth. The last time I saw his name was in connection with the Wrexham job he applied for many months, maybe even over a year ago. Then the name sank back into obscurity. I took note of this re-appearance because Burnley owes an enormous debt of gratitude to Jimmy Mullen. It's a name that sadly became much maligned in his final year but prior to that he took the club to two promotions in the space of three years in the early Nineties.

His start as manager was marked by nine consecutive wins. We thought the Messiah had arrived. In his first season the London Clarets wrote that he transformed the club from a shambles into fourth division champions. He was a breathe of fresh air playing attractive football using two wide players and in addition to that he had Steve Davis who was possibly the best player in the division as the bedrock of the side. His relationship with the fans though was always frail and by the next season there were already chants for him to go. It was in the next season though that he took Burnley to the Wembley play-offs after a stuttering win-here-lose-there kind of season. The signing of David Eyres from Blackpool was a masterstroke and yet still there were cries of Mullen Out. Nevertheless another signing, that of Ted Tin Man McMinn, helped Burnley finally secure a play-off place, in which they beat Stockport 2-1 to reach Division One. The following season Burnley went straight back down but that's another story in an excellent book (*Burnley Were Back* by Stephen Cummings, Janus, 1996).

In my belief Jimmy Mullen was cruelly treated. Two promotions in three years at a club with limited resources is a fabulous achievement. It may well be that relegation in 94/95 was the result of a good lower division manager reaching one level too far. It may have been lack of resources. It may have been (according to Stephen Cummings) successions of bizarre team selections and tactics and some poor player purchases. But, whatever the reason Mullen was subjected to intolerable levels of insult and persecution and the last straw allegedly was an incident in a Chinese restaurant when he and his family were publicly abused.

Long before Stan Ternent ever invented the description, Burnley fans have always wanted champagne football on beer money. Maybe Rochdale fans are right. Maybe we do have ideas above our resources. Mullen was a victim of that and was subjected to some disgraceful treatment. It is my belief that he worked two miracles at Burnley, which is why when I see his name appear in a brief newspaper snippet I look and see what he is doing now and if I ever met the man I would shake his hand in gratitude.

****

Saturday, December 14

Today there will indeed be a one-minute silence in memory of the Forest fan murdered in Burnley last weekend. It's a brave decision by the club and not without a measure of controversy.

One view is that yes, no matter what the circumstances, there should be a tribute. A life was lost and it doesn't matter what the situation behind it is. This was a tragedy and nobody should lose their life because they went to a football match. That is the view I share. The second view is that a few questions need to be asked about the incident first.

Today's silence in my mind is in memory of not just a murdered boy just a few weeks before Christmas, but also the stained reputation of the town of Burnley and, perhaps more importantly, a gesture to the boy's family. Then finally, it is for this; it is a demonstration that I along with other ordinary Burnley fans disassociate ourselves from all football hooliganism and in doing this we show our condemnation of all violence.

The club probably cannot win on this one. Hold the silence and the critics raise the question as to just what is it for and is it appropriate bearing in mind for the moment nobody knows a thing about the lad or his part in the events? But not to hold a silence would bring about cries of insensitivity and indifference. And if the silence is marked by noise or protest then more shame heaps itself on the club. Having chosen their course one can only hope that it is observed properly.

Today's game is against Rotherham and it's as gloomy and soggy a day as there's been for weeks; and believe me there have been endless dank days this November and December. There is the suggestion by Tony Scholes that spectators will need to sit up on the roof of the stands on the assumption that that's where the ball will be most of the time. My mind goes back to Millmoor. There should have been a Government warning on the tickets. Health warning: There is no football inside this ground.

I note from the Rotherham club website that they have been invited to play in next season's Isle of Man Festival. They seem to be thrilled and obviously take this as a compliment. Have they never been to the Isle of Man before? Surely today's game cannot be as dire as the one at Rotherham just four weeks ago. I fear another 0-0 is on the cards.

Sunday, December 15

Bradford, still in existence, at last won after a run of seven defeats.

Man U won their seventh game on the trot.

Gary Lineker gets the go-ahead for his consortium to take Leicester over.

And we applied the four-goal rule yesterday, that's the rule that says when we are 4-0 down we can leave immediately. For the London Clarets it is a three-goal rule. That must account for the sudden mass exodus not much more than halfway through the first half when Rotherham slotted home their third. For us it meant leaving a good twenty-five minutes before the end when we decided our time could be better used doing some Christmas shopping on the way home. It was in a bookshop half an hour later where we heard the faint crackling commentary announce it was 6-2 at the end, yes I repeat…

BURNLEY 2 ROTHERHAM 6

So much for 0-0: funny, I had an odd feeling about this game when I saw these big bruisers jogging out in their blue and black striped kit, the vertical stripes making them all look a foot taller. Bearing in mind they're all six feet tall to start with, made of solid brawn and Yorkshire pudding, they looked bloody enormous.

In short, Rotherham, strong and powerful, could do nowt wrong today and we could do nothing right. To add insult to injury ex-Burnley players Lee and Mullin scored four of the six goals. Shame they couldn't do that when they played for us. Sod's Law does indeed exist. Prior to this, Mullin hadn't scored all season. In their black and blue kit, we then did all we could to make Rotherham look like Inter Milan.

Cox came back into defence rusty and totally out of touch after his lay off. He and Davis looked and played as though they had never met before. In between each of the six goals Burnley managed to play a few minutes of their own brand of neat passing football, sometimes passing the ball to a teammate, but mostly neatly passing the ball to the scrap metal men. Rotherham must have thought it was Christmas come early. They were just bigger and better. The only consolation is that it will be they and not us going to the Isle of Man next August… or are we?

At half time, to combat these menacing blocks of mobile towering Yorkshire granite, we then bring on Moore (Alan) and Tony Grant, who compared to these Wrestlemania muscle-bound hybrids from the cloning labs of Rotherham, looked like delicate orchids.

Some time before the end came the icing on the cake that is Claret. With the score at 4-0 we somehow contrived to score two goals and with ten minutes still remaining there was still time for two more. Sadly it was the Incredible Hulks who scored them.

One of the revelations of Stan's new book just on sale is that he resorted to sprinkling holy water from Lourdes onto the pitch and the goalmouths to try and change things round when results were particularly bad a while ago. The team then went on to a run of eleven unbeaten games. If it's that good maybe he should dunk the whole of today's team in a barrel of the stuff, although to be fair you could argue it was another horrible freak result that Rotherham won't repeat till the next Millennium.

In their early days the embryonic Burnley, then known as Burnley Rovers, who also happened to be a rugby team, washed in the freezing River Calder after each game. It is perhaps time, after this lamentable display, to revive this tradition. Of this game we will say little more and banish it to the dustbin of memory save for saying that the very moving one-minute silence was observed impeccably.

Nagging questions begin to emerge though. The group the lad was with were in town from 12.15 onwards. Just what was a group of away supporters doing in the town centre so early, three hours before the match was due to start? Were the police unaware that such a group was already in the town? Yes, the silence was necessary. Yes, a death is unacceptable. But why was that group of Forest fans in Burnley so early?

Rain buckets down. The Sundays and the websites make for gloomy reading and Stan is brutally honest:

> *"Every now and then we tend to throw in a performance like that and it's difficult to explain why. It was a very frustrating and disappointing afternoon. I can guarantee one thing: we'll be better than that next time."*
>
> *"We were second best all over the park in the first half when all the damage was done... we have no excuses, we were well and truly beaten."*

Here's an interesting statistic. Of Rotherham's seventeen shots, thirteen were on target. That kind of percentage happens maybe once a season for any team, let alone Rotherham. It happened yesterday at Burnley. And that's what being a Burnley supporter is all about: it only happens at Burnley.

> *"We were overrun all over the field - they wanted to win more than we did. Without exception we were terrible."* (Paul, London Clarets)

> *"We were unspeakably inept. We didn't want it and they did. We played like a load of pansies."* (Michael, London Claret)

Tuesday, December 17

It occurs to me that Saturday was the halfway stage of the season. We have played 23 games and things stand like this.

Played 23, Won 9, Drawn 5, Lost 9, Scored 33, Against 41, Pts 32

1. *There are few occasions of a club at the halfway stage with 32 points being relegated. There are equally few occasions when a team with 32 points at the halfway stage has been promoted. It is reasonable to say we could either be promoted or relegated or finish up in the middle somewhere.* (Tony Scholes Claretsmad).

2. We are seven points behind a play-off place.

3. In addition to this, we have Payton and now Davis and Briscoe injured.

4. We are still in shock from a 6-2 thumping. *"It may still have been eleven days to Christmas, but Burnley managed a pantomime performance on Saturday that was more in keeping with a 'Two Ronnies' Christmas Special than a first division match. The difference was that no one was laughing.* (From the excellent London Clarets match report by Cozzo)

5. The accounts and forecasts made public in Saturday's programme make gloomy reading, but we are still here and there is no further talk or rumour of administration. There is no mention of players not being paid for Christmas though it is unlikely they will be given a turkey.

6. The Gawthorpe training area is a swamp but profits from Stan's book, which had sold 734 copies by the end of Saturday, are going into the reclamation and welly fund.

7. Perhaps the find of the season so far is McGregor who at last has been given a chance to show more of what he can do. He has yet to let the team down.

8. The Government has announced it will give people the right to carry on working after the age of 65 and still get a pension. This is good news for Paul Cook and Andy Payton.

9. Having come in for much criticism in early games it is significant that our two best players at the halfway stage are Roberto di Blakio and Grahamissimo del Branchio. Both get better every game. There are signs too that Weller is getting back to something like the player he was. And in four years time, if we are all around by then, there might be another Tony Grant goal to look forward to.

10. *And so far it's been a very strange season.* (writes London Claret Igor Wowk in his piece Halfway House). *This year the Clarets looked badly affected by the ITV Digital Gloom and the statement of the obvious that everyone was for sale and the Beresford/Broomes farce played its full part in the ensuing pre-season chaos culminating in one of the worst Burnley performances I've seen for a long time on the opening day. Basically they were not ready for the start of the season and Stan's very public and fairly uncharacteristic lambasting of the team and certain individuals was not a good sign... the Clarets have often won games they were not expected to win, only to lose games they were expected to get a positive result. At the moment they are completely unpredictable...*

It's a long piece that Igor Wowk writes in which he wonders if Papadopoulos would be a better partner for Robbie Blake even though Gareth Taylor is one of the best headers of a ball in the division. He berates the Burnley public for not turning out more than they do, only appearing when the likes of Ian Wright and Paul Gascoigne are brought in. Then like all of us he bemoans the appearance of the hard core of 'nutters' whose only interest is aggression and opposition baiting. Finally, again like all of us, he would be relieved to see a top half finish bearing in mind financial restraints and the limited room for manoeuvre.

In conclusion he ends with, *"Let's get fifty points in the bank a.s.a.p, crack on from there and see where it takes us."*

Wednesday, December 18

Stan himself has certainly not given up hope of a play-off place and remains determined that he and club will one day make it into the Premiership. After Saturday's debacle we are not so sure but in The Burnley Express prior to Saturday his aims were crystal clear saying he wants to manage in the Premiership and his ambition is to get Burnley there.

> *The players here now have the same ambition as me, to get into the Premiership... I made promises to the fans when I came here and I am determined to keep them... in my heart of hearts if the ITV Digital situation hadn't happened, it would have been a reasonably level playing field in the First Division, and if I had been able to strengthen, I think we could get in the Premiership... The chairman is the best I could have. If he had more money he would give it to me... But if anyone is to blame, it isn't ITV, clubs, chairmen, managers or players. The people who agreed the contracts are responsible. The contract should have been watertight, but all of a sudden the clubs are left with egg on their face...*

But bad news hits the club today. We knew Davis and Briscoe were injured but not the extent of the damage. Steve Davis will be out for up to two months with a knee injury sustained in Saturday's nightmare game. Details emerge that it was in a block tackle later in the second half that the harm was done. He will have a scan later this week to discover the extent of the damage. "I'm very disappointed and gutted to be missing the Christmas period, the third round of the FA Cup and all the games after that," he said.

In a word, this is a disaster, both for him and club. It was Davis, now in a brace for the next few weeks, who scored both the Burnley goals on Saturday. With Cox still ring-rusty it remains to be seen what the back line will be for the Gillingham game. The word inspirational is an understatement when describing the role of the Burnley captain. The injury demonstrates the tightrope the club walks in terms of size of squad and loss of key players.

To that we add a groin injury to Lee Briscoe which keeps him out until the after the New Year. Paul Cook's shoulder injury sustained in an earlier game now needs an operation.

Suddenly three players are missing in an already small squad. Just sixteen players remain for selection.

Thursday, December 19

Third Division York are to go into administration (*Daily Telegraph*, Sport Thursday) and may be out of business by their match against Swansea City on January 18 unless they can persuade someone to take over a business which is losing £20,000 a week... the York players who have recently received help from the PFA have agreed to play for nothing over the festive period while their employers, who are £500,000 in the red, look for a buyer.

But on to Gillingham: where if memory serves me right we have a habit of drawing. Gillingham is a small Kentish town but this is not the delightful Kent countryside of which we speak, the Garden of England, the county of fields, pleasant landscapes, picturesque villages, country lanes and high-speed rail tracks.

This is industrial Kent or what there is of it, in an area of maritime traditions, with terraced rows and little back streets. Apparently it is a favourite watering hole and away destination of the London Clarets. It possesses the only pub in the land where the help of a parrot and a mobile phone was enlisted in order to get a landlady out of the bath in order to unlock the pub doors. The Will Adams is highly recommended but there's also The Frog and Toad, the Dog and Bone, and... The Upper Gillingham Conservative Club.

My worn and battered AA Gazetteer of towns and cities in England has absolutely nothing to say about the place other than it having a population of 79,740 and connections with Charles Dickens. Further intensive research however has brought to light that it was Elizabeth First who founded the dockyard and Nelson's Victory was launched from the slipway. Will Adams was a ship's pilot who one day landed by chance in Japan, which doesn't say much for his navigating and seems an awful long way to go to lose your way. Years later Gary Lineker landed there and hurt his toe. General Gordon's folding chair, the one he used at Khartoum, is on display in the museum. All this information I am sure will send people flocking to Gillingham for a fortnight.

Gillingham's founders were the Excelsior football team who played on a ground called the Great Lines, known for its downward slope and nearness to a huge manure heap. I make no comment on the current Gillingham, save to say the ground is much improved and the manure heap has gone.

The reserves had a rare game last night in Arctic temperatures. With eight first team squad players in the team including Coxy and Arthur and Moore (Ian), Grant and Papa, there to gain match fitness, or re-kindle lost form, we still lost 3-1 to Preston.

Friday, December 20

The family of Nathan Blake have sent a message to the club:

> *Hello and a big thank you to all who have left messages in Burnley. At this sad time for our family and friends, we find it so difficult to comprehend the mindless act of violence that took place on December 8th, 2002. All Nathan wanted to achieve that day was the enjoyment of a game of football with his friends, after all, it is only a game. We have received messages from far and wide and all are standing united as we try to come to terms with the tragic loss of a grandson, son, brother, boyfriend, friend and football supporter. Please don't let Nathan's death be in vain. Always think of 'Nathan from Nottingham' at all future sporting events. Once again a big thank you to all.* The Shaw Family

There is nothing else to say other than the words 'Nathan from Nottingham' will be indeed etched into our minds for a long time to come.

Saturday, December 21

Chairman Barry Kilby is to meet Stan to discuss the possibility of team strengthening according to *The Lancashire Evening Telegraph*, now that the club's meagre playing resources are so stretched.

"It is safe to say I will have to talk to Stan about it," admitted the Chairman. "We will have to assess the situation and any move will depend on the finances involved. If anyone comes in it has got to be someone we want but also someone we can afford. At the moment we are looking at the situation and if we identify targets we will see if it is possible to bring them in. We will keep an eye on it and Stan is always welcome to ask about players, but we have also got the kids who are trying to break into the squad."

Barry Kilby also commented on the drop in attendances and the loss of around £15,000 a week because of the smaller number of walk-in paying customers at the turnstiles.

The dilemma is simple. Fail to strengthen, lose players to injury, results deteriorate, team slides down, crowds get smaller. Only by moving up the table into the play-off places is there any possibility of increasing crowds and that means spending money the club just doesn't have.

Stan has reiterated the necessity to sell if a good offer comes along for any player (Burnley Express) with the club £5million down. On top of that is the news that two more players, in addition to Davis, Briscoe and Cook, are out Saturday's game, Armstrong picked up an injury in this week's reserve game and Moore (Alan), injured last Saturday. Youngsters will have to be brought in, but who?

> *This is as tough as it has been in my time at Burnley, I had hoped such days were behind me. We will have to throw a couple of youngsters onto the bench. But there's no point moaning about it, life is hard work, and you just have to get on with things. Who knows what might come out of adversity?* (Stan quoted in Lancashire Evening Telegraph)

Sir Brian Mawhinney will become the new Football League Chairman. Formerly Secretary for Northern Ireland, he now takes on the even more dangerous job of presiding over the 72 Nationwide chairmen. His predecessor, Keith Harris, resigned in August after a furious row with League chairmen following the Digital fiasco. Harris left saying he was handing the asylum back to the inmates. Mawhinney earned his reputation as a tough negotiator between 1990 and 1992 in Northern Ireland and is a dedicated supporter of Peterborough United.

AND TODAY'S SORRY RESULT:

GILLINGHAM 4 BURNLEY 2

Sunday, December 22

Who would true valour see, let him come hither,
One here will constant be, come wind come weather,
There's no discouragement, Shall make him once relent
His first avowed intent, to be a Claret.
(John Bunyan 1676)

In Dickensian conditions: fog and mist swirling in off the Medway, which would have given a fine riverside backcloth to any film or TV production of *Our Mutual Friend*, Burnley's *Hard Times* continued. Any *Great Expectations* we might once have had for this season now seem well and truly buried as we went down this time 4-2. Our season would appear to be falling apart. Furthermore the banana skin that is the Grimsby cup game lurks just around the New Year corner.

The Burnley goals came from Gareth Taylor and a Robbie Blake penalty.

Gareth Taylor and Dean West were sent off. When the third goal went in the dog looked at me and I looked at him. He sat under my feet as I listened to the commentary and being a smart kind of mutt nudged me with his snout to say that's it, that's the third, let's go out. We did.

We are now down to fifteenth in the table and the last away win was back in October. The bubble has burst and the team seems well and truly off the rails. As well as injuries there are suspensions which will result in West, Taylor and Little all missing the Grimsby cup game in addition to the already injured Davis, and probably Briscoe and Cook.

Notwithstanding a very poor referee display, the Clarets in the gothic gloom were dispirited and lacklustre, resulting in plain and blunt condemnation on the London Clarets Vox Pop web page:

> *It was pretty grim. There was no commitment and a disappointing lack of team spirit. Gillingham thoroughly deserved their victory and our ineptitude was only bettered by the referee's. He was atrocious but that didn't influence the result.* (Dave)

> *We deserved to lose. I have no problems with Gillingham but the ref was absolutely diabolical. Before Taylor was sent off there were two fouls against our players for which the ref could have stopped the game. One of the fouls was on Taylor and the guy who fouled him should have been sent off. When the ref went off at the end he was smirking, and seemed quite happy with the way things had gone. Stan tried to speak to him but the stewards wouldn't let him.* (Cozzo)

> *We were completely outmuscled in midfield. We caused them problems in attack, but defensively we are naïve. The shallowness of the squad is there for all to see. Gillingham are a big strong team and (as with Rotherham) we can't control big strong players. I'm hoping that Stan can do something in the transfer window, even if it's only a loan signing...* (Woody)

> *We played poorly but the referee was as bad as you can imagine. As far as Burnley were concerned, Taylor won lots in the air but the ball wasn't finding anyone. Little didn't get involved as much as he could have done. The defence got the ball in good positions but then just hoofed it up the field...* (Russell)

Stan was certainly unhappy and commented on sloppy defending, the standard of refereeing, players who aren't playing as well as they should be, and the need for squad strengthening. He acknowledged that there were Burnley people who had travelled 300 miles there to see the team perform and who had paid good money to do so. Without any additions such as loan players he predicted a long hard winter.

Within the space of just seven days a definite crisis has arisen. Ten goals have been conceded in just two games. There is a treatment room full of the injured. Suspensions are looming. Stan has publicly stated that certain players are off form. Any other team that is big and powerful brushes the midfield aside. On top of all that Wolves are due on Boxing Day, a team that traditionally gives us a good hiding in every game be it home or away.

Stan would seem to have few options other than playing two goalkeepers or getting the bottle of Lourdes water out again. The target of 50 points now seems a long way away - eighteen points in fact, or six wins. I have no doubt we can win four between now and the season's end and scrape a couple of draws but it's going to be a damned close thing on the evidence of the last two games. And yet there is that nagging little part of the brain that reminds you it's a funny old game and it would be just like Burnley for a patched up side to win for the first time in years against Wolves on Thursday.

December 26 - Boxing Day

Man U are red, City are bluish
If it wasn't Christmas, you'd all be Jewish.
(Ancient Hebrew proverb, circa AD 25)

And miracle of miracles, indeed they did win.

BURNLEY TERRIERS 2 WOLVES WHINGERS AND MOANERS 1

Which means five more wins for safety and four points from a play-off place.

It has been said by some that being born a Burnley supporter is punishment for something done in a previous life. There is much truth in this. We saw them play superbly in the first half, saw them score two great goals, saw them play Wolves off the park, and then the punishment theory took over as Wolves dominated the second half. This was classic Burnley stuff. True to form Burnley vanished, the midfield evaporated, Wolves scored and we then had the customary final five minutes of backs to the wall stuff and then four more of injury time where nails were chewed to the bone, heartbeats were missed and nerves were shredded. So what's new? This is what life is like as a Claret. It would be dull if it were any other way.

This is the side that has conceded ten goals in the last two games, we said, as we drove over in torrential rain. This is the side that has been brushed aside on the last two Saturdays. But this is the side we said that defies logic, does the unexpected almost to order and one day, just one day, Wolves must be beaten when the law of averages will come into play, and the curse will be lifted, thus ending the horrendous run of results against them.

No grumbles today. We had eleven heroes, none more so than McGregor at left back (Branch was injured) who was outstanding; Cox back to his gigantic best and Taylor who won everything. Have we at last found another left back in McGregor? It means that Branch can be released to play as a wide left midfield player. What justice and irony that Taylor's opening goal was a superb header, reminding all of us of his header last year in the same game, which was disallowed for no reason anyone or any camera could see.

West scored the second and the crowd then sat back, scoffed their pies, and enjoyed half time two goals up.

"Better if it was three though", we all agreed plaintively as the second half began and classic Burnley took over, the Burnley that don't really know what to do when they're two goals ahead. We have two teams at Burnley. There's the Burnley who are superb, like the one in the first half today. Then there is the Burnley who flounder in places like Grimsby and Gillingham.

Consider the facts. Burnley hadn't won a Boxing Day game since 1993 or taken maximum points from Wolves for 39 years. What right had we to think we could win this game? It's simple. As ever, as in any football supporter's mind, there's that little glimmer of optimism, that bit of the psyche that says the jinx must end one day. Today looked a certain win for Wolves, but in football there's no such thing as certainty.

In his programme notes Chairman Kilby, clearly with the last two results in mind, reminded us of just how far we have come over the last five years since a drab 0 - 0 Boxing Day draw against Chesterfield. Five years ago today Burnley were fighting against relegation. Today we sit in mid-table security. Promotion looks unlikely but then so does relegation. No one can say that this year has been the best of years but today victory was sweet - and on my birthday as well. They say you can remember what you were doing on every birthday. This one I certainly shall.

Friday, December 27

Which Burnley team will get off the bus at Brighton tomorrow, the good or the bad, the Jekyll or the Hyde? Both Beresford and Little took knocks yesterday. Brighton are much improved since a long run of defeats anchored them into the bottom three following their opening day win at Burnley.

Brighton has a lot to answer for. For those who hate swimming in a cold sea, you can blame Dr. Richard Russell who started it all in his book. In 1750 he said that sea air and bathing at Brighthelmstone was actually beneficial and healthy. Before him, nobody had really thought of it that way. It was just a place where you caught fish, got wet and sometimes drowned. Sunbathing hadn't been invented yet. Word got round of course and in 1783 The Prince Regent decided to come to Brighton to dip the royal toe in the briny. Feeling better immediately he set up camp in Brighton, bought a farmhouse, added on various bits and pieces, and this eventually resulted in The Royal Pavilion, basically a big house with knobs on, which today the uninitiated would simply assume with its domes and minarets, is a very large Indian restaurant.

George IV, as he eventually became, enriched Brighton with culture, art, architecture, music, theatre, painting, gluttony and the pleasures of the flesh. Sadly he put very little money into the football team, which is now hanging on grimly for its existence, at the awful Withdean Stadium, where there is a ban on music, parking, and speaking in any voice above a whisper. Norman Wisdom was a director for eight years until 1978.

There is one fan known as The Rocketman at Brighton who lurks in the trees around the stadium and lets off rockets every time they score or win. On an occasion when Zamora scored a hat trick one landed on the pitch and it was decided it was time this danger to society was caught. Local residents in this exclusive suburb are far from pleased that this former quiet peaceful athletics track is now a soccer stadium and their homes are subject to rocket attacks.

Brighton today is very much a sort of extension of trendy London with a three-mile beach. Some people can walk on hot coals and some on Brighton Beach, much of which is made of feet-crippling rocks and stones. If memory serves me correctly, Mods and Rockers used to meet here regularly years ago to exchange insults. One bit of it was the first ever official nudist beach and the ancient West Pier is about to collapse into the sea.

> *It offers a jolly day out. There are some good pubs and for once a decent variety of non-drinking options on offer... Let us not forget that Brighton were the Wimbledon of their day, a cause celebre behind which football fans of many colours united. Owned by dodgy sorts who were in it for the money, their ground was flogged, and the usual kind of shops occupy that once sacred space. Brighton were left homeless and seemingly heading for oblivion. That they have not just survived but flourished, and that they have returned to Brighton after a spell in exile at Gillingham, is a kind of miracle...* (Firmo London Clarets)

We saved the box of Burnley Christmas crackers till yesterday. It seemed an apt and fitting tribute to a good result. Quality stuff, might I say. Not in these crackers the usual tatty tissue paper hat that slides down over your eyes making consumption of a plate of turkey and veg difficult if not impossible, but instead there is a bright and attractive adjustable card hat, which oozes style and class. The gifts are pretty standard but the piece de resistance are the quiz questions. Here are just a few and the answers I'll give just as soon as I can find where I've put them.

1. Who were Burnley's opponents in Frank Casper's last match before he resigned?
2. To which club did Burnley sell Billy Ingham?
3. Which ex-Claret was born in West Sleekburn?
4. Who was assistant to Adrian Heath after John Ward left?
5. Which was the last non-league team to play at Turf Moor in an FA Cup tie?

Saturday, December 28

"Football, Bloody Hell" (Alex Ferguson)

That sums it up. As at Bradford though not for the same reasons we threw away a two goal lead with just minutes to go.

BRIGHTON 2 BURNLEY 2

Two nil up with just five minutes left and Brighton score two in a minute. We sat listening to the commentary; open-mouthed and feeling like deflated balloons like all air had been sucked out of us. Not many teams give away two goals in a minute in the dying minutes of a match. Burnley do and I'm still sat here three hours later brain dead.

The bottle of (sale price) Lanson was in the fridge waiting to be opened and eaten with the fine freshly home-made golden-crusted turkey pie. It just didn't taste the same.

Crisis? What crisis, I'm thinking. We're back on track, two wins in a row. We're set up nicely for the game at the hellhole that is Bramall Lane on New Years Day. Our depleted troops, (with two youths on the bench again), playing with strains, knocks and niggles are going to pull off another good win. Like hell.

Supporter's views were direct and to the point:

It really is difficult to quite work out just how we lost two of the three points on offer but basically the answer is we threw them away in a game that should have been dead and buried long before any late drama...(Tony Scholes, Claretsmad)

The way we gave two points away today was nothing short of disgraceful. The only comfort after the Bradford debacle was that the team might have learned something. Today they showed they had learned nothing. If there are any Burnley players reading this could they please take note that the game of football lasts for ninety-plus minutes. We were 2-0 up against possibly the worst team in the division who had offered nothing and looked like relegation fodder, when we relaxed and gave two points away. To concede that first goal was unfortunate... but to concede a second was simply unprofessional. I am so angry. I was thinking of those Burnley people who have to get on the coaches back to Burnley. They deserve a team that plays for ninety minutes. Tonight I'm thinking about those two dreadful draws: at Bradford and at Brighton. Those should have been wins and we would be comfortable in this division now. I so much hope that we won't regret it. The team should apologise to everyone who turned up today. Brighton are going to go down and we've only taken one point off them. Pathetic. (Firmo. London Clarets)

And so we threw it away. That dear reader is Burnley and sums up nicely and ends fittingly, the frustrating and exasperating year that has been 2002.

Sunday, December 29

The West Pier at Brighton collapsed today. There are strong suspicions that it was the rocketman.

Christmas is over, the turkey finished, the presents packed away. This year there was no repeat of what I thought last Christmas was a brainwave, when I bought the good Mrs Thomas a selection of items from the club shop. I showered her with videos, Kings of Europe, Season's Highlights, books, and a framed picture of the ground. There was a Burnley shirt, (and you all know how much they cost), sweets, pens, biros and other sundry items. I thought she'd be pleased. With what I spent Burnley could have bought a small player. She was not impressed. Let's just say this year I stuck to the tried and tested - a course of treatment at the local beauty parlour which goes under the original name of Nails 'R Us. When it first opened I thought it was an ironmongers.

JANUARY

New Year's Day - Wednesday, January 1 2003

Today we are at Sheffield United. Only one good thing has ever come out of Sheffield and that's the road back home. Oh, and Super Johnny Francis.

I wrote in last year's diary after last season's game the words *abject*, *dire*, *bereft*, *dismal*, *dreadfu*l, and *numbing*... and that was just the pies. Burnley were even worse. We were well and truly stuffed. It was where all of us realised that the shadow that was Gazza was not going to take us to the Promised Land. There are just a few details to mention. It is nineteen seasons since we last collected a point at Bramhell Lane. Burnley have not scored a league goal there for twenty-five seasons. It is twenty-nine seasons since Burnley actually won a league game there. Sheffield United haven't conceded a goal in their last five games and only one in the last eight.

I confess to an intense extreme dislike of Hellhole Lane. It oozes South Yorkshire antagonism, hostility and belligerence. Currently it is the home of Mustapha Bin Warlock and his Sheffield branch of the Al Qaeda. As a general rule, nay empirical, the cave dwellers and terrorists from Bramallistan have been far too good for our brave but simple Claret-wearing Lancashire Fusiliers. They're a hard lot in the concrete streets of Sheffield and little old us usually get a good hiding. Their ground gives the same feeling that a blood-filled Roman Arena must have done two thousand years ago.

Regrettably I have to report that Sheffield are a pretty good side this year. They have some cracking players - Peskisillyladdo and Ndlovu (pronounced erndlurve with a kind of Barry White drawl). They booted Leeds out of the Worthington. They are in the semi-finals of said competition. They sit high up in the play-off places. I expect nothing from this game other than a thick ear.

I am an ex-headmaster so therefore I am intelligent and rational, (well I think so even if the staff didn't). I know all my times tables and can spell words like disleckšia and dilinquunt. I am wise and sensible. Nevertheless I have a totally irrational dislike of Sheffield United.

Bramhole Lane had its origins in cricket grounds that were leased from the Duke of Norfolk in Victorian times. Football came in 1862. As a condition of the lease the good and noble Duke insisted that sport here 'be conducted in a respectable manner'. One hundred and forty years later this request has been well and truly forgotten and the poor old duffer would turn in his grave if he knew just what the Blades got up to here. Last season in their infamous game against West Brom they had three players sent off on a day of utter ignominy.

They should build an asylum there instead of a hotel, said one newspaper under the headline Thuggery Rules at the Lane of Shame.

In programme notes earlier this season Crystal Palace chairman Simon Jordan wrote about Sheffield United:

> *Hopefully this time, they will give us proper balls to warm up with, showers that are not cold, ball boys who adopt the same policy for both sides and tea at half time.*

Ah well, it may just be sour grapes, but I have to say I just don't like 'em and I don't want to be beaten by them at Buggerall Lane.

Well done to United Chairman Derek Dooley though who was awarded an MBE in the New Year honours list. After a bad injury as a player many years ago he had a leg amputated. Then years later, as manager of Sheffield Wednesday, he was sacked on Christmas Eve. Yes, they're a hard unsentimental lot in South Yorkshire.

Thursday, January 2

We didn't lose at the Sheffield International Centre For Violent Activities. After all the build up and anticipation, the game was postponed because of a waterlogged pitch. I suppose you'd say that's a good result. The arguments for and against winter breaks are raised again. After the deluges of rain these last couple of days the only games that took place yesterday were those on Mt. Ararat. So instead of discussing how we got a real pasting yesterday, let's take stock now that the New Year is here.

This time last year we were top of Division One, we thought we were on our way up but nobody really knew of the slide that was to come. Maybe we had over achieved and excelled ourselves as the moves came off and the goals went in.

2002 was a typical Burnley year, that is to say both annoying and maddening. Again it was winter weather that disrupted the season in January. After that we lost games we should have won and sometimes we just gift wrapped the points and gave them away. Then we won the difficult games quite unexpectedly. Referees decisions, or the absence of them, in certain games cost us dearly. They say they even out after a season. In our case I don't think they did. Losing a play-off place by just one goal was heartbreaking and we still think of goals missed and silly goals conceded. The club bemoans the loss of ITV money and we think what might have been if that money had allowed us to retain David Johnson.

The truth is that what we have is a basically good bunch of players who sometimes play above themselves and convince us that they are better than they really are. mid-table is probably about right and we do well to be there in relative safety, but how infuriating to think that maximum points at Bradford and Brighton would have us just one point behind the play-offs.

It is probable that given the opportunity by Chairman Kilby, Stan would bring in two, maybe three loan players, but according to the Claretsmad website on December 23rd Stan and the Chairman hadn't spoken in weeks though that possibly sounds more sinister than it really is. After the Gillingham game Stan referred to supporters travelling 300 miles, giving up their last Saturday before Christmas and that the club owed it to them to see if wages could be found for new players.

> *If we can't bring anyone in, it will be a long hard winter. I understand the Board's position, but if we don't strengthen, we won't get results and the gates will drop off. We need to sit down and draw up our priorities.* (Stan in The Lancashire Evening Telegraph)

Chairman Kilby was cautious in response, saying that it would depend on cost and availability and that there was no guarantee they could bring a rabbit out of a hat. But at least this was not an emphatic *no* and the hint at the most recent Board meeting was that emergency money might well be found from somewhere.

The possibility of another cup run generating more income is just a week away if we can overcome the dreaded Grimsby at Brooding Park. But it's a game we shall play with a team decimated by suspensions and injuries. Fail to win or force a replay at Turf Moor and income dwindles yet further. To be knocked out by the fishy ones just doesn't bear thinking about.

There is no doubt that loan players are available in abundance. Five hundred players are without clubs. The player's union and its benevolent fund supports dozens of them and tries to find them new clubs. Some are still in their prime and they sit by the phone waiting for a call. There are stories of former big name players who can no longer even afford a Christmas Turkey without Union help.

According to Gordon Taylor:

> *There is a cold wind of financial crisis blowing through the game and we have dug deep to help out, but our cash supply has run out.*
>
> *Many of the 500 out of work have gone part time, but there are many who are being turfed out of their homes. There are youngsters who have not made the grade whom we are subsidising through university. Paying their fees because they can't afford it. Our grant to players is £2m. We are helping out two dozen clubs with loans close to £6m*

How ironic it is that in three games this season loan players have taken us to the cleaners - Proctor at Bradford, Kabba who ran us ragged at Grimsby, and Sidwell at Brighton who mugged us with a minute to go.

Saturday, January 4

Michopoulos has returnedoulos to Burnley from his loan spell at Crystal Palos. Earl Davis has been recalled from his loan spell at Stalybridge. Stan's book has now sold 3000 copies. Tom Clancy is getting worried. Will Tony Livesey be showered with critical acclaim for what is being said to be a masterpiece of its genre? West and Taylor have failed in their appeals against their sendings off at Gillingham. Burnley at Grimsby in the FA Cup 3rd round today are therefore without the two of them plus Little, Davis, and Briscoe.

Life must be so simple if you are a Grimsby supporter. I say this with the greatest respect but in general they don't expect much, a win every now and then, survival in the bottom six of the division. An occasional away win and that's another season over. Aspirations are moderate at best, and the hope is simply to stay in Division One. Ground capacity is low. Gates are poor. They haven't won any of their last five cup games. The 6-5 win against Burnley probably had them dancing in the streets for a fortnight. A point at Brighton for Grimsby would be an achievement. For us it was thoroughly disappointing.

How much more complicated and tension filled it is to be Claret. Unfortunately we are blessed, if that's the right word, cursed might be better, with dreams of grandeur. We want champagne. We have expectations and ambitions. We have a fine ground. We have a history. We have been champions and we have produced great players. We have seen the light and tasted glory. At Burnley we have scaled the heights and seen Europe and the Isle of Man.

And thus, even though we never actually do, we expect to beat teams like Grimsby in their quaint little ground where the wind whips in off the sea and the front rows of spectators are spattered by passing seagulls, some of which are just inconsiderate, and others do it deliberately. We might appreciate them doing this on a Blackburn supporter but not on ourselves.

'Three miles of boggy turf' was how Lord Torrington in 1791 described the strip of land where Grimsby play. Today it is called Cleethorpes. If you come across a pub quiz question that asks you which team used to change in bathing huts, the answer is Grimsby. If in the same quiz you are asked which supporters in 1982 kicked out the back of the Osmond Stand and urinated into the gardens behind, the answer is Leeds United. Charming.

From the top of The Findus Stand/Stones Bitter/or whatever it is now called, there is one of the finest panoramic views in football. The view of the moorlands and outer areas of Burnley from the top of the James Hargreaves Stand on a clear day is grand enough, but that at Grimsby, of the Humber Estuary, the sea, passing tankers, Spurn Head and the North Humberside peninsula, especially under a clear blue sky, is unsurpassed. One almost doesn't mind drawing or even losing.

Sunday, January 5

And draw they did again didn't they? Threw away a 2-0 lead and it all ended up

GRIMSBY 2 BURNLEY 2

It is just unbelievable that any team could do this again.

But as we are Burnley we will continue to muddle along as we have done for the last 25 years. (Brent. London Clarets)

Do we not know what to do when we are 2-0 up, we ask for the second week running? For the fifth consecutive game Burnley score two goals and yet have only won one of those five games. Even with half a team missing we play them off the park for forty minutes or so, could, should have scored a hatful, and then in the second half are just plain abysmal. Total domination in the first half, said Claretsmad, then dreadful in the second. Add to that a penalty for Grimsby given for something unfathomable to all but the referee (ridiculous decision, said Stan) and a giveaway goal just three minutes from the end when a mesmerised defence let an eighteen-year-old dance and waltz (always waltz, never tango) around them, across them, in between them, all over them, and then at will fire home at leisure from the edge of the box.

Moore (Alan) and Weller scored the Burnley goals after which the Burnley fans chanted we want six, classic Claret optimism.

The only consolations are more gate money on the 14th, our name in the hat on Monday (Tottenham, Everton, Newcastle, Man City, Birmingham, Villa and Middlesbrough won't be), we don't go there again for another year... oh, and it's quicker to get home from Grimsby than Brighton. To have been a supporter at both of those games doesn't bear thinking about.

The view from the other side (abridged) came from Tony Butcher on the Grimsby website Electronic Fishcake.com. If we think we at Burnley have problems then who'd be a Grimsby supporter?

A cold cloudy afternoon with about 1,000 Burnleyites gathering in shivering groups to keep warm. And sing which is a lot more than the Town fans did...

About three fans bothered to cheer when the Town players were announced and it took 57 minutes for the Town supporters to raise anything other than the old favourite, the Grimsby Grumble (six teenagers singing 6-5 twice doesn't count). No atmosphere, no magic in this cup. Vast swathes of the ground were bereft of humanity; it had the aura of a particularly dull pre-season friendly. It was as if those Town fans that were present resented being there...

Burnley kicked off towards the Pontoon, retaining possession and absolutely refusing to kick it out of play...

Ah, the scoreboard back working today, with no messages in code, so it was a waste of time bringing the enigma deciphering machine in, wasn't it..?

Burnley attacked, Town panicked. That's the story of the next twenty minutes. Burnley confused Town by passing then moving, which was not what certain Town defenders wanted to see. So they stopped looking...

The programme sellers were more challenging opponents...

A brief meeting with a lost Burnley supporter provided vital pre-match intelligence - that their centre forward, Dimitrios Papadopoulos, known from now on as Mr. Pap, had an inner ear imbalance and was thus often unable to remain standing...

Oh well, I might as well get the pain over with now. Their goals...

A Moore took the ball straight forward a stride and caressed it under the leaping Coyne from about eight yards out... three or four minutes later it got worse... I Moore unmarked and about ten yards from the bye line carefully crossed into the middle of the goal. Coyne dived out and from the middle of his six yard box parried the cross out towards the edge of the area. Straight to the unmarked Weller who carefully placed a volley down the centre of the goal...

The rest of the half was absolutely terrible, for Burnley stopped. That's the only way to describe it. If they wanted to humiliate Town they could have, as there was no coordination or in some cases will to succeed in their monochrome opponents. Back passes were under hit, shoulders shrugged, players left unmarked, runs not made. Stagnant, sour and shocking, this was a poor advertisement for non-league football....

Just as the crowd mood was about to explode into a horrid torrent of abuse at the players, the referee's random decision maker came up with the jackpot. I couldn't see the ref's eyes spinning but I assume they were...

McGregor challenged Campbell, who fell rather feebly as he tried to turn. The ball rolled to another Burnley defender and they cleared. Play stopped, the referee's arm was horizontal and pointing towards the penalty spot. After a second or so the crowd realised it was in fact, in reality, honestly, a penalty. Wahey! We hadn't even asked for it either. Who would take it? Yes who? No-one appeared to know, least of all the team...

Cooke trundled forward and cracked the ball into the bottom right hand corner as the keeper dived left. The crowd chuckled at such fortune... Burnley continued to treat the match as a done deal, often getting into exceptionally dangerous positions, but lackadaisically wasting the opportunities, mainly by mishitting shots straight to Coyne...

The game was gone, lost, awful; shocking, dreadful, dinners were on tables when Town won a throw in, under the Smiths/Stones/Findus Stand. Gallimore lobbed it to Mansaram about twenty yards out in a big muddy bog. Mansaram turned infield and meandered across the face of the box. He beat one player, came to another and beat him, all the time going laterally. The crowd were beginning to grizzle, expecting a shot or at least a pass out to Cooke. By this time Mansaram had gone beyond the other corner of the penalty area. Instead of passing he came back. Oh here we go, a Keystone Cop ramshackle journey across the pitch to a land that time forgot. Woooah! Mansaram lifted his left leg, and whacked a supreme shot low into the bottom left hand corner. Foot like a traction engine. Bang, bang it's in. What a shocker, what a stinker for Burnley...

Lucky, very lucky. An almost indescribably bad performance, collectively and individually, but undefeated. Burnley have only themselves to blame for not winning 8-0...(Tony Butcher. Electronic Fishcake.com)

I have to confess I am a great admirer of Fishcake writing.

Monday, January 6

Paul Weller out injured for the next couple of weeks or more following the Grimsby game, to add to the list of those in the treatment room. This is a real blow. Over the last few games he has come back to the form that made him player of the year two seasons ago and he has been captain in Davis's absence.

Marlon Beresford's current monthly deal has now expired and it is the Ipswich game in five days time with no extension currently sorted. Rumours continue that he is going to Arsenal as cover for their current keeper crisis, or more realistically to Preston who have a fetish for taking our disused players. With Michopoulos backoulos there is clearly no intention to raise the offer to Beresford that is already on the table. The transfer window has been open now for seven days and little or nothing has happened anywhere.

Today there was a welcome return to an old tradition, the draw for the next round of the Cup on a Monday lunchtime - and on the radio to boot. What has it been over the last few years, Saturday midnight, Sunday before breakfast, middle of the afternoon... on Sky TV? Years ago we huddled round the radio with ears glued for what was always a big event. Hearts raced, pulses increased and there were always those black and white grainy newspaper pictures in the paper the next day of the team gathered round a radio big enough to stand on. Ah memories... The Goon Show, Journey Into Space, Friday Night Is Music Night...

Having said all that, I watched on it on BBC2.

It's Brentford away in the next round of the Cup IF we beat the cod heads next Tuesday. There will surely be some grumbling if we don't. And if we do then it's a banana skin nothing game we face where there isn't even the bonus of a good payday for the coffers. Brentford knocked out Derby this weekend so they must fancy their chances at their stadium beneath the Heathrow flight path.

Tuesday, January 7

To Burnley today to get tickets for the next two games. Ah, the bliss of retirement when one can do these leisurely things.

"Phone them," says Mrs Thomas who suspects that it is just an excuse to have a large bacon bap in the club café.

But no, I want to drive over to see the snow and ice-covered landscapes over the hilltops and moorlands between Hebden Bridge and Burnley, where isolated farms lie marooned in a desert of white as far as the eye can see, where ruined stone walls and gaunt trees are silhouetted against the skyline and sheep huddle in sheltered hollows. Such a drive works up an appetite for the bacon bap.

The car is parked in the deserted club car park and I'm walking towards the ticket office. My God, who's this walking towards me in trousers with a crease sharp enough to slice bacon, immaculate shirt like it's just come out of the Christmas wrapping paper, a tie and smart casual windcheater looking like he's just stepped off a yacht moored at Cannes? The face is tanned and weather-beaten. It's definitely an out-of-doors face. This is a man who obviously spends his time in the open air.

My God, it's Stan. He looks bigger than I thought. I must tell him about my book. Shall I say well done? Shall I say keep up the good work? Shall I ask is he signing Lee Bowyer? No, I must grab the chance to ask about visiting the training ground for half a day. I must ask about sitting on the bench for a game. I must ask can I interview him one day. I am a mature ex headmaster. I can do these things. I have spoken in meetings, dealt with blazing parents and smoothly fobbed off irate education officials asking where has all the money gone. I am no tongue-tied numbskull.

We approach. In a friendly tone he speaks first. "How do you do?"

I reply breezily as we pass by. "Good morning."

My mouth opens to speak again but no words come out. We pass. Blast. That's it. That's my conversation with Stan. How do you do? Good morning. Is that the best I can do? Write out one hundred times… I am a pillock.

Ah well never mind, maybe he'll be in the café. I'll buy him a bacon bap and pluck up courage to try again. No he isn't but there inside is a whole bunch of athletic, good looking (well some of them) healthy looking (well some of them) blokes in black training gear. They look like SAS rejects. Normally the café is full of the old who have been trying to keep fit or rowdy school kids in mid-soccer tournament. Just every now and then there is a crocked first teamer who has been having treatment. Anyway this black-garbed crew who look like gods (well some of them) on a football field, close up here in the cafe, look distinctly more human with their knobbly knees and hairy legs.

They've been training in the gym because Gawthorpe is frozen solid. Now they're going to watch a video. The Munsters? No, the Grimsby game. Then I see a familiar face. Well, it's half familiar; the other half is buried beneath a bobble hat. Then it beams.

The face looks at me and I call out. "Dean?"

He calls back. "Mr. Thomas?"

And yes, it's the lad I used to teach twenty years ago. The last time I saw him he was only this high. He comes over with a grin like a Cheshire cat. He's friendly, good natured, modest and sociable. He's the only lad in twenty years who made it into football out of all those I used to coach on a wet Saturday morning or a freezing afternoon after school. The lad who more or less single-handedly won us second place in the schools league in his final year against schools twice as big as my little village school on the edge of Leeds. And the lad covered in mud, who I once told jokingly after a game somewhere in the murky backwaters of Wakefield, and believe me there is some deep murk in Wakefield, I'll get you a trial at Burnley one day. I don't think it impressed him. The early '80s weren't exactly our vintage years.

Well I must have taught him something right (everything except the offside rule) all those years ago, before schools became impossible places in which to work. Today they are places where a third of the workforce, according to a new survey, plan to leave within the next five years. I was lucky, I left the asylum seven years ago.

We sat and chatted for ten minutes about old times and the village before he went off to watch the video. God it was cold at Grimsby he said. He hadn't played - just sat and froze. My bacon bap arrives. They do two sorts, undercooked and nearly black. I always ask for the black. He can't understand why they can go ten games unbeaten and then go to pieces. Yes, Glen Little never stops eating as we watch him shovel toast down as fast as he can. Yes I can ring him anytime and if there is a book launch he'll be glad to be there with a couple of the lads and if I want to come up to the player's bar after a game that'll be fine. Then he has to leave. The gaffer wants them all.

"And stop calling me Mr. Thomas in front of the other players," I tell him, "Sir," will be fine.

I finish my coffee and ponder. I bet there are many ways in which being a football manager is like being a headmaster, The only difference is I could never sack people on the spot or tell them they were sh*te.

Wednesday, January 8

Marlon signs for another month. No other club is coming in for him, and neither is there an increased Burnley offer on the table. According to Claretsmad.com, Beresford is happy enough with the deal and said:

> *I'm really pleased about this because it suits me and I think it suits the club as well but hopefully we will be able to review things before the end of this month because I need to think about my future. Ideally for me it would be better to get something sorted out long term with more security. That is my hope but the chairman's away at the moment. Hopefully we'll be able to discuss it when he returns. The ideal scenario for me would be to stay at Burnley. Without a doubt Burnley is a club close to my heart and I'm sure everyone's aware of that so to stay here as long as possible would be great. But at the same time you've got to sign a contract that you're happy with because you have a family to look after.*

Thursday, January 9

It's an interesting fact that Paul Weller is the only youth team product in the current first team, in other words the last of any of the youths to have made any lasting impression at the club. Paul is twenty-seven, which begs the question, what has happened to all the rest, of which there must be many.

It's an interesting fact that the last youth team product to have true star quality was Trevor Steven and he was sold to Everton in 1983. This is a sobering thought. We all know that Burnley was a club that had a production line of wonderful young players in the '60s and '70s. Books other than this have listed them extensively.

Trevor Steven was certainly special and more or less leapfrogged straight into the first team although only eighteen. John Bond eventually sold him but then any manager at the club would have struggled to hold on to him. He went on to win league titles in three different countries and played for England. He was a supremely special player.

Paul Weller signed as a professional in 1993. Others since then have played small bit parts, or sat on the bench, or moved on or just faded from the scene. Paul Smith had everything but illness cost him dear. At the moment there is no young player at the club who could command a regular first team place.

I am therefore, with great sadness, inclined to agree with Stan Ternent's views that the youth set-up at the club could be disbanded. In cost effective terms it seems to be money down the drain. All the more galling is the fact that our neighbours at Blackburn are now producing quality teenagers on a regular basis who can slot into their Premiership first team. But then they have an academy, and we don't. Jack Walker's millions: Out with the old, in with the new, bugger the cost, I read somewhere.

Stan commented on the youth set up at the club's recent AGM at which Barry Kilby was re elected chairman. His views were reported widely in the press and on websites:

In my view it would be better to have one team of twenty players and then trawl the academies and get young players in at eighteen and nineteen. At the moment the failure rate at Burnley Football Club is too high. We need to have academy status but the minimum charge to set one up and get Gawthorpe right is somewhere in the region of £3 to £4million. The youth team is a very complicated and a long-winded item of discussion and it is a subject close to my heart. The problem is that Burnley Football Club can't attract the best young players. Forty years ago, thirty-five years ago, the club would go out and get the best because Burnley was in the top flight, in the European Cup, champions of England. The situation now is that young players want to play for Manchester United, Liverpool and Arsenal. Clubs like Sunderland have just spent £12million on their academy; all the other clubs have them while we, at this moment in time, can't. It is a case of finance and wages. Our rivals Blackburn can take a kid and offer him an apprenticeship and long term deal on wages some of my first team aren't on. That's why we can't attract the best kids. Even if we did get a Dave Thomas or a Leighton James, whichever youngster was your favourite, we would not have them two minutes before another club came in, took him and just pay compensation. To me football is a seven days a week job. The kids are in college all Monday and most of Thursday, Saturday they play and Sunday they have off so that leaves three days. You can't do much on Friday because of the game on Saturday, that leaves two days, Tuesday and Wednesday, to be a professional footballer. The board and chairman understand where I am coming from. We are not producing kids. It is hard for people to take because Burnley was always known for bringing on their own players. I was one of them. I was part of it. In the '60s it was all home grown and I remember when we signed Frank Casper it was a rare thing. Since then the club has gone down the divisions and the best kids want to go to the Premiership. It is a real minefield and already in football there are hundreds of very good players unemployed.

The sad and awful thing is you can't really argue with that. Here at the moment with a string of injuries and suspensions (six players out again on Saturday), there is not one youth team player who could walk straight into the team and fill one of the slots.

The 'reserves' i.e. the youth team, plus Gordon Armstrong, lost 4-1 at Huddersfield yesterday afternoon. Reports suggest in fact they gave a good account of themselves and were playing against a very experienced Huddersfield side. Sadly though in the Burnley ranks there appears to be no 'star' waiting to burst onto the scene like a Trevor Steven, a Dave Thomas or a Brian Flynn who all those years ago exploded into the team on their teenage debuts.

But here's a thought. Since the golden group of Beckham, Scholes, Butt and the Nevilles et al emerged years ago from the Man U youth set up, when was the last time Man U unearthed a real star. Wes Brown? Hardly. John O Shea? Not yet. Not much of a return is it over the last few years for the millions they have laid out on their academy? The Premiership and Nationwide is littered with their youth team rejects. Good enough for another club but not good enough for us, was and maybe still is, a Man U maxim. Yes, I agree with Stan. Take a few Man U rejects when they're nineteen and twenty. After all, David Johnson was one.

Friday, January 10

My neighbour, Bradford John, still doesn't know if his beloved Bradford will be in business by the end of the season, or even next month. I try to put myself in his position and say a prayer of thanks that at The Turf we aren't as desperate as they are and the good ship Claret, though in deep water, is skippered well by Cap'n Kilby and Bosun Stan.

We sank a bottle of Ivory Label Lanson last night (on special offer at Safeway) while John went through all his woes. We'd shopped in the club shop at the weekend (and say it quietly) I went along with him and spent a few pounds there. Think of it as charity I said to myself.

The shop was sad. It's a huge place presumably part of the now vanished Geoffrey Richmond's misplaced ambitions. It's the size of a Marks and Spencer's and has two floors which used to be full of flash designer gear, golf clubs and skiing equipment. The latter seemed a litte optimistic since it hardly ever snows in Bradford any more. At the weekend the upper floor was closed down. Downstairs everything was marked down to half price in an attempt to clear stock. It was tempting to phone the Burnley shop and tell them to bring a lorry over. A few sad looking kids were on duty clearly wondering would they have a job on Saturday. I bought a couple of T shirts for summer and a woolly hat, which almost looks claret. I felt thoroughly guilty thinking this was money I could be spending at Burnley but then what else could I do with my neighbour so distraught and dejected. And anyway if Bradford folds, he can come to Burnley.

According to John the stadium is built on the site of an old holy well, not that it's done them much good. Obviously the Lourdes irrigation system we use to water the pitch at Burnley is more effective than Bradford's sacred hallowed water.

**Early in the season and things weren't too good.
A Burnley fan props up the newspaper headline.**

Bradford City vs Burnley games are a big day in the Bradford calendar. Burnley gifted Bradford a last minute equalizer and Bradford supporters thought they'd won the Cup.

It's tough at the top. Dave plans how to avoid another home defeat and wonders if anyone else is turning up today, or, alternatively, if he has come on the wrong day.

Do that again and I'll...
vs Brighton.

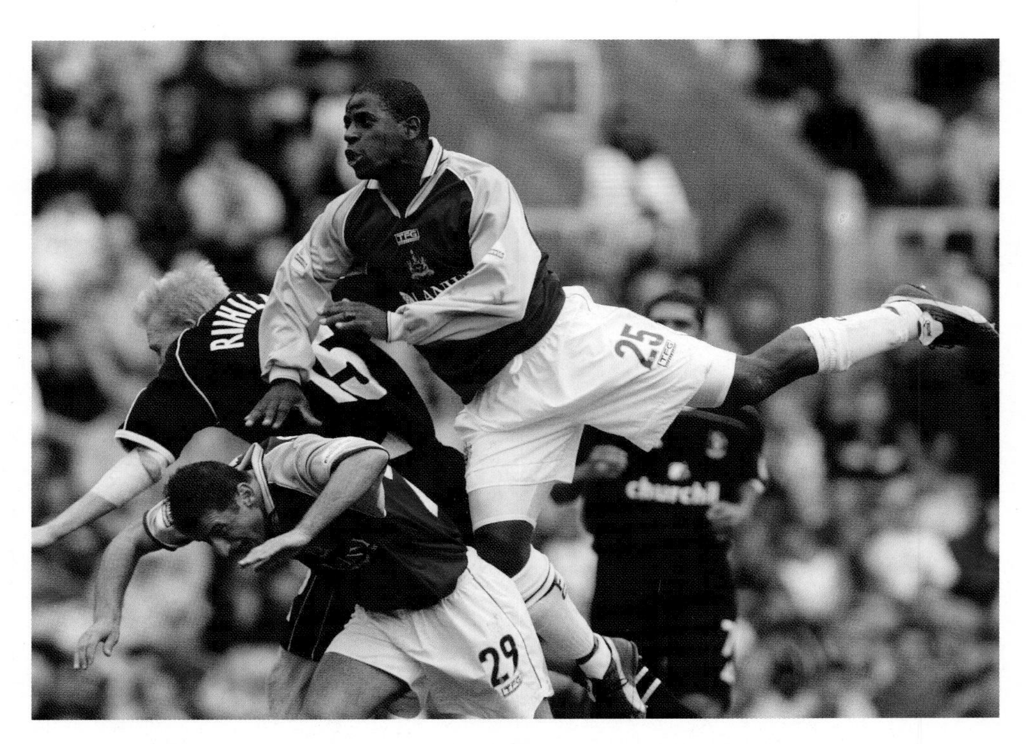

Lennie Johnrose takes off against Crystal Palace.

The Boys...having a little celebration.

Dimi Papadopoulos scores a stunner against Stoke City.

Graham Branch outpaces champions Portsmouth.

TFG
LANWAY

TFG
LANWAY

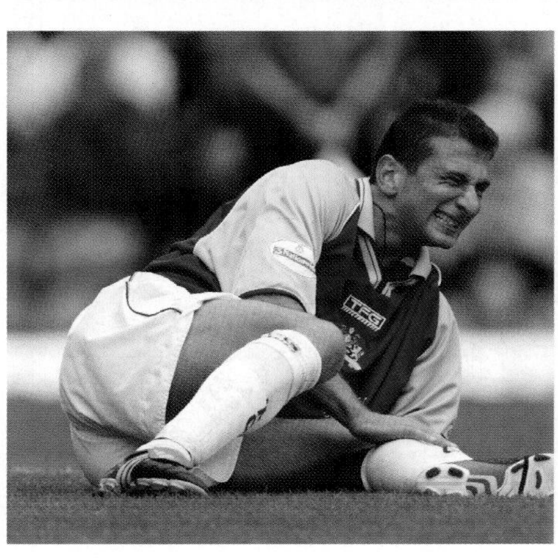
TFG

LEFT: (clockwise from top left)
Ian Moore versus Brighton.
Arthur Gnohere versus Brighton.
Robbie Blake baffles a Blackpool defender.
Paul Weller versus Portsmouth.
Dimi Papadopoulos goes through the pain barrier against Crystal Palace.
Dean West against Brighton.

Steve Davis celebrates his goal against Tottenham.

Stan Ternent... time for a Silk Cut, maybe...

Gareth Taylor outleaps Silvestre against Man Utd in the Worthington Cup.

Come on lads, earn your money... and Robbie Blake, stop dreaming and concentrate...

Glen Little's stunning individual goal against Grimsby in the FA Cup.

Happy days are here again.
Gareth Taylor and Tony Grant against Wolves.

Mrs T. is surprised to learn that Drissa will be wearing his best suit for the game against Gillingham.

Master and pupil, Mr T. with Dean West.
Dean stopped smiling when Mr T. asked him for his missing homework.

Graham Branch, in disguise, explains to sponsor Emma Fielden how he's having his best season ever.

Ian Moore, in disguise, welcoming matchball sponsor John Fielding.

Legend Andy Lochhead explains to Gillingham sponsors, “Sorry folks...this is Mr Kilby’s room. You lot get pie and peas.”

A Burnley family take their seats early at Watford. Nobody was smiling at quarter to five.

Send 'im off ref...
During the great 3-0 win against Fulham in the FA Cup.

Bees in flight.
Bertie and Bumble celebrate a honey of a win against Fulham in the FA Cup.

John worries that when Bradford finally collapse Mr Mumtaz will buy up the ground and land. Mr. Mumtaz's fine restaurant is famous throughout Bradford. My neighbour loves a good curry but not to the extent of seeing The Pulse/BradfordBingley/Valley Parade/Richmond Park/ Holy Bantams or whatever it is called, becoming the world's biggest Indian Restaurant.

"We can't pay Lombard, we're behind on the payments," moaned John as he began to demolish a Stella six pack, "we couldn't pay the players before Christmas, we sacked our assistant manager, we've still got players on Premiership wages, the shop is closing down, we've players we can't play because their old clubs want appearance money, the club cat is half starved and Mumtaz wants the land. We're doomed."

I returned home wearing my new woolly hat, the Lanson having made me feel quite mellow in spite of my neighbour's depression. The hat fits very tightly and has a sort of woolly bubble on the end. Mrs. Thomas looked aghast.

"You can't wear that," she announced, finishing off the evening perfectly. "It looks ridiculous. You look like a condom."

Friday, January 10

Yesterday Stan strengthened the squad by signing a player from bankrupt Belgian club Mechelen. Not just English clubs then is it? Claretsmad Tony Scholes our man with the spy glass, reported the arrival of not a nineteen year old midfield player from Sunderland as per expectation but a central defender, Drissa Diallo, from the land of the Walloons, thirty years old and a free agent as Mechelen have gone bankrupt. Mechelen can't be that bad having won two titles in recent years with Diallo a regular. He has previously played for Brevannes, Sedan, and Tilleur Luik. Today's geography question, boys and girls, is take out your atlas and find where these places are. You have five minutes and no help from me because I don't know either. The third one sounds like it might be vaguely Mongolian.

Born in Mauretania, plays in Belgium, has a French passport, 6 feet tall and hopefully speaks fluent Lancashire with a smattering of broad Geordie. Gawd bless yer Stan. Where do you find 'em? If he's another Coxy he'll not be bad.

Today was the funeral of Nathan Blake from Nottingham. Chief Executive Andrew Watson and club secretary Cathy Pickup represented Burnley with players Gareth Taylor and Ian Cox. There seems little else to say other than hooliganism is high on the agenda at next weeks meeting between the Board and representatives of supporters clubs.

Saturday, January 11

York City have ten days in which to find a buyer or face closure. The PFA had to pay York's £70,000 wage bill in November and the players in the first team squad, of whom one is ex-Burnley Chris Brass, have not been paid since. Chris Brass, who belongs to the same year group as Paul Weller, was always unlucky, I thought, not to have become a regular at Turf Moor. He always impressed me but suffered probably from being one of those jack-of-all-trades who was asked to play in a variety of positions, never being able to make one his own, in spite of being a thoroughly decent perceptive player.

Ipswich are £30million in debt and some time ago laid off eighteen of the back room staff to trim costs. This week they sold Jamie Clapham to Birmingham making it another one less on the wage bill. Birmingham made a loss last financial year in excess of £6million.

We are home to Ipswich today for the first league game in twenty-seven years. Six players missing; Davis, Briscoe, Weller, Taylor, Cox and West. I'll take a draw. A win will be a massive bonus. Ipswich are undefeated in six and have won four of them, one point above us and inching towards the play-offs after a poor start. They're on a definite run and are one of my bets for a play-off place. George Burley was sacked there early in the season. It looked like the job was Peter Reid's. Then there was a phone call to Rotherham's Ronnie Moore offering him the job. Ronnie took it very seriously and had just about packed his suitcase until discovering it was all a very convincing hoax. To supporter dismay Joe Royle was appointed. He used to play for Norwich. Ah, the politics of football.

Perhaps they are starting to think more kindly about him. They call him 'BFJ' from the Roald Dahl book title BFG Big Friendly Giant. Apparently BFJ neither likes nor dislikes it, seeing it as a term of endearment, but he said in the *East Anglian Daily Times* that he can't believe that Ipswich fans think he is fat.

Sunday, January 12

BURNLEY 1 TRACTOR BOYS 1

Not six regular first teamers missing yesterday, but seven, when there was no Marlon Beresford in goal as we took our seats. Instead it was Nikos Backfromloanoulos who returned to a loud and prolonged welcome. Initial conjecture was that this was Stan playing mind games with Beresford on account of the unsigned long-term contract. In fact after the game, in the players lounge, we learned it was because of a training injury sustained on Tuesday and resultant sciatica.

With so many players missing we came away afterwards feeling well satisfied at taking a point from the current in-form team. Both teams could have scored deciding goals; both teams had dominant spells. The Ipswich goal was entirely against the run of play and must have surprised them as much as it did us… no… correction… no goal against us surprises us this season and this one came courtesy of Burnley standing admiring an Ipswich corner in preference to doing something about it. From then on the middle third of the game we spent assuming this was going to be a 1-0 burglary for which under new Home Office guidelines first time offenders will not face imprisonment. Blake's penalty changed things and we spent the last third of the game watching both teams squander chances coming their way.

Two thoughts linger. One, we miss Gareth Taylor. Two, Glen Little misses Paul Weller and Dean West.

We ran our socks off, none more so than Alan Moore. New man Drissa Diallo (looks more like a Harlem Globetrotter basketball player than a footballer) had an excellent game making a goal line clearance that bordered on the miraculous. He tackled well and all in all looks a good acquisition. McGregor was excellent. Branch was my man of the match. Ian Moore was back to his pacy best. No grumbles from me then, and afterwards it was off to the players lounge to find Dean West.

Players' Lounge is a bit of a misnomer. It's more of a cupboard under the stairs: nothing glossy or superclub class about this place deep in the bowels of the Cricket Field End Stand. There's a sort of a pinky striped wallpaper peeling away in one or two places and a few framed pictures and faded newspaper pages on the walls. A flickering telly screen is on Sky Sports and the results programme. In one corner there's a tiny bar. It's basically whisky, brandy or lager. A huge hot water urn balances on a small table from which there are hot drinks. Basic indeed but the atmosphere is warm and friendly as we wait. Player's wives wait in a huddle around a low table, but not for these girls slinky lingerie, low cut dresses and plunging necklines like Chardonnay on ITV - well not in here anyway. One by one the players begin to arrive. In grey suits, shirt and tie they drift in to meet family or friends. Interestingly, I don't see one player with a drink.

Dean eventually arrives and I ask him what dressing room opinion is. He says it could have gone either way and Ipswich are a good side. I sense there is satisfaction at a point gained rather than two lost. We chat away and seeing and listening to the players who come in is a reminder that these blokes have just the same feelings, frailties, mortgages, families and emotions as the rest of us. Perhaps those so-called fans in the crowd who abuse our team might care to remember that.

Mrs Thomas is beside herself at the appearance of all these athletic heroic blokes in such close proximity. Mrs. T likes Paul Weller but I'd said to her wait till you see Gareth Taylor. Shucks, she won't see him. He's got his little boy with him so he's gone straight home. Dean is clear to play on Tuesday but makes no assumptions that he'll be straight back in.

I've taken an old school photograph of us all at school twenty years ago gathered round the school's first computer trying to figure out how to get Sky. There's Dean looking like a little cherub.

Mrs. T, who knows a little Greek (on our travels in Greece we've noticed not many Greeks are over 5 feet 5", ha ha), wants to practise her language skills on the unsuspecting Dimitrios Papadopoulos who is standing with two other Greek guys, one of whom we take to be his father.

"Signomi?," she says. (Excuse me?)

"Milau poly ligo Ellineeka." (I know a little Greek).

Dimi who close up looks about seventeen years old is clearly startled by the appearance of this strange beaming lady with a drink in her hand, in her middle fifties spouting garbled Greek at him. He looks puzzled, smiles politely and looks at his dad for help. I think she tries to tell him he has played well, but who knows what she says, and I don't think he does either.

Drissa Diallo comes in. Ahem. I speak quite a bit of French.

"Drissa," I smile at him.

"Aujord hui vous etes tres bon." (Today you are very good).

I mumble a few more things at him, impressing myself more than him, while he patiently smiles and nods. It's only later when I get home that in hindsight I feel a bit embarrassed. In my efforts to put him at ease, I realise I have told him I love him.

We left Turf Moor and the Players' Lounge well pleased. Mrs. T clutched the programme signed 'Best Wishes to Mrs. Thomas from Dean West'. He didn't want my autograph. He already has it - on his school report - and I promised him I wouldn't say a word about that.

****

And who is this today on Sky Goals On Sunday? The pundits are none other than Peter Reid and our own gaffer. Stan once referred to these people as the claptrappers union. He looks grandfatherly, comfortably relaxed, at ease and prosperous on the red settee in his grey roll neck sweater, slacks, brogues and woolly socks. It's well known that he and Peter Reid are the best of pals although they spend most of the programme with each saying that the other is the most miserable.

"I'm not miserable," says Stan.

"Well who've I been drinkin' with these last 15 months, it must have been yer twin." says Reidy.

Example of Reidy Scouse wit.

"You were a World Cup player, what do you think of Maradona?"

"Yeh... she's a good singer."

Stan says again that he'd love to manage in the Premiership preferably with Burnley and that he didn't see the Digital thing coming. Letting Kevin Ball, Mitchell Thomas and Gazza go at the end of the season plus two or three others saved £1.3million on the wages bill and was done to clear the way to bring a couple of others in that he can't name. Thanks to Digital these others weren't brought in (We assume maybe that one was David Johnson). He says that he gets on pretty well with everybody in the game except just one person but won't go into that. Somebody asks, "Is it yer Mrs?", which has them all rolling about on the settees for half an hour.

The highlights of the Burnley game are on. They show how smart the Ipswich goal was and then Blake's nice little textbook penalty. Yes Ian Moore was well and truly clattered but Stan gives him 10 out of 10 for use of the arms in the fall.

Monday, January 13

How close are Huddersfield to administration this morning? According to *The Daily Telegraph* they are £6million in debt with a wage bill of £3million. On Saturday they lost at home to Peterborough 1-0 in front of another poor crowd. Chairman of the Los Angeles branch of the Huddersfield supporters club is Patrick Stewart, otherwise known as Captain Jean-Luc Picard of the Starship Enterprise. He is, not surprisingly, the only member of the Los Angeles Huddersfield Town supporters club. The next attraction at The McAlpine is An Evening With The Hamiltons, which sounds a whole lot better than an afternoon with Barry Fry or an evening watching Star Trek.

Huddersfield could well be one of the 50% of football league clubs Man U chief executive Peter Kenyon predicted would not survive the current financial crisis. Of course ITV Digital is seen as the cause but in truth it goes deeper than that with club boards and management unable to control club costs long before the TV money fiasco arose. Yes there is money to be made in football but this money is in the hands of just a small group of Premiership clubs. Ex-jockey Willie Carson, now chairman of Swindon, another struggling club, is reported to have said that if football were a proper business you'd shut it down and walk away.

Plenty of clubs were in debt long before ITV Digital kicked the ladder from under them. 80% of clubs between them could tot up £134million in debts. David Gold of Birmingham City has said that in his mind clubs were in trouble before Digital. Then along came the extra money and instead of using it to stabilise and adjust, almost all of them went out and spent the lot in advance of receiving it, awarding players long lucrative contracts to counteract the Bosman rule. It becomes a spiral. Clubs spent money in advance of getting it, to pay players they couldn't afford, in an attempt to reach the top end of their league, and having done that, then spend yet more money they hadn't got in order to stay there.

Complicating all that is also the fact that income from player sales has plummeted. And where players have been sold it is at knockdown prices - witness the January sales at Leeds United. Bowyer and Dacourt have gone. Ferdinand and Keane went earlier. Others look set to follow and all at prices that are but a fraction of what was paid for them or what their supposed value was a year ago. Leeds would appear to be bending backwards to get rid of Fowler and his alleged £45,000 a week wage, at a knockdown price. Clubs once counted their players as part of the assets. Not any more, when many are a liability, overpaid and in many cases distinctly average, most of them negative equity and many of them from overseas and bought without enough thought.

The only hope is that sense is beginning to prevail, that there is a new air of realism and that those clubs which do survive - and clubs over the years do seem to have a habit of muddling through and surviving - will not fall into the ambition/overspending trap again. Whilst once upon a time clubs by and large went and spent and hoped it would be all right at the end of the day, now it might just be that more clubs are moving towards better budgeting and cost control. The era of massive wages may be at an end.

At Burnley there are two years of belt-tightening ahead and switching the lights out every time you leave the room. The price we are paying is that we look set to just float around in mid-table and eke out the pennies. Better that though than Coventry £60million in debt, Derby £30million, Ipswich £30million, Chelsea £99million, Leeds £60 or £75million depending which paper you read, and Bradford £36million with Lombard knocking ever harder at their door.

Tuesday, January 14

Gordon Taylor today thinks that capping player's wages will cause more problems than it solves. He too blames club boards and mismanagement for any financial crisis, not the players. He believes salary capping will encourage creative accounting, including paying player's wives. He has produced a paper 'Salary Caps - not a panacea for football's financial problems' and says that players should not be the ones paying for Directors' mistakes. He emphasises that while many continue to blame ITV Digital, transfer windows and player's wages, it is in fact financial mismanagement which is the root cause which is now resulting in fewer players in the game and being paid less. Clubs have spent more than they have earned.

The typical short-sighted approach by the very people who have misdirected the clubs in this way is to lay the blame on players and look to cut salaries which in their opinion would bring the club back to a solvent position...

We are wary of further problems, such as creative accounting, payments being driven underground, or being made outside the club...

The job market for player's wives could increase too. Market forces will dictate that at the end of their contracts the vast majority of players will be looking for new deals on less money than they receive now...

There has to be protection for clubs from key individuals in top positions whose bad practice has left them in an exposed and vulnerable position...

A code of conduct should be set in place... we would recommend a financial propriety committee to be established...

Salary capping appears to be a knee jerk reaction to the financial mess a number of clubs are in. Common sense needs to prevail and clubs need to live within their means.

Grimsby meanwhile have taken back Michael Boulding on loan from Aston Villa to whom he went at the end of last season. Boulding is the player who tore through Burnley like an Exocet last season at Grimsby and effectively ended Burnley's play-off hopes. Bearing in mind the impact loan players always have in games against Burnley his appearance in tonight's cup replay fills me with some trepidation especially as he scored at the weekend. Cox and West are available for tonight's cup replay having served their suspensions. With those two in contention again it will be interesting to see what Stan does with the back four with McGregor having played so well on Saturday. Still out are Weller, Taylor, Davis and Briscoe.

Wednesday, January 15

BURNLEY 4 GRIM GRIMSBY 0

Last night we witnessed the disappearance of any last lingering glamour or appeal the FA Cup might once have had. In front of a paltry 5,436 crowd who shivered, pulled woolly hats tightly down over foreheads, rubbed numbed hands together and clutched scarves around windswept necks, Burnley eventually scored four goals to make the scoreline look a proper reflection of their dominance and skill.

In a three-quarters-empty stadium, with the sounds of players' voices echoing around the ground, the top half of the Jimmy Mac Stand empty, the atmosphere bizarre and surreal, the bottom half of the Longside empty, tonight there was a super show from Ian Moore, lovely intricate passing moves from all and sundry, another fine display from McGregor in defence, more great work from Branch, a typically consistent and ever dependable display by Dean West and by the end of the night four classy goals.

On the other hand, there were innumerable instances of the one-pass-too-many syndrome, shot after shot wide or high, endless over-elaboration in the penalty area, and sadly and more importantly, thousands of missing spectators. To be frank, when we left the shelter of the pie zone and emerged into the Hargreaves top tier as the game kicked off, the sight before us was just astonishing, with row after row of empty seats and half the ground closed. If there are over 11,000 season ticket holders then why could 6,000 of them not be bothered to buy a cup tie ticket especially as there are no more home games until early

February. Is it that this competition isn't exciting any more? Is it the cost at £19 a ticket? Is it the traffic jams at Cardiff being less appealing than the twin towers of a now half demolished Wembley? Whatever, we sat there amazed, quite numbed and disbelieving.

OK, so Burnley v Grim Grimsby isn't the greatest attraction to a neutral, but we aren't neutrals are we? This was after all a cup game. Not for one minute did any of us surely think there would be anything approaching a 15,000 crowd but surely something over 9,000 seemed a reasonable guess. In gate money terms then, this was hardly worth switching the lights on for. Only the £50,000 win money made it financially worthwhile.

As for the game: Grimsby were the worst, most hopeless side I have ever seen. Michopoulos did not have one save to make all night: truly, not one save all night. How futile and depressing it must be to come all that way and chant Come On You Grimsby when your team is so inept. Boulding in fact did not play (nor did Diallo for us) because of FA registration rules.

For us, Deano Van Westhurst was back making run after run down the right, and McGregor was at centre back. Ian Moore's opening left foot twenty-five yard goal was simply stunning. Blink and you missed it. Little's goal came when he beat fifty-seven men in the penalty area, changed direction seventeen times, confused and beat himself four times, had a dizzy spell, stopped to ask for directions, enquired did he have time to go and get a pie, finished up facing the wrong way, and still whacked the ball home from about six yards. Blake's tidy penalty was the result of Papa going down in the area after a blatant shirt pull (shirt pull outside the box, the fall two yards inside but then this is Classic Greek Drama and what Dimmy is good at). The fourth goal was as good as any you'll see when Ian Moore took the ball at pace down the middle of most of the Grimsby half, beat two men with ease and then another two with disdain and coolly slotted the ball home with a plum, (no, that should be aplomb). And then for good measure we had the Padiham Predator on for the last ten minutes and the crowd, though I use the word loosely, willed him to score.

Rumour has it that at the 1-0 stage Stan yelled, "For God's sake, don't score two." Once the 2-0 arrived all of us sat back and waited for Grimsby to come back and equalize. Not tonight. The codheads were well and truly put in their plaice.

Thursday, January 16

York City are on the brink of extinction. They now have only until 12 noon today for a buyer to step forward and contact the administrators. Failing that, it is the end, and even if the club is saved they must leave Bootham Crescent at the end of the season when Persimmon Homes will construct 93 luxury homes. The York share of the ITV Digital loss was £102,000 and the team has played for nothing since November. As ever, there are undercurrents of letdowns and sellouts.

Burnley boss Stan Ternent wants to sign Blackburn midfielder Alan Mahon said *The Lancashire Evening Telegraph* yesterday. The Clarets boss has been in touch with Rovers about the out of favour midfielder. A loan deal is possible if the two clubs and the player can come to an agreement. Graeme Souness has indicated that the player has no future at Ewood and a number of clubs have made enquiries. Reactions to a deal bringing a Blackburn player to Burnley would be mixed. Adam Blacklaw made a move in the other direction many years ago but such moves have been few and far between.

The Minister for Tourism and Leisure, The Honourable David Cretney MHK (wow), has announced that both Burnley and Rotherham will head the list of teams taking part in the Isles de Manne Steam Packet Company Football Festival this coming summer. In addition to Burnley and Rotherham (aka New Milan), there will also be Rushden and Diamonds, Blackpool, current holders Wrexham plus the Isle of Man. Sadly, winning this tournament does not guarantee a place in the Champions League. As ever, for some peculiar reason Burnley are immediate favourites to win the trophy. Sky never televises this one. I wonder why?

At a meeting this week Division One clubs voted unanimously in favour of creating greater autonomy for themselves and having their own Chief Executive. This would give them greater commercial and administrative powers and opportunities to remarket themselves. But to do this they need a 75% vote of all three divisions of the Nationwide. Separate television and commercial rights for Division One clubs in the same way that the Premiership has control over theirs, would appear to be the target. Division One chairmen are stressing that their intention is not to split the Nationwide but that their proposals will in fact help the lower divisions. A higher Division One profile is seen as essential making it "the flagship of the Football League". Or a poor man's Premiership Division Two perhaps.

Burnley's Andrew Watson said,

We have tried to keep a system that does not affect the income or voting powers of Divisions Two and Three. The clubs were getting fed up with directors changing all the time, and the idea behind this move is to employ a chief executive who hopefully stays around to add stability.

He insisted there was no intention of breaking away from the lower divisions.

Critics of these moves however insist that they are only a greed-based reflection of the setting up of the Premiership ten years ago and that it is indeed an attempt to break away from Divisions Two and Three. In doing this, Division One would have the opportunity to create more money for itself, albeit on a much lesser scale than the Premiership, and thereby solve many of the financial problems of its members.

Friday, January 17

Grimsby Town's fine independent website ElectronicFishcake.com and their reporter Tony Butcher had these things to say, amongst many others, about Tuesday's exhibition by the Clarets...

...Whole sections of the Burnley stands were closed with barely discernible patches of humanity dotted about the vast acres of claret and blue plastic...

Burnley had Jack-be-Nimble (Blake) and Jack-be-Quick (I Moore) up front...

Town players moved in strange and unusual ways, like they'd never met before. Burnley started like they had at Blundell Park, a whirling dervish of flicks and tricks...

Burnley surges, Burnley crosses, Clarets to the left of them, Clarets to the right of them... More crosses, more blocks, the occasional slice of cheese as Burnley danced round the edges of the Town penalty area...

...The game had the tension of a geography lesson on a wet Tuesday in June and the fascination of the Inner Ring Road in Scunthorpe, unlikely to be the subject of a sonnet...

More crosses, more quite frankly poncing about by Burnley. Shoot dammit and get it over with.

... Over, gone, finished. That was the first half. Town had looked what they were: a mish mash bunch of odds and sods, thrown together with no rhyme or reason...

Town were unable to keep up the high tempo sleepwalking of the first half settling into a groggy, stumbling, barely conscious lethargy. Burnley plainly got a rollicking from Stan the Man, foregoing the tip tap showbiz XI football until they got inside the Town penalty area...

... Burnley players were intent on scoring the perfect goal, wishing to walk the ball in only after each player had touched the ball once. They swirled in dizzying patterns that confused the old and infirm, which was half the Town team of course...

Burnley, Burnley, Burnley, - all up the other end. If only they could shoot straight they'd be seven up by the hour mark.

... more Hollywood football, with party tricks brought out from the closet. Was I mistaken or did Glen Little whip out a pair of spoons and play "My Old Man" whilst drifting past Mr Gallimore...

All in all it's best to draw a veil over this game and get on with the rest of our lives.

Saturday, January 18

A stay of execution for York City: their Supporter's Trust will keep them afloat for another two to three weeks. There wouldn't be a Burnley supporter anywhere who wouldn't be saddened to see the demise of Bootham Crescent. On 28 April 1992 it was where Burnley clinched the Division Four championship with goals from Deary and Francis.

Bradford City players can be paid. The club have sold Benito Carbone's old house, which was certainly rather more than a two-up two-down back-to-back with an outside loo in Manningham. Apparently it was a £750,000 smart pad in Alwoodley, one of the more desirable areas of Leeds. My friend who knows about these things tells me it was sold cut price.

Clarets boss Stan Ternent was yesterday remaining tight-lipped over speculation linking him with a move for Blackburn Rovers out of favour midfielder Alan Mahon, reported *The Burnley Express* yesterday.

Crystal Palace today. There aren't too many things you can say about Crystal Palace except that they don't actually play at Crystal Palace. Their ground nestles in a maze of side streets in suburban south London where there is little of distinction and is just about the hardest ground to find anywhere without getting well and truly lost. Their highest ever attendance, 51,482, was against Burnley in season 78/79. This was nothing to do with the glamour of Burnley, it's just that we were the sacrificial lambs making up the numbers when Palace clinched the old Division Two title. We finished thirteenth. In their early history at a previous ground they once had near railway yards, there is a legend that when they were losing, a friendly steam engine driver would conveniently let off clouds of steam and smoke which drifted across and enveloped the pitch thus disrupting the game. And last year this is the ground where Ian Moore Moore Moore broke his 13 game duck and scored both goals in a 2-1 win.

Ian Moore prior to the Grimsby game was certainly looking to regain his regular first team place.

"It's up to me now. I have to take the chance," he said in *The Burnley Express*. "I've said all I can off the pitch and I've got to start doing it on the pitch."

He'd obviously had a few words with Stan. "They haven't been quiet meetings, but I seem to go in and come out none the wiser."

A win here would be the hundredth league and cup victory for Stan Ternent during his time at Turf Moor. Ternent was a coach at Palace in the Eighties and it was there that he began his long association with Ian Wright and says that he is probably the best player he has ever worked with. With Steve Davis and Paul Weller the only currently injured players, it is now a case of who to select rather than who is available. Neither have there been any big money offers for Glen Little. A £3million move to Southampton was being hinted some time ago but seems unlikely now - if it was ever true in the first place.

Graeme Souness speaking on Sky Sports confirmed that Burnley were one of a number of clubs interested in Alan Mahon.

AND AT 4.50 IT WAS CRYSTAL PALACE 1 BURNLEY 1

Sunday, January 19

The opening surprises yesterday were the absence of Little because of back spasms following the Grimsby game and McGregor left on the bench in spite of consistently excellent performances over the last few weeks. Diallo took a place alongside Gnohere, for his second game. Briscoe and Taylor returned. To accommodate Taylor, Moore (Ian) took Little's right wing role, the one he doesn't like. The ever-dependable Cox was not even on the bench.

We can't grumble at a point can we? Or can we? Crystal Palace are a form team and we haven't exactly excelled ourselves away from home since the 1-0 win at Leicester. Most pressure came from Palace but it is galling to think that a 1-0 Burnley lead was lost to a highly debatable penalty when Adebola went down under a Beresford challenge.

View one, is that it was outside the area anyway. View two is that Adebola dived over Beresford who never made any contact. View three is that from the referee's viewpoint it looked like a penalty. The fact of the matter is that Adebola after the game told Stan and his staff that Beresford never touched him.

> *We looked good for the three points though, until the referee gave a penalty, which was never a penalty. Dele Adebola has said that Marlon has never touched him. He said that to me and my staff, but the referee said that from his angle it looked like a penalty...* (Stan on the official Burnley website)

On top of all that was Blake hitting a post and the ball bouncing back into the keeper's arms, and Grant, in a one-on-one with the goalkeeper, electing to pass when a first time shot might have scored. And then in the final minutes came two clear penalty calls, the first when Papa's shirt was blatantly pulled but Papa elected to stay on his feet and the second being a Palace player steering a Burnley shot wide of the post with his hand. As we have said before, such decisions decide play-off places.

A fair result - not a great game. Taylor was superb. Things don't quite seem to be coming off for Blake at the moment. Another good performance from Diallo. I felt sorry for McGregor being dropped to the bench. A point's not much good to us but I'm happy with the performance. (Cozzo, London Clarets)

The game could have gone either way. Palace missed some easy chances to win the game but we had two clear penalties denied to us by the referee. A mid-table draw. (Woody London Clarets)

I'm pretty happy with today's result. I thought we showed pretty good commitment. Golden Bonce was excellent again. He won everything in the air and as well as scoring the goal he was a good defender for us - a most underrated aspect of his play. We missed him last week and it was good to see him back. (Firmo London Clarets)

The London Clarets Vox Pop sums up the referee in one word; '*tosser*'.

And so we plod on to the magic fifty points. Ridiculous though it is, play-off aspirations remain, even though we drift around in sixteenth place having picked up just 6 points from the last six games. Yet still a play-off place remains just five points away, tantalisingly close, only two wins away, and with other teams above us continually taking points off each other it is still within the bounds of possibility. Portsmouth the leaders are stuttering. Leicester in second place lost at Gillingham. Sheffield United and Ipswich are the teams on fire. Any team that can put four or five consecutive wins together can do it. With everyone fit and if key players are playing well, there is no reason why we can't do that. The season is still alive and well. Don't write us off just yet. And there's a possible Cup run. I'm enjoying this season.

Monday, January 20

Gazza has flown off to China to find somewhere to play, hoping for a £500,000 a year contract with Liaoning of Beijing. There is an inherent sadness and pathos in all this. If China is not the answer, if there is rejection there, then where next, after all other avenues and destinations have failed?

There is quite simply nowhere else. It's still hard to think that Gazza was only last season a Burnley player but we are constantly reminded when newspaper pictures usually show him in a Claret shirt. He arrived and was paraded before us at the Preston game with all of the razzamatazz and fanfares of a circus. All of us roared and acclaimed this man/child in spite of all his misdemeanours, foolishness and impudence. He didn't play that night but there is no doubt that the inspiration and mood he brought fired us to a badly needed win. We took him to our hearts and willed him to rediscover the talent he once had. But it was not to be. At every ground he went to in a Claret shirt, when he ran onto the pitch the applause and greetings that met and welcomed him from other fans was astonishing in its generosity and affection. It was as if it was a thank you for the years of genius and skill he had displayed for their entertainment. It was as if everyone knew they would not see Gazza play again. It was as if Gazza was a player who belonged not just to one team but to all of us. We won't forget his tears at Italia '90. We won't forget his goal against Scotland in Euro '96. We won't forget other stunning goals and weaving runs, and bursts of acceleration, and pieces of audacious skill that few other mortals can ever hope to copy.

His stay with us was brief and came to nothing but we still think back to his first game against Bradford when just as in the final Coventry game, it was only fingertip goalkeeper saves that stopped him from scoring, and just one goal would have taken us to the play-offs. If only... If only he could have recaptured just some of the form that made him world class. If only the gamble had paid off. If only his body had still been quick and sharp. If only time and drink and mad escapades hadn't ravaged his instincts and skills... If only...

Of the Bradford game, his first for Burnley, some reports were derogatory and callous. I prefer to hang on to the ones that were kind, forgiving and generous:

> *His evening may have ended in anti-climax, but at least the clown prince is back in business. Paul Gascoigne clad in Claret and Blue, swaggered into Burnley last night to help his new teammates squeeze into third place in the bottleneck at the top. The former England international's debut may have been low key - two speculative free kicks and a second half booking provided the highs and lows - and strangled by Claus Jorgensen's equalizer for Bradford City near the end, but his influence was there for all to see. If Gascoigne does nothing else, he will inspire those around him. Burnley are asking for nothing more.* (The Guardian)

> *The years have not been kind. His hair is thinning (well whose isn't?), his waist thickening, but there are still few things better than a bit of Gazzamatazz. Burnley may be the last stage for Paul Gascoigne but it will be fun while it lasts and he will draw a crowd to the end. But for a couple of saves from Alan Combe including one out of the top drawer from a fabulous late free kick, Gazza would even have had a goal in a bright start to his new career, a mazy run here, a clever pass there... and almost added to his legend with an early quickly taken free kick that Combe did well to fingertip wide at his post...* (The Daily Mirror)

But sadly even in China it doesn't look good for him with reports that he is less than fit. From Washington DC to Gillingham, Exeter, Colchester, Carshalton, Dundee, Partick, New Zealand, with mentions of Romania and St. Pauli of Germany: Maybe now the end of Gazza's final journey is not too far away. What none of us want is Gazza reduced to the football equivalent of Alex Hurricane Higgins, now playing snooker for £30 a game in unknown pubs to make ends meet.

Tuesday, January 21

My neighbour Bradford John has sent me up the middle pages of *The People*. He knows I want to read Stan's book and can't get one anywhere. It's a sell-out in Burnley. *The People* are serialising it however and here it is. It gets straight to the nub, no fancy Pulitzer frills here. This is not designed to be a bodice-ripping, heart-panting *Pride and Prejudice* literary masterpiece but a hard-hitting explosive story of the hitherto unknown secret face of football. *The People* is keen to show us that football seems to be an everyday story of violence and bloodshed.

In just a few hundred words I read that Stan seems to have been in more punch ups than John Wayne and that not even a STRICTLY PRIVATE FIRE EXIT ONLY metal door in the Bramall Lane dressing room is safe from a kung fu attack. Apparently someone from Sheffield United, we read, was on the other side, to whit, one Kevin Blackwell who Stan smacks and nuts for good measure, sorting him out big style as the saying goes.

This is great stuff. I read on.

At Bradford he is naffed off by Ron Futcher's efforts at training. Futch messes up once too often. No carrot and reward system here. No gold stars like kids get at primary school. Guess what. Yup. Stan butts him bang on the nose. Futcher doesn't go down though (Stan seems surprised) and there follows what may be vaguely described as a two-man scrimmage until they decide it's a draw. But what we learn though in this story is that apparently whenever Stan loses a gold chain he goes aaaaargh, a common reaction in my experience. Thus having lost his gold chain and yelled aaaaargh the tussle continues. Beware then, dear reader, of Stan going aaaaargh for it could well be the prelude to the onset of a chinning. Vanish quickly is my advice.

And there's more. Brill.

Burnley lose a game 5-0 and Glen Little yells something sarky to the debutant goalkeeper. Stan reacts, after all he is the manager of a team that has just lost 5-0. Yup. Glen gets the treatment. We don't know if Stan yells aaaaargh but Stan hits him hard on the head with a bottle. Good job it was his head I bet someone wanted to yell, but probably thought better of it. It is not the only time Stan has battered Glen: no wonder Glen isn't as good looking as he used to be. Alex Ferguson gets out the hairdryer. Stan gets out a bottle. I should have tried this man management style in staff meetings when I used to be a Head, or with Smith minor from 4c whenever he had a stroppy and went to sit up on the shed roof in the playground instead of doing his sums.

Next paragraph. Can't wait.

Now he's with Carlisle in Benidorm. This time there's a mass brawl and suddenly Stan is alone, abandoned, deserted and is booted down some spiral stairs. At the bottom he is bottled. I'm new to this fisticuff stuff. Does this mean they push him in a big bottle and leave him in there, or hit him with one? Somehow he survives, well he must have, he's here at The Turf now and getting his own back on Glen Little.

And still we haven't finished. In a parking space someone is less than helpful when Mrs. Ternent is parking her car. Stan, yup, you've guessed it, attacks him, glasses go flying, dust everywhere and the fight continues. The Plod arrives. You can tell how sharp the Plod is in Burnley. In the cells they ask him to take the laces out of his slip-on shoes. Smart, huh?

Stan's one-man mission to clout everybody in sight continues in Doncaster where a fan is giving him some stick. The fan offers him a ciggy, then whips it away and gives Stan a rude sign. Stan leaps over the wall and sets on him. Sam Ellis drags him back but not before Stan has done serious injury to the Doncaster fan's Embassy Number 6. Now correct me if I'm wrong here but didn't Cantona do something similar years later and chalk up a lengthy ban. Good job for Stan his little bit of GBH was only at Doncaster and not on Sky.

I can't wait for next Sunday to get part two. This is a stonking good read and makes my own scribbling efforts here look puny. Maybe I should inject some aggro and give our postman a good kicking and write about it. Then there's the milkman who I could wallop except he comes at 4.00 in the morning. He'll be awake and I won't which will give him a distinct advantage. Or I could chin the paperboy. Which one though? The one who comes on Sunday is a strapping teenager; the one who comes on a weekday comes with his dad. Should I give my neighbour a knuckle sandwich? We're the best of pals and he is forever drinking all my Stella Artois but at the end of the day he is I suppose fair game. After all, he is a Bradford supporter.

There are lots of words I don't understand though. Words like f*****g, I suppose it could mean fizzing. Then there's b******s, which I guess must be bollards, it crops up quite a lot. 'You c***' has me baffled. There's only one d in cad, unless it's cade.

I've nearly finished reading the double page spread: Just one more bit to go. In Sutton Coleslaw Stan manages to insult Pavarotti although Pav isn't there to hear it. Pavarotter is twice the size of Stan but given Stan's track record when it comes to belting people he won't worry about that. Stan won't put his fag out; it's a Silk Cut. Nice bit of product placement (a marketing term) there for which Silk Cut should pay Stan a bit of extra dosh into the Gawthorpe Fund. Pavarotti is due to walk through Stan's cloud of smoke any minute and nobody wants that in Sutton Coldsore otherwise his voice might wobble. Guess what Stan says to the minion who has the nerve to ask him to stub his ciggy. Yup. You've guessed it.

"Bollards to Pavarotti."

I have to say I find this bad language stuff upsetting. In my other Headteacher life I was told to fuck off by parents several times. The thing is though, they always said 'fuck off Mr Thomas' and said it very politely.

Wednesday, January 22

Alan Mahon has decided not to join the Clarets but has gone to Cardiff City instead. I wonder if money has anything to do with it? Tut tut, silly me for thinking that. I wonder if anyone has the same thought as me - give McGregor a go in midfield.

The big story of the moment is Michael Owen and his gambling losses. Michael bets on a whole lot of things including Burnley to win at Grimsby last week. If he's betting on Burnley to win at Grimsby then no wonder he's losing.

Here's an extract from Alan Wilkie's book *One Night At The Palace, A Referee's Story*:

The season started with a game at Rochdale against Burnley. I always try to do my homework to establish whether there are any 'leftovers' from previous games and there was nothing to indicate any bad blood from this particular match. It was obvious right from the start however that this was a grudge match. I had to produce the first of five yellow cards after just 24 seconds for a nasty late challenge.

Among all the nastiness an amusing incident happened halfway through the second half. As the ball was played upfield I automatically looked towards my linesman to see if there was an offside. I saw straightaway a flash of yellow above his head. Automatically I blew the whistle and awarded a free kick. My linesman looked at me incredulously and couldn't understand what I was doing. I then realised that in fact the flash of yellow was an inflatable banana being waved by a fan behind him. I am pleased to say that the players had a bit of a laugh when I told them what had happened and we re-started with a dropped ball. The assessor was not amused however.

For the record this was the opening game in season 1989/90. Burnley lost 2-1. The crowd was 5,420 and that season ended with Burnley sixteenthth in Division Four. Ah, happy days, they seem a lifetime away.

Thursday, January 23

Bradford John came racing up tonight. He's only two doors away. One of the rooms in his house is a Bradford shrine. Shirts and memorabilia adorn the walls. Rows of books on all football subjects fill the miles of shelving. Old black and white framed Bradford pictures hang from every space. There's a signed football, piles of programmes, heaps of City Gent, souvenirs, prints, scarves and all the paraphernalia you'd expect from a Valley Parade fanatic filling every corner. His second home is the Bradford FC Superstore although since its semi-closure it's more of a corner shop.

Of course he wants one of my Stellas and damnit I'm down to the last five but he's brought a couple of books up with him. He is the only man I know who bought not one but six signed copies of ex Bradford man John Hendrie's book, *Don't Call Me Happy*. Why any sane man should want to buy six copies is beyond me. But where football is concerned I suppose, sanity deserts us all, does it not, whatever our team. He also brings up a copy of ex-Bradford man Stuart McCall's book *The Real McCall* and by this time he is on the second Stella Artois. Bradford John also drinks brandy in the same copious quantities but fortunately not mine.

John has marked the appropriate pages and they refer to Stan's time at Bradford in the mid Eighties. This, dear reader, is called research and in matters Bradford, John is my right hand man and a fund of inside info. McCall's book describes how Terry Dolan and Stan brought new thinking and new style both on and off the pitch to Bradford. He reveals that Terry was so laid back he often fell over while Stan was the aggressive one and the motivator. Presumably that means it was Stan who applied the kicks up the backside and yelled aaaaargh every now and then. There is no mention of the Futcher incident.

But lo and behold, in Hendrie's book yes, there it is, but not quite the same as Stan tells it. In fact it's the other way round. Hendrie describes Stan as being the fiery character and that he would regularly have big arguments with certain players. But spirit was good, this kind of thing was never a problem in the dressing room, Hendrie adds, and bitterness was never a problem. Hendrie is complimentary about Stan and thanks him for the tactical switch of playing him as a central striker.

Both McCall's and Hendrie's books are a good read and full of insights. There is a total absence of words such as s**t and f**k and f*****g and c***. They're books a nun could read. In fact there's a complete absence of b******s in these books but then they weren't ghosted by Tony Livesey.

Ron Futcher became a Claret from November 89 to July 91. My memory of him is that he played like Stan says he trained - barely raising a sweat. For this he became fondly known as Rocket Ron. But, in a total of seventy games he scored thirty-two goals, which is good going by anyone's standards. He left suddenly at the beginning of the 91/92 season and in the season prior to that his eighteen goals helped Burnley reach the play-offs when we lost out to Torquay. This was in fact a personal best season for him. Clearly Stan's earlier unusual coaching style at Bradford had paid off. Rocket Ron made a big contribution to Burnley FC with his strike rate. The less kind would ask if he was a striker or on strike, but one goal every two games was his answer.

Meanwhile I've been wondering about this two-footed kung fu leap at the doors at Sheffield. I'm dithering on this one and decided to run a test and see if it is actually possible to perform a stunt like this and come flying through the other side, landing on your feet in the upright position ready to bray somebody. The test failed. I took a leap at the garage doors, first making absolutely sure they weren't locked, yelled aaaaargh loudly and hit them at 20mph with both feet smack in the middle. Instead of me exploding (Liveseyspeak) into the garage with the doors opening as per intention, they remained firmly closed and I landed flat on my back in a moaning crumpled heap on the tarmac, big style, as the saying goes. The word b******s might have inadvertently slipped from my lips. Further tests would appear to be necessary.

Friday, January 24

There is a story that football was invented in Brentford when Julius Caesar, shortly after 55BC, kicked an Ancient British skull across the River Brent. It said that on the other side handsome but eccentric centurion Paulus di Canius trapped it on his thigh, flicked it over his head, did a backward somersault, and caught it on the back of his neck. This is the first ever mention of this Italian genius. It took 1,800 years for the new game to catch on, which either means that people in Brentford are a bit slow on the uptake or there was a shortage of skulls.

Today the football ground, Griffin Park, is famous because there used to be a pub in each corner - The Griffin, Royal Oak, Princess Royal and The New Inn. Now there is a rumour there are only three. For a brief spell in their early days Brentford players used to change in The Griffin. Like other South London clubs it is surrounded by rows and rows of terraced houses and cottages. Some of them find the steel uprights of the ground very handy for hanging their washing lines on. In 1999 EasyJet painted the advertising slogan 'We've Got The Balls' on the roof of a stand. Charming.

The average price of a house in Brentford (with or without washing line) is £278,000 pounds. In Burnley you can buy a street for that. I read recently that 47% of people in Brentford are satisfied with street cleanliness, which I am sure you feel a lot better for knowing. Burglary is three times the national average, which should make you feel a lot better about living in Burnley.

The M4 raised up on stilts, with its stunning architecture and unending traffic, wends its concrete way through the town and dominates the Brentford experience. At some point it goes past the Fullers Griffin Brewery. Fullers produce my favourite beer, London Pride. The fact that the only other beer I drink is Rolling Rock will tell you that in hard drinking terms I am at wimp level. Nobody could say that Brentford is the most exciting place in the world; it's just a chunk of West London joined on to other chunks that then become the vast sprawl that is the capital. Once upon a time it no doubt had its own separate identity and character but now it has been swallowed up lock, stock and Griffin Park resulting in what would probably be total anonymity but for us hearing the name Brentford on the football results once a week.

The only other thing of note in Brentford (not counting the burglaries) is The Aquatic Experience. This is at Syon Park and according to their blurb we can

Discover the fascinating world of the rainforest, the lungs of our planet and take a journey into the Juassic (their spelling not mine) world of fish, reptiles and amphibians (actually I thought you could do this at Bramall Lane). You can smile at our crocodiles seeing them swim underwater and amaze at our cute monkeys swinging in the trees. (which you can also do at Blackburn). To make the day really memorable you can touch and hold snakes, lizards, insects, birds and even baby crocodiles - an experience to remember.

Personally I'd rather go to a football match.

Saturday, January 25

It's twenty years since Burnley got through to Round 5. Surely by the law of averages it's time we did. This time last year it was genteel, Regency Cheltenham with its yellow and white stuccoed houses, mineral springs, balconies framed by delicate ironwork, crescents and elegant avenues, who disposed of a lacklustre Burnley side who by all accounts thought all they had to do was turn up. Reports from that game make for gruesome reading so we won't go into them here. Oh go on then, maybe just a couple…

'Humbled and Humiliated', said *The Lancashire Evening Telegraph.*

'Shambolic and Shameful', said Claretsmad.

'If you were at the game', said The London Clarets, 'you probably won't be reading this - lucky you. For anyone still desperately clinging to excuses, please be assured that the pitch, the weather etc, were all fine. We got beaten fair and square by a far better side. The phrase giant killing is totally inappropriate, because the so-called sleeping giant was a comatose pygmy'.

"No disrespect to Brentford, but we'll be in the last sixteen and will come up against a good side," says Lee Briscoe this week. He's obviously forgotten Cheltenham. Does this man not know that nothing at Burnley is cast in certainty? Well I hope he's right. It is reasonable to assume that Stan will not be best pleased by this show of cockiness. Such words serve only to wind up the opposition and demonstrate a very short memory.

But fear not, by the end of the day it was...

BRENTFORD 0 BURNLEY 3

...and Lee Briscoe got away with his moment of brashness which, had it backfired, would certainly have left him with egg on his face.

Sunday, January 26

"A masterly display of finishing," said David Oates on BBC Five Live. 'Football is a cruel game… the result was an absolute travesty', said the Brentford website. "But we're in the hat and it's nice to be there," said Stan.

Let's be pleased here and say well done. OK, some might say that Brentford are 'only' second division but the Cup doesn't work that way. This was a great win against a Brentford team ravaged by injuries before the game, ravaged further when two key players went off injured as the game went on, but who still played out of their skins and dominated much of the game, so much so that for long periods it was described as the siege of the Alamo. Their manager Wally Downes said he was choked for his players. Only world class saves from Marlon Beresford, stout defending from all the back four, and yes a masterly display of Burnley finishing (what, us… really?), three goals from three chances, two of them from Brentford individual errors, won us this game. But this is the FA Cup, and it's the brutal way this competition works. Witness Dagenham and Redbridge going out in the last minute 1-0 at Norwich. Brentford must be wondering just how they lost and deserve full credit, but so do Burnley.

Today the team for the second consecutive game was Beresford, West, Diallo, Gnohere, Branch, Briscoe, Grant, Cook, Moore, Taylor and Blake in front of 1,700 Burnley travelling fans. Little came on late in the game. It was Blake, Cook and Little who scored the Burnley goals, with two of them in the final five minutes which in itself has a certain irony given our current talent for giving goals away in the final minutes.

The statistics tell the story. Brentford had twenty-two shots to Burnley's ten: thirteen corners to Burnley's five and 57% of possession to Burnley's 43%. Beresford was by far the busier of the two goalkeepers and was man of the match. Drissa Diallo's was the name heard most often on the commentary. But at the end of the day it's the Clarets who march on and hope now for a home tie, big money and further progress to the magic last eight in the sixth round. Who'd have thought a little while ago that we'd start to think of the possibility of fixture pile-ups in a potentially overcrowded March and April; maybe an extra televised game and yet more excitement? It's more than a Claret can stand.

London Clarets report extracts…

This was only my second game after the Watford defeat when the referee was rubbish…

…The ground itself is going to be knocked down which is a bit of a shame for Brentford fans but not for anybody else. The away end had all the aura and charm of an abattoir, and was fresh out of cheese and onion crisps, which is disgraceful…

…Burnley fans were speaking a language with which I am not familiar. I had to cover my ears for some reason…

…Half time was a bit of a hoot with space for possibly six people in the toilets for the whole of the away end. I should have worn my wellies. There was an earthy odour apparent which could not have come from a bottle, but more from a deep aversion to showering…

…I really enjoyed today and as I am now officially a lucky mascot until we lose, my dad might take me to more games. I particularly like the Brillo pad who has a particularly good head-butt; and Arthur, who is crackers, but my favourites are Glen

and Blakey who both had a great effect on the result. As I am bored now I will finish with a question from this week's homework. How can you tell when you are out of invisible ink? (Max Heagin, aged 9, with help from his dad)

What a find Drissa Diallo has been, or was it he who somehow found Burnley, the story being that having turned down Portsmouth he miraculously found his way to Burnley by train unaided and alone. God forbid, for anyone to reach their destination by train these days is a minor miracle let alone a total stranger to the UK. Well done Drissa although there is a rumour you were actually looking for Barnsley.

Monday, January 27

This may be the last entry for this month as flu descends and I force myself to stay on my feet to watch the Cup draw at 1.30. My other favourite team, Bradford, seem to have found their financial salvation with a sudden deluge of scarf sales. Bradford scarves are the same colour as Hogwarts and if you don't know where or what Hogwarts is, then I can only ask where and what have you been doing for the last few years. There is a rumour that Bradford are considering changing the name of their ground from the Pulse Stadium to Hogwarts Parade.

Regarding the Cup, discussion centres on do we want a nice home draw and a local derby against our neighbours Rochdale or a financially juicy away tie at somewhere like Liverpool? A home tie against Chelsea would be attractive and a cert to be televised. Leeds at The Turf might be nice if it would enable us to put the final nail in their Elland Road coffin: what distant memories that would revive. And as for Man U, let's save them for the final at Cardiff. This is where it all gets exciting and the dreams begin. Get through this and round six is within touching distance - the last eight and the real excitement.

****

And who have we got? The anti-climax of bloomin' Fulham away: another anonymous nothing game. It's a dull unexciting tie with nothing to light the imagination or set the pulse racing. It won't be played on a Saturday because Fulham share QPR's ground and QPR are at home on the Saturday against Port Vale. It won't make any significant money for Burnley because it's hardly likely to raise a crowd anywhere near 15,000 and you can bet 2,000 of those will be Clarets. Yesterday when Fulham beat Charlton in an all-Premiership all-London tie there was a just paltry 12,000 crowd. And for sure it's hardly likely to attract either BBC or Sky either, is it? What a depressing draw and no doubt Fulham think they are on an easy home win result. It is Burnley's fourth consecutive away draw. The more confident of us will think we can draw down there and bring them back to Burnley. But with this Burnley side, when we never know which team is going to play, the good or the bad, you can never make a firm prediction. I actually think, with Gnohere, Diallo, Little, Blake, and Beresford at their best, it's a game we can win.

And now, with the flu descending at speed, I am off to bed for three days, so at this point we shall take a break from these gripping, can't-put-down diaries. When I wake we shall see if Leeds have sold Woodgate to Newcastle, if England are going to play cricket in Zimbabwe, if the FTSE has reached rock bottom and if Bush has nuked Iraq. Watch this space.

FEBRUARY

Saturday, February 1

My eyes flickered open yesterday at about midday. For three days I have sweated, shivered, tossed, turned, moaned and groaned and that was just thinking about Liverpool swooping in to take Beresford away now that they need cover for Jersey Dogood. I had the flu as well which didn't help. When I woke…

Marlon (world class saves at Brentford my speciality), to our relief is still with us. On a wider front (who says these diaries aren't topical?).

Woodgate has left Leeds, who lost on Tuesday, and gone to Newcastle. Leeds fans are on the point of rioting in the streets.

Fowler has gone from Leeds to Man City after changing his mind and then changing it again.

Lennie Johnrose is now at Swansea.

Gazza has found a club (not the Beijing Tropicana) but struggling Chinese second division side Gansu Tianma, which until now I always thought was something fishy from a Thai restaurant. Reports say it is a one-year deal involving coaching. Gansu I read play somewhere near the Gobi Desert, which is about as far away from The Kettledrum in Burnley as you can get.

The reserves won 3-1 against Sheffield United (very satisfying for all of us) at Chesterfield. Andy Payton scored twice.

West Ham won their first home game of the season on Wednesday.

Glenn Roeder is still there as, according to reports, West Ham can't afford the compensation package involved in sacking him.

Ditto Mick Wadsorth at Huddersfield (apparently).

Bradford City have been taken out of administration. It must be the Hogwarts scarf sales.

The cricket team still agonise and dither about playing in Zimbabwe.

And the plunging line that is the FTSE, like my flu, recovered just slightly.

Better still is the copy of *Stan The Man*, which arrived while I fitfully slumbered. Semi recovered I sat up till gone midnight last night reading and got half way through in one sitting. I am relieved and pleased that it is a far better book than the chunks *The People* selected. They're just the gory sensational bits. If ever a book reveals how a man's mind works and the emotions he feels, this is it. If ever a book reveals despair, it is the time at Chelsea bit. If ever a book reveals the state Burnley was in when he took over, this is it. If ever a book reveals the strength of a man and the strength of his family, this is it. And if ever a book shows a man to be Claret through and through, this is it. It makes for salutary reading. But then there are the genuine real laugh out loud bits. Not too many books make me roll about on the settee. This is one.

Of course there are bits you take with a pinch of salt. Stan, did you really drive up the motorway for sixteen miles at ninety poking another car through the window with a crutch? If so, expect a knock on your door from the 'ello, 'ello, 'ello squad quite soon.

Were you really listed one of the top ten best looking footballers in 1914? And if Lourdes water is so all-powerful, which it obviously is, can I have a gallon to top up my petrol tank?

Nope, this is a pick up, can't put down, read all night, finish in one go, thoroughly enjoyable book and should be compulsory reading for all trainee managers. Meanwhile I've been trying to work out who those two centre halves were; one was colour blind and the other just blind. I laughed till I ached and should a publisher one day discover my own little contribution to the world of literature (as if) I have found a title on one of your pages.

IT'S BURNLEY, NOT BARCELONA

Brilliant. It sums us up beautifully.

However, I still shiver with this dratted flu and the question is do I drive forty miles to Burnley today?

To go, or not to go, that is the question:
Whether 'tis nobler in the mind to suffer
The slings and arrows of outrageous influenza,
Or to take Lemsip against a sea of sneezes,
And by opposing, end them?
(William Shakespeare. Hamlet, somewhere in a castle)

And on top of that there is the road through the Calder Valley to negotiate. To the uninitiated this may seem to pose no problem, but between Halifax and Hebden Bridge, or Hebden Bridge and Todmorden there are usually roadworks festooned with traffic lights around every other corner, every journey we make.

There are holes for the gas, for the electric, for the water, for the telephones and sometimes holes just for no reason at all. They have hole-digging training days round here and men in white helmets and yellow jackets and big brown boots lean on shovels and admire the holes that have just been dug and then fill in forms and write about them. It is the most dug up stretch of road in the universe and it lies between home and the game. Sometimes men will gather just to think about digging a hole. Sometimes the hole gets there before them. Holes here are sometimes like crop circles in a field of wheat. They materialize as if by magic and nobody knows who put them there. Then of course when the holes have been dug and filled it is all re-tarmaced. Sometimes the holes have gone but the lights stay. And then when all that is finished, they start all over again.

I sometimes wonder if the boys in the team ever think about the efforts we folk make to get to a game. I've got the flu and face twenty-seven sets of traffic lights and a road dug up with 'oles round every bend. But how can I not go? They need me.

Reading today! It's kind of a defining moment for the season so far. Reading in August was the low spot of the season and that was a long, long time ago. Today is almost a test of how much better we are. And the fact is simple; a string of four or five wins will see any middling club into a play-off place. Reading have only won one in ten. Burnley are undefeated in seven but the last league win was Boxing Day and the other three league games have been draws. I'm just desperate for a win. The ten goals by Rotherham and Gillingham seem an age ago. Robbie has been here exactly a year. Drissa and Arthur look good at the moment and in *The Lancashire Evening Telegraph* Stan said, "Drissa is an out and out defender, he is different to Arthur. No one else understands them, but they are OK."

Reading not too long ago were part of that geographical south-central part of the country where football consisted of second rate small town struggling teams like Oxford and Swindon… and Reading. Now they have a benefactor in John Madejski who made his money with the *Auto Trader*, which he sold according to reports for £260million. They have a spanking new stadium complex, a half decent team up at the top end of Division One and when last seen Mr. Madejski drove a dark blue Rolls-Royce. A man with sense though, he doesn't lash out funding players left, right and centre or waste millions buying substandard unknowns from Europe where there is this myth that they are all better than Nationwide players. Not for him the wild intention to buy his way into the Premiership. Forget the name, Mr Madejski was born and bred in Stoke but left a week later, it is said, because he couldn't stand the place. For 200 years Reading have done precious little other than win Symod Cup in 1988. And if you can remember what that cup was about then you know more about footie than ClaretTony.

Sunday, February 2

Please explain to me why the words it only happens at Burnley are so apt. No, don't. I know why. It's because of scorelines like

BURNLEY 2 READING 5

I really thought we might win yesterday but instead of the good feeling that a win produces we drove him fuming, not so much at the defeat, but at the circumstances and decisions creating that defeat. We saw things yesterday that have no place on a football field, from missile throwing to a linesman's decision, so appalling, so blatantly wrong that it was outrageous. This then lead directly to Reading's opening goal - which in itself had more than a suspicion of offside about it. Cook kept the ball in play. The linesman flagged it out. Reading took the throw and while Burnley stood and fumed, went on to score.

Football is full of ironies. Reading haven't won an away game since November. In their last home game on Wednesday they were tanked 3-1 by Leicester. And then with that Sod's Law inevitability that we all know too well it was Sidwell now signed by Reading, who scored the goal, the same Sidwell who scored the two last minute goals against us at Brighton when we threw away two points. Sidwell again it was who put the rebound home to score Reading's fourth after Beresford had saved the penalty.

The referee missed a blatant handball penalty for Burnley early in the second half. With Blake still on the pitch at that stage it was conceivable it would have been put away. Blake was off the field when we were awarded a penalty for another handball. The Reading goalkeeper saved Papadopoulos's effort. It looked like Cook was going to take it until Papadopoulos got his hands on the ball. That would have made it 3-2 and game on with plenty of time remaining. Greek Tragedy.

The Reading penalty came from another little comedy, this time of the Brian Rix Farce variety. The Burnley defence, just outside the area, is playing the ball out nicely. Two

Burnley players collide; one of them totally misses the ball. The ball runs loose and is picked up by a Reading player who bears down on goal. Beresford successfully steers him wide. Oops, Marlon brings him down, or did he? Or was it as Phil Bird describes it, a dive of the Fosbury Flop variety? Bingo, penalty.

On top of all this the Reading goalkeeper Marcus Hahnemann, after Reading scored their first goal, then proceeded to give a display of the most atrociously deliberate unashamed time wasting I have ever seen in forty years of watching any football. This went on for nearly two thirds of the game from the 37th minute onwards. Equally inexcusable was the referee's (Roy Pearson) total inability or interest in doing anything about it. That this display of unprofessionalism didn't cause a crowd riot behind his goal is a total mystery. In fact his aggravation and behaviour did incite the throwing of various objects onto the pitch in his direction by a group of mormons, sorry, morons. It would be tragic if Burnley were to face a fine because of this man's provocation. Hahnemann at every opportunity wasted half a minute walking round the back of the goal taking the longest route possible to place the ball usually on the opposite side of the goal to where the ball went out. It was sickening. Then, more wasted time as the ball was placed, then moved, then placed again, then the slow amble back several steps before he eventually took his run and kick. The referee ignored all this when a yellow card might have stopped it. That no one rushed onto the pitch to throttle this man is a miracle and a tribute to the self-control and discipline of 14,000 home spectators.

Nobody is saying that this is a game Burnley could or should have won. But with circumstances such as these (and Sidwell haunting us again) this game was beyond them from the minute that an incompetent linesman decreed that Cook had taken the ball over the line. Until that point neither side looked like they would score if they played till July. It only happens at Burnley.

We won't begrudge Reading their victory entirely. We won't say that their victory was undeserved, but the sour taste left behind will not go away.

We left the game with the score at 4-1. At the end of the game with the score at 5-2 (and it could have been six had Reading not hit the bar), with bizarre surrealism our celebratory anthem Tom Hark blasted the ground from the speaker system. To add insult to injury we missed the small consolation of Dean West's 90th minute thirty-yard screamer. Such is life I suppose.

Monday, February 3

"To be honest I'm a little bit lost for words... Burnley always seem to throw in a bad performance every now and then... The crowd were leaving early and I don't blame them," said Stan after the game. "I wish I could have joined them."

But while we descend into melancholy dejection, Bradford continued their recovery, celebrating the lifting of administration with a fine 2-1 win over Ipswich. That's five wins from the last seven games for them and all dating back to the upsurge in scarf sales. My neighbour phoned to ask what the Burnley debacle was all about. I told Mrs. T. to tell him I had gone to bed with a migraine, being in no mood to talk about it.

Barnsley meanwhile sink lower and lower into the mire and even with the Mayor of Barnsley having taken them over, all is far from well and the question is being asked will there be a Barnsley in a month's time? Huge debts, administration, demonstrations, suspicion and reported to be losing £200,000 a month. Fan's distrust centres around the suspicion that Oakwell will be sold off and a supermarket built to replace it. The new owner said recently they were paying Premiership wages and playing Sunday league football. There were reports that people were fighting at the annual Christmas party. Peter Doyle is now reported to have announced he will bankroll the club until the end of the month and is then open to offers. Kind of puts Burnley's financial problems into some kind of perspective.

According to the club website today Burnley are now searching for and asking for help in identifying the idiots who threw objects at Hahnemann on Saturday. Hahnemann was exasperating beyond belief but throwing objects at him is not the answer. Meeting him in a dark alleyway after the game and giving him a good Stanning, maybe... Objects lobbed at him and identified included a pie and a banana, a bottle, a pound coin, sandwiches and a bag of something unidentifiable. Most people's opinion is that it is the pie which would have caused most harm and what a waste of a quid. When the pie was handed over to the referee he too refused it, but took the pound.

With a pie, sandwiches and a banana, Hahnemann was only two tomatoes short of a picnic.

Stan has announced that he would like to get both Marlon and Drissa Diallo signed up long term this week before somebody else does and will be speaking to the Chairman. He identified Drissa as one player who did have a good game against Reading on Saturday.

Wednesday, February 5

The dog got a longer walk than usual today as I attempted to walk off the state of depression. The goals I watched again on Sky yesterday. I hadn't been there to see them score the fifth.

There's usually a punch-up every hundred yards be it with any other dog, stray joggers, the crows on the field, or any duck by the canal side daft enough not to get out of his way.

When I was a Head I used to take kids on nature walks (now I take the beast), in the good old days before National Curriculum put every teacher and pupil in a straitjacket and told them what to do every minute and how to do it. We also had time for Games every Friday in those days as well and none of us begrudged doing after-school football.

For a longer walk when my head needs straightening we head off down to the canal where I tell him about all the things we see. I find that talking to the dog is a great way of getting rid of the stress of a bad result. By now he must be the best-educated Scottie in North West Leeds. He ambles and drifts along at a snail's pace just like the bunches of kids who used to do exactly the same years ago.

A Scottie is the perfect dog for a nature walk. The words *speed* or *quickly* are not in their vocabulary. If you want a dog that leaps and bounds around like Dimi, dives about like Marlon, or chases everything like Moore (Ian), then a Scottie is not for you.

However, if you want a dog that wears itself out doing nothing, that plods along like an old man before its time or that won't chase a football, like some of players the Gaffer cleared out when he arrived, then the Scottie is the dog of your dreams.

This dog is called Scamper, a pleasant enough name his previous owners bestowed upon him. This name however belies the general outdoor unpleasantness and aggressiveness of his nature. If dogs played football a dog like this would make a fine midfield player in the Kevin Ball mould. A better name would have been Snapper or JustLookAtMyTeethPal. It will set about anything bigger than itself just like Brian O'Neil used to do. In fact given the chance to rename this dog or christen a new one, Brian would be a perfect choice.

To unwind and clear my brain, the walk we do takes a familiar route. At the end of our lane we turn right and proceed downhill (a bit like Barnsley I suppose). There's a cottage down there and in it live two sheep dogs which in the absence of sheep round up small children and old ladies who happen to pass by. They have a penchant for nipping ankles. We call them Norman and Jack, aka Hunter and Charlton, who also used to bite people's legs. Norman and Jack tried it on us once and received short shrift from short legs. Jack allegedly used to have a famously-named little black book in which he wrote the names of players he wanted to sort out at a later date. My dog I suspect does the same when he gets home. Having escaped them we take the sloping road down the hill and turn right after a few hundred yards and head towards the canal, taking the old industrial flagged track towards the remains of a canalside factory area. On the way, in a field alongside the track, live two doddering old donkeys, which must be a hundred if they're a day. We call them Howey and Blatherwick and always lob them a crust or two although how they chew them is beyond me, seeing as neither have a tooth left.

Across the bridge over the canal, fortunately behind a tall fence, live Dervish and Lurch, two elephant size dogs, which bear no resemblance to any known breed. They guard the old millowner's house now converted into a trendy des. res. Dervish and Lurch in the nicest possible way remind me of Martin Keown and Sol Campbell.

There's about a mile to walk along the canal and after this it is but a short stroll back to the main road and our house. There is just one more obstacle to negotiate and that is the pub we have to pass. The landlord here has a large hairy Alsatian. It goes by the unusual name of 'yer bloody thing', which is what we used to call John Bond. I know it is called this because one day it ran out and set upon the small one obviously thinking, 'ah here comes lunch'. The small one gave as good as it got and gave the bully a good seeing to in just the same way that Brian Flynn used to sort out blokes twice his size. As the Alsation began to look bewildered at the ferocity of the hairy one's response out raced a couple of blokes with arms covered in tattoos yelling "Ged in 'ere yer bloody thing".

Yer bloody thing obediently obliged as Braveheart gave one of its back legs a final nip. The whole thing reminded me of a set-to between Kevin Ball and Jason Roberts when big does not mean better.

Thursday, February 6

The January Transfer Window Sales bonanza never happened. Between September 2001 and January 2002 clubs spent £114million. This January £30million was spent of which £9million was on just one player, Woodgate of Leeds. At Burnley only Anthony Shandran went out - to York and only Drissa Diallo came in - free. It's just another indication that there isn't the money around in football any more for clubs to lash out and buy, buy, buy. The biggest sellers were the ones in deepest financial trouble. Leeds United cleared out Woodgate, Bowyer, Dacourt and Fowler plus other sundry lesser players. Ferdinand and Keane had already gone. If ever a club has descended into a nightmare, from Champions League semi-finals to near bankruptcy in just two years, under the chairmanship of Peter

Getridofemsdale, then Leeds is it. Leeds have just reached settlement with the sacked David O'Leary. Out goes a wad of the Woodgate money. Terry Venables has agreed to stay till the season's end. With bad luck such as Lucas Radebe injuring his knee again slipping on the ice at home putting out his dustbins, Leeds supporters must think that every gypsy curse on the planet has come back to haunt them.

Quote of the week so far came from Gillingham chairman Paul Scally who had no sympathy for Leeds' money troubles and scathingly told them they had chased the golden goose, which unfortunately had not laid any golden eggs. Leeds then scraped through to the next round of the Cup beating Gillingham 2-1.

Derby cleared out Poom, Christie, Riggot, Higginbotham, Carbonari plus others. All of them went at bargain prices, nothing like the prices they would have fetched just months ago. Only Newcastle seem to have the big money to play with. Elsewhere it's short-term deals, loans or nowt.

Friday, February 7

Both Marlon Beresford and Drissa Diallo have signed contracts which keep them at Turf Moor until the end of the season.

The caring Clarets are now aiding the Samaritans having teamed up with them to launch a new campaign. With Glen Little taking a leading publicity role, posters will be displayed at Turf Moor reminding fans that when depressed or suicidal they can call The Samaritans. Mr Edoardo Abbis of Burnley FC said, "This is a valuable community project. We are delighted to work with the Samaritans." An unnamed source said: "At Burnley this week we need all the help we can get. After the Reading game everybody was suicidal."

A spokesman for the organisation said that he was aware that currently there was a great deal of depression at The Turf and August had been a particularly busy month. September and October had showed a drop in calls but they had risen after that. Interestingly dozens of people phoned on Boxing Day at around 5pm to say how well they felt.

A local volunteer said, "We want people to give us a call when the problem starts and maybe we can help them before things get too bad. It's also possible that one or two of the players will be phoning us the way things are going at the moment."

Refinance Package Now In Place At Turf Moor, says Tony Scholes on Claretsmad.com:

There has been much speculation over recent months as to the financial stability of our club and had we listened to The Daily Mail then we wouldn't have been in business now.

Much work has gone on behind the scenes and finally this week it all came to fruition when a refinance package was signed sealed and delivered, bringing to an end seven months of hard work. In a recent meeting Chairman Barry Kilby heaped praise on two people for their commitment to bringing this about, accountant Roger Spencer and Vice Chairman Ray Ingleby, but this is only the start of the rescue.

Basically the club have been boosted by a £1million loan from the Chairman and a further £1 million guarantee from the other directors but more importantly the creditors have now signed up to an agreement that gives us a two-year holiday regarding our payments to them. All this will help the club as it tries to cope with the loss of over £5million over the next two years. This was money that was budgeted for and money the club were assured of with the Football League telling clubs that the deal with ITV Digital was a secure contract.

The hard work starts here now and over the next two years the club will have to bring costs down in line with the new level of income. There have been recent suggestions from the club that there is currently a shortfall of £50,000 per week, which will reduce next season to £30,000 per week. In two years time it has to have been reduced completely to then allow us to re-start the payments to creditors. Chief Executive Andrew Watson spelled it out this week that without this package the club would without doubt have been in administration. He admitted that we were very close to being in administration.

He did though also thank the fans for their support, through attending matches and through commercial activities such as lotteries and the club shops. Without that he said the package could not have been put in place. So the first two of the difficult years are reducing costs whilst the following two years are repaying the creditors. What all this really means to us, the supporters, is that we can expect Burnley Football Club to be playing league football in the 2006/07 season and beyond.

Saturday, February 8

To Coventry today: memories of our tanking last Saturday have faded. The football fan is a resilient creature. Coventry too are not exactly setting the world on fire at the moment and were nicely booted out of the FA Cup by our dear neighbours at Rochdale. So, with that eternal hope and buoyancy that things can only get better, it's on to the next game. As things stand now Burnley are placed seven points below a play-off place and while things remain mathematically possible then so does optimism. Come on... the season is by no means over.

Coventry was once a thriving medieval town and it was Jimmy Hill who took them into the twentieth century. It was a place where people had the habit of riding around naked on horseback, the most famous being Lady Godiva. In spite of being told to stay indoors by Lord Leofric, local yobs, yokels and voyeurs followed her around, the most famous being a lad named Tom whose other name was Peeping. Today these same yobs and yokels follow the football team. The story is that Lady Godiva agreed to ride bareback to persuade Leofric, her husband, to reduce taxes and the price of admission to Highfield Road. There is no record of any nudist horseback riding in Burnley.

From a tiny village, a city and trade centre grew and grew. While Burnley was still a bit of a swamp, Coventry was a bustling place of medieval timbered leaning buildings, dwellings, market places, temples, guildhalls, hospitals, cathedral and churches, which were rearranged by the Luftwaffe in WWII. In just one air raid forty acres of the city vanished. Following its flattening, the city is now a mass of concrete, ring roads, flyovers and windswept shopping precincts. My AA Road Book 1966, says it is a city of industry and manufacturing but 1966 is thirty-seven years ago. Today I don't think we have any cities famous for industry and manufacturing. Something else happened in 1966 but for the moment it escapes me. The cathedral was also redesigned by the Luftwaffe but was eventually rebuilt and opened by Her Majesty. It was rumoured at the time that Jimmy Hill was first choice. In it there is a memorial to the Coventry Martyrs of the sixteenth century. This was the season Coventry were first relegated. In 1641 the city police refused admission to Charles I on account of the Royalist hooligans he brought with him and the fear of damage to city centre shops and property by his Burberry Boys. The blue kit of Coventry City reflects the fame of the blue dye once manufactured in the town by a secret process, which kept the colour from fading. It might work on the shirts but hasn't done much for the team.

The team, now Coventry City, once began life as Singers FC. This was not Ron Atkinson and Terry Venables doing a duet, or Hobble and Twaddle on Top of the Pops, but a bicycle factory works team. Until 1958 one word summed up Coventry City - crap. And then James W. T. Hill arrived and transformed them into a promotion-winning club eventually reaching the old First Division. If it was new or innovative you found it first at Coventry City. Jimmy Hill resigned as manager in 1967 but joined the Board until 1983. He is now registered as an official National Treasure and is occasionally wheeled out on Sky TV. Coventry in the Premiership in recent years toyed seriously with the idea of relegation on more than one occasion and eventually got their wish, which is why we visit them tomorrow and hope for something better than last Saturday. Like so many others they are now seriously cash strapped, a result of never really adjusting to life in the Nationwide after living the dream and leading the good life in the make believe land of the beguiling, delusion-inducing Premiership.

I predicted a 3-2 win for us but the result was...

SKY BLUES 0 CLARET BLUES 1

If you'd asked me to forecast a score, one with a clean sheet would be the last I would have thought of. Three names recurred over and over again on the web commentary - Michopoulos, Cox and Diallo. It sounded like a great win as we sat, as ever, biting fingernails and cursing as the referee somehow found four extra minutes to add on and then extended these to six.

Sunday, February 9

Played 30. Won 11 Drawn 8 Lost 11 Points 41. Position 15th. 5 points from a play-off place

Burnley enjoy being sent to Coventry and have won their last 4 league games against them. Did you know... in Civil War days (ugly Cromwell versus the dashing King in case you've forgotten), Royalist prisoners were sent to the Church of Saint John in Coventry to be imprisoned, hence the expression sent to...

By all accounts this was not the prettiest of games on a lumpy bumpy threadbare pitch. 'Dreary weather, dreary match, dreary city. Surely one of the dullest places in these islands... even people who were born and bred there agree it's awful...' (Eddie Lea. London Clarets). Cox scored the goal with a glancing header from a Blake free kick.

Cox replaced Gnohere, sent home to Paris with his family for a few days because said Stan, "Il pete plus haut que son cul", or put it another way, "Il a la tete dans le cul". Both mean just about the same. "He has his head up his backside", although the French themselves would be more likely to use the former, which actually means he farts higher than his arse. Trust the French, so much more sophisticated and cultured than us.

Marlon (wife in labour), was replaced by Nikos, who had a storming game and made some superb saves. Glen Little had an abductor strain; sorry you'll have to look that one up. Consider this - with those three missing, plus Davis and Weller, we can still put out a team that wins.

"We did well today," said Stan on the official website. "We played well all over the pitch and we scored a really good goal... we defended well on a difficult pitch... All in all it was a good team performance and it's difficult to single anyone out because they all played to their capabilities and in some cases even more... I had a call from Marlon this morning and his wife had gone into labour but in Nik we have a capable deputy. I have sent Arthur home to France for a few days for some rest. He's still only young and he's foreign and I feel he needs a rest mentally. So he's going back to Paris for a few days with his wife and child to see his parents and I'm hopeful he'll come back refreshed and ready for the Cup game."

Monday, February 10

Begone dull care. I prithee be gone from me.
Begone dull care. Thou and I shall never agree.
My wife shall sing and I shall dance, we'll merrily pass the day,
I hold it one of the brightest things, to drive dull care away.
(Ye Olde Tudor Top Twenty Chartbuster)

This was indeed a fine weekend win to liven the spirits with Nik the Greek, Cox and Drissa in the team of the week.

Tuesday, February 11

Stan has been a bit more explicit about sending Arthur home to France for a few days. On the official website he had this to say:

> *I have sent him home to rest for a week, he needs to take his family back to France, see his parents, dodge around for a few days. You sometimes get this with foreign players but he is a young lad who has done extremely well for us. I felt this was a good time for him to take his missus and kiddy back to Paris. I hope that he will come back nice and refreshed and I have still got great faith in his ability and Arthur is OK with it. He is still a very important part of the squad but I decided that rather than having him sitting at home he should go across to France. It's a long week before our game on the Sunday and he will be back for the Fulham match.*

Ipswich Town's plight deepened yesterday when the club filed for temporary administration. This is not the same as full administration and the Ipswich Board retain control of day-to-day running of the club. David Sheepshank the chairman said:

We have sought strenuously to avoid this eventuality by all reasonable means. However it has proved impossible to cope with the immense financial burden caused by relegation and what followed...

Oldham Athletic are the latest club to express worry about finances, saying that they cannot afford to withstand £50,000 losses every week and that Ian Dowie will have to cut costs and backroom staff.

It makes Burnley's success in avoiding administration and the introduction of their seemingly solid four year plan all the more admirable. The latest London Clarets magazine Something To Write Home About, makes the point that current AGMs are very quiet sedentary affairs, nothing like the near riots of the Teasdale era, because it is perceived that the club is now in relatively safe hands,

The new Something To Write Home About also gives some insights into the Meet The Board Evening that took place in January, which was attended by Cozzo reporting for the London Clarets magazine. A whole range of issues was covered including the language in Stan's book, the current financial situation, the death and funeral of Nathan Blake, hooliganism in general at Burnley games, the image of Burnley both as a town and club, and the current youth system.

The problem is that it is a big step up for the youngsters in the youth and reserve sides to play in the first team. The vast majority will not be good enough so perhaps we do need to look at players released from the Premiership academies.

A question was raised regarding the Gawthorpe Fund. How much has been raised? How are the plans going? Apparently £8,000 has been raised out of the £800,000 needed. The plans have all been drawn up and a proposal put forward but approval is still awaited.

The development of the Jimmy Mac void and of the Cricket Field Stand was raised. The club seemed to feel that the cricket field was a crucial project as it can be funded privately and so funds would not need to be diverted from elsewhere. Much was dependent on the cricket club moving and a possible site had been identified but the redevelopment plans of Burnley Council have an impact and these are due out in April. The club appeared hopeful of progress but frustrated by the slow pace at which things were moving.

*One point that did make me laugh was when a representative said he had been asked to complain by a member who had bought Stan's book for his seven year old nephew and had been disgusted by the foul language. So it has 'You fat b*stard' on the cover and was co written by the editor of The Sport and the Sunday Sport newspapers. What did he expect?*

The Burnley first team squad have been in Portugal since Sunday. Money has been found from the holiday money jar on the boardroom mantelpiece, a big bottle full of pennies on the bar at The Cock and Pullet, a few pound coins down the back of the sofa, and the gas meter. With a week to spare before the cup match on Sunday Stan thought it a good idea to get away and have a break, said Chairman Kilby. He added that the weather and pitches at Gawthorpe haven't been too good recently, so we had a look around, managed to find some money and went for it. It should do us good, he went on, with a quarter of the season to go, still hoping to be in the play-offs and the FA Cup game to come. The team come back on Friday. Very nice too, but what's wrong with the Isle of Man, which I'm told is very quiet at this time of year and much cheaper?

Wednesday, February 12

Has somebody come into some money at Burnley all of a sudden? Now there is talk of loan signings. Claretsmad Tony Scholes reveals all:

Chairman Barry Kilby has said today that we are looking at a number of players who would be available for the league games and that our aim is still to get in the play-offs. He believes we have a very good chance. Speculation has started but for once the Burnley chairman himself started the ball rolling by naming Birmingham midfielder Bryan Hughes as one of the targets and he added that there could be at least one new face in the squad for the game against Derby...

...As soon as news was settling down on that one came another link, this time causing even more discussion when Blackburn boss Graeme Souness decided to tell all and sundry our business and admit that we had made an enquiry for Matt Jansen...

...We have as in the case of Hughes made an enquiry. Nothing more, nothing less and that makes the headline in one of our local newspapers this evening just downright ridiculous when they claim that, 'Stan Wants Rovers Star'...

The same paper then likens this possible signing to those of Ian Wright and Gazza and says a Jansen deal would top both of those. Somehow I don't think so...

Whether Hughes or Jansen or both do arrive at Turf Moor or not in the near future we cannot even guess, but it does look as though the club are ready to make a move and bring in a couple of loan players to help us push towards the top six.

On the club website Stan says, "I've spoken to Graeme about it and I would like to sign him. My only concern would be the fan's reaction as I don't have any worries because he is a good player who is not in their side at the moment. Blackburn would be paying part of his wages and the chairman is going to speak to them now so the matter is out of my hands. I just have to wait and see what the two clubs and the player decide between them."

Thursday, February 13

England 1 Australia 3. One is just speechless, there is just nothing to say. And Jansen chooses Coventry.

Friday, February 14

From *The Times Educational Supplement*, today's issue:

BURNLEY WINS SOUTHERN HEART

You need empathy for this one. Imagine you are on the terraces, wearing the claret and blue of a certain Lancashire soccer team. Now raise those fists and chant: "We are Burn-ley from the north!"

Not inspired? Well you're probably not from Burnley. So why are a bunch of kids - from Milton Keynes in fact shouting for the Clarets? The explanation lies with Burnley-mad Jim Hudson, head of Two Mile Ash Middle School. He has spent a decade brainwashing his young charges into supporting his beloved team. Perhaps he's done them a favour: chances are most of them would otherwise have ended up supporting Manchester United.

Anyway Burnley now has a thriving fan base in Milton Keynes with 50 pupils, staff and parents regularly travelling to away matches in the Midlands and South. The match they're really looking forward to is the end of season clash against Wimbledon. The Dons have plans to relocate from South West London to Milton Keynes, hoping to find a bigger fan base there. They'd better not count on Jim Hudson's school though - it's providing Burnley mascots for the game.

Saturday, February 15

Fulham, our Sunday opponents, started as a church team in 1879 and played on wasteland. In 1894 they moved to Craven Cottage, another wilderness. And currently they play at QPR another ...

Geography and location apart, Fulham and Burnley in terms of history and a bygone era of Sixties accomplishment could be twinned, up to a point. Both are clubs that were up there with the best at one time decades ago. Both were clubs that then hit the depths, and drifted up and down the divisions for many years. Both settled down in the Nationwide First Division - and there the similarities ended as the Duke of Harrods came along, one Mohamed Al Fayed, and began to sink his patronage into the club. Much as we love our Barry Kilby who has pumped much of his own money into Turf Moor, he himself would admit that he probably pales into insignificance alongside Mr. Fayed.

Once upon a time so legend has it, Fulham was a predominantly working class area. Indeed as recently as the 1970s and early 1980s, the area provided the setting for the TV series Minder featuring loveable West Londoners Arfur Daley and Terry McCann. Don't however expect too much in the way of diamond geezers ducking and diving in the manner, or indeed, the manor, of Arfur and Terry now. These days Fulham is seriously upmarket. Fair enough it's not quite Chelsea, let alone South Kensington, but the hot topics of discussion on the mean streets of SW6 are more likely to be the relative merits of Ferraris vs Porsches rather than 4-4-2 or 3-5-3. That's not to say that Fulham supporters no longer exist in Fulham, it's just that most of them have been priced off the manor by city traders called Jeremy and Caroline. (Firmo, London Clarets)

Mention Fulham and you might think of Johnny Haynes and Jimmy Hill (again). Correct me if I'm wrong but didn't Tommy Trinder have some connection with them? If you're under forty you won't have a clue who Tommy Trinder was. For a while they had a spell of playing fantasy football with a team containing the likes of George Best, Rodney Marsh and Bobby Moore. Enter next, some years later, one Kevin Keegan, then Tigana. Hello Premiership, Now it's lollypop sucking Jean Fulham and his Tigana Brass kindly provided by Mr Al Fayed who take centre stage - if you can call Loftus Road centre stage.

Controversy, supporter's suspicion, doubt and accusations now fly back and forth. Plans to rebuild Craven Cottage, or build a brand new stadium, or ground share at Chelsea or stay at QPR float around on a weekly basis. Mr Fayed at this point in time has decided that the cost of redeveloping Craven Cottage is now too much (£100million). It is a listed building and in a conservation area. English Heritage wants a whole list of things retaining. Building problems and logistics are immense because of the size of the plot and nearness to the river. There are added things like riverside walks and even widening the river at one location involved. On top of all these there are challenges from local residents, objections from the sailing club, traffic management issues, noise problems, the depth of excavations, electricity supply difficulties… and finally restrictions on the use of a new ground to football on match days only, thus knocking out other essential income from potential conference and banqueting business. And there's more… sponsorship is not what it was, corporate long-term revenue is not what it was, TV revenue is no longer guaranteed.

Doesn't it just make you glad to be Claret, where life is much simpler?

Sunday, February 16

And so not to Fulham and Craven Cottage but to QPR… a drab, box-like, claustrophobic ground… and West London, either Shepherd's Bush or White City, depending on where you're coming from… It's surrounded by blocks of flats and rows of houses in a not too prosperous area… It's impossible to hear the words 'Shepherd's Bush' without launching into the theme tune from 'Steptoe and Son' and thinking of Oil Drum Lane, whilst White City is somehow redolent of a 1950s world of rationing and false hopes. And just look at the names of the streets round here: Bloemfontein Road, India Way, South Africa Road. It positively reeks of Empire. Indeed although you kind of know that the ground is on Loftus Road, it isn't; the club's offices and therefore postal address, are on South Africa Road. Perhaps it was thought politic to conceal this in the days of Apartheid? (Firmo, The London Clarets)

Never mind politics. Today was carnival time with 3,000 supporters determined to outdo the legendary support given to the Clarets when they visited Derby in a replay in 1992. On that occasion the support and volume of unceasing noise and singing was so astonishing it is etched forever into club history; and that was on a day that Burnley lost. Even the newspapers yesterday and today got in on the act and instead of ignoring us, as they usually do, there were little features and snippets about the game and our players. Most unusual.

The supporters at Derby clapped and cheered a defeat. Legend says it went on for twenty minutes after the game. Today 3,000 supporters clapped and cheered and saluted and were rewarded with a final score of

FULHAM HARRODS MILLIONAIRES 1 BURNLEY BARGAIN BASEMENT 1

Words like marvellous, wonderful, fantastic and fabulous are all in order after a great, great, great display of backs-to-the-wall stuff once Fulham equalized. Nobody was less than heroic today; nobody was less than magnificent against the Premiership side but maybe it is possible to pick out Diallo and Cook as being super-heroic. The team, for the record, was Beresford, West, Diallo, Cox, Branch, Briscoe, Cook, Grant, Moore (Ian), Moore (Alan) and Taylor.

At the game's start there was no place for Blake, who was on the bench, and no Little who was still injured. Weller was back on the bench after his lengthy lay-off and Stan elected to play five in midfield and just Taylor up front. It worked and it's back to the Turf a week on Wednesday and into the hat for the 6th round draw. Alan Moore gave Burnley a fourth minute lead with a simply stunning goal, pouncing on a Fulham lapse, picking up the ball and running thirty yards at pace before slotting the ball home. From then on the Burnley team, which included eight players who cost nothing, outthought, outfought and outwitted the Harrods millionaires who were ensnared by Stan's tactics and formation. It is over 50 seasons since Fulham have ever won at Turf Moor and they cannot be happy about the replay, especially as Tigana is rocking the Fulham boat demanding answers from Mr Fayed about Fulham's future prospects. Their entente at the moment is less than cordiale.

Monday, February 17

Not a newspaper wasn't fulsome in its praise today.

David Miller wrote about echoes of the past and history lying thick on the ground at Loftus Road, in *The Daily Telegraph* and likened the current side and the football it plays to that of Harry Potts in the early '60s. He makes an analogy between Burnley and the engineering of Brunel's Iron Bridge, the latter he says an example of 19th century ingenuity and resolution still capably functioning today. Work that one out if you can. Nevertheless you could see his admiration for us simple Lancashire lads.

They played some of the most attractive football West London will have seen this season and were seldom under pressure until a minute before half time when Malbranque cancelled out the fourth minute goal by Alan Moore... resourceful opponents who defended so effectively... and under Ternent their future remains promising.

"They are a typically English team and very difficult to play against", said Jean Tigana in The Mirror, which went on to say Saha and Sava were snubbed out magnificently by the power of central defenders Ian Cox and Drissa Diallo with pumped-up Burnley running rings around the Fulham team…

The Daily Express began with :

They came in their thousands, roared themselves hoarse and after 90 minutes of high octane football Burnley's magnificent support could celebrate a money spinning replay. The club deserve every penny... each and every player in those famous claret shirts covered themselves in glory...

"This was a glorious cup-tie", begins *The Times*. "Do not let anyone tell you that Burnley were lucky... Burnley were architects of a well-deserved draw. The moral of this tie was that opportunism, allied with determination and fine organisation can reap dividends".

"And Fulham? Just a small town in Egypt", said Firmo of the London Clarets.

Our reward, if it is one, is certainly not a glamour tie against Chelsea or Arsenal. We sat listening to the car radio in a supermarket car park. No, not a local derby against Leeds. Nor is it a home tie. Fortune deserts us again. It's Watford away in the next round if we beat the Egyptians in the replay next Wednesday. Sheffield Utd staggeringly have their ninth consecutive home tie (against Leeds) whilst for Burnley it is now the fifth consecutive away tie. Nobody can say that reaching this far has been easy. The other ties are Arsenal against Chelsea and Southampton v Wolves. But even if we don't progress beyond this round how marvellous it was to see our name on the screen as part of the last nine in the draw. It was a rare sight and it looked so damned good. The Twin Towers of Wembley are now no more, demolished only days ago and in our dreams it's Cardiff that creeps nearer.

The name Man Utd was absent from the draw having lost 2-0 at home to Arsenal. Ferguson was livid afterwards and kicked a boot across the dressing room in his fury, which left Beckham with a cut on his head needing two stitches or butterfly strips depending on which paper you read.

Wednesday, February 19

There is a good feeling at the moment and it's time to take stock. So maybe we are well down into the bottom half of the table but we are still only five points away from a play-off place. At the top remain Portsmouth and Leicester who are pulling away but Reading creep into third place after beating Sheffield Utd last night, for whom it is the third consecutive defeat. Well what a shame.

We are in the draw for the sixth round and a bumper house for the Fulham replay, which is on Sky, should swell the bank account nicely. I read somewhere it's £265,000 for a cup-tie.

The games now come fast and furious and from Derby onwards on Saturday it's more or less two games a week for the foreseeable future with postponed games to fit in and the Cup replay. The major worry here is further injuries and suspensions causing problems with the small squad. It was hoped that a loan player would be signed but this has not happened.

3,000 supporters at Fulham showed what Burnley support is all about and the vibrancy and volume will surely be the same again next Wednesday. This time the cry is not on with the masks as per Fulham it's out with the scarves for a riot of colour. Beat Fulham - and Watford should, could, ought to, see us at least bring them back to Burnley for another replay. And if we don't beat Fulham then it's still been a damned good cup run, the best for years. No grumbles from me.

And finally, consider this... the result at Fulham was achieved without Davis, Little and Blake. Who would have predicted that? Reported Whitto for London Clarets:

Burnley were magnifique. We battled for the whole 92 minutes, fought for every ball, were tigerish in the tackle and showed no respect. This was a good old-fashioned cup-tie. This was Premiership quality against the First Division's most inconsistent and frustrating side: £40million versus the usual ragbag of free transfers and journeymen with the odd £1million pound man thrown in. From the very first whistle our intention was clear: give Fulham no time to play their fancy football, close them down and don't give them the ball. It worked a treat...

Friday, February 21

The money could soon be rolling in. For winning in the third round of the FA Cup Burnley have already received £50,000 prize money. For beating Brentford it was £75,000. Beat Fulham and they earn another £150,000. For the Fulham game being televised Burnley receive £265,000 from Sky. Beat Watford and the club receive £400,000 prize money and the game will be televised on BBC2. Then it's semi-finals and the dream becomes mouthwatering. Tomorrow is the bread and butter Derby game but our minds are on Wednesday. Glen Little will be absent for both, a week away from fitness.

Few present supporters will remember much about the semi-final Burnley played in against Newcastle in 1974. Two Malcolm McDonald goals saw us off with a crocked Frank Casper suffering from the Norman Hunter tackle in the previous week's game. There was a carnival atmosphere with both sets of supporters mingling amicably and making their way down the hill to the Hillsborough ground. Burnley never really got going in that game and it was difficult to watch as the side that had outplayed Leeds a week earlier with slick stylish football struggled against Newcastle. Hard to think that nearly thirty years has elapsed since then.

I fished out the old programme from the box I keep them in. It cost 10p. 1974, electricity and the telephone had just been discovered in Blackburn. Explorers had uncovered ancient civilizations in Accrington. Bacup and its strange people were revealed to the world for the first time. Trains ran on time. You could fill your car with petrol for what it would cost now for a litre. Chas and Dave were already in their fifties.

On the front of the programme are Martin Dobson and Bobby Moncur with the obligatory ears covered by hair fashion, the de rigeur style of the age. Referee was Headmaster Gordon Hill, considered to be the best referee of the era. On the way Burnley had beaten Grimsby (aaargh, they didn't mess about with us in those days), Oldham, Aston Villa and Wrexham. There were illustrious names in the team then - Alan Stevenson, Peter Noble, Colin Waldron, Keith Newton, Martin Dobson, Frank Casper and Leighton James. Semi-final day on March 30 1974 was not one of their better days and Malcolm McDonald had a day to remember when he was just too much for centre half Jim Thomson to cope with. Jimmy Adamson was manager then and earlier had said Burnley would be the team of the Seventies. Burnley immediately slipped into the second division as soon as he said it. Newcastle had stuttered and lurched to the semi-final needing three replays to do it and one of these needed extra time. Burnley had progressed smoothly and efficiently. Alas, it all counted for nothing and the dream of Wembley faded into memory. For some of us it begins to stir again even though we realise the mere notion is ridiculous. And at least people can now see where they are going in Blackburn.

Saturday, February 22

BURNLEY 2 DERBY COUNTY 0

Up several places to eleventh but now seven points behind a play-off place because Wolves played an extra game and won in midweek.

We called at The Kettledrum on the way to the game. Readers of Stan's book will be well familiar with the famous bums that have sat on those hallowed seats - Gazza, Ian Wright, not to mention Stan himself. It's a fine pub and is a kind of gateway to the fog--shrouded moorlands beyond the steep road behind. Old cottages cluster around it and others nestle in the hollow before the narrow road twists and turns up the hill. Old barns have been converted into attractive properties. This is not the cloth-capped, cobbled alleys, terraced rows, dark gloomy mills, derelict streets image that comes to too many minds when the name Burnley is mentioned. This is the other picture. Around the town if you know where to look are green meadows and pastures, woods and streams, the Cliviger Gorge, mile after mile of moorland and wild beauty where there are tiny villages and picturesque hamlets made up of cottages dating back centuries.

The Kettledrum has a fine menu amongst which you'll find Bury Black Pudding and "Jon the Pieman" Suet Pudding. And in what other pub, complete with low ceilings, rustic beams, nooks, crannies and secluded corners, could you enjoy a choice of three different types of sausage (Rustic, Lincolnshire or Irish Farmhouse) in the Sausage and Mash whilst upstairs there's a funeral going on? Anyway, a fine lunch ended with Sticky Toffee Puddings and compensated for a strange sort of game at The Turf today where we had a total of just seven shots all afternoon - and still won.

A good first half, two well taken goals from Moore (Ian) and Gareth Taylor set the scene against a woeful, almost disinterested, Derby side (Rams looking sheepish I suppose), for what we hoped might be four or five by the end of the afternoon. Er no, this is Burnley don't forget and for the second half we watched and squirmed as Derby took over the first twenty minutes or so and penned us back. Other than a superb Ian Moore solo run from the half way line which deserved a goal, and a couple of shots high over the bar from long range, Burnley were invisible. John Gregory was flattering, saying Burnley in the second half showed his team how to defend. Stan too was pleased with the defensive qualities. In truth we could do little else. As for Derby, Ravioli was their best player and Giorgi Kingofthekhazi ran up more cul de sacs than a council estate. And boy was it bloomin' cold. We left the ground shrammed. The Kettledrum in comparison as we drove by on the way home, looked warm and inviting and another plate of sticky toffee puddings was very tempting as a thick swirling mist descended on the moorland road. Three more points though are very welcome from what might be described as a routine win and a nice warm-up for Wednesday.

London Clarets Vox Pop sums things up:

The first half display was absolutely excellent - we scored two goals and could have scored more.... Dermot

We performed very well especially in the first half. We didn't allow Derby anything and they probably wouldn't have scored if they'd played until midnight. Roll on Wednesday... Paul F

Burnley played well in the first half. Alan Moore, Paul Cook and Tony Grant were brilliant... Chris

An excellent first half, with Alan Moore, Gareth Taylor and Tony Grant all playing well. The second half was perhaps a little bit disappointing in comparison but Drissa and Coxy were excellent again. It was good to see Taffy (Leighton James) back on the pitch. He's 50 now so those of us who remember him playing are showing our ages... Mike

Yep, I saw him play and still recall how he effortlessly ghosted by and around players so deceptively. Deceptive sums him up, maybe. He had deceptive pace and subtle deceptive skills. He drifted by opposing full backs with smooth and fluent ease, as often as not turning inside and unleashing a twenty-yard shot from the edge of the box. Or, he went by them on the outside and chipped over a perfect accurate cross. For five years he was a regular in a side that came back into the First Division, missed Europe by a point and reached an FA Cup semi-final. Derby signed him eventually for £330,000 and from there he went on to QPR. Then it was back to Burnley in '78, then after two years on to Swansea. From there it was up to Sunderland. In 1984 there was a season with Bury, which in that year was almost entirely made of ex-Burnley players. Meanwhile Burnley were heading inexorably on towards the Orient game of '87 and he played in that game and the result you know by heart. He finally ended his Burnley career in '89. It had lasted on and off for nineteen years, 336 league games, 66 goals and 23 full caps for Wales. The story goes that there are an awful lot of Burnley fans now in their fifties, who named their sons Leighton. His sportsman's skills didn't only include football. He played cricket for Burnley and Lowerhouse with his best innings in a victory against East Lancashire. His was a priceless talent, exceptional and unique. He came on at half time to a prolonged and standing ovation. Yes he was a one off and will be one of that small, rare assemblage - a Claret legend.

Tuesday, February 25

Barry Kilby's programme notes outlined the possible changes to the play-off system next season. There seem to be strong moves to introduce something new. The proposal is this:

The play-off places would be extended by two to include seventh and eighth places. The first round of the play-offs would be one match only with position 5 at home to position 8 and position 6 at home to position 7. This gives home advantage to the side that finishes higher in each pairing. The winners of those games would go forward to a second round, where position 3 and 4 in the table would be at home, also in one match deciders. The winners of these round 2 matches would contest the final place for the Premiership.

The advantage of this system would obviously be the extended play-off positions of 7 and 8 in the league, but also the abolition of the two-leg system to sudden death would be a much better spectacle for the fans and TV. The teams in positions 3 and 4 would only be one home game away from the final whilst the lucky eighth play-offs contender would have to win two away games and the final to reach the Premiership.

Wednesday, February 26

Fulham, or to be precise Tigana, are worried by tiredness. They have played four games in eleven days. Wily fox Stan thinks this is a load of old tosh. There are hopes that Glen Little is fit and will at least get a place on the bench. There are doubts that this will be anything near a full house. Fewer than 10,000 tickets have been sold of which 500 are Fulham. Messageboards are on the gloomy side talking of how expensive it is, it is on Sky on big screens in the pub, and how many people in Burnley have this kind of money to throw around? Fair point. It's a game sandwiched between the Derby home game and Stoke away - the latter traditionally a game Burnley take massive support to, it being handily just down the M6. And then on top of all this, arguments rage as to the declining glamour and appeal of the FA Cup. Images of the Grimsby game and acres of empty terraces are still vivid. Not even Spurs in the Worthington could raise a decent crowd. People will only fill the ground for a big game a la Man Utd. Counter arguments are that we are within sniffing distance of a semi-final. The income from Sky and prize money becomes increasingly huge. And at the end of the day, if by some miracle Cardiff was reality, Burnley would be empty for the day and the town would go wild. As the saying goes, we'd have our fifteen minutes of fame.

Me? My little heart is skipping the odd beat this morning in anticipation of tonight's game. I loved seeing our name in the hat for the last nine. I love seeing the extra little snippets in the paper about the club that only Cup progress brings. The game is being shown in the USA, Canada, and South East Asia. It's 1951 since Fulham won a game at Turf Moor and Winston Churchill was Prime Minister. I'm thinking now about Leeds in a semi at Old Trafford. I'm thinking now, shall we stay overnight in Cardiff? Football is based on dreams and maybes and that's why the FA Cup is still a magnet for the likes of us.

Thursday, February 27

If I wrote flowery prose for a living I suppose I'd write now about the mists of time and a long gone era last night rolling back to reveal an evening belonging to a previous age which is now only a dim and distant memory in the psyche of older men. I'd write that for some, this golden period of long ago is only something they read about or are told by their fathers and their fathers before them. I'd write about the stirrings of a sleeping giant, slowly wakening from its torpid anonymity in a Northern town hit hard by decline and neglect over the last four decades. I'd write about the ghosts of mythology and legends of ancient times gazing down from their seats in the heavens, smiling with approval and pleasure. And I might write about a club earlier this season being just two days from administration, £4.5million out of pocket, marooned at the bottom of the league at the end of August and belonging to a town stained by the heartbreaking murder of a Forest fan. And why would I write all that. Simple; the score last night was

BURNLEY 3 FULHAM 0

AND WE ARE JUST SO PROUD AND ELATED

The team (for the history books) was Beresford, West, Diallo, Cox, Branch, Moore (Ian), Grant, Cook, Moore (Alan), and Taylor. Scorers were Taylor, a poacher's goal, Moore (Ian), a chip over the goalkeeper from a delightful dink over the defence from Deano Westissimo, and Drissa Diallo with a thumping header from a perfect corner.

Little teasing and twisting, back to fitness, came on for a cameo final ten minutes, but in truth he wasn't needed. Weller replaced an exhausted Cook who had run himself into the ground. Sponsors man of the match was officially Moore Ian, but it could have been Taylor (Sky man of the match), Grant or Diallo. If those four were superhuman then the rest were not far behind. Diallo must be the find of the century. Not a man wasn't on top form, denying Fulham space and time to breathe. Beresford hardly had a shot to save. Let's be honest, this wasn't samba football, or the neat intricate dazzling stuff that ripped Tottingham apart. This was what we might call power football, gritty, resolute, determined, all hustle and bustle and then a little bit of showboating at the end. Tigana accused us of setting out to 'break' his star player Boa Morte but that was a rubbish claim.

None of us could have predicted such total superiority and the best score of the season. Never mind Fulham moaning that they were tired from Monday's game against Totteringham, they chose not to postpone that game, preferring the money that Sky TV brings. Never mind them moaning (along with Andy Gray on Sky) that the sending off of Davis was harsh. He could have put Grant out of the game forever with an appalling tackle. The pundits agreed (Mark Lawrenson on BBC was gushing), the better team won and only one team was up for it. As for their big names, Finnan was more finished. Legwinski was Legweary. Boa Morte was more Boa constricted, Saha was more haha, Sava was anything but, Djetou was more Djetwho, and the rest were just anonymous. Tigana went through his usual twenty pack of toothpicks and whinged about the refereeing. Boa Morte went off with an ankle injury after colliding with an advertising board, which Tigana thought should have been booked. For what it's worth Inamoment the Japanese lad was their best player and Tigana must be in a state of shock. Was Mr Al Fayed there? I haven't a clue. Turning Craven Cottage into luxury flats is probably that bit closer after tonight.

Burnley dismiss fractious Fulham with panache, said The Times Sport and went on to describe Fulham's humbling by *Burnley's blood and guts approach.*

Fulham fold in front of Ternent's finest Clarets, said The Grauniad, *superior in every department... Fulham thoroughly outplayed and left with aching limbs and the match fee... clueless in defeat... Burnley's muscle and endeavour unsettled Fulham though rarely illegally... too strong throughout... the smattering of visiting fans huddled shivering and dejected, must have wondered why they bothered...*

The Mirror was typically tabloidesque...*from the kick off Stan Ternent's troops had their bayonets fixed and Fulham did not like the cold steel as they slumped towards their second cup defeat by a lesser light in Lancashire...*

The game ended with cries and singing of "Can We Play You Every Week?" ringing round the ground. Marvellous. Just marvellous.

What a memorable season this is turning out to be. Who would have thought it? Just bloody amazing. So to celebrate, in a fit of madness this morning, I booked flight tickets (with free champagne and canapé reception - naturally) for the away trip to Portsmouth at the end of March. Am I mad, or stupid, or do I have the IQ of a banana? Stan wants to fly the players down there so to fund the flight there are seats available for mugs, I mean supporters. The voice on the end of the Business Centre phone was reassuring and assured me the plane would not be an old Hazard Airways twin engined Dakota. I put the phone down wondering if is this the feelgood factor or just insane extravagance. But Mrs. T wants to fly with Gareth so...

Friday February 28

...You cannot drink tea out of a teacup without the aid of the Five Towns... you cannot eat a meal in decency without the aid of the Five Towns. For this, the architecture of the Five Towns is an architecture of ovens and chimneys; for this its atmosphere is as black as its mud; for this it burns and smokes all night... for this it lives crammed together in slippery streets where the housewife must change white window curtains at least once a fortnight if she wishes to remain respectable...(The Old Wives Tale, Arnold Bennett)

There are those, like Firmo of London Clarets, who are of the opinion that the art of living is to visit places like Stoke as infrequently as possible. I am not in a position to agree or disagree. Tomorrow will be my first visit to a place once characterised by mile after mile of 'pitheads, chimneys and kilns, tier after tier, dim in their own mists'. Philosophers have pondered long and hard trying to fathom is it a town or a number of towns? Is it part of the North or South or Midlands... or is it just Stoke. And is Stoke a conglomeration of five towns or six? There's Burslem, Tunstall, Fenton, Longton, Stoke and Hanley. But Arnold Bennett (of *Clayhanger* and *The Old Wives Tale* fame) always called it The Five Towns. It's confusing. Whatever... it is accused of being an utterly grim place and years ago, the centre of the pottery industry, it was a drab industrial landscape bad enough to rival any Northern cotton town.

Mention Stoke and we think of Stanley Matthews and it's where Jimmy Mac, after he fell from grace, was banished by Bob Lord. And of course there's Josiah Wedgwood, mass cup and saucer manufacturer, but best known today for the pottery ornaments we give to people when they retire or get married, or have an anniversary (the pale blue posh stuff with classical white designs).

A little while ago it was the Icelanders who descended on Stoke City FC and took it over. It became a sort of extension of Reykjavik United. A lot of Stoke City supporters however remain generally grumpy according to reports, their demeanour untempered by the injection of Icelandic phlegm. They play now at The Britannia Stadium, one of those new stadiums that look like any other, a replacement of the old Victoria Ground. Their early history is interesting. They started as The Stoke Ramblers. They still ramble quite a lot. It wasn't that long ago since sheep used to graze on their pitch as a cheap way of keeping the grass cut. And this was before the ITV Digital fiasco. One ground they played on in their embryonic infancy is now a cemetery. They currently occupy bottom place in Division One and their situation is grave to say the least. They were hammered last weekend 6-0 away at Nottingham Forest but football is a funny game and Sod's Law will no doubt decree that they will extract revenge on the next team to turn up, which just happens to be our own inconsistent heroes in Claret. OK, so we've just trounced Fulham but such is life as a Claret fan, we always look on the down side, our glass is always half empty, never half full. A 5-2 or a 6-5 defeat is always lurking around the corner for days when we have become over confident. The word pessimist was invented for us. We've had too many kicks over the years. Not for us a quick impromptu verse or two of 'Always look on the bright side of life… di dum, di dum, di dum di dum di dum…' And when the term 'wet blanket' was invented by Dr. Johnson, Mrs. T. says it was with me in mind. Wake me up; kick me on the shin… Fulham was a dream…

Here's some more interesting bits and bobs about Stoke. There are 7,800 litterbins and 516 miles of streets are swept each week. The best bit comes from the Stoke-on-Trent City Council official website which says that last year 129,963 tonnes of household waste was collected from residents bins, streets, and recycling sites. This is enough, it says, to fill the Britannia Football Ground. Well, they said it, not me, although it doesn't say if this is with or without the football team. Nationally there's a 3% increase each year in the production of household rubbish. In Stoke it's only 1%. This I suspect means that householders in Stoke are not filling their bins for collection like the rest of us but doing one of two things:

1. Lobbing it into the neighbour's garden, or
2. Dumping it in the Britannia Stadium.

Whatever is happening, there's an awful lot of rubbish in Stoke. And that's official.

MARCH

Saturday, March 1

We enter a month that could be one of the most momentous and memorable in Burnley's history. Nobody could ever have imagined back at the end of August when things looked so despondent that at the beginning of March we could be on the brink of a record-breaking end of season run-in. As things stand at the moment a play-off place might still just be attainable with a good run of league wins. Burnley sit eight points behind sixth place but there are games in hand and the top teams will continue to take points off each other. All Burnley players bar Steve Davis are fit giving a near full squad to carry the load. If there is such a thing as a gathering momentum then you can almost feel it increasing following the wins against Derby and Fulham. Winning breeds success and confidence, which then breeds further success. March begins a period of nine games. It's an exhausting and demanding tall order; suspensions, fatigue and injuries could wreak havoc. And of course the month includes the Watford game, a quarter-final. Victory there and it's on into the semi-finals and the huge financial rewards. Knees are knocking.

To date the cup run and victory against Fulham have had enormous financial consequences. Burnley can expect to bank at least half a million in TV money from this week and next week. Then there's prize money and added to gate money would mean another half million minimum from the Watford game. After Wednesday Stan said, "That was really a £750,000 football game."

Nine games in a month would tax even the strongest club. It's a make or break month which will end in joy or disappointment. If it's the latter we'll applaud them all the same. The high spots we've had so far have brought us pleasure and pride enough and if we don't win another game it will still be a season to remember.

Here we go then… the biggest month for decades if things go right… glory or gloom, happiness or heartache… delight or dejection… and I'd hate to say which it will be.

Sunday, March 2

Blow, winds, and crack your cheeks! Rage! Blow!
You cataracts and hurricanes, spout,
Till you have drenched our steeples…

Go on have a guess who wrote this… yep… William Shakespeare, King Lear.

The first of the nine games ended well yesterday and we can't ask for anything more.

STOKE 0 BURNLEY 1

It wasn't pretty and it wasn't pleasant and Mrs. T. wouldn't let me have a pie. It was dour, gritty and tough to watch. It must have been even tougher to play as wind and rain and hail buffeted the ground and slammed onto the stand roofs. The Britannia is exposed enough as it is on even a warm summer's day but on a day like yesterday it was no place for the fainthearted. It's where Scott practised for his trip to Antarctica.

"The wind was so strong we just couldn't get the ball out of our half," said Dean West when I phoned him. "The wind just blew it straight back."

Away supporters were lucky, with the wind coming from behind us and the rear walls of the stand providing shelter. Only the flags nearly blowing off their poles on the adjoining stand, and the sight of home supporters at the opposite end running for shelter as the hail came down gave us the picture of what it was like out on the pitch. The word grim hardly does it justice. Accordingly, the football too was dour and the first half performance from Burnley had more than a touch of After The Lord Mayor's Show about it. In truth Stoke did to us what we did to Fulham on Wednesday. That plus the horrendous weather penned us more or less in our own half for long spells. More than once I thought back to that ghastly day at Rotherham, but at least here we sat in a decent modern stadium with all mod cons and lightbulbs that worked.

Stan put out the same team for the fourth consecutive game so that again Blake and Little were on the bench. What we offered in the first half cried out for one or both of them to be brought on. Little was about to come in shortly into the second half but then out of nothing from a half-cleared corner, Deano Westo hit home a right foot shot from twenty-five yards (some say thirty) which was in the back of the net before he could open his eyes. Goal of the season?

'A thing of beauty is a joy forever...' said John Keats in 1884.

By God this wasn't just a beauty, it was a peach, a rasper, a screamer, an absolute thunderbolt which Vulcan the blacksmith of the gods couldn't have bettered. From our away end we watched it fly off his boot and bend away from the Stoke goalkeeper into the top right hand corner. It had to be a goal like this which would settle the game. When you're a bottom club like Stoke, it's the kind of goal that kills you off and makes you think just how bloody unfair life can be.

After this, Stoke huffed and puffed, but Coxy and Drissa, Branch and West, snuffed them out with ease and there seemed little doubt that Stoke would never score if they played till Christmas.

This visit to Stoke was a first. Where we parked was a first for me - in a sort of farmyard, except strangely there weren't any animals, down a muddy unmade lane after we left the half-finished new road system that presumably one day will go somewhere civilised. By now we found ourselves at the foot of the hill with the ground looking down on us. The Britannia seems to be built at the top of the most exposed windswept peak in Stoke. At the entrance to the house (reminiscent of the Norman Bates motel in Psycho) was a huge rough sign, 'Beware of the very mad dog'. A huge woman stood by the gate and held out hands the size of shovels to receive the £3. She assured us the dog was locked up somewhere but for a while the temptation was to back out of this strange forlorn place and park elsewhere. Round the back stood her even bigger husband, directing traffic and rubbing his giant mitts at the thought of all these £3 parking fees coming his way tax free. On a dark stormy night you'd be thinking about *Legend Of Sleepy Hollow* stuff here.

From there we trudged up the slope to the ground above, crossing over the canal which Giant Haystack's moll had assured us was very picturesque and we'd just missed a barge. Up to the barren summit we went whereon stands the gleaming white concrete Britannia.

Forget Rule Britannia, this is Bleak Britannia. With weather conditions like this we can only suppose that it makes the Icelander contingent at Stoke feel very much at home.

Never mind, thankfully it's three points in the bag and we can do no more. Unfortunately other teams (Wolves and Sheffield) above us in the top six won again so we still remain eight points behind Sheffield Untidy in sixth place. Fourteen games remain and it's fair to suppose we need to win ten of them. It's a tall order and looked at in that way it does seem unlikely. But that's three league wins on the trot now, plus Fulham, and not a goal conceded.

Shock of the day... the half time announcement that all 4,200 tickets for the Watford game were sold out in forty-eight hours to shareholders, foundation members and season ticket holders. Who says the cup is dead? There is the faint but unlikely hope that Watford will send more tickets.

Monday, March 3

I picked up the new *When The Ball Moves*, number 23, on Saturday. Barnsey has clearly seen sense and stopped trying to offload the job lot of masks he bought for the Fulham games. But if you do ever see a shifty, suspicious looking bloke at car boot sales or the prom at Blackpool with a large holdall stuffed with Union Jack masks - that's Barnsey, bless 'im. In the new issue there was a good piece about the cost of attending extra cup games. One very unpleasant four-letter word sums up why gates have been so low for the FA Cup home games and that word is c o s t. Only 11,000 turned up for the Fulham game. We all thought it would bring at least 15,000. The chatrooms, message boards and now WTBM all say the same. Once you've bought a season ticket, another £19 for another unexpected game for which you have not budgeted becomes very difficult and it comes down to a choice between a ticket or tickets, and the week's housekeeping and mortgage payments. It's back to the current problem with corporate football. Slowly but surely low income supporters, the traditional bedrock of football clubs, are being priced out. There's clearly a dilemma here. Raise prices again next season and attendances could drop further. Peg them at current levels and the club's own housekeeping is stretched. The answer can only come from alternative revenue sources generated by commercial activities and off the field revenue sources. A figure of £20 a ticket is a kind of barrier. Turf Moor crowds remain a wonderful mixture of the young, the old and whole families. At clubs like Newcastle or Chelsea, where seat prices are astronomical, fans come from the under-thirties high earners category. The working class man or the unemployed are squeezed out. At Stoke on Saturday I looked around and saw an amazing age range of Burnley support from toddlers to Grannies, dads and lads, dads and daughters and whole families. It must be quite unique and cost them a fortune. Premiership prices would destroy this.

The Times this morning made Paul Cook man of the match. Dean West who was supporter's player of the season last year, ironically never got a man of the match award or a bottle of champers. If he scores a thirty-yard Exocet special at Watford he can have a bottle from Mrs. T and me.

From the Stoke programme in which manager Tony Pulis describes Stan and Sam as 'old stagers' (I'm sure they're delighted at that), there's a piece about a campaign to have Jimmy McIlroy awarded a knighthood. Well fair enough, if Tom Finney can have one why not Sir Jimmy? The Central Lancashire Clarets supporters club has started a petition.

Jimmy Mac is clearly revered in Stoke just as much as in Burnley and the petition has already stirred passions in Northern Ireland where the Irish FA have signed it. McIlroy played 116 games for Stoke, scoring 19 goals, and helped them win the old Second Division title. He left Burnley and enjoyed three more good seasons at Stoke. Who knows what might have happened if he had played those final three years at Burnley.

Andrew Watson spoke recently of the impact of the money made so far from the cup run:

> *We are having a Board meeting on Monday where we will be discussing what will happen with the money. We have negotiated a payment holiday with creditors but those agreements did refer to us having a windfall such as we have at the moment. It may be a case that some of the money will go towards reducing our debts and that will be a very good thing as we want to be a debt free club as soon as we possibly can.*

But Burnley also have several players out of contract this summer. There's the dilemma then: pay off the debts or retain key players? Sunday's game v Watford has massive consequences. For one club distinction awaits and financial salvation. Only Mike Parry on Talksport, speaking disparagingly about lame donkeys such as Burnley and Watford enjoying cup glory, sours the moment.

Tuesday, March 4

But first there's Millwall. The pace is now relentless, without respite for the coming weeks. Millwall have lost four on the trot whilst we have won four and haven't conceded a goal in those games. That Millwall have lost the last four games is of no consequence. The New Den is still an intimidating and difficult place and teams that have just lost 5-0 (to Portsmouth) have, unfortunately for us, the Sod's Law habit of coming back to win the next one, plus of course they have one of football's best assistant referees, bless him, Steve Claridge, who has performed at more clubs than Bernard Manning.

Mention the name Millwall and images of trouble and violent fans immediately spring to mind. It has been closed more times than any other ground as well as having innumerable fines imposed. The F Troop at Luton years ago caused mayhem in a televised riot. Firmo of London Clarets has four rules for any away supporter going to this game: Don't turn up drunk, don't talk back to police or stewards, don't wear your colours, and keep your mouth shut. The ban on away support has been lifted.

Neither is Millwall in Millwall, if you see what I mean. Millwall have moved from the Isle of Dogs (the bit you see at the intro to Eastenders) and now play south of the river in Bermondsey. There isn't a trace of the old ground left now that flats and houses bury it. It was situated on Cold Blow Lane and never did a name sum up a ground better. Simon Inglis' *Football Grounds of Britain* says the ground was special. It was rough and tough and wild… but proud, like the people who lived around it. Whilst Leeds United and Elland Road was once a centre of the rhubarb industry, some would say it still is, Cold Blow Lane used to be a vegetable plot where potatoes grew. Workers in a jam factory started the club in 1885. Like many football grounds, railway lines surrounded Cold Blow Lane and engine drivers regularly pulled up to watch the game from somewhere near the corner flag.

When the Old Den played its final game there were pitch invasions in protest and the

Directors had to hide as turf, debris and rubbish was hurled at them. The New Den was opened in August 1993 but this didn't stop further instances of pitch invasions and riots. Old habits die hard. New Den, Old Bill, a match made in heaven. It would be too much to hope that we could pinch another 1-0 win tonight in the second of our five consecutive away games on our round Britain tour.

Wednesday, March 5

We didn't. It was a website commentary special last night which we sat and squirmed through. 206 Burnley fans were there and saw

MILLWALL 1 BURNLEY 1

They saw Ian Moore score and then Millwall equalize with just six minutes to go with an offside goal and 6 Burnley players booked. It was Millwall's first goal in something like five games. In the second half from the Phil Bird website commentary it sounded like Burnley hardly had a kick. Organisation and defensive solidity looked like it would result in another three points but it was not to be. The Burnley website described it as a scruffy game in a ghostly stadium. With the inevitability that only football brings, Millwall's Sadlier replaced the ineffective Claridge, and scored the scrambled giveaway equalizer in his comeback game after a lengthy absence through injury. Such is football. We creep one point nearer the play-offs and are now seven points behind the sixth team Wolves. Other results last night did not go kindly and the top five all pull ahead. I suppose it's a measure of our progress and faint expectations that there is disappointment at the loss of two points. But Stan was furious with the refereeing;

> *It wasn't a fair result. We should have won 1-0 because their goal was offside. We looked a little leggy and tired tonight but we're disappointed with 1-1. We could have scored two or three goals in the first half but in the second half they had a lot of pressure. With all due respect that was a woeful refereeing display. They can fine me but I won't pay because I'll show them the video and they'll probably fine him. He did exactly the same thing to us at Crystal Palace not too long ago and there is a season's work at stake here. If that's his best he should be on Hackney Marshes. He booked six players and there wasn't a bad tackle in the game... Millwall is a difficult place to come to and maybe we had one eye on Sunday, but I felt we were cheated... I thought my players were the victims of woeful refereeing... Millwall had a little help... let's put it that way... a blatant penalty which he doesn't give... an offside goal which he does give...* (Burnley website)

They say refereeing evens itself out over a season but I sometimes wonder. This referee, Mr. Cooper was the same referee who awarded a dubious penalty against Marlon Beresford at Crystal Palace just weeks ago. In the two Burnley games he has refereed he has booked a total of ten Burnley players and cost us four points.

"He's just arrogant," said one of the players to me, "he's done it to us again."

Five consecutive away games, that's an awful lot of travelling.

"So we have to spend a few hours in a coach but that isn't hard work," said Dean West. "There are a lot of people who would like to be in our position, people who do a proper job…"

Watford rested six players last night at home and Preston beat them 1-0. Sheff Utd and Nottingham Forest both won. The countdown to Sunday begins now and I shall find out tonight if I have two tickets courtesy of my contact deepthroat, who knows somebody who has tickets… shhh... it's all legit and above board. Honest.

Thursday, March 6

Deepthroat came up trumps last night, when I phoned him and I have to meet him tomorrow to get the tickets. I said I'd be the bloke with the moustache and the claret and blue scarf eating a bacon bap at the table by the door in the club cafe. Each of us would wink three times. Wolves got another point last night so are eight points ahead in sixth place but we have two games in hand. Reading won 1-0 and are well clear in third spot. I watched them on Sky. They looked ragged and messy in a dreadful game. How on earth did they win at Burnley 5-2? Ah yes, they had a helping start from a clueless linesman.

There was an impassioned plea from Tony Scholes on Claretsmad this week. It's worth a read in full but in essence he says:

Just over a year ago, disappointed with falling reserve team crowds, Claretsmad launched a Roll Up For The Reserves campaign when we took on Preston at Turf Moor… it was a major disappointment to us that the following reserve team crowds then went back to normal with many people not even knowing about them due to lack of publicity… but with our keen interest in youth development and seeing the younger players come through we wanted to be very much part of raising the profile of the reserves… three weeks ago we lost 2-1 to Tranmere and the official attendance was just 122… we would have liked to have launched a high profile campaign to try to restore interest in the reserve games and to try to attract people to the games… we were due to play Oldham, a week tomorrow… then we heard last Friday that it was to be brought forward a week and would be played in the afternoon… There has been much debate recently about the way forward for Burnley FC in terms of player development… and now the profile of the reserve team has been lowered by shoving a fixture out of the way and playing it in an afternoon… the reserves are facing relegation this season at a time when our youngsters need to be playing against the best opposition possible… to a division with just one First Division reserve team with the rest from the lower divisions and even the Conference… we are a First Division Club but these sort of decisions put us on a par with a non-league club…

Stan has gone on record as saying that there should be five permissible subs in a game plus the goalkeeper. It is at this time of year that it makes some sense, as tired players, congested fixture lists, and two games a week takes its toll.

Lennie Lawrence of Division Two table toppers Cardiff has admitted to trying to sign Glen Little on loan, but Stan said no.

Saturday, March 8

Burnley will appeal against an automatic fine of £5,000 imposed for the six bookings at Millwall on Tuesday. Gareth Taylor spent the game looking for fellow players to tell the referee to calm down but couldn't because they'd all been booked.

The papers are full of us today. Our fifteen minutes of fame begins now. There's a big feature about Glen Little in *The Express* and his time at Burnley. Yes, he mentions Stan hitting him with a bottle and other altercations. He says he would have preferred a flying boot. *The Telegraph* homes in on Stan. Blimey we're talking about Europe here. The losing Cardiff finalists could well get a UEFA spot. Burnley v Barcelona, now there's a novelty. Can my heart cope with this? In *The Telegraph* there's a small item that says in August, when all the players were transfer listed, it was because none of them would agree to a wage reduction to counteract the Digital losses. I've never seen any reference to that until today. Is there any substance to this, surely it would have come out into the open long before today or has the club kept this quiet? Earlier in the season Andrew Watson said that no players had been asked to take a wage reduction.

At the club yesterday when I went to collect tickets for the next half dozen games (and shhh Watford on Sunday) it was quite evident that cup fever was mounting. Friday is press day anyway but this time at the training ground there had been BBC, Sky and Chris Kamara their effusive, voluble pundit. The Boot Room too was crammed with reporters, cameras and journalists with Stan penned in a corner. Did I hear him say remember we're not Barcelona?

Upstairs in the club offices (I'm seeing people about this diary being published) it reminded me of the days when I had a proper job and was a Head in a manic office, where the phone never stops, racing round in circles, everyone has five things to do all at once and to have them done by yesterday. Some of them looked like they'd hadn't slept for the last three days. Only the Business Centre seemed calm and quiet when I went in. Chief Executive Andrew Watson was slumped on a chair in a corner looking worn out.

"I've had five hours sleep in three days," he said.

He had that ashen, exhausted look they call Executive Grey in the Dulux catalogue.

I went in to sign the papers that said I would not carry alcohol, sharp items, and aerosols, and would behave in a proper manner at all times on the plane to Portsmouth. Mrs. T had difficulty in agreeing to the last on account of the proximity of Gareth Taylor. The small print promises a refund if there is severe weather but doesn't say what happens if we hit it halfway there. Nor does the price include an umbrella for if it's pouring down at the uncovered away end. It seems an awful lot of money just to get drenched.

****

Shopping, cultural enlightenment, eating out or relaxing in one of our many parks... Watford has it all... Shop until you drop... or dance the night away in one of the many nightclubs... Did you know that the babies and young children's store Mothercare first started in Watford with a large factory in Cherry Tree Road? Official Guide To Watford.

Philosophers and historians have pondered for years as to why Watford is Watford. Apparently it just is. In Anglo-Saxon the word 'wath' meant hunting and a ford was where you crossed a river. Anyway here we are again in this place where my pen pal Firmo says that his extensive research has shown up absolutely nothing of interest at Watford other than St Albans to the north being much much nicer with its real history and cathedral and scenery. Back in Watford the Romans, Saxons and Vikings came and saw and went, beginning the tradition that nobody stays long in Watford.

Nineteen years ago Burnley played Wrexham at Turf Moor in a quarter final (we won 1-0). Bob Lord banning BBC cameras from the ground made the occasion memorable. Apparently he wanted a fee of £10,000 and said they should pay for what they got along the lines of that's what they would pay to get Morecambe and Wise. They had got football on the cheap for far too long he said. In this respect who is to say the Butcher of Turf Moor wasn't just a man forty years ahead of his time? He refused to have Welsh anthems played prior to the game on the grounds that he'd then have to play Scottish music or Irish music for other occasions. Personally I agree, the thought of Chas and Dave over the speakers when Tottenham came or Elton John when it's Watford is too unbearable to contemplate. Then he took a storm of flak from fans incensed at the price increase from 40p to 50p for the game. Doesn't that just take you back, what does 10p buy now at the Turf… a trip to the loo if ever they decide to charge for that. Sssssh, they're always looking for revenue streams. It was shortly after this that he made his famous anti-Semitic remarks about the Jews who run television at a sportsman's dinner in Liverpool.

And thus game three of this marathon month looms, the big one. The piddling name Watford begins to look far larger than usual. We can't afford to crack lame jokes at their expense this weekend. Except perhaps to tell you that way back in the mists of time they started life at a place called 'The Bog'. Then in 1916 after wandering around Watford they ended up with no ground, no players, £3 in the bank and assets of just £30 - and today we think we've got it bad. Anyway they eventually ended up on the site of a former gravel pit so that in later years large holes, the result of subsidence, would appear on the pitch at regular intervals and players would fall down them. Fans as old as me will remember a tiny, wily player called Tommy Harmer, only marginally bigger than Tom Thumb who really did disappear down a hole in 1961 when playing against Grimsby (them again). Tiny Tom eventually went to Spurs and became part of their great team, playing the same kind of devious, schemer role that Jimmy Mac played for us. In a newspaper report of the time he was alleged to have said he left Watford because he'd had enough of falling down holes. Even as late as the '80s a hole of moon crater proportions appeared at one end of the ground. At Stoke it was sheep that used to wander on the pitch but at Watford it was a goat that ambled on during a game and began to neatly trim the grass oblivious to all that was going on around it.

Today Watford is synonymous with illustrious names such as Elton John, Graham Taylor (give him credit, he worked miracles there), Luther Blisset, and Gianluca Vialli, now suing them for all he is worth under the heading of 'potential lost income'. They reached a Cup Final, dallied with Europe, flirted with the Premiership recently and now appear to be stabilised in mid-table much the same as us, counting the pennies and no doubt thinking, having beaten West Brom and Sunderland so far, that fate is on their side and that destiny, the semis and a pot of gold awaits them, not us. They beat us back at the end of November 2-1, somewhat fortuitously one has to say, ending the notion that for us Vicarage Road is a good ground. BBC2 could hardly have imagined that when they bought the rights to screen a tie this weekend that they would be rewarded with Watford v Burnley. Still, they shouldn't grumble. It could have been Grimsby v Walsall. Bob Lord will be smiling down from heaven above when he hears how much they're paying for this tie.

Watford are planning to make the home ends a sea of yellow (yuk) says the London Claret web. Now gathering momentum is a suggestion across various message boards that Claret fans should sport flat caps (you know, like your dad used to wear) during the game, which will make a dignified contrast with the ghastly Watford yellow. Plus we'll have something to throw in the air if we win. Just remember say the London Clarets that if you are actually over seventy and wear a flat cap you are not making an ironic statement about northern stereotypes - you are one. Whippets are optional but if you take one along don't put it on your head or throw it in the air, whippets don't like that kind of thing.

The Watford website *Blind, Stupid and Desperate* and Matt Rowson, as you would expect, takes an offensive line about Burnley which is a shame. Apart from geographical location, shoot me down if you want but I personally feel a kinship and an empathy with little old Watford who have all the problems that we have. A quarter final is a special occasion and unworthy of some of the abusive stuff written about Stan Ternent in particular. I'm not suggesting that after the game both sets of fans should sing Auld Langs whatever it is, arm in arm on the pitch, but at management level a most amazing deal, according to *The Express*, has been agreed to share the £400,000 prize money regardless of who wins. Both clubs are desperate for money but unlike the above named website are not blind and stupid.

Sunday, March 9

Who so beset him round with dismal stories,
Do but themselves confound, his strength the more is,
No lion can him fright, he'll with a giant fight,
But he will have the right, to be a Claret...
(John Bunyan, 1676)

Twenty-two idiots chasing round after a ball in the freezing cold (Garry Nelson's words, not mine), is what football is. Not today, I have to argue. Today football is about fate and fortune for two average clubs and possible fame and distinction for maybe a handful of the twenty-two players who hold the hopes of two towns and thousands of people in their ability to get a round thing to go into a large net at one end of a field and at the other end do just the opposite.

If the game is decided by just one goal, then the one player who scores that goal will be a hero for life. Or, the game today is about the notoriety that waits for the player who is fated to give away a penalty or scores an own goal, or who is sent off. Fate is a funny thing and it's what makes football what it is, that you just don't know what providence will bring until it arrives. Destiny has already decided the winner who will go into the semi-finals. It has made its choice. It is an odd thought that the progression of connected events that has lead up to today began weeks and weeks ago as part of some predetermined process. There's a sort of Thomas Hardy, Far From The Madding Crowd aspect to all this; that all these things are the result of universal cosmic forces over which we ourselves have no control and in which we are mere puppets. Fate, fortune, luck, the run of the ball, may well have singled out already which player or players will win this game and what the outcome will be.

What is luck? It's the bounce of a ball one way or another in one split second, a ball that hits a divot and hits a player's hand, a ball that bounces off a post to a forward who scores rather than the goalkeeper who saves, the toss of a coin and which way it lands. It's the luck of the draw; it's the name that comes out of the hat first - Sheffield Utd with their ninth consecutive home draw... Burnley with their fifth consecutive away...

My God, I got carried away there didn't I? It was sitting on the old bench today in a bit of warm sunshine at my favourite spot along the canal, while the dog chased squirrels and barked at passing barges, that these thoughts began to occur. Enough of this deep philosophising, it's only a game innit, just twenty-two blokes running up and down a bit of grass trying to win a tin pot? Time for bed said Zebedee.

And indeed I did climb into bed drained and exhausted by the journey, the game, the emotion, the day and the score. I'll tell you tomorrow how it ended. For now it's late and I'm b*****ed.

Monday, March 10

WATFORD 2 BURNLEY 0

We lost 2-0, but we have no complaints. This is not a day for unkind words or the barbs of hurtful criticism. If you believe in chains of events leading up to a predetermined end, over which we have no control, and in which we are just the playthings of the Gods, then this was just such a day. The last time we felt like this was at the end of last season when even though we had beaten Coventry 1-0, we still missed the play-offs by just one goal. It's as if someone up there, some unkind influence, some manipulative unseen being, just plays with us for His or Her cruel sport. I feel the same today as I did then, flat and so disappointed not just for other supporters and me, but for our team as well.

In the cold light of day, which fittingly is wintry, grey and dull, I can write that we didn't win, didn't deserve to win, didn't play, didn't create a single worthwhile chance and gave their goalkeeper absolutely nothing to do all afternoon. So much hope, so much to play for, so much anticipation and then so much anti-climax. I wrote at the beginning of these diaries about supporter's feelings and emotions. Today, it's what this page is all about. Will we ever get so close to a semi-final again?

We can't grumble at the day, the atmosphere, the sense of occasion, the colour and spectacle, the passion of supporters, the camaraderie and bonhomie of opposing fans, the sunshine which bathed us in its spring like warmth and softness, or the effort and commitment from our team. We can't say that any Burnley player played badly or let the side down. We came home just as proud of them as we did after the Fulham game; at the game's end we gave them a standing ovation, and the message that they and us were as one in our heartfelt dejection. They trudged off disconsolately. Can we imagine what must have been going through their minds? We drove home silently but still full of pride thinking of the wonderful games they played and the efforts they made to get us as far as this.

We sang, we cheered, we roared, we clapped, we made a thunderous noise that could have been heard twenty miles away and we did that for ninety minutes and more. But it just wasn't to be. The fates, divine intervention, call it what you will, that indefinable and inexplicable thing we can only call the run of the ball, that moment when a ball bounces one way and not the other, falling into someone's path at the right time in the right place, were on the day with Watford… and Tommy Smith. Chance decreed that it would be his day.

The game itself was all about twenty-two players giving each other no time or space to do anything of class or style. It was a game we knew would be settled by maybe one solitary moment of quality, or one bounce, either their way or ours, one stroke of misfortune, or one moment of madness… or just one corner. And it was Watford who had all the corners and the pressure that comes from them.

And that's how it happened. A corner, not cleared, flailing legs and feet, the ball ricocheting around and continuing to Tommy Smith who falling, poked it home from just a few yards so that it slowly, agonisingly, scruffily, trickled under a despairing Marlon Beresford. This was Tommy Smith just back for his first game for four weeks after a car crash. Tell me now that these things aren't worked out in advance in a ready-made script. After that their second goal was a sort of undeserved irrelevant postscript and just as inevitable as the first, coming from a free kick put straight over the wall by a player who was only in the side because of injury to another and who has been told already he will not be retained next season. Irony heaped upon irony. And then another twist of fate, we failed to score for the first time in twenty games since way back in December, three months ago.

Today the media is cruel and callous:

One of the worst spectacles of football this stage of competition has witnessed for a long time… until Tommy Smith broke the deadlock in the 74th minute the match had been bereft of just about everything… (Telegraph Sport, Monday)

The tie, played out in swirling wind and on a poor pitch, was tense with few real chances created - especially in a first half where the ball was in the air so often it put to shame the hundreds of balloons that littered the pitch… if you happened to be stuck outside the stadium you would have been suffering spasms of envy. It sounded fantastic. The fans were passionate, desperate, raucous, bursting with cup fever, but it all had little to do with the fare on offer on the pitch… (The Times, The Game section)

A desperate quarter-final tie bereft of drama and entertainment or anything resembling quality or class… you can fully understand the nervous approach from both sides as there was simply so much at stake… but this was a pitiful last eight tie… and Burnley were downright ordinary and it was hard to believe that both clubs had knocked out Premiership opposition… (The Mirror)

Alan Hansen used one word, 'dire', on the BBC.

The only consolations come from knowing that it is Watford, a club so small and similar to ourselves financially, that will benefit from the semi-finals and that two sets of family oriented fans combined to make it a day free from violence and confrontation and aggression. The approach to the game and the streets outside as people made their way to Vicarage Road were festooned with smiles and colour, friendliness and mutual anticipation. The sun shone from a blue sky making the colours dazzling and brilliant and bringing out the best in people's good nature and openness. There was indeed a sense of occasion and importance and such days don't come often. That it didn't continue out onto the pitch and provide us with a thrilling dramatic game was just one of those things. I shall remain convinced forever that for us it was never in the stars and never intended to be a day of glory for Burnley.

One further consolation is that Gareth Taylor today was a giant at both ends of the pitch. If ever a player has grown and developed in stature over the last season it is he. The BBC pundits picked him out over and again. He covered every blade of grass, won header after header, and cleared from our own penalty area half a dozen times. In truth he was all we had to offer on a day where wellying it in the air or hoofing it to Gareth's head seemed the only recognisable tactic and the ball, according to Mark Lawrenson, must have been crying out for mercy until it was kicked up onto a rooftop where it remained and another one introduced.

For now, play-off hopes linger. A quarter of the season remains. To Sheffield and Warnock's men on Wednesday and who is to say these inconsistent, unpredictable, ageing, near-exhausted Clarets can't come away having pinched a 1-0 win or a battling draw. It would be just like them wouldn't it?

Tuesday, March 11

The draw for the semi-finals yesterday is a reminder of what we have missed and though there is no resentment, good luck to Watford, the sense of deflation and what might have been continues. Watford will play Southampton. Sheffield United, who knocked out Leeds, will play Arsenal or Chelsea. Seeing the name Watford in the newspapers, hearing it over and over again on TV, rubs salt in the wound. For us, no more limelight, no more cameras, no more spotlights. It was nice while it lasted. The recurring thought, which as yet will not go away, is that this could have been us and the words if only... begin to appear in our thoughts... if only we had used Little, Blake and Weller from the start, been positive and bold and played the football that we know we can produce... if only...

Of course the papers pick out the irony that Tommy Smith was lucky to be playing let alone score. Bits and pieces of the game come back - how it was all Burnley in the first twenty, twenty-five minutes, Watford just weren't there. But not a chance was created other than one close header. How Branch and West could do nothing but punt the ball upfield because there were so few options. How West desperately misses Little and Weller in front of him. How the few moments of real danger and excitement came when Little came on and started to make a few runs. How the intricate little passing patterns, triangles, flicks and movements, which then draw West into the game more as an attacking full back, increased once Blake joined Little. How in the whole game we had just three on target shots. How the in-roads we made into the Watford penalty area didn't really begin until the last twenty minutes: by then of course, all too late.

Burnley fans may not wish to read of Watford elation and joy but I logged on to their website *Blind, Stupid and Desperate* to see their reaction. I'm glad I did. I found a piece so readable, so full of the euphoria, and what it is like to be a football fan, any football fan, at a time like this, that it sums up what all of us feel and what chaotic, incoherent thoughts burst through all our heads on our good days. It's what we at Burnley felt after the Tottenham game. It's what we felt after the Fulham game.

The best of it is this:

Oh, come on. You don't expect details do you?

Not while it's still swirling round in my hungover head, all fresh and vivid and ridiculously potent. Not while it's all still there, ready to come rushing back as soon as I close my eyes and summon it up. It's much too soon, much too soon. Even after watching the video into the early hours of the morning I can offer precious little insight into how it happened and what it means and where it all went so spectacularly right. Details? No, not now. Not for a long time.

The only details that matter are circumstantial. These are the things that you'll hang your memories from, that'll enable you to conjure up the images and sounds and emotions of yesterday for many years to come. These are the bits and bobs and odds and sods that combine to make football (and this competition in particular) more than just the game itself, more than just the broad, bland sweep of history...

The personal stuff is what makes you part of it, rather than merely a spectator. In the days leading up to the match it's the way your body seems to jolt suddenly and momentarily when your thoughts drift away from whatever you're trying to distract yourself with. And it's the increasing impossibility of finding anything to distract yourself with, until you finally surrender entirely to dreams and imagination and superstition and all the rest...

It's all special... eating an enormous breakfast at Doug and Kim's just around the corner from the ground and that the way that the jovial banter round the table fails to hide the gnawing anticipation. Then out into the crowded streets on a bright, warm, early spring afternoon... and it's magical, whatever's about to happen. Just savour everything, every moment.

Even the unbearable anti-climax of a defeat - or perhaps worse still, a draw - would have faded away eventually. We would have looked back with regret, and then remembered all those wonderful details. Those personal, joyful memories... It makes you hungry for more of course... but that doesn't mean you can't enjoy what you have. And yet as the team emerged from the tunnel for a second celebratory bow in front of ecstatic rejoicing supporters, I couldn't help but look at the handful of Burnley supporters still in the Vic Road end, unable to tear themselves away. And I wouldn't have swapped places for anything.

Because this was utterly unmissable. So many more of those precious little details that could easily have been lost in ghastly disappointment. The two goal celebrations... particularly the second, when all of the nervous, exhausting expectation was suddenly and spectacularly converted into glorious certainty... And applauding until my shoulders ached, and shouting and singing until my throat was raw... and noise and colour and great beaming smiles everywhere and just wanting to stand in the middle of it forever.

If football fans have a heaven of their own, then it's probably a bit like this...

This was a largely dour, unattractive match that, while typical of much First Division fare, probably shocked a fair number of onlookers. Sod it though. The whole beauty of the FA Cup is not merely that it creates upsets and surprises and unlikely heroes, but that it includes the kind of variety of qualities, styles, approaches and philosophies that's utterly impossible in a single league, then randomly tests them all against each other. Sometimes that's going to result in a mediocre, boot- and- boot - again scrap. So be it.

...Burnley were thoroughly beaten... and although four minutes of injury time did the nerves no good we knew that we were safe as soon as Briscoe had directed a free header straight at Alec Chamberlain from Little's free kick. Then, we could really celebrate...

And it ends there almost. Except, of course that there's more to look forward to. And a whole month to savour it, imagine it, lose yourself in yet more daydreams. Yesterday no matter how much we tried to pretend otherwise there was a great deal to lose. From here on, there's nothing at all to be frightened of.

Just enjoy it. Every single second. Every little detail. (Ian Grant, Watford Website, Blind, Stupid and Desperate)

Yes, I was one of the handful at the Vic Road end unable to tear myself away. It was as if we didn't want to let go, didn't believe or accept the mind numbing ending, as if by staying there it meant the result wasn't real, wasn't final, that the clock could be turned back and that it could all be played again with a different result. Leaving our seat, standing and leaving, signified acceptance and we didn't want to accept it, did we?

'This is the way the world ends', wrote T. S. Eliot, 'not with a bang but a whimper'. How right he was. He must have written that with Sunday in mind.

One last thing about the day: Entrance To Cardiff Road Blocked said a street sign near the ground. If I'd seen that before the game maybe I'd have driven straight back home.

****

In Sunday's *News of The World* there was a little more about the August decision to listen to offers for the whole first team squad. It is alleged by the newspaper that Burnley's cost cutting measures included asking the players to revise the bonus system. Struggling to make ends meet, Stan Ternent it is said, put the entire squad on the offers list when they refused but now believes it may have underlined morale in the camp.

"Having thought long and hard about it I may have made a mistake," he said. "I asked the players about revised bonuses but they decided to stay on what they were earning. I said if that's the case, everyone's for sale. I wouldn't do it again."

One wonders how much more there is to come out regarding this story and how it was kept so quiet in August or indeed if there is in fact any truth at all in it. If there is any substance to it then what upset and disquiet did it cause and why is it only now just emerging? Does this explain the poor run of results in August with presumably a disgruntled squad of players and a fair amount of friction and resentment? Putting the team on an open to offers list was public knowledge but no mention was ever made of wage arguments.

If the cup windfalls ease our financial problems a little, Huddersfield's continue. Their chairman, David Taylor has warned that his club, £6million in debt, is on the brink of closure. Several players have not been paid in full since December. *The Telegraph* reports him saying that

> *We need help and at the moment there is no help. If people don't come forward soon they may find it's too late. Nobody takes the grave difficulty of our situation seriously. They assume we are going to carry on but there comes a time when you can't carry on and that time is fast approaching.*

Coventry, £23million in debt according to *The Telegraph*, have dismissed their chief scout, their youth coach and their commercial manager as part of cost cutting. The Coventry situation is dire, as they slide down the table after early hopes of being amongst the pacesetters.

And Sunderland after just twenty games have sacked Howard Wilkinson and Steve Cotterill after only two wins in those games in charge. This was what they announced as the dream team just months ago following the dismissal of Peter Reid. More than one Sunderland supporter I know announced it more nightmare than dream at the time. How would we feel in the unlikely event of them offering the job to Stan T? Temporarily the acting manager post has been given to Kevin Ball.

Wednesday, March 12

Funny how under certain circumstances long-dormant tribal instincts can emerge and become apparent. It was obvious at Watford that allegiances are all based on what Desmond Morris called *The Soccer Tribe*. It's all to do with a sense of belonging, allegiance, kinship and if not blood ties then those that come from having one common interest. For ninety minutes, or indeed from the minute you see a fellow supporter on a motorway flying a scarf from his car, that sense of tribe, clan and family begins. At Leicester Services we pulled up alongside a car festooned and decorated with Claret and Blue. I'd never seen these people in my life before. Yet we began a conversation as if we were long lost brothers. That's what football does. If painting your face claret and blue isn't a tribal custom with it's origins going back thousands of years to our primeval ancestors, then nothing is. It was many years ago Desmond Morris wrote his book over 300 pages long about this phenomenon describing the rituals, the gatherings, the invasion of another town, the defending of territory and the symbolism and celebrations.

One suggestion that is fascinating is the attempt he makes to analyse the reasons why people vent their rage and frustration on players and on the team - any team. We're not just talking Burnley here. He suggests that in all of us there is always pent up, unreleased anger (nothing new about that) which comes from our everyday lives, that these are all stored up and then wait inside us ready to be released in some visible form. Morris suggests that for those of us who go to a football match, it is here that the trigger occurs which then acts as safety valve and out comes all our rage, gestural aggression and emotion. Funny how it's socially permissible he says, to scream and shout at a football match but not at your desk in the office or behind the counter in a shop. The spectator who yells abuse, is in fact licensed to do so, he says, by the nature of the occasion that he is attending and the context of the sporting event.

Ah I hear you say, but all that's rubbish. The other side of the coin is this. You go to a football match feeling on top of the world. But then you watch a load of rubbish (any football ground I'm not talking Burnley here). As a result, aggression and disgruntlement, which wasn't there in the first place, is aroused as the game goes on and you get angrier and angrier as a direct result of the game.

Speaking of tribes, yes, it's Sheffield tonight. It's them. Blades fans will not thank me for reminding them that they have a lot in common with Rotherham - they are all descendants of the Brigantes Tribe, a fierce, grumpy, uncultured, warlike clan, prone to violence and throat cutting, who gave the Romans what for and have been causing trouble ever since in pubs, clubs and Sheffield city centre on a Saturday night. Bramall Lane aggressiveness is thus part of a longer history. Anyway I digress. Later on by the river the Saxons built a settlement, and then the Normans arrived. The Domesday Book contains a fascinating reference to a 'ffielde wherein ye younge men of the village of Sheaf do kicke and punt a boars head and trye thereof to kille or maime any man theruponne who shalle stoppe them'.

It is much the same today.

In medieval times the place grew and grew and in 1297 it was granted a charter so that the buggers, sorry burgers of Sheffield expanded and prospered. Industry increased in Georgian times, exploded in Victorian times, then the Luftwaffe flattened it all and it has now with its concrete canyons risen again like a phoenix… rather similar to Sheffield United this season.

I'd have preferred a home game against someone we might expect to beat. In truth, away to Sheffield Utd is not really what the doctor ordered as a means of restoring morale after the disappointment that was Sunday.

I seem to recall already writing about Sheffield in less than charitable terms. My feelings haven't changed much but whilst Sheffield Wednesday arouse no thoughts in my head at all, Sheffield United do just the opposite. Let's be honest here, I think it's just resentment, or that we can never win there. I can't warm to them. I can't find anything to say that is generously affectionate about them. One of the newspapers yesterday carried a big spread about Neil Warnock and how there are several managers who would cross the road rather than speak to him. But we must begrudgingly admit he has fashioned one hell of a team mixing experience with youth and Premiership academy cast-offs, and that he has transformed their fortunes since he took over when they were heading like a stone to Division Two. On Sky last night in his pundit role he came across as the amiable, pleasant good-natured bloke you'd be happy to have as your neighbour. Just what does he do then to wind other managers up so badly? That's the bit we never seem to find out.

Stan too was generous in his comments at yesterday's press conference; "Credit where credit is due, I think Sheffield United have had an amazing season and all credit to everyone there, the players and the staff."

Not only that, Stan indicated that team changes would be made, a couple of the lads needing games, some of them needing a rest.

"There will be a few changes but I have a good squad and I think I'll give one or two of them a head and we'll see what happens."

Unfortunately, it is nineteen seasons since Burnley took a point at Bramall lane. We have not scored there for twenty-five seasons and haven't won there for twenty-nine seasons (2-0 with goals from Martin Dobson and Doug Collins), and it was still a cricket ground. Sheffield's last home league win was in mid-January so you can be fairly sure that they'll put that right tonight.

Yup. They duly did.

SHEFFIELD UTD 4 BURNLEY 2

Thursday, March 13

Half a league, half a league, half a league onward.
All in the valley of Death, rode the six hundred.
"Forward the Light Brigade! Charge for the guns," he said.
Into the valley of death, rode the six hundred.
(Alfred Lord Tennyson. 1809 - 1892. Charge of the Light Brigade)

And that's what it felt like last night. Except we didn't quite charge, it was more of a limp. This quite frankly was Blades against blunt spoons. It was as if we were beaten before we even got off the bus at this graveyard ground. We were beaten by a team with pace, muscle, athleticism and skill, and on top of all that, the prodigious shooting power of Michael Brown. If we'd played this game on New Year's Eve by the way as per fixture list, he would have been suspended.

Cannon to the right of them, cannon to the left of them.
Cannon in front of them, volleyed and thundered...

And that's how it seemed as the game progressed and Sheffield could have had a cricket score. As if annoyed by our impudence at pulling a goal back to make the score 2-1 Sheffield then effortlessly turned up the power and volume another notch and Erndlurve scored two more scorchers from their left side, conveniently made vacant and empty following the substitution of Dean West. Robbie Blake scored a consolation goal at the end but by then Mrs. T. and I had applied the four goal rule and left.

Stormed at with shot and shell.

Well not exactly shot and shell, just the loudest tannoy system on the planet, which has United coming out to the Star Wars theme. I'm not sure what would have been appropriate for us last night - perhaps the theme tune from Steptoe and Son. To make full use of the tannoy they then have a man with a mike. Now, in my experience of these things there is nothing worse than a man full of himself with a microphone in front of a big crowd and this man at Sheffield is no exception to the rule. You know how bad it's going to be when he announces the team as The Red and White Wizards... My heart sank. Following that, every Michael Brown goal was followed by a long advert for this season's video of his goals - and this is while the game is going on. Surreal.

The massed ranks of Claret fans were amazingly there in numbers again illustrating once again the theory that being a Burnley supporter is a penance for something done in a previous life. With nothing else to shout about they proceeded to deride Warnock as often as possible with a few banal chants but this was about all we had to offer on a night when we were cruelly exposed as an ageing, disheartened team. The people next to us had driven over from Grassington. To appreciate the devotion of that, you must take out a road map and trace the route.

The legacy of Watford was plain to see. Perhaps the saddest sight was seeing the legend Steve Davis, struggling, clearly only half fit, in a midfield role again, run ragged by younger, fitter players who over and over again left him stranded in their wake. Stan did indeed change the team around, in came Little and Weller (and Davis of course), Blake came on later. But it was to no effect.

And yet again: five more bookings, these being largely the result of crude attempts to up-end disappearing Sheffield players as they sped happily away from our shocked Light Brigade and headed on down towards Marlon. We could of course attempt to pitch some blame onto a trigger-happy referee who seemed more than anxious in the first half to assist Sheffield at every opportunity, and ignore blatant fouls on our gallant Clarets, but sadly it would only serve to mask a night of shellshocked shortcomings. Sadly too it all adds up to yet another victory for Darth Warnock over the forces of good in the shape of Luke Ternentwalker and Sam Chewbacca.

It's probably fair to say that our season, barring miracles and ten wins from the last twelve games (ho ho), is over and it is Sheffield who have done it again to us for the third season running. The only difference this time is that they have done it early with twelve games remaining. Wolves won last night and are now eleven points ahead in the sixth play-off place. Reading are thirteen points ahead and we have three games in hand on them. Our two games in hand on Wolves are probably irrelevant but Reading remain just about catchable if they drop points. Walsall on Saturday is the last chance saloon.

In a bizarre, masochistic way I'm glad we went, predictable and painful though it was to watch. I think we saw at first hand the end of this season's dreams and maybe even the beginning of the end of the line for several players who have served us so well over the last few seasons. It surely must be the time now to go back to the drawing board, for thinking about just where do we go from here, and for thinking about new players in the summer. We were given a lesson, it's as simple as that. In truth though, it has been a bonus this season to have had any dreams at all. All of us at the beginning of the season would have settled for survival financially, and staying in Division One. These two targets have certainly been achieved.

Today on the club website Stan individually criticised Ian Cox for "an unbelievable rick" he made leading up to their third goal. Out of interest, wasn't Glen Little clattered by the touchline just prior to this? Individual criticisms are something I don't like, but well… if you want to apportion ricks, then OK, Marlon made an unbelievable rick of the second goal. Lee Briscoe, with the score at 0-0, made an unbelievable rick of a glorious first half scoring opportunity, one on one with the goalkeeper, and Stan made a rick selecting a half fit Steve Davis and leaving out Robbie Blake. Hindsight is a wonderful thing, which is why, frankly, individual criticisms should not be put in print. All in all you could say the whole thing was a rickety mess and it's best not to pick on individuals.

The only plus, was the warm welcome and applause given, as his name was announced, to former United player Gareth Taylor by the Sheffield crowd. Very sporting. Maybe they're not so bad after all.

Friday, March 14

Last chance at Walsall then, eh? Lose tomorrow and that is finally it and win at Walsall is something Burnley didn't manage last year.

Walsall, The Saddlers, play at The Bescot Stadium, which was once fondly known as the biscuit tin stadium on account of its tin construction and appearance. The construction of a new two-tier stand behind one goal has changed that. Walsall are one of those middling-to-bottom Division One clubs happy to survive another season on low crowds, which for them I suppose is success. Their one claim to fame is that they are the home of the renowned Chicken Balti Pie, beloved by football fans everywhere. Situated in the gloomy industrial Black Country (are we allowed to call it that in these politically correct times?), right by the M6 and the glass RAC Control Centre, the current ground replaced a former stadium called Fellows Park which is now the site of yes, you've guessed it, a supermarket. When the game is dull at the Bescot you can nip out and watch the traffic jams.

The Bescot, interestingly, was built on the site of old sewage farms. These were then named the W.C. Fields. For many years this is why Walsall played crap football. 400 seats and some of the floodlights from the old Fellows Park were sold to Padiham FC. You need to live in Burnley or indeed Padiham to appreciate that little snippet.

The diversity of Walsall industry has given it the name 'The Town of 100 Trades' of which one is football - just about. Trade number 99 is the regular Car Boot Sale in the club car park, which was the financial salvation of Walsall FC for many a year, and might still be for all I know. My research tells me that Walsall unless things have changed are one of the few financially solvent clubs in the Nationwide. The moral of this is, don't knock car boot sales in the club car park. Burnley aren't allowed to organise them thanks to local trading restrictions. Last year we lost 1-0 at this depressing place and the Walsall team even included the legendary Don Goodman, who must have been forty if he was a day and wearing on his head what suspiciously looked like a pineapple.

And so what else complimentary can we say about Walsall? Vehicle thefts are 8 per 1000 vehicles (above national average). Burglary is 2 per 1000 householders (above national average), missed bin collections are 7 per 100,000 (deserving of the highest praise), 1.3% of streetlights do not work (might explain the car nicking and burglaries), 5% of population do not bother to pay council tax (might explain why street lights don't work), and wait for it this is dreadful, the percentage of council house repair jobs carried out where an appointment has been made and kept is 0. Personally I think I'd stay in Burnley with all its problems if I were you.

But Walsall does have a nationally renowned art gallery and collection full of pictures and paintings by an illustrious list of names, including Picasso, Gainsborough and Vincent Van Dulux. It is also the birthplace of some of Slade; that raucous pop group of Noddy Holder fame with that awful and loud Christmas hit to which we are subjected every Yuletide, the name of which I thankfully can't remember but no doubt you do. And it is also the birthplace of Jerome K. Jerome who wrote Three Men In A Boat. And if you knew that one you could confidently enter Who Wants To Be a Millionaire? as long as you don't cough too often.

Saturday, March 15

Let us begin today's cheerful entry with the news that Walsall have lost four of their last five home games. In short they are easy meat, piss poor, not much better than rubbish, built on sewage and not that many points away from the bottom three. With characteristic generosity Burnley therefore immediately allow them to win and all our play-off hopes are now consigned to the dustbin. I am therefore rapidly succumbing to bouts of both depression and Irritable Male Syndrome (IMS).

Today's good news is...

WALSALL 3 BURNLEY 2

...thus producing three dreadful defeats in seven days that have changed the whole nature of our season. If there are pivotal moments then these last seven days have provided them. Just seven days ago there was all to play for, both FA Cup and Division One play-offs. We began the month of March by suggesting that we headed for glory or gloom, delight or dejection, happiness or heartache. We now know which it is to be. We suggested that this could be the most glorious month in Burnley's long and illustrious history. The word bollocks now springs to mind.

Alan Moore returned to the lineup. Blake and Little began on the bench. Dean West was this week's sacrificial lamb on the altar of culpability. Phil Bird expressed disbelief on the web commentary at the 0-2 stage that somehow we had contrived to be losing having had all the play and chances: M***** again responsible for one of the goals, that's 3 in 3 games now where the fickle finger of fault might be dogging his footsteps. It's unfair that goalkeeper's mistakes are remembered. Striker's misses are soon forgotten. Blake and Little came on for the second half and both scored to bring a 3-0 scoreline to near respectability. Burnley's fifteen shots at goal and twelve corners were double those of Walsall. It's an interesting exercise to count the number of times a name is mentioned on a commentary. Today the names heard most were Branch and Taylor. An M6 pileup and closure had already given Burnley fans a lengthy detour to begin the day happily and some of them were still trickling in at half time. Oh to be stuck on the M6 on the way to Walsall now that spring is here. Walsall, bloody Walsall. Everybody beats bloody Walsall except us.

With the postponement of the Portsmouth game there are now five consecutive home games. Portsmouth have had players called up by various Mickey Mouse countries for international games. Our flight with the players then is cancelled. I have to say I am mightily relieved. With things being as they are at the moment, had it not been postponed, we might well have flown down as per plan but gone shopping instead of bothering with the football. Five consecutive home games might give cause for optimism at some clubs, but sadly not at Burnley at the minute. The glorious win over Fulham seems years away now.

London Clarets Website Vox Pop:

All those Clarets who travelled to Walsall today should be given a refund. When will you realise that to get points you have to WIN matches? There is no excuse for this capitulation. Today summed up everything that is bad about Burnley. We were a disgrace and we deserved nothing. (Whitto)

Here was our season on a knife edge. Win and we'd still be in the play-off picture; lose, and we'd be out of it. So you'd think we'd go for a win, yes? As if. Today was a piss-poor, ineffective, defeatist rollover. Walsall are crap but our performances made them look like world beaters... (Paddy)

...we needed to win today, but instead we picked a defensive line up. We let a poor team score soft goals against us. Our reaction to defeat at Watford has been very disappointing. Some teams seem to respond well to a setback - not us. We deliver another series of setbacks... the season ended today. (Firmo)

Stan was furious according to the official club website.

We got what we deserved today and that was nothing. We had two or three chances early on, but after that, we were woeful by our standards. We were 3 down and in the last 15 minutes we might have got something out of it, but it's too late. But the performances today and in the last week have been totally unacceptable and the players are under no illusions how I feel about it - they are having a laugh. They are not playing with enthusiasm, there is no spark and there was no brightness. Something has to be done about it and I intend to get to the bottom of it. I can't kick the ball off the line and into the goal, so it's the players. If the cap fits, wear it.

Who'd want to be on a plane trip to Portsmouth with Stan in this mood? Thank God it's cancelled. Clearly there's trouble at t'mill. Whatever the rot is, it set in by all accounts at half time in the Millwall game. Nothing has gone right since then and spirit seems to be at rock bottom.

Monday, March 17

CASE HISTORY

David is 58, a retired Headteacher, and has seldom experienced any health problems. He was successful in his work and now enjoys his garden, some part time teaching, walking the dog, and writing. He has written articles for The Times Educational Supplement and a series of short stories for The Dalesman magazine. Recently however he has become listless, his spelling has gone to peeces, he has had problems sleeping, is becoming disinterested with things in general and very reluctant to answer the telephone. His doctor was called but an examination revealed no abnormalities even though David confided in him that he felt a complete failure, particularly on Saturdays. His wife has become increasingly alarmed and was particularly concerned when David got up one morning and called out in a stressed voice that he just couldn't go on any more, that life was no longer worth living, and that he couldn't face going to The Turf again.

EXPERT MEDICAL DIAGNOSIS BY DR. U. R. LOWE

David is clearly a Burnley supporter and the symptoms of depression are all too evident. There are feelings of hopelessness and despair. This comes when optimism is replaced by feelings of gloom and pessimism. Anxiety is common, and comes from never knowing whether it will be the depressing 4-5-1 that has been so poor recently or the more adventurous 4-4-2 or even the dashing but vulnerable 4-3-3. Mood swings are frequent and will continue to be so; the highs of a good result are now replaced by the lows of constant defeat. Social withdrawal will happen when David can no longer face visiting Turf Moor even though many of his friends are there and the Balti Pies are first class - when you can actually get one. Fatigue is a common symptom of Depression and David is not sleeping at all well, especially now that he worries about getting his money back for the cancelled plane trip to Portsmouth. And finally lack of concentration becomes all too evident now that he cannot look at the results and league tables and Ceefax for more than just a few seconds without bursting into tears on a Sunday morning.

Depression can be triggered by all manner of things, which come under the heading of stressful life events, or can be the side effects of drugs, medication, hormones, menstruation or postnatal problems. In David's case a more likely cause is Seasonal Affective Disorder (SAD), which happens when the season at Burnley begins to go downhill and everything seems very dark and gloomy. When this happens in the space of just seven days the effects are all the more pronounced. SAD has occurred at Burnley now for the second consecutive season and is all too common in this part of Lancashire.

DR. LOWE'S SUGGESTED TREATMENT

Psychotherapy may help - talking to other supporters who have similar problems or joining a good messageboard. Medication i.e. anti-depressant drugs may help, perhaps a pie at half time, a few drinks both before and after a game - though these should be closely monitored because drink itself is a depressant, or an aspirin and a lie down in a darkened room after a particularly bad game. In extreme cases of depression electroshock treatment may be helpful but an expert should always be on hand to make sure you put your fingers in the socket properly. Good diet is essential and an increase in consumption of oily fish such as salmon, herrings, sardines, tuna and mackerel can work beneficially. Eat more turkey. This is low fat meat and contains L-tryptophan and actually acts as a sedative, which is why we all fall asleep after Christmas Dinner.

DR. LOWE'S EXPERT'S PROGNOSIS

David could do a number of things. He could stop reading the Sunday sports pages for a while. He could stop going to watch Burnley for a few weeks and resume next season. He could continue to attend and hope that things will pick up (keeping a supply of turkey sandwiches and tins of mackerel with him). He could seek counselling or start going to Blackburn.

Tuesday, March 18

There are now inevitable muttered mumblings on the websites and messageboards, and in newspapers like *The Observer* where supporters can have their brief say. Questions are being asked about current team selection and tactics. Questions centre around Blake and Little being left on the bench and the continued use of the defensive negative 4-5-1 formation, even against teams as poor as Walsall. The words 'hoof' and 'punt' appear frequently. *The People* match report for the Walsall game gave the lowest ratings I have ever seen to the players of any team, let alone Burnley. Marlon was given a 2. My God, I haven't seen a 2 out of 10 since my days at school in woodwork and the wobbly lamp I handed in.

But even Stan has told the *Lancashire Evening Telegraph* he would rather walk away than watch any more of that: "I am absolutely sick to death of it. They are nicking money while people are paying their hard earned cash to go and see them... That was the worst week in my time at Turf Moor without a doubt. I am not going to keep carrying the can for the players. If I can't shake them up then I don't know what to do. They have got to shake themselves up; it has to come from within the players. They are not having a go and they are bone idle."

> *The three defeats have without doubt been appalling and the distressed and disappointed looks at Watford have now turned to anger and rage. Certain players have been picked on by the fans although there is no doubt that Ternent himself has not come out unscathed with supporters beginning to wonder about the style of play, in particular at Watford where there seemed no real attempt to try and win the game.* (Tony Scholes on Claretsmad)

> *So all in all a bad couple of weeks. One point from three league games and a non-performance at Watford in the cup. I'm worried now that we've been found out after three decent seasons in this league. Plan A seems to be team spirit, work hard, close down the opposition, hoof it to Taylor. There's not much evidence of a Plan B. The facts show that whatever the permutation we've got a fairly useless defence. The squad just continues to age - and where are the eager, young, fresh faces banging on the first team door. There are none. It doesn't bode well for the future. After a rotten start this year we dusted ourselves down and got it sorted (sort of). Next season could be very difficult.* (Eddie Lea, London Clarets)

In fairness it must be said that for every piece that is critical about Stan on the websites, there are others that spring to his defence, reminding us of what he has achieved, the rescue job he has done, the limited resources he works with, the ambitions he has, and that his blood is true claret and blue.

However, just when I was relieved not to be taking the plane down to Portsmouth with Stan and the players because of the postponement of the game (that's the good news), we are given (here comes the bad news) first refusal on a rearranged flight to Norwich for which, to my amazement, I am told there is a waiting list of punters with money to burn. Apparently there are sixty-five other supporters just as daft as me.

Wednesday, March 19

Here's a scene from the Turf last night as we sit in our seats, and in spite of three current defeats, enjoying being back at The Turf. Behind us to the right is a large fat bloke stuffing a pie into his mouth whilst standing up hurling abuse at the players. His face is a mask of fury and bile. His eyes are narrowed and venomous. He is a large bloke, twice as big as me, so I stay mum. What's interesting though is that this tirade is during the warm-up. The game hasn't even started. It's still ten minutes to kick off. For this he has paid £19, oh and whatever it is for a pie these days. Most of the pie has finished up on the collar of the person in front of him. God forbid that we lose. The whole pie might come back up.

BUT LOSE WE DID. BURNLEY 1 LEICESTER 2

Stan rang the changes for this one and we came home tonight pondering on that age-old football feeling, just how did we lose that one? In the previous three games we had deserved nothing. Tonight football was all about us being mugged, with Fatman behind us silenced by the better football we played, the passion, competitiveness and spirit. To put it succinctly, this was a bloody good game. Stan shuffled Davis back to his rightful centre back role instead of Cox, Gnohere was at left back instead of Branch, West returned, Little and Blake were on from the start, Taylor was suspended… and the ball to feet football flowed all night. This team at Watford would have won. It might have been swept away at all-powerful Sheffield, but would probably have won at Walsall - who let Preston score five against them last night which kind of tells you how bad we must have been at Walsall.

Blake and Little demonstrated that with them in the team anything can happen. There will be a 50% success rate, or better, in all that they do. Some of what they do will not come off and they will lose the ball. But for the rest of the time they will cause havoc, create chances and excite us all. Sometimes we will groan in frustration when things break down, but for the rest of the time they will put the fear of God into opposing teams. With these two you have to accept the bad with the good. The latter will win us games. Spontaneous applause burst out and rippled round the ground time and time again last night at the lovely passing moves and the exhilarating forward runs. Pieman behind us was silenced even though we lost.

Duff shooting and an inability to defend from two late corners cost us this game in which Leicester, currently second and looking certain to go up, were totally outplayed. Of fifteen shots, just three were on target. Apparently Stan asked for ruthless finishing. Perhaps they misheard and thought he said toothless. Chance after chance was skied over the bar or yards wide.

Remember when Rotherham came here and clattered us 6-2? Of their seventeen shots, thirteen were on target. There's a moral in there somewhere. Moore (Ian) might well have had a penalty when he was baulked and sandwiched in the box (ooh very painful) by the brick wall that is Taggart and Eliot. They remind me of that legendary pair of Bolton players and hard men, Tommy Banks and Roy Hartle - now that shows my age. Not even Kevin Ball would wanna mess with them down a dark alley in Padiham on a Friday night.

Thursday, March 20

So things at the moment are like this: Portsmouth and Leicester occupy automatic promotion places. Sheff Utd, Reading, Nottingham Forest and Wolves occupy the play-off spots. Burnley are in thirteenth place on 48 points, 12 points behind Wolves with two games in hand. Ten games remain. A run of ten consecutive wins should cement a play-off place with 78 points. Stan has said this has to be the target. One of those games by the way is away to Portsmouth who currently score goals for fun and play a brand of football that is of Premiership quality.

The official website has the following piece:

Burnley manager Stan Ternent hit out at claims he was ready to quit his job following the match with Leicester City. Several national newspapers reported on Tuesday morning that Ternent would walk away from the Turf Moor job if his players failed to beat Leicester City at Turf Moor following an earlier story in the Lancashire Evening Telegraph. Ternent was far from happy with the reports and angrily denied the stories.

"I have got no intention and never said at any stage that I was considering leaving Burnley Football Club," he said.

"I talked about the players and everyone has picked up from there so I would expect a full retraction and redress of the balance. It's totally bang out of order."

Yesterday in the *Lancashire Evening Telegraph*, Stan added:

I have not packed anything in, in my life, and I don't intend to start now. I have no intention of leaving but I did make comments about the players. But as far as leaving Burnley Football Club it won't be under my volition.

They are capable of being a top six football team. They have been in the top seven for the last two seasons. We still have an opportunity to do that if we can win the last ten matches. That has to be the target. I have not given up on the play-offs not while it is mathematically possible. Even if it isn't I want to finish as high as possible.

There are reports that Nationwide clubs face further financial blows if their Internet partner Premium TV continues with its problems.

The Daily Telegraph reported some days ago that clubs face a £35million blow if their website deal crashes. Premium TV announced new redundancies amid fears that it could close down. The company has already renegotiated its original £65million deal which was for a twenty year period. If the reduced deal collapses the Football League's official website faces closure and another source of revenue becomes lost to Nationwide clubs. Football League officials are concerned that there is no 'shareholder liability', the same loophole that allowed Granada and Carlton to avoid meeting the bill when ITV Digital collapsed. Last summer Premium TV changed the terms of the deal to link payments to the number of 'hits' on individual websites.

Friday, March 21

From Breaking News, Official Website.

Burnley Football Club's Catering Department is looking for pie and hot dog connoisseurs to help us decide on our pie and hot dog suppliers for next season. Burnley fans are amongst the largest percentage of pie eating supporters in football, and with your help, we would like to keep it that way. The catering department are looking for supporters to come to The James Hargreaves suite on Wednesday March 26th at 12.30 pm to taste the different products from various companies and then give us their honest opinions.

We will serve complimentary tea, coffee and soft drinks to help wash them down and the results of the tasting day will help us decide which company will get our business next season.

For more information call the Catering Department.

Now that's what I call consultation.

The news was interesting when I phoned. Apparently Everton FC think that they are the number one pie scoffing club with 19% of their supporters buying a pie. But catering manager Chris Gibson disagrees and claims that Claret fans are the No.1 customers with 25% of any crowd buying a pie. Chris says that last season over 100,000 pies were sold. A disappointment though has been the Balti Pie introduced by popular demand. Oddly enough, it has not been a best seller. Clearly this is traditional pie country and old habits die hard with consumption of meat and potato, steak and kidney and cheese and onion retaining the top spots. Chris had no information regarding the correlation between pie consumption and heart disease in Burnley.

Saturday, March 22

Though these are football diaries, there is a world outside. Yesterday the invasion of Iraq started in earnest. We mention this because it is right to do so. Out there are Burnley boys and while we watch our football match safe from harm it could well be that in some dry, dusty, God-forsaken hole in the desert of Iraq some poor lad, from Lancashire, or Iraq, or anywhere for that matter lies dying today while we grumble because we've missed another chance. Give it some thought. There are bigger, more important, things than football and moaning because we've lost again. The first eight British deaths occurred yesterday when a helicopter crashed. Kind of puts things in perspective. I don't know about anyone else but my mind is not exactly a hundred percent on football today. Bill Shankly once said football is more than a matter of life and death. We know what he meant, but in truth it isn't.

+++War latest, says The Express front page +++Rumours Saddam is dead +++Allies in Baghdad by Monday +++B52s launch terrifying blitz +++Britain in mourning for our hero Marines +++Iraqi soldiers wave white flags+++

Leeds at last sack Terry Venables. Peter Reid is appointed on a caretaker basis for their last eight games. Leeds are seven points from the bottom three with a daunting collection of final games. They are by no means clear of trouble. Peter Reid though, according to one newspaper, will not be picking the team. The bank manager does that. Poor Terry Venables. The holiday brochure that was Leeds Utd was not exactly accurate as he perused it before taking on the job. Within two weeks of arriving Ferdinand was sold to ease crippling debts and the sales continued from thereon. Peter Getridofemsdale remains as chairman with every football commentator in the land wondering just how this man clings on to office. Handsome compensation will be paid to Venables and Reid is reputedly on half a million if he keeps Leeds in the Premiership. My chums and neighbours in this city who are Leeds supporters are shellshocked on an almost daily basis. Today's game against Grimsby ended

BURNLEY 1 GRIMSBY 1

Of this for the moment we will say little, for there is little to be said.

Sunday, March 23

'Well that's the end of another season', writes Barnsey in *When The Ball Moves*, and that's before yesterday's game. 'Yes, I know there are over ten games to go. Yes, I know that mathematically we have a chance of making the play-offs. I know we have a tendency to make late spurts up the table. I know you can never write us off. Well usually you'd be right, but then not much about this season has been quite so usual for us, has it?'

Tony Scholes on Claretsmad after yesterday writes, 'Where do you start? After some improvement on Tuesday against Leicester, despite the defeat, we were back to square one yesterday with what has to be the worst performance of the season'.

There is little to add, save to say, the sun shone beautifully and we got half a suntan. During the first half I read the programme from cover to cover. The chap behind me actually fell asleep (honest, I do not make that up). Pigeons settled happily on various parts of the pitch there was so little to disturb them. In fact sometimes they settled on a player's head. Grimsby were so bad it is a mystery they aren't marooned at the bottom already ninety points behind the rest, and this had all the ingredients, passion and interest of listening to Ian Duncan Smith. This was the classic end of season game that neither players nor crowd were interested in.

In the *Lancashire Evening Telegraph* on Friday evening Chairman Barry Kilby warned that if gates fall lower, then boss Stan Ternent will be severely limited in his budget and in what he can offer any of the nine players whose contracts expire this summer in order to retain those he wishes to retain. Barry Kilby expressed the concern that with gates sinking any lower, the club stands to lose £10,000 a game over the last six games.

Back on Claretsmad Tony Scholes suggests that he will have great difficulty getting some people to turn up again after being treated to almost ninety minutes of passionless garbage. It was another poor turn out; in real terms less than 11,300 and it was those that didn't bother that made the right decision… for Burnley it is going to be a difficult period. With the club set to announce increased season ticket prices and the Chairman warning the fans of the consequences of not turning up it will do nothing to persuade people to come… Attendances will continue to drop and season ticket sales could drop alarmingly… Somehow we have to find some better form than this, the last two to three weeks have been nothing short of a horror story that have seen us pick up two points from fifteen and go out of the FA Cup with a string of awful performances.

Actually yesterday I thought it was more than ninety minutes. This game seemed to go on and on and on with a procession of time-consuming injuries, Grimsby's Stacey Coldicott broke a leg, Alan Moore pulled a hamstring, and constant substitutions. For the first time that I can remember it was gone five o' clock when the referee mercifully blew his full time whistle.

The Grimsby site Electronic Fishcake.com is recommended reading. I quote;

To the huge delight of those present wearing black and white spectacles, real or imagined, the Burnley players didn't seem particularly bothered. Oh sure they wanted to play pretty football, tippy tappying the ball around, trying to score a perfect goal for the end of season video compilation, but getting stuck in wasn't priority number one, all other priorities rescinded... huge expanses of time were taken up with nothingness... Oh sure Burnley sometimes had shots, but so weak and wide that they have asked that for the sake of their families, the individuals are not identified and the details not released...

On this showing I dread the Portsmouth game, which your genial scribe and Mrs. T have every attention of attending seeing as Mrs. T's sister lives but an hour's drive away in rustic gentle, deepest Sussex in an olde house where log fires and huge roast beef and Yorkshire Pud dinners are the order of the day. Come on, there has to be some kind of incentive.

Quote of the day:

the main area of concern is the engine room. At the moment it seems that we are operating with an 899cc Cinquecento engine, whilst other sides have at least a 1.6 Golf under the bonnet... (Barnsey, When The Ball Moves Editorial)

Ian Moore was the mobile phone man of the match. Pardon? Let me explain. This is the latest money-making wheeze the club have introduced. You can't blame them in all honesty. You dial the number and type in your choice for man of the match. It costs 50p. What will they think of next? The possibilities are numerous. We could type in what we think of the referee. We could type in a player's number and then what we think he should be paid. We could type in who we think should be substituted or sent home for an early night and told not to come back till next week.

What a stunning game we have to look forward to on Tuesday at home to Bradford, two struggling teams battling for mid-table inferiority. It could well be an exercise in futility although being a local derby with a smidgeon of grudge to it, it might just produce something better than yesterday. Burnley 3 Fulham 0 seems a hundred years ago.

Monday, March 24

Does it really matter in the great scheme of things? Maybe there are more important things than moaning about a 1-1 draw with Grimsby.

Let's remind ourselves of bigger matters.

+++RAF Tornado shot down+++ Allies just 95 miles from Baghdad+++ ITN Newsman killed+++ casualties and deaths+++ American prisoners executed+++ Missiles go astray+++

Stewart Binns programme notes on Saturday try to make sense of the whole thing. Binns is one of three regular contributors. His pieces are measured, studious, informative… Alistair Campbell is the passionate fan who dips into nostalgia and when I were a lad… Tony Livesey Editor of the *Daily Sport* and co-author of Stan's book is tabloidspeak, tubthumping and batters us into being less critical, better supporters… all three are the eternal optimists.

Life in general and football in particular goes on and we are right to make sure it does. In World War II, football continued on a regionalised basis with star players turning out for whatever club was nearest to them, wherever they were stationed. For a while Aldershot (whatever happened to them?) were the Real Madrid of their day. Sport is escape and a diversion, be it from boredom, work or from the horror of events in Iraq, which we can watch 24 hours a day on TV if we choose. And let's not forget those Claret lads out in Iraq whose first question late on a Saturday might well be 'how did Burnley do today?'.

Tuesday, March 25

Prior to tonight's game against Drabford City, Stan has been remarkably low key in his comments about Saturday's performance. We can only assume that he has run out of the will to publicly demonstrate his ire. His only comments have been along the lines of players not performing to their capability, of being a little off colour (terminally ill according to a doctor sitting behind us), and on the club website:

> *There comes a time when you have to back players. Everyone goes through a dodgy patch regardless of what you do for a living so I think it's important that you show faith in them.*

Bradford webs are suspiciously quiet at the moment. Remember there is no love lost between Bradford and Burnley. They seem to think for some reason that we are a team of kicking, brutal, cheating, ugly cloggers. Mention the names Dean West or Dimi Papadopoulos and you are likely to be taken to some dark alleyway in Manningham to have your nose rearranged. Remember that for Bradford fans this is their big game of the year. My neighbour Bradford John has taken today as a holiday to prepare mentally, and tomorrow to recover. I do believe that Burnley are disliked even more than Sheffield United and Sheffield Wednesday. Only Leeds inspire deeper loathing. Remember we have not beaten Bradford in the league since 1937. Their Fanzine *City Gent* had only this to say but which I thought quite devastating in its understated simplicity:

> *We have commissioned an independent cultural survey to review Burnley. This is his assessment... 'The town centre is like Shipley, only not as sophisticated'.*

Wednesday, March 26

BURNLEY 0 DRABFORD 2

Last night. Let us say immediately that this was possibly undeserved… possibly. Lady Luck smiled on Bradford, said the Yorkshire Post this morning. Even the world famous and renowned Bradford Telegraph and Argus questioned the disallowing of Burnley's 'equalizing' goal and that's a paper where the sports pages are printed in Hogwarts claret and amber.

Take away two controversial decisions, the first to allow a Bradford goal which Diallo looked to have cleared from under the bar, the second disallowing a Burnley goal for nobody knows what and it is possible that we might have got something from this game. Reliable sources of undisputed honesty sitting near this linesman insist that he only raised his flag for a Bradford goal when Bradford players turned to celebrate and that after the game several Bradford players questioned whether it was over the line or not. On the other hand it could also be said Bradford probably just about merited this win if only because of their judicious mix of the very young and the not so old, out-running, out-tackling and out-defending Burnley's mix of the ageing and the very aged. Prior to the game Stan had called this 'half a derby' and the Clarets proceeded to play it that way, only coming into the game in the second half. Of our thirteen shots only four were on target which is seems a fair average over recent weeks and is the reason why we have now lost five out of the last six games and drifted down the table since Boxing Day, this month's dreadful run in particular beginning next to the cemetery at Watford.

With Blake on for the second half Burnley played football, passed to feet, looked lively, pressured Bradford for most of the half - and still contrived to give them a second goal after poor old Arthur was sent off for a second bookable offence. "Quelle domage".

These are bad times and the month ends on feelings of just where do we go from here. A month that started with such hopes and aspirations now grinds to a close with supporters wondering just where the next points will come from, and wondering if in fact we might well continue in freefall and fail to win another game this season. It seems unthinkable given the forward attacking skills we can display but there is now such pessimism, such a feeling of letdown round the place, that it is possible that for the next game there could well be a crowd of under 10,000 and fewer and fewer people will renew season tickets if this continues. The prices are announced on Friday… and even more worryingly who the hell will buy my book?

When freefall occurs like this it is sometimes difficult to pinpoint exactly why. In the case of a club like Leeds Utd this season it is blindingly obvious but in our case just exactly what is it? It began at Watford; no it began in the game before at Millwall at half time, and has continued ever since with manager Stan seemingly unable to stop the rot. Hard words, kind words, make no difference. Team shuffling makes no difference. Changing of formations and tactics makes no difference. In the game where he did what we all cried out for, beginning with Little and Blake, the latter was so ineffective he had to be taken off at half time and not a person in the crowd would have argued with that. And then of course there are referee's decisions. When a team hits the skids, key decisions go against you and that's before I mention a good penalty claim in the second half when Moore was brought down and another incident where Little's shirt was clearly pulled. Linesmen seem to miss these things yet manage to disallow what seemed to everyone else a perfectly good goal which left Moore beating the ground in despair and my irritable male syndrome language hopefully reaching the referee.

Stan on the club website commented that a break now until a week on Saturday will do them all good, that overall Burnley were unlucky and didn't get the breaks going their way. He questioned the two controversial decisions and commented that Bradford weren't two goals better. If there is a lesson though to be drawn from last night it is perhaps that Bradford and Nicky Laws came with their superb current away record and maybe demonstrated the need for some young legs at the Turf. In Ben Muirhead he has found an 18 year old from Man U who could well become a very good player. Supporters are asking, why don't we manage to do this? Their young teenage players Forrest, Muirhead, Bower and Francis, I am reliably informed by somebody who knows somebody's dad, are playing for the princely sum of £100 a week.

Bradford, bearing in mind the state they were in just months ago with seven consecutive defeats, relegation looming, financial chaos, administration, the sacking of coaching staff, crippling injuries, their very future and existence on a knife edge, and no Whiskas for the club cat, are now on the up and their supporters can't wait for next season. We, meanwhile, will now settle for Division One continuation for another year, plus financial survival and stability and we have our memories of moments of cup glory to keep us warm. But next season worries us. Eight games remain, four at home and four away. Would that we could find the confidence to go out and win some of them.

Firmo's excellent London Clarets Grimsby report ends with...

It's a truism but we are where we deserve to be. We are a mid-table side. At no point this season have we been higher than eighth so why would we think we ought to make the play-offs? This has been a season characterised by lack of consistency. We have been brilliant and dreadful and in between there's been a fair amount of boredom. It's frustrating now because a couple of weeks ago we looked to be on the threshold of something unlikely and exciting but then we ballsed it up. I do say that every season we stay in the First Division is a success, and that after four games when I thought we were doomed I'm happy to have avoided that by miles but there is part of me that thinks that things have got stale and need a shake up. The summer will be important.

You could end any of this month's reports with these words. The summer will indeed be important, and interesting with ten members of the first team squad up for contract renewal or otherwise - Branch, Cook, Payton, Armstrong, Cox, Briscoe, Diallo, Michopoulos, Beresford and Davis. Seven of them played last night. In addition there are five younger fringe players who have yet to feature at all in a first team game.

Thursday, March 27

The view from the away end, kindly provided by my neighbour Bradford John: the truncated version rather than the 1 hour 30 minute monologue I endured earlier this evening after he had consumed several celebratory Stellas. My protestations that linemen's decisions change games and how on earth could anyone possibly tell that the ball had crossed the line were swept aside by his tide of Bantam euphoria. I never knew that beating Burnley meant so much to smaller teams.

Pies... excellent; sale of beer from separate outlet... excellent; knee room... excellent. View... excellent save for one post in the way. Police and help given outside ground... excellent. Stewards inside ground... absolutely excellent; atmosphere and chanting in away end excellent, Burnley support and chanting... poor. Final result... excellent. Burnley... one dimensional until Blake came on. Bradford's first goal, definitely a goal (But he would say that wouldn't he even though he sat half a mile away); Gnohere's dismissal... had to go. Urinals... disgusting, only to be visited once, then best avoided, and probably never cleaned out since the days of Martin Dobson, much better to use the car park when it gets dark. Local crumpet as seen from car window in Colne, worse than Keighley... Local totty as seen in Keighley from car window... worse than Barnsley. (Personally I would say Leeds market). Question; why do Burnley have so many people in the dugout and who are they all?.. that must be where a million of your wage bill goes... you could get rid of half of those and get players instead...

And Nicky Law's view of the Burnley disallowed goal from the esteemed and revered *Telegraph and Argus:* "After I got up from the floor from the shock I agreed with the linesman."

****

Who did eat all the pies then? This was in truth a freebie to excite the taste buds yesterday. Has there ever been such an assemblage of distinguished mouthwatering pies and perfect crusts as there was in the JH suite? Wherever you looked, from the moment you reached the top of the James Hargreaves stairs, it was pies, pies and yet more pies. Twas enough to send a man dizzy. Truly for the pie aficionado (pieionado) this was a day to remember. The words of William Wordsworth came to mind as I tried hard not to over eat but what the hell, this was important research I was undertaking .

I wandered lonely as a cloud that floats on high o'er Turf Moor's Vale, when all at once I saw a crowd, a host of golden crusty pies...

Four different types of hot dog and six types of pie were there to be sampled. I personally found that Hot Dog E and Meat and Potato Pie E were my tip top tips. The Steak and Kidney I sampled (better not reveal which table it came from) was binned. The Cheese and Onion from Table X was delicious but I'm still tasting it.

Catering Manager Chris Gibson was clearly pleased by the success of the event and revealed that one particular pie had swept the board but only the chefs knew from whence it came. As a lad years ago I used to work in an uncle's bakery (ha ha, if only you knew what went on in a bakery, best that you don't). They tell me things are better now. My money is on Meat and Potato pie E... firm, round, well filled, nice to hold, visually perfect... golden tan, great body, something to really get your mouth round, take it slowly and then build up to a real climax... then pause to savour and re-live the experience exhausted for the moment, yet eager for more... Only the absence of a nice Chardonnay spoiled the occasion.

Burnley sold 102,000 pies last season, of which 78% were meat and potato, 6% Balti, 8% cheese and onion and 8% steak and kidney. The town of Burnley I have read is noted for its high incidence of heart disease, although Chris Gibson had no figures for this or any information regarding correlation between pie consumption and chest pains, and neither was there a doctor in attendance.

First in the queue of eager punters at the top of the stairs I can report were the half starved impoverished members of the Burnley Leisure and Community staff, with legends Ashley Hoskin and Vince Overson well to the fore. Vince Overson is on a diet I believe and I have to say I did at no time see him with a pie. I was momentarily reminded of the queues of asylum seekers who line up at the plush reception centre along Kirkstall Road in Leeds to receive their benefits. (Most of them turn up in taxis actually). Also in attendance were assorted workmen off the street, members of the fire brigade (never ones to miss out on free food in my experience), a bloke who looked suspiciously like the club caretaker, a miscellany of club administrators who we can only assume are so underpaid that they seek humanitarian pie aid, reporters and photographers, another group who seem to have the uncanny knack of finding free groceries, and an assortment of somewhat portly fans. I saw no players while I was there so we can only assume that Stan told them to keep well clear of this deadly cholesterol stuff and stick to pasta. Mind you, I've seen them eating plates of chips in the club café but mum's the word.

I understand these events are every two years. I have applied for my next invitation already.

Friday, March 28

Yesterday Burnley FC announced to the world that Glen Little had been transferred to Reading for the remainder of the season. The world at large hardly gives a toss, but in Burnley... there is uproar. On the Richter scale it doesn't quite compare with the banishment of Jimmy Mac or the sale of Martin Dobson but Glenno is the nearest thing we have to a B-list celebrity. With eight games to go and 24 points to play for, it would appear that the towel has been thrown in and the club is admitting the season is over. And there are rumours surfacing that Blake may go to Wigan and Gareth Taylor turned down a loan move. The timing of Little's move is immaculate, being the day before the press release outlining new season ticket prices. It is already common knowledge that season ticket prices will go up but nobody knows by how much. The announcement outlined that Glen Little's loan move is a cost cutting measure, there is a saving of his wages, presumably considerable, and according to Chairman Barry Kilby the deal is worth £100,000 to the club which helps rebuilding for next season.

If the date was April 1 I would treat this with disbelief. But no, this is for real. It makes sense for both clubs says Barry Kilby. To say this is a surprise move is the understatement of the century and leaves some people with the same open mouth with which we all received the news that Dobbo was to leave for Everton thirty years ago, and that Jimmy Mac was to leave for Stoke nearly forty years ago. Yes, it is that much of a shock, even though we have known all along that all players at the club are on the open to offers list. It is the unexpected stark suddenness that is stunning. All we can do is try to understand the club position and place our belief in both Glen and the club's words that he will be back for next season.

"Everyone knows I am happy here," he says.

Burnley have clearly taken a calculated gamble, that the savings they make will balance the possibility of reduced gates caused by his absence, and that there will not be too drastic a reduction in attendances. And to think, all this was going on while we were happily scoffing pies lulled into a sense of well-fed bonhomie. Yes it makes sense financially, gates are falling anyway, and losses are still critical following the Digital shambles. The wage bill is £7.5million a year. The chance to get one of the very highest earners at the club off the books temporarily is clearly seen as too good to miss and is perhaps unavoidable.

But what of supporters? There are arguments that a season ticket price freeze would be a great morale booster for already stretched supporters and might just ensure that most present holders would renew their subscription. Instead for the moment, there is just an offer that season ticket holders may bring a friend free to the Gillingham game. Mouthwatering. There are those who will refuse to renew season tickets until they are sure that Little is back. By then the special reduced rates offer will be unavailable. They will then maybe decide not to renew.

The *Lancashire Evening Telegraph* says that there is no doubt Stan Ternent will want him back for next season and that this will give him the opportunity to take a look at a couple of other players and systems. Pardon me but what other players? As for coming back, consider this; what happens if Reading make the play-offs, Reading win the play-offs, Reading reach the Premiership? Then will Glen Little return to Burnley?

For the Bradford and Grimsby games the club announced that there were only around 200 pay on the day customers, well less than £4,000. Clearly these are disastrous figures. It was inevitable that Glen Little would go if an offer came.

Saturday, March 29

About SuperGlen the London Clarets website writes…

The news didn't exactly fill us with a surge of unbridled joy... underlying it are two major worries. Firstly are the club's financial problems worse than we believed? Is it worth letting a key player or players, if the Blake rumours can be believed (to Wigan on loan), leave the squad for the sake of a few week's wages? What happened to the money from our cup runs? And secondly, what impact will the move have on the motivation and cohesion of the squad. The club's longer term financial stability depends on how well things go on the pitch and it's hard to see how loaning out Glen Little will help in that regard.

A Claretsmad e-mail response came up with the point that by definition season ticket holders have already paid to see Little play, his transfer is therefore a slap in the face. Fair point. Suppose you bought a ticket in advance for the stage show Chicago, then six months later you find it cancelled. Don't you get a refund, or am I being simple here?

Another from Claretsmad in support of the club suggests we are still paying the price of gambling on Gazza and David Johnson in the back end of last season and that was a gamble we all applauded at the time.

Yet another Claretsmad message makes the point that it only needs 300 adults not to renew season tickets and the supposed £100,000 savings on Glen Little are wiped out.

From Happy Claret…

The Glen Little episode for me is the final straw. It may well be good business for another club to pay his wages for a few months, but with all the injuries and all the suspensions looming, what kind of side are we going to field in the one match that has any meaning in the final games? (Preston). Local pride is at stake, and that means a lot to those who are dyed in the wool. I have paid out for my season ticket under the impression that I can watch the best side that Burnley can field in every game. This however is no longer the case. I really am disappointed with the way things have gone over the last three weeks or so but this has put the lid on it. Preston must be rubbing their hands in anticipation...

My own view is that it is quite likely that the club made a calculated decision that even with Glen Little, ticket sales would be vastly reduced following such a declining end to the season. The writing was on the wall already that there is growing disinterest and disillusion; ipso facto Glen had to go. My God, how we are paying for that dreadful day at Watford and the loss of another half million income. What a thoroughly awful month. March 2003: a month to remember… or forget… if you can.

****

Season ticket prices announced yesterday. Increases are minimal, so small as to be almost negligible at under a pound per game. In the James Hargreaves Stand there is an actual price freeze. Most website responses express relief and a petition is started to get Stan Ternent to give Andy Payton one last farewell game before the season ends. Today should have been the day we flew to Portsmouth with the team. Wouldn't that have been a jolly day? Thank God it's off.

+++Little's loan move doesn't even get a single line in most newspapers+++ events in Iraq do+++ Iraq allegedly executes 2 British soldiers+++ kind of puts Little events and ST prices into a bigger perspective+++

But never have two things coincided to produce such a flood of messageboard arguments and responses. Here's another from Claretsmad. It defends Chief Executive Andrew Watson who is sometimes criticised. My own comment is that his job reminds me of mine in my other Headteacher life, both being jobs where you spend your time trying to keep a place solvent, wrack your brains to think of ways to raise money to recruit and retain staff, identify ways to provide extra income to raise standards, and in doing so demonstrate the age old adage that you can't please all of the people all of the time. Basically it's a thankless job and the terrible thing is you know in your heart that yes, you are taking money off the same few people.

...how can Andrew Watson be told that his time is effectively up? (writes Drissa Diallo's Head). *If Andrew Watson wants to state that season ticket prices will increase year on year then so be it. It is his job to decide that. Football is unfortunately a business and has been for a good five years at least. With all the problems of the last 12 months there has never*

been a more crucial time to have a Chief Executive who can look at the cold hard facts without being affected by the Claret and Blue cloud that would blur our judgement. Just because he says he will raise prices each season doesn't mean that he has to, and to insinuate otherwise is doing the man a great injustice. It is part of HIS business plan and that means it can change at any time - it is a flexible approach to how he intends to run Burnley Football Club in the future. I too feel disappointed that next season it will cost more money to see the same (or worse) Burnley. But does a weekly shop cost the same every year? We could argue that it would be better to freeze, or drop, prices...

...Yes it would make a couple of thousand people slightly happier but those smiles would turn to tears when we are in liquidation. Who would be blamed then, I wonder

... One day Barry Kilby might say enough is enough... Goodbye Burnley Football Club. Then what do we do?

Sunday, March 30

Lennie Johnrose scored for Swansea to lift them out of the bottom two in Div 3+++ I read that Maylett was M. O. T. M+++ Swansea are now managed by Burnley legend Brian Flynn. Swansea in the Conference seems unthinkable+++ Gunshot and stab wounds in dreadful running battle+++ No not in Iraq but England yobs in Leichtenstein where England scrape a poor 2-0 win.

Gazza, our adopted son of Burnley, is now in China playing for Gansu Tianma of Lanzhou, a brash, sprawling, messy industrial city of three million people on the banks of the Yellow River fifty miles from the start of the Gobi Desert. He played his first competitive game and scored. Reports say his goal was mesmerising. He clowned, urged his teammates on and was cheered long after the final whistle. Gansu won 2-0. An army band played *Happy Days Are Here Again*. His goal was a classic, dummying two defenders before firing a low shot from the edge of the box into the corner of the goal. His celebration was classic Gazza, stripping off the shirt, punching his chest and yelling to the ecstatic crowd. His coach Gong Lei said afterwards "Today he was like he was before...fantastic." Gazza, Gazza give us a wave.

On the claretsmad message board;

To try and get a terrible month finished with as soon as possible I have just turned over my Burnley FC calendar to see which Burnley stars are going to grace my wall for April... Who is it? Glen Little! A month of a reminder that Glen is not in a claret and blue shirt... was this planned? (Lord Lucan)

Maybe you can get the head of another player and stick it on. (Slats)

This really makes me furious. People bought these calendars in good faith and now a 12th of it is ruined. (Robo)

Monday, March 31

Irritable Male Syndrome has set in, the result of this awful month, Glen vanishing, the club in turmoil, and it wouldn't go away no matter how many times I walked the dog round the field. The poor bugger was exhausted by the end of the weekend and now lies inert in its basket. Scotties are not athletic at the best of times and this one is worse than average. Irritable Male Syndrome (IMS) is when a bloke's testosterone levels suddenly drop. Symptoms are fatigue, depression, wrinkles, aches, pains, irritability, extreme grumpiness and the point blank refusal to go anywhere near IKEA on a Saturday. Famous luminaries are Victor Meldrew and that well-known gladiator Max Maximus, aka Russell Crowe. The only difference between a male and female with IMS is that the latter will happily go to Marks and Spencer's and buy a new frock at any opportunity. It was tests on sheep that first uncovered this syndrome when it was discovered that testosterone levels in rams rose in the spring mating season and fell in winter. As levels fell, rams lost the ability to remain calm and rational. According to doctors, men run low on testosterone in their fifties (yup that's me), and gradually lose the ability to do handstands, lift a small car over their head, and by and large stand in need of a good dose of Viagra every now and then. Apparently it is much the same with Indian elephants.

Now, as my IMS subsides, a few intelligent entries can appear for which I am indebted to Phil Bird on the official website;

Alan Wiley refereed our FA Cup quarterfinal against Watford. He was in the news when he was in charge of the critical Arsenal/Everton game at Highbury. As big Duncan Ferguson ran onto the pitch during the 2-1 defeat it is alleged Alan Wiley told one of his linesman to "keep an eye on him." That comment has left Everton manager David Moyes demanding an explanation from the Premier League and the referee's panel.

Apparently Moyes spoke to Philip Don (referee's big wig) and he claimed 'the referee warned the linesman that there would be more aerial challenges from Everton'. That's victimisation and is completely wrong; you cannot pre-judge players. It makes you wonder if his assistants were given the same message regarding Gareth Taylor at Vicarage Road. We had a disjointed game when Wiley (like so many refs this season) seemed to pick on our Welsh international pulling him up for innocuous fouls time and time again.

Phil Bird also writes;

We are at a crossroads. A top thirty side for the last two seasons, we are near that goal again but you sense changes are necessary. A lot of players are out of contract this summer; we need some younger, fresher legs. The wage bill needs to be cut. The transfer market is dead. No fees will be exchanged this summer. Wheeling and dealing is the name of the game. I've got faith in the gaffer - he is as good a manager as any in the Football League. He knows where he needs to strengthen the side. He knows the midfield has been without a battler since Kevin Ball left last summer. With everybody's support he can keep us in that top thirty position and with some changes in personnel, we can even push for a top six slot in 2004.

APRIL

Tuesday, April 1

I hear at long last there are plans to solve the vexed problem of where to re-settle Burnley Cricket Club so that Burnley can redevelop the Cricket Field Stand and the vacated land behind. It's an old plan that has been brought out of mothballs. It was first announced on the Claretsmad website exactly a year ago but has been refined since then, I am told. It is stunningly simple and doesn't necessitate the cricket club moving out of town. All that is involved is the digging up of a large part of the Turf Moor pitch in the centre area exactly 22 yards square. Two prepared rolls of what is known as multituft will be kept for use at the correct temperatures (in a purpose built greenhouse), depending on whether the game of the day is cricket or football. Scientists have developed a new strain of almost indestructible multituft. It is based on the weave used in men's hairpiece manufacture. Having solved the problem of it blowing away in the wind they are 100% confident it will last for several years. For cricket games the multituft will be unrolled into the prepared gravel and loam based hollow square and will be ready marked out with the necessary white lines for cricket. For football the prepared multituft will be marked out with the centre circle and it too will be unrolled into its position when required. At the end of the cricket season it simply stays in position and the rolled up cricket lawn will be stored under the James Hargreaves Stand. The pavilion for cricket games will be The Bob Lord Stand. Seats on rollers will be kept behind the proposed new Stand/restaurant/hotel/-supermarket/Mothercare store, which will replace the old Cricket Field stand and the awful urinals. These mobile seats can then be rolled round on match days. For big football matches i.e. against Man Utd, these seats can be positioned around the perimeter of the pitch to provide extra seating at premium prices. Since these plans first appeared a year ago there have been additional ideas. Officials at the club are said to be so excited about this, that they can one day envisage staging Test Matches. Then there is the further potential for utilising the square by laying temporary flooring for Line Dancing nights. Instead of Opera In The Park the marketing department are pencilling in Singalong At The Turf evenings and Robbie Williams has been pencilled in for the first Pop Night At The Turf.

The club have appointed new accountants 'Dolittle & Diddlum' and have asked them for advice on ways to expand and maximise the club's income-generating base and increase the brand clients (fans).

Wednesday, April 2

Hobgoblin nor foul fiend can daunt our spirit;
We know we at the end shall life inherit.
Then fancies flee away; we'll fear not what men say.
We'll labour night and day to be a Claret.
(John Bunyan 1676)

In pubs and on websites and messageboards the Glen Little controversy and Season Ticket debate continues;

Would he have been loaned to Sheffield Utd? asks one fan.

How long have the club known, when did negotiations start?

Food prices go up, petrol goes up, council tax goes up, get real, why should Turf Moor be different?

Do you also think this is the thin end of something bigger? writes one supporter. Like Stan Ternent leaving before the end of the season?

Instead of bringing a friend free to the Gillingham game with my season ticket, can I have a refund instead?

I think I've seen Glen Little's house up for sale.

The Board are doing their best; the predicament they are in is very difficult.

It's a good move, he hasn't played consistently well anyway,

Of course money, money, money is the issue; we were two days away from administration back before Christmas for goodness sake. We now exist on a knife-edge. What else could the club do?

My season ticket has gone up £20, my council tax has gone up £110. One gives me pleasure and the other… stop whinging and moaning, show your colours .

I think Glen's departure is the tip of an iceberg, something is going on. Just what is the financial truth at this club we all follow?

Would Glen really have earned £100,000 in just eight weeks? That's £12,000 a week.

Why don't the club come clean and tell us?

Just what is the reality?

What a mess we would have been in without the Cup runs. It doesn't bear thinking about.

The Directors and Barry Kilby deserve our trust, they put money in and don't take a salary.

What were the pies like? Delicious, especially Meat and Potato Pie E.

George Burley is appointed interim manager of Derby following John Gregory's suspension some days ago.

Peter Ridsdale resigns as Leeds Utd Chairman. Now £79million in debt and only a handful of points above the relegation places, their situation is one of potential disaster. Peter Reid has just seven games to save them. How would they cope with relegation to the Nationwide? Just imagine a Burnley v Leeds Utd derby game… mouthwatering, isn't it? In his press conference their new chairman Professor John McKenzie referred to the club as a business. There's a lesson there for all of us. This is no longer sport; this is business, with brands, revenue streams, cost bases, projections, accounts, finances, spreadsheets, business plans, bank managers and creditors. They speak in language we don't understand. The Leeds debt however makes Burnley problems almost insignificant and makes the savings on Glen Little's wages appear almost inconsequential in financial terms.

As the dust settles and the message boards quieten down, one thread seems to be that in terms of loss of goodwill and probable lost income from season ticket sales, not to mention increasing disillusion and disinterest in the final four home games the effect is extremely damaging. Had all three players gone - Taylor, Blake and Little - then money-wise the savings would have been enormous and in that respect you might have argued worth doing... but then the football outrage would have been gigantic.

On the other hand the alternative view is that it is a perfectly good move, that Little has not had his most consistent season, that an interim change will do him good, and that the money saved is critically important. The club had to do something.

As things stand at the moment at the commencement of the final month, Portsmouth and Leicester occupy the two automatic promotion places. Sheffield United, Reading, NottinghamForest and Wolves hold the play-off places. At the bottom lie Sheffield Wednesday, Grimsby and Stoke City. Burnley after 38 games are in sixteenth place with 49 points, 12 points above the relegation places and seemingly safe for another season in Division One assuming we can win just one more game to take us above the magic 50 points line. How ironic it is Watford here on Saturday.

Anthony Shandran will remain at York City on loan until the end of the season. In twelve games he has scored twice. Dimi Papadopoulos scored a hat trick in last night's U21 Greek side against Northern Ireland in Belfast. Reports on April 1 from Claretsmad that the club would charge 10p for each visit to the toilets next season, and that a season convenience ticket could be purchased, proved to be nothing more than just a mischievous leak.

Thursday, April 3

Huddersfield are now in administration. Some of their squad have not been paid for five months according to *The Telegraph.* Chairman David Taylor has asked season ticket holders to donate £125 each and admits that there is a 50% chance the club will go bankrupt. The players backed by the PFA in fact lodged the application for administration. This was after one creditor threatened to issue a winding-up petition. Well perhaps season ticket holders at the Turf should be relieved not to have received a similar request from the Burnley Board.

Sky Sports News announced that the £17.2million Leeds loss for the last six months is the largest ever loss for any club. New Chairman Professor John McKenzie made an interesting observation when he said that the new Chief Executive to be appointed would be a businessman first and a Leeds supporter second. The modern executive is not there to be sentimental. They are there to keep a club afloat, to be objective and understand the complicated world of finance. Did you know that Terry Venables job at Leeds wasn't called a job, it was called a service agreement?

Leeds have attempted to control their debt by 'factoring'. No I don't know what this is either. Leeds accounts would have been worse but for the fact that they included the whole of the £26million they received for Rio Ferdinand in their statement. This was even though they only received just half of it, £13million, up front. This they did by selling the remaining £13million debt Man U owed them to another company and received it ahead of time. But they have had to pay commission. Are you as lost as I am by all this? Factoring is not uncommon in the hard world of big business and you can add to that the way in which players are mortgaged to a bank or loan company in just the same way that we buy a house. In simple terms it's spending tomorrow's money, today, which at our own different levels we all do.

At Burnley the mortgaged players are Blake, Ian Moore and Papadopoulos and this is now common practice in football. At Elland Road it is alleged that seventeen non-playing staff have been made redundant saving £3million. One wonders how players at that club on £20,000 and more per week, feel about this. Frankly, if it were me I wouldn't sleep at night. Leeds are now looking to increase revenue through new investors or increased use of the ground.

It begs the question at Turf Moor. Are the potentials of the facilities at Burnley FC fully maximised? How else could they be used? What other events could it stage which would not necessarily take more money off supporters? In the Jimmy Mac there is the undeveloped void between the two tiers. All kinds of ideas have been put forward for it including a Business Centre, Casino and Restaurant. But such projects need funding or partnerships or loans to get them off the ground. The club is hamstrung to a degree by Burnley trading rules and restrictions. These, if my understanding is correct, prevent the club from holding Car Boot Sales, Trade Fairs, Markets, or anything that takes business from Burnley traders. Some towns enforce these restrictions rigidly, some don't.

The Leeds debacle should in fact make us all at Burnley feel better. There is a set of Directors here who put money in and don't take a salary. If I am correct Ridsdale was on something over £300,000 a year at Leeds. At Burnley Andrew Watson said that the debt is now approximately £3million, a manageable amount if prudence is exercised... look at Leicester and Derby. Prior to his arrival, he said, there hadn't been an increase in admission prices for five years, and it was this in itself which necessitated an ongoing programme of rises and which explains the fact that some of the rises were bigger than people would have wanted. Regarding Glen Little, he said, there hadn't been a player sale at Turf Moor for 5 years. And Andrew Watson added for every letter criticising the Glen Little loan, he has had one in support. Significantly, in his early years at the club, the ongoing message he received from supporters from all areas was that people wanted to see this club run as a business so that it then might flourish. But now that proper business practices are in place the club is accused by some of being nothing but moneymakers and concerned only with balance sheets. You just can't win.

Street battles, injuries, violence, confrontations+++ no, not Iraq+++ England supporters at the international last night in Middlesbrough+++ Leeds supporters well to the front+++ what barmpot at the FA decided to hold an England - Turkey game so close to Leeds?+++ England won 2-0+++ Burnley reserves 2 Rotherham reserves 1. Damien Hindle scores two+++ Suggestions that he should be given at least a place on the first team bench before end of season+++ Notts County have been warned that they will be expelled from the League if they do not come out of receivership by May 27. The oldest club in the country will have their status terminated unless financial problems are resolved in the next 53 days.

Friday, April 4

'Show the colours', Cozzo, London Clarets, writes at the beginning of his just posted report of the Bradford game:

No chance of the play-offs, and little danger of relegation, it promises to be a more relaxed final few games than we have enjoyed for several years. What we wouldn't have given for that after five games of the season when we only had one point and the prospect of relegation loomed large. So overall, it's been a good season. Safely in the First Division and two good cup runs that have brought in greatly needed cash after the much vaunted collapse of ITV Digital. Anyone who wouldn't have settled for that at the start of the season was living in cloud cuckoo land.

I learned today that some supporters had stayed away from Pie Day last week as soon as they knew that Sky cameras would be there. I can understand and appreciate why. Sky have this habit of presenting Burnley as the land of cloth caps and whippets. Remember the time we signed Ian Wright? Sky interviewed two fans at the gates to Gawthorpe. And whom did they find to interview? Yup, two blokes with the broadest Burnley twang imaginable, and accompanied by whippets. If I remember it rightly, one of them wore wellies and a cap. It makes you want to cry. To my dismay meat and potato Pie E did not win. I can only imagine this is because by the time people had sampled A B C and D they had no room for an E. I have learned since that the makers of Pie E provide the pies at Man U. I may have to change teams.

The *Lancashire Evening Telegraph* has reported this week that Barry Kilby is ready to sit down with Stan Ternent and start planning for next season's campaign. But he has said that whilst the £100,000 saving on Glen Little will help the manager, the bulk of the Cup run money will help pay debts. First team squad members out of contract will be Davis, Diallo, Beresford, Michopoulos, Branch, Cox, Cook, Armstrong, Payton and Briscoe. Barry Kilby added that the aim is to get out of debt as quickly as possible but the club is now in a position to give Stan Ternent a budget with which he can decide how to proceed. With that budget he can get the best players he can:

We can now make an accurate assessment of what the income will be for the rest of the season... But while we start making decisions about players in the near future it is likely that it will be a while before any new faces come in. I think that with the financial situation everybody will be leaving it later. Discussions will take place but no one will want to bring any players in until July 1st when their previous contract ends.

Significantly Barry Kilby dismissed rumours that Blake and Taylor might have been offloaded on loan along with Glen Little:

I have not even heard the suggestions that Robbie Blake and Gareth Taylor were going to be allowed to leave. But I can say categorically it was never even an option. No one contacted us about any other player, it was just Reading wanted Glen.

Posted by herts-claret on claretsmad messageboard:

For the next three weeks or so I am off to Devon tomorrow morning, then getting married on Saturday. Following that we board a 747 from Heathrow on Monday bound for Hawaii. Season will be all but over by the time I return. Chin up and fingers crossed for a positive end to the season.

Reply from Eli: *How can you do that before we've reached 50 points?*

The BBC used the Turf Moor Leisure Centre for its political debate programme Question Time last night. The temporary studio was erected in the sports hall and a nice fat fee came Burnley's way. The programme was filmed throughout the day and then broadcast in the evening at 10.35. Questions ranged far and wide but no one asked was Ian Moore, Moore, Moore's goal against Bradford really offside?

Saturday, April 5

The Glen Little furore subsides+++ Reading versus Brighton last night on Sky+++ Glen made his debut+++ a shot and a header+++ a few touches+++ Final score Reading 1 Brighton 2+++ Whoops+++ Stan has his budget from Barry Kilby and says he will study it over the weekend+++

Tony Livesey, *Daily Sport* Editor, programme contributor, writer of Stan's book and local lad made good, posted a message this week blasting the critics:

As they say in all the best Baghdad knocking shops... stone me! Here we are heading for our fourth season in Division One and you lot are stringing yourselves up. I'd hate to think how you'd react if we were relegated. It's Glen Little who's gone not your wife. I'm not sure some of you realised how critical this season was for BFC. Clipped with debt - however much we like to think our individual season ticket purchases help - the club was only going to EVER limp through. Survival was the only real option. Of course Stan wanted more, who wouldn't? But taking stock now: two decent cup runs, safety, recouping well over a million that ITV picked from our pockets, you have to admit the season is a success. Yes! Success! Don't kid yourselves either. Next year will be more of the same. If we can possibly survive that, contracts can be re-negotiated and the club we love may just have a future. As it is, take a look around. Derby, Ipswich, Coventry, Sheffield Wednesday, Bradford... all wobbling. I've watched Burnley for 33 years. It's a long haul folks. I've read on here about people wanting a protest or going to Ewood instead or not buying a season ticket next season. It beggars belief. I for one will be in the Turf Moor trenches for the next 33 years, God willing. Does that make me a mug? Nope. It makes me what I am. A Burnley fan. Not a boo boy, not a fair-weather supporter, not someone who expects to win every game. Just a fan who recognises that if some of your howls of outrage reach the ground on matchday, you may well frighten away the people who currently keep our club afloat. Don't forget I am the man who organised the 3.33 protest. I recognise failure when I see it. I don't see it at Burnley. But I do see it in the attitudes of some impatient, impractical supporters.

Ten day break over. Several players write or comment that it should have done them good. Sadly it won't do Paul Cook much good who has an ankle encased in plaster, is a player shortly out of contract and thinks he may have played his last game for the club. A bad late tackle in the Bradford game, unseen by the referee, saw him taken off. He will be missing in all likelihood for the rest of the season. He spoke candidly in the *Evening Telegraph* this week...

I am not sure the supporters really appreciate the problems Stan has had this season. Things have not gone well in the last few weeks but you have to remember he has not been able to buy a single player all season. We have still had two good cup runs and had a chance of the play-offs and that has been a good achievement. He loves Burnley, he loves the club, and he loves the town and every decision he will make will be aimed at getting the best for the club. In a way if you have success and it comes quickly, people forget what went before.

Cook spoke of his future. He would love to stay on if needed, doesn't see himself playing for another league club, feels he can play a bit longer and is frustrated to be sidelined with the ankle in plaster for four weeks. He has played almost 150 games for the Clarets, has a UEFA B Coaching badge, would like to go into coaching and feels privileged to have been in the game so long.

Paul Cook, if you have indeed played your last game for the club - we salute you and offer you our grateful thanks. You have played no small part in our successes of recent seasons.

The Watford website *Blind, Stupid and Desperate* previews today's game. The preview includes:

The Claret's league form since the quarter final has been every bit as miserable as our own... with the crucial distinction that they don't have travel arrangements to Villa Park... The knife has been turned in the wound with the offloading of chief entertainer Glen Little to play-off chasing Reading... players and fans alike have gloomily written off the season with some particularly lacklustre displays... Stan Ternent's biggest problems are in midfield where injuries and loans conspire to reduce his options to virtually nil... Ian Moore referred in a website interview to how the Cup-tie left a bad taste in the mouth and the Clarets should have been in the Semi-Final apparently. Such a bugger when you get outplayed and outfought isn't it? Burnley is never a favourite destination at the best of times... it'll be a select few making the journey to Lancashire where a rare win would secure our First Division status. Leaving us free to concentrate on the Cup. Tee hee.

B******ds. Wouldn't it be nice to stick six in against them?

Sunday, April 6

Well er no... not six... we only managed four. Trouble is they scored seven... yes folks... sorry... you heard it right, seven.

BURNLEY 4 WATFORD 7

After this game we drove home laughing at the absurdity of it and thinking what good value for money it is at the Turf these days... eleven goals, two hat tricks, incidents galore, lovely weather... you could almost get to like it. Then bewilderment sets in and you get to think hey, it's not supposed to be like this. We're not claret and blue any more, just clattered and blue. Not since the days of Queen Victoria have Burnley let seven in at the Turf. But this is not the time or place to give you a quick Victorian History lesson though the bit of Headmaster still in me is desperate to do just that. Oh go on then… did you know the origin of the word crap comes from the inventor of the flush loo, Thomas Crapper?

Anyway, back at Chez Thomas… we down a couple of bottles of the falling over water, we consume a large, very large, Chinese takeaway, we watch the funniest film in years, *My Big Fat Greek Wedding,* and we laugh till we hurt… and then we remember we had been to a home match and lost 7-4, to a team that hadn't won a game since they beat us in the quarter final. Fortunately, full of the Vino Expensivo, it all came back as just blurred, indistinct images. There are no prizes for guessing what the views of fans are. We were outclassed, outpaced, outrun, and humiliated.

'This was a return to the dark days of the mid--eighties, lethargic ferrets on a spring picnic', writes Whitto in his extensive London Clarets match report.

Cries of SuperGlen predictably rang round the ground though it must be said they didn't last long. Marlon Beresford was shamefully barracked, and yet this is the same keeper who has kept us in more than one game this season. MOTM Gareth Taylor scored a hat trick (plus hit the post) and one can only assume it was this and the warm soporific sunshine which resulted in an ending to the game unmarred by prolonged crowd anger and spleen venting. This in truth at the end was a shell-shocked crowd that didn't know what to do, shed tears, boo the team off or cheer Gareth. Thankfully it chose the latter. How interesting that Michael Chopra, a player Watford have on loan from Newcastle, scored four of their goals. This is now four times this season that loan players have haunted us.

A strange thing happened though and we all had to look twice. Stan brought on one of the youngsters. Matty O'Neill made his first appearance and it was undoubtedly his excellent debut, brief though it was, that appeased the crowd. I can't speak for ten thousand others but I left that ground thinking 'my God, we do have youths who can play. We do have a future'. This lad actually looks like an athlete; lithe, slim, quick, with a prodigious throw, a couple of tricks in his locker and he had me leaving the ground with a glimmer of hope. Tony Scholes on Claretsmad has already sung the praises of several of these young lads. O'Neill looked at ease, comfortable, a good 'un, a natural.

Lord only knows what must be going through the minds of Barry Kilby, Andrew Watson and Stan Ternent after this debacle. There is no doubt they are desperate for fans to invest in season tickets so that there is then a clear idea of the money to play around with for new contract discussions. This can be the only reason for the April deadline for reduced price tickets as opposed to June, which all fans prefer. In The *Lancashire Evening Telegraph* Stan said:

I have spent most of my life in the town and what I am hearing is that people are talking about not buying their season tickets again next year. All I know is that we need the help of our fans and if they stay away it will be detrimental to our club. The chairman has already put £5million of his own money in and if it was not for him there might be no club. If the fans don't back us then we run the risk of not being competitive next season. I would love to see them come to the matches and support the lads and I would love to see them renew their season tickets. I will not be in a position to talk to players about signing new contracts for next season until the end of this one because it will all depend on how many season tickets we sell this month. Who I keep, who I let go, who I bring in, it all depends on the amount of money we get from season ticket sales.

Here then is the classic Catch 22 situation. The biggest PR move the club could make at the moment is to extend the season ticket reduced price deadline into June or late May. But an earlier, unpopular April deadline gives a budget indication as soon as possible.

The scenario becomes worse every game and heaven help us all if we lose to Preston on Tuesday. But Stan joked with the press afterwards,"They reckon that Bin Laden and Saddam Hussein were having a chat and they both said they wouldn't fancy that Stan Ternent's job."

If Stan had the press in stitches, Watford had the team tied up in knots. This has to be rock bottom… or is it? There's a new poster being designed. Gillingham got 4, Reading got 5, Rotherham got 6, Watford got 7, roll up, roll up, and see if Preston can get 8. It looks possible that this team will not win again this season. Not that long ago we looked upwards to see how far away from the play-off places we were. All of us now nervously look to see if Grimsby, Wednesday and Stoke have won. That tells its own story.

Spare a thought though for Essex fan Paul Johnson. Drives all the way up here to watch us lose 7-4 and then drives all the way back home only to have a puncture on the M11 just ten miles from home.

Monday, April 7

Images of Saturday afternoon occasionally flickered across the mind as dog and me sauntered along the canal bank watching kingfishers and herons. Geese have come back to start nesting along the edge where the fields dip down into the water's edge. I wandered along wondering what it must be like to be at work in Burnley this morning.

The handful of Watford fans who came up on Saturday were as bemused and bewildered as the rest of us:

This is a lesson for all those who claim there is something peculiar about going to Burnley on a Monday night (2001), Preston on a Thursday (2002), Sunderland on a Tuesday (1996), Plymouth on a Tuesday (1997) or even the Isle of Man! For you just never know what will happen. The assembled souls will always remember this game. It was history, and while memories fade there will always be the books and the videos and maybe even a DVD of the match to give the memory a little jog from time to time. What can never be found on a TV or in a book, though, is the experience of travelling 300 miles with no hope, and travelling back with a huge grin, an inner giggle and the knowledge that you had been part of something totally chaotic, totally frantic, totally unforgettable. This was what being a Watford fan is occasionally about. (Pete Fincham. Watford website. Blind, Stupid and Desperate)

London Clarets Vox Pop is not quite so effusive:

Thank goodness for illness. I spent a comparatively pleasant day and watched the game on Ceefax. Probably the best way to watch it. (Pauline)

Tuesday, April 8

There are warnings that scores of players will be released this summer in cost cutting exercises. One unnamed Premiership chairman has told players to "brush up on their dustman's skills," as he warned of more than 800 footballers being kicked out in the coming months. There are warnings of a brutal cull, that wage bills must be reduced, and that the flood of cheaper footballers from the ever-expanding EU will continue to undercut English players. Last season hundreds of footballers failed to find new jobs. Aston Villa Chairman Doug Ellis said, "Players and their agents have got to realise they are not living in the real world."

The same newspaper, the *Daily Express,* carries the story of Chelsea player Winston Bogarde, reputedly earning £40,000 a week and who has been more or less a permanent reserve there for the last three years. Then Chelsea wonder why they are allegedly £90 million in the red. If Chelsea cancel his contract as expected it will cost them £2million for the remaining year.

Back at The Turf, assistant manager Sam Ellis says "If we keep scoring four we might win a game."

We only scored two, but it was enough.

BURNLEY 2 PRESTON 0

Wednesday, April 9

Reports of my death have been greatly exaggerated
(Mark Twain, Groucho Marx, or John Lennon?)

Pride, dignity and a new lease of life (we hope) returned to Turf Moor last night. With a decimated squad, with three kids on the bench, Pilkington, O'Neill and Chaplow, with the spice of a local derby, and all of us wondering what the night would hold… they come up trumps and never looked like losing. The team, deserving of a mention…

Michopoulos, West, Branch, McGregor, Briscoe, Moore (Ian), Weller, Davis, Blake, Taylor and Papadopoulos.

At The Kettledrum where we called before the game the landlord said Stan had been in Sunday night complaining of a headache, he'd had so many season tickets thrown at him on Saturday. At the cash turnstile a gaggle of supporters stood trying to sell off unwanted season tickets. After Saturday who could blame them?, but I hope they stayed on and came in and saw the display put on tonight. If they didn't they must be kicking themselves. After Saturday just one more win this season looked impossible but as Tony Scholes says on Claretsmad:

> *It's been doom and gloom around Turf Moor for the last month but that's all been lifted tonight after we deservedly beat Lancashire rivals Preston with two goals from Dimitri Papadopoulos and Robbie Blake. Sometimes I think I have just about worked out what Stan is going to do next and I honestly thought he would stick with the same team, but never could I have worked out his changes tonight. There were only two in personnel.*

Not surprisingly, Nik Michopoulos replaced Marlon Beresford in goal and Dimitri Papdopoulos came in for Tony Grant. But even with the eleven names it was surely impossible to believe that he would play Graham Branch in the centre of the defence and move Steve Davis into midfield. And could he employ four strikers and then employ a 4-5-1 system? Yes of course he could. But that's why Stan's the gaffer and I have to buy a season ticket (despite the Watson increases) every season. I could never have come up with that and presumably could not have come up with tonight's performance either. It was cheese to Saturday's chalk in every way possible...

Roberto de Blakio's goal came from a thirty yard free kick of Beckhamesque quality. Dimi's goal was from an angle so acute (the Greeks invented geometry) it defied description. Not a single player didn't run and chase and tackle like tigers. Blake was official man of the match but for me m.o.t.m was the pacy Branch who was a giant at centre back. On top of all this the backing from the crowd was loud and sustained. It was as if the nightmare of Saturday and recent weeks was expunged from all our collective memories before we even set foot in the ground. Magic moment of the match... at the end when Gareth Taylor turned to the Jimmy Mac End and proudly held up his shirt. One last thing... 52 points... now we are safe. There'll be some smiling faces in Burnley this morning.

Sunderland announce total debts of £26million+++ Bury players club together to pay their coach's wages+++ Earl Davis stays at Southport till end of season+++ Ceefax says Stan and Sam announce personal wage cuts to help financial situation+++ the truth here, in spite of one newspaper reporting to the contrary way before Christmas, is that Stan and Sam took a pay cut at the beginning of the season.

Thursday, April 10

Sunderland announce the need to restructure+++ that's a nice way of saying 'sack people'+++ mass redundancies expected with a pool of forty playing staff reduced to twenty-five and up to eighty-three non-playing staff facing the axe+++ Chief Executive Hugh Roberts on Sky says they have a bright future+++ He has the same cheerful optimism as Iraq's Information Minister now renamed Comical Ali, he's the one with the Frank Spencer beret+++ He's the one who said, with an American tank right behind him, we are now crushing the Americans+++ efforts to keep Notts County afloat continue to flounder with administrators rejecting another bid for the club.

Onwards then to Norwich, the island in a bog. I'm one of the ones flying down. I can't decide whether it's the team that needs me, or the accountants need my money. Let's be honest, it's the latter. Thank goodness we have a win at last though, the mood should be a whole lot jollier and perhaps I will have that glass of champers and scoff a few nibbles. The tickets and itinerary have arrived with instructions from the airport people to bring a passport. Now I know Norwich is a long way away and Norfolk's a funny place, but I didn't know it was that far. Newspapers say that American tanks are now within two miles of the city centre but there are no reports of looting. It may be a gentle, rustic place well fed by the blessed Delia, but it was in days of yore a pretty violent place with lots of revolting peasants put down mercilessly by their landlords with about as much consideration for their well being as Saddam used to give his loyal subjects. The name Norwich first appears on coins minted in the reign of King Athelstan, no relation to Ourstan. When the Normans arrived it already had 5,500 inhabitants desperate for a footy team. In 1381 the peasants were just as revolting as ever and executed the mayor. It was a Bishop who next sorted out the peasants, as Bishops were wont to do in those days. Again in 1549 it was noticed how revolting the peasants were and again they were crushed. God, you'd think by now they'd have learned their lesson. With football not invented yet, a Saturday afternoon watching peasants hang at the castle was the in thing with a picnic for afters. So as you can see, violence and riots have occurred frequently in this area as the years have rolled by and, latterly in their Premier days, very often when Leeds United or Tottenham turned up.

I'm not saying what this caper is setting me back. But for the price, me and the Mrs could have a weekend in New York, four days in Paris, seven days in Corfu, three months in The Isle of Man, or six months in Knott End. Thank God we won on Tuesday is all I can say. Apparently the game is a sellout. They must have heard Mrs. T is coming.

Friday, April 11

Sunderland manager Mick McCarthy has put ALL Sunderland players on the open to offers list.

Whilst trawling through the *Lancashire Evening Telegraph* archives looking for some particular info about Burnley I came across something far more interesting. The cost of funerals apparently went up 25% in Burnley a year ago. That's what's known as dead expensive. Seems to me that Turf Moor season ticket increases give far better value than a plot at Burnley Crematorium.

Tony Livesey posts a question on the Claretsmad messageboard, the gist of it being should Glen come back or do we prefer three or four new faces with the money saved? Logic, reasoning and acceptance replace the raw emotion and outrage of just a few days ago. From the twenty-four replies seen so far the general view is that yes, if he does not come back, it should be seen as a positive opportunity and it could benefit the club. Richard Oldroyd's balanced piece on Claretsmad, *Taking A Step Back*, is excellent.

> *Players come and go but Burnley FC remains, that's how it's been, that's how it is, and that's how it always will be...* writes Claretsmad Tony Scholes.
>
> *There will be other heroes again,* writes BabylonClaret.

I have a hunch the Gaffer is relishing the summer to come and the chance to wheel and deal and bring in new faces. On the official website he talks about knowing which players he will retain, the ones he will retain if they accept what he has to offer, and having irons in the fire with regard to new players coming in as well. He doesn't expect to be paying out fees, says there will be a lot of good players out of work this summer and this summer will be a watershed. There will be a lot of good players knocking about, he adds. I think players and agents know what the case is now after twelve months of it, but if the penny hasn't dropped yet, it will in the summer.

It will be interesting, he says. Hmmm, exciting is the word I'd use.

Mrs T is wondering what to wear tomorrow for the plane trip. She has asked if we should take the small suitcase or the large. Now she's looking for the Greek holiday phrasebook we have. I tell her tomorrow is not the time to ask Nik the Greek 'ekete angee na res avgho lemona stin Taverna?' (Do you have artichokes with egg and lemon dressing in the Taverna?).

Saturday, April 12

Blimey it's only 9:10 and we've been to Naarch and back.

The signs were good this morning, an early start and Mrs. T has chosen the black leather coat for today, casual but elegant, and the blue jeans - four Eddie Stobart lorries on the way to the airfield, a black cat crosses our path, my lucky £2 coin in my back pocket… no trouble finding the airfield… a brief look at the sea at Lytham, ah, forgot the tide never comes in here, it's always about three miles out. Lytham is the posh end of Blackpool. Visitors here do not wear hats with Kiss Me Quick on the front. There are no shops selling artificial willies. Flowers in hotel windows are real not plastic.

People are milling about arriving at Warton; Stan is outside Reception having a fag. Inside, the players are in a separate lounge away from the drink. The champers and Bucks Fizz goes down nicely. I've done a million school trips in my other life and I can recognise worry and anxiety on an organiser's face a mile away. Graham Branch grinning is charging round looking for the rest of the team.

All of us, players, fans, directors and stressed-out organisers fearing the wrath of Stan should there be any cock up (didn't a cook once get soup hurled all over him in Stan's book?), move on and mingle together in the tiny departure lounge. Ah there's Phil Bird. Surprise of the day - he's a lot taller than he looks on the radio. Stan and Barry chat away in a corner. Ah there's Deano. The casual but elegant black leather coat works its magic and gentleman Dean gives Mrs T a peck on the cheek. Yes, I always taught my pupils respect for their elders. Some players chat and joke. Some are decidedly quiet and pensive. The three young kids who will be on the bench look nervous and apprehensive. They're probably wondering does everyone have to give the lady in the black leather coat a peck on the cheek?

How do we know what these players are thinking? Tomorrow could have been the Cup game against Southampton, the biggest day of their lives. Some of them must be wondering about contracts. For some of them, when will there be something to eat?

The flight is short, just an hour, just time to eat a breakfast before descent starts and the plate is whipped away and the last bit of sausage. We shall forever judge plane trips now in sausage time. Warton to Naarch is two sausages.

"Dave, Dave, we're landing in a field full of turkeys!"

"No dear, there is a runway at the end of the field full of turkeys."

Quote of the day. We've landed and we are coming down the wobbliest tin aircraft steps onto the tarmac. Behind us a voice says, "So this is what it's like being in Europe."

The airport is grandly called Naarch International Airport. The bus the team is on has the registration KAC 1. Not good.

We're into Naarch by just after 11 or thereabouts and we wander up to the cathedral area in the old part of town along narrow winding cobbled streets. Coffee in a Café Uno.

The middle comes out of the middle of my £2 coin: Definitely not good. Have you ever before had the middle come out of your £2 coin when you pay for a coffee in a Café Uno in Naarch with a very camp maitre 'd. Ooh I say darling, look, your middle's just come out…

A bloke with a yellow and green scarf yells out, "Burnley hah! Worse defence then Baghdad airport." I'm about to tell him to f**k off but I remember I'm in the cathedral precinct. Then I notice he's wearing a dog collar.

More wandering round, on into the cathedral where a choir and organ are rehearsing for a concert: Beautiful, just beautiful. We're in a Cathedral so might as well have a quick prayer for a Burnley win. Lunch in the sunshine at the Cathedral café, music wafts out into the outside air. This is agricultural England innit? It must be. I eavesdrop a conversation at the next table.

"Apparently rouwnd 'ere they use' ter grow mustrrd as ferrrrtloizer…" an old bloke is telling his even older Mrs. Well I never knew that. Lunch and wandering over it's down to the ground. It has been a perfect day so far in warm sunshine. Everybody seems to dress in yellow in Naarch, which is indeed a nice City.

And there dear reader it sadly ends. 1,500 or so Clarets found out that the prayer in the cathedral wasn't long enough. Lighting one candle wasn't enough. 50p in the offertory box wasn't enough. God always remembers he who has sinned or more importantly he who is stingy. Within three minutes we have gifted Naarch the perfect start, a headed goal from a corner. From then on it is all uphill with the same team that won against Preston. But we play well, run hard, chase everything, create several chances, Blake is on form thriving in being the playmaker, Papa plays well, Niko has little to do, much of the first half is all Burnley until Brisser is flattened by a late nasty challenge which goes unnoticed and is stretchered off. A more observant ref than Mr. Conn would have sent Kenton off. For good measure Kenton later almost ends Weller's career. Armstrong comes on and goes off. Enter young Chaplow. Off the pitch he looks about sixteen and frail as a twig. On the field he proceeds to have a fine debut and looks another good 'un, another natural. He does fine.

Second half and then another of those cursed referee decisions that have haunted us all season. The ball strikes McGregor on the elbow. For good measure he has his back to the ball as well. Mr. Conn for his next trick awards a free kick not far from the box.

I write on a postcard;

Dear Referee
If ball strikes arm it is not free kick, it is free kick when arm strikes ball. Did you not lurn this at skool? I am writing this very slowly cos I know you kan not read very fast.

In the ensuing melee sixty seconds later Naarch score their second, thank you ref, end of story. Again McGregor is penalised when the ball hits him again. A Norwich player is then hit on the arm by the ball. Mr Conn waves play on. Conned again. Is it any wonder referee's are above traffic wardens in the I-do-not-like league. But overall we are not disgraced and the team are applauded long and loud. Goodbye perfect day.

Ah well, a swift drink in Frankie and Benny's. Thirty minute coach drive back to airport. Meet up with mainly dejected players in arrival area, spontaneous applause for Chaplow who can't weigh more than about six stone, and is pushing a mammoth trolley laden with three tons of kit. Brisser is OK. The leg is not broken, just rearranged. Deano has one shoe on and one shoe off; blisters. He must have covered a marathon this afternoon. Mood quiet, a bit sombre and down. It cheers up when we find out there are sandwiches on the flight home. Things thaw out. Lots of pictures and chit chat.

Mrs. T plonks herself between the two Greeks and tells them she knows a little Greek. His name is Takis. Ha ha I think I've done that joke before but I never get tired of telling it. There is just time on the plane to eat the four sandwiches and the scone and gulp the thimbleful of coffee before the plates are whipped away again and the wheels hit the tarmac. For the players, just another day I guess, and I know they're pleased to be able to get home early instead of in the small hours. Portsmouth on Tuesday is a long coach journey there and back in a day. Maybe, just maybe, more than one of them was thinking it could have been them in the semis tomorrow. For us, would we do this plane trip again? Yes. Beaten but not disgraced.

NARCH 2 BURNLEY 0

Tuesday, April 15

Portsmouth and Farting Park: I went there once. It's where Charles Dickens was born and it's the home of the British Navy. We used to have a fleet the envy of the world but now money and fuel are so tight that only one boat at a time can go out. If two boats go out they can only get halfway there. Portsmouth and Nelson are synonymous. After his death, which reports say was fatal, his body was brought home in a barrel of brandy. I know people who are alive who would like to come home in a barrel of brandy. There are still bits of olde Portsmouth which Nelson would still recognise if he could get out of the barrel. If you walk around the Point you can smell the tar, hemp and rum of the olden days, hear the long gone shouts of seamen in taverns and feel the tramp of the press gang along the cobbled streets. Sometimes though it's just the Plod carting away Millwall supporters. It's a place full of history and museums. Fratton Park is one. Also associated with Portsmouth are national treasures such as Sir Arthur Conan Doyle, H.G. Wells, Rudyard Kipling and Paul Merson. Don't skip these education bits. They might come in handy some day.

We're staying with Mrs. T's sister in nearby gentle Midhurst, a place of tearooms, waxed jackets and green wellies. A couple of thousand people live here, which is good for green welly sales. It's a picturesque little place on the River Rother, characterised by narrow streets, olde worlde cottages and red tile roofs. Burnley and Midhurst; chalk and cheese, about as different as you can get. Cowdray House is 16th century but was burned down in 1793. Its owner Lord Montague was then drowned the following week in Germany, which is as fine an example of 18th century bad luck as you'll find. Midhurst and the surrounding areas are further characterised by, and famous for, the revolting muck yellow that Lord Cowdray paints his dozens of properties. He doesn't actually paint them himself of course; lackeys do it. I can only assume there is an intense personal satisfaction in driving round the countryside in one's 4 x 4, what ho, being able to spot all one's properties, from twenty miles away if the light is right, or even in the dark for that matter. A wealthy man, is Lord C. We should invite him onto the Board at BFC Towers. But then we run the risk I suppose of him painting it yellow.

This is Polo country to boot and Prince Charles had the odd chukka or two until gout set in, restricting the donning of the royal jodhpurs and the quick rubdowns in the horsebox afterwards with Camilla.

If you're a football fan there is sod all round here, the nearest teams being Portsmouth some miles hence and Brighton - and we won't go into that. Essentially this is fox hunting, golf, polo, Women's Institute, homemade chutney and country pursuits territory.

Sister-in-law lives down a charming country lane, but don't ever think, dear town dweller, that life in the countryside is quiet and relaxing. Cows, diggers and lorries, scowling, belligerent, wild-haired farmers and tractors are on the move from first light. Birds sing and trill non-stop. Pheasants cackle. Woodpeckers tap at anything resembling wood. Double-barrelled shotguns go off all day long. Then there are chainsaws, hammers, combine harvesters, milk tankers, delivery vans, the clip-clop of horse's hooves, dogs barking, hunting horns, private helicopters landing in private fields, and that's not to mention the incessant full volume of the farm labourer's (there's only one) transistor radio. Quiet, the country is not. Personally, I think I prefer city life. All you worry about there are the double-barrelled shotguns.

Wednesday, April 16

Fratton Park is a time warp. The first thing that greeted Mrs T and me were the acres of graffiti all over the walls at the approaches to the away end. Charming. I never knew you could spray and decorate the word f**k so many different ways.

> *Fratton Park is disgraceful in every respect. Surely the time when you could get away with these relics has now passed. Just getting in is hard enough. You tend to get stuck in a queue trying to pass through a couple of turnstiles shoehorned in to a corner of the ground. Once in, don't assume that just because you've got a ticket with a seat number on it and are aiming to sit with your mates you'll be able to. We've had 'sit where you like' here before. And those seats of course are stuck on an end with no roof. Hmm lovely. Only one thing's worse than standing in the rain and that's sitting in it. Not bad for 16 quid! As for amenities you're joking right? You will not get anything to eat or be able to get to the toilet at half time. In fact you'll struggle whatever time you go and if there's a queue down the steps as seems likely, get in it, and go to the food hut or the toilets depending on which you happen to come to first. The gents are tiny, and on the last visit the ladies were through an unmarked door. And if you can't get a pie, count yourself lucky. I did, and it might once have aspired to being lukewarm. Disgusting. All this from a club which played in a higher division than us for many years. Lord knows we've had lean times, but the chronic lack of investment in this place just stares at you. Still it amuses me to think of pampered Premier League fans on this away end next season so good luck to Portsmouth.* (Firmo, London Clarets)

Ground apart, this was Portsmouth's night. Again it was a scratch Burnley team with Branch and McGregor at centre back, Gnohere at left back, Davis in midfield, Papa midfield wide left, Moore (Ian) in the place he doesn't like, midfield wide right. Maylett, recalled from Swansea, came on and was hauled off soon afterwards. O' Neill and Chaplow eventually came on as subs. Brisser went off at Naarch having been clattered, at

Portsmouth it was Papa's turn early on with a knee in his back which just about dislocated his hip. There was no sub goalkeeper on the bench, Beresford was said to be ill. As at Naarch Burnley ran, chased, harried, tackled and put everything into their efforts to spoil the Portsmouth shindig. It looked like we might pull off an unexpected 0 - 0 draw. T'was not to be, as Portsmouth simply wore us down and eventually scored to make the result

PORTSMOUTH 1 BURNLEY 0

No journey by plane for this game for the players. Just a long, gruelling, boring journey by coach during the day with the prospect of an overnight journey home after the game: the footballer's dream. This was the night Portsmouth were supposedly expected to make easy work of the division's second worst defence. What were we there for if not to be the fall guys, the patsies and the sacrificial lambs as Portsmouth rattled in the goals and clinched promotion in style? Not so. We made them work, struggle, puff and pant. Again Chaplow and O'Neill showed that there is young talent at the club. Merson, very much the difference between the two sides, missed a generously given penalty, we had chances of our own, and in fact the first half belonged to Burnley. Stan claimed we should have had a penalty when Moore Ian went over but referees these days are becoming immune to Mooro's diving impersonations of a man on the end of a foul. To be fair, Redknapps' shrewdly collected thirty-somethings eventually deserved their win. They had the better chances and celebrated their promotion after the game raucously and joyously, as we scurried away into the night, licking our wounds, and leaving them to their celebrations and blaring car horns which no doubt went on well into the small hours. The noise from the Portsmouth fans had been deafening throughout most of the game. When was the last time we heard noise as incessant and thunderous as this at Turf Moor? It rolled round the ground all night in continuous cascades and waves and was surely worth an extra player. But Burnley refused to give in and it was only in the 75th minute that Portsmouth at last broke down Burnley stubbornness with McGregor and Branch superb all night. Weller was back to his best in midfield. Niko too was in constant action and almost saved the Todorov shot which brought Portsmouth to their Premiership target.

Will they survive? We wish them well for like us they are not the biggest of clubs. They have won promotion with shrewdness rather than a flash wallet. And how can you not like 'arry Redknapp? Sure, chairman Milan Mandaric has money but he has used it wisely. It has gone on free transfers, loan signings and salaries, allegedly £12million a year, rather than big money purchases. How it has paid off. There is talk of moving to a new ground to be built on nearby disused railway yards. Mandaric talks of funding new players to help retain their place in the top flight. And the irony; as Redknapp takes Portsmouth up, his old club West Ham, who sacked him, look certain to come down.

Ah well, beaten but not disgraced, just as at Norwich. On the showings of these two games all is certainly not doom and gloom and the more I see of the two youngsters the more I like them. Both are fast, agile and slim. They look and move like footballers and have a relish for the game and getting into the action. You can't help thinking that at a club like Nottingham Forest they would be given an extended run so that they would grow and blossom. What struck me too at the game was the amount of support Burnley has that is southern based. We seemed to be surrounded by London, or West Country or south coast accents. Our little corner of the ground was packed and more than just a few had made the horrendous journey down from Burnley. On one coach going home was a Lancashire-based Portsmouth fan. At least one person went home happy and we don't begrudge him that, one bit. One interesting thing, according to the Pompey programme Gnohere apparently is Irish. We shall have to rename him O' Hery.

Friday, April 18

Tigana gets the chop at Fulham+++ Francis gets the boot at Crystal Palace+++ Chairman Simon Jordan says he's had f**k all, or words to that effect, for the £30million he has invested in the club+++ He wants, nay demands, Premiership football at Selhurst Park+++ For £30 million he's got Palace just three points more than Burnley+++ Burnley got three more points today but alas they were on Robbie Blake's driving licence which he must now do without for six months on account of doing 36mph in a 30mph zone in Padiham.

Saturday, April 19

It's our big day. Me and a friend are sponsoring the match ball. My pal imports and supplies those motorised invalid carts for the aged and infirm that softly hum round Asda and M&S and Safeway and such like places. I make no comment other than to say if Stan doesn't get the average age of this team down this summer there might be a few of these machines here at the club soon. Anyway, we are to have a day of luxury with the toffs in the Bob Lord best seats. I've followed this club since 59/60 and never once have sat on this side of the ground. It's a strange feeling walking in there. We're due to meet official legends Andy Lochhead and Tommy Cummings and have a three course nosh. We've gotta wear a shirt and tie, not eat the peas with our knife or finish up the gravy with a spoon or drink tea out of the saucer. This is VIP country.

We are to enjoy the game in style. There's free this and free that, pens, programmes, pictures… most unusual for Burnley... have they forgotten they owe millions?.. there must be a catch somewhere… Oh yeh, the price.

My gawd we've even got a reserved parking space. And best of all we're playing… wait for it… Gillingham. Talk about value for money. This is the team that is such an attraction that today every season ticket holder can bring a friend free. And here am I paying a fortune to get in. How do I do it? Pillock!

Suddenly the warm summer-like weather of the past few days has been replaced by icy, cutting, winds from the east. In the Bob Lord stand any wind from the east blows straight up yer trouser leg. Not nice. But inside the Sponsor's Lounge the warmth is comforting and best of all there's our own bar. Here are our hosts, Tommy Cummings and Andy Lochhead. Tommy still looks like Tommy and Andy still looks like Andy. I say that because many football legends, a la Georgie Best, you have to look twice to remember who they are when age has been unkind to them. Age has in fact mellowed and softened the craggy features of Andy Braveheart. There's now a gentleness and roundness, the edges have become softened. This is not to say he doesn't still look hard as nails and could probably head a ball, or me, half the length of the pitch.

In the Chairman's Lounge there is a framed newspaper report of the greatest goal ever scored at Burnley - the goal by Tommy Cummings when he took the ball the complete length of the field, beat every man in front of him, some of them twice in fact, had a cup of tea, and eventually smacked the ball home after the most mesmerising run in Turf Moor history. It was remarkable because Tommy was a centre half. The Chairman's lounge is all carved panelling and a throwback to Victorian times filled with memories and nostalgia and the history of yesteryear. But in the corner inside a polished cupboard is a computer linked to the ticket office so that the Chairman can see how the cash tills are ringing at any minute. Oak panelled it might be, but this is business. It has to be.

It's Andy Lochhead who takes us round the ground. At the foot of the stairs in the main entrance hall we pass the portrait of Bob Lord, the one where the watching eyes follow you as you walk by. You can sense the respect and even affection as Andy speaks about him, of how he made the club, was far thinking, a butcher by trade and a butcher by nature, according to some.

"I only got sent off once and that was in a reserve game. As I came off Bob Lord glowered and growled at me. I never got sent off again," said Andy.

Then it's on into the tiny dressing room where kit is hung up ready for the team. Andy holds up a pair of briefs.

"We called them jockstraps in my day," he says in his soft Scottish burr. "Mine were made of asbestos. They had to be. They had a big job to do." You believe him as well.

We walk out onto the pitch down the tunnel and that's some spectacular sight at the far end as the Jimmy Mac Stand rises up into the sky. I'm a kid again running down the tunnel and looking at that far end, pretending it's massed with supporters shouting acclaim…

On we wander, through the pressroom. "This is where Stan takes the credit if we win, and if we lose…"

I pick up a Nationwide Newsletter. There's an interesting statistic inside that Paul Merson leads the list of players with the most assists, twelve to be exact, but Robbie Blake is only three behind that.

Eventually we're back in the warmth of the Sponsor's Lounge. Tommy is doing the time of the first goal. I pick 28 minutes. Memorise that; you'll need it later. There's always a goal scored in the 28th minute in the Nationwide. The food is good, the company excellent. Andy and Tommy are two first-rate hosts. Could you ever imagine that a man as hard and intimidating as Andy on the field could be so gentle off it? They say Norman Hunter is the same. As we eat, on the TV in the corner Rangers and Motherwell are kicking lumps out of each other. What more could you want while you eat Yorkshire Pud? Well, what Mrs. T wants is Gareth to be motm so she slopes off to the Man of the Match sponsors and suggests they choose her hunky pin up.

"Why… are you his mother?" asks one of them.

Outdoors, she actually collars him by the touchline as they are warming up and over he comes. I'm beginning to worry though that back in the dressing room they'll be saying, "Hey guys, you know that lady in the black leather coat, the one on the plane at Norwich, the one in the corner at Portsmouth, the one in the coat that's elegant but casual… well… she's here again…"

She is over the moon that whilst at the touchline he says to her, "How are you?" Sadly I have to report that according to reliable witnesses, it was actually, "Who are you?".

What more could you want, I was asking? A win would be nice. And win they did.

BURNLEY BABES 2 GILLINGHAM 0

Sunday, April 20

In truth, today began badly. The omens were not propitious, the signs gloomy, for what did that dog do before we left? Huh, unspeakable things. We have not mentioned him on these pages recently but today, as we were about to leave the house dressed to the nines, looking like fully qualified VIPs, all set to go, what does he do but hoik a large dead fish out of the pond, a very old, dead, smelly fish and proceed to carry it triumphantly to the lawn. On the lawn he pats it around for a while, plays football with it, lobs and tosses it around, heads it, juggles with it, jumps on it, and then rolls all over it, wallowing in the pong. For good measure he then eats it. The entrails when I examined them would have given an Ancient British soothsayer hallucinations for a fortnight. Another defeat seemed to be the forecast.

If you could give prizes for names Gillingham would be up there at the top somewhere with Nyron Nosworthy, Mamady Sidibe, Akwasi Edusei, Perpetuini and Jones Awuah. I bet none of them come from Ramsbottom. Didn't do them any good though. Even with another scratch team, the fish intestines predicting otherwise, Deano injured, and Weller going off injured, all ended well. Drissa was back, and Branchy gave another towering centre back performance. O'Neill was in the starting line up and four other youngsters were on the bench. This, once we scored, was a game where the result never seemed in any doubt. A Taylor volley put Burnley ahead in the 28th minute… the 28th minute. Nobody was more surprised than him. His last volley went over the stand at Norwich and finished up on the airport runway. It took him several minutes to get over the surprise of this unusual feat of foot and then to stop showing Sam Ellis the boot, left I do believe, that had brought about this phenomenon. It seemed at this point his new magic footwear would indeed earn him man of the match; but ah dear reader, not so. For so majestic, so commanding, so unbeatable was the lightning quick Graham Branch that it was he who was duly selected for the honour. And rightly so. He is being referred to now as Der Kaiser Branchenbauer, a far cry from the different shouts he was hearing a year ago.

Drissa scored the second from another O'Neill long throw and let us now discuss this second phenomenon of the day - the O'Neill throw. Quite simply it is as good as any corner and heads unerringly for the penalty spot where unsuspecting defenders seem mesmerised by its trajectory. It goes like an arrow. Taylor scored his goal courtesy of an assist that resulted from an O'Neill throw. He had an excellent game. So did Chaplow, and did any Claret fan ever expect to see the day when Stan would have four young 'uns on the bench and would end the game with three of them on the field? Stan is turning his own theories upside down.

We return to the comfort of the Lounge. As we do so my pal John and I walk in the footsteps of Jimmy Mac. We go weak at the knees.

Branchy comes in to receive the man of the match award:

Graham Branch quite simply got nothing wrong; he won all his headers, countless tackles and made great use of the ball. I'm not sure I could have envisaged Branchy playing in the middle just a few short weeks ago but he looked comfortably at home there today. (Tony Scholes, Claretsmad)

Emma, 24, slim, attractive, one of our group, had a different view; "Doesn't he scrub up well?"

"The time of the first goal was 28 minutes," boomed microphone man from behind the bar somewhere. "And the winner is DAVE THOMAS." Brilliant, here's a game I could have got into for free but at least I've won a ball I can put on the mantelpiece.

Only just over 10,000 attended today and that's a shame. Today we might just have seen a glimpse of the future and if we don't win again this season we are now as safe as houses for another year. And next week, the dog can have another fish.

Monday, April 21

Not much left now, is there, as we head on to Nottingham Forest who ride high in the play-off places and should in theory give us a walloping. In ye oldene days when it was two points a game, there were always three games over the Easter period and that was when championships were won and lost, or promotion gained. Few teams ever got a maximum six points and players and management played three games in four days, without a murmur. Nowadays, any team who had to do that would be horrified, especially our pampered Premiership prima donnas.

The City Ground is the only ground in the country (correct me if I'm wrong) where swans can occasionally be seen gliding across the pitch. 'Tis true this only happens when the River Severn floods and the last time this happened was in 1947 when the water was so high that even the goalposts disappeared. And we grumble about Gawthorpe. Tut tut.

Today though memories are stirred of the game at Turf Moor earlier in the season in December when Forest fan Nathan Blake was killed. Our thoughts are with him and his family again. There is little more to be said for the trial is still pending. All of us hope and wish for a trouble-free day.

Nottingham is of course steeped in history. The castle is no longer a castle but a Mansion House built over the ruins. Kings came and went, Edward III, Edward IV, Richard III, Charles I and King Brian the Clough. The legend of Robin Hood is mostly made up. His real name was Kevin Costner. Beneath the castle is the world's reputedly oldest pub Ye Olde Trip To Jerusalem. The rooms are carved out of the rock on which the castle stands and it is said to date back to Crusader times, 1189 to be precise. Knights would gather here for a kickabout before setting off for their favourite pastime, that is to say, trotting off to the Holy Land for a couple of years to sort out the infidels. Today it takes about two weeks. The Olde Trip specialises in giant Yorkshire Puddings filled with sausages or meat and veg. And speaking of Yorkshire puddings, guess which team were playing Nottingham Forest in 1968 when the Main Stand burned down… yup… Leeds United.

Raleigh bicycles, Boots the Chemists and Player's cigarettes all started in Nottingham. It was in 1877 that John Player cigarettes first appeared. Boots cough lozenges appeared ten years later… honest, I kid you not.

The City Ground (surely one of the most unimaginative of football ground names), is another of our graveyards. Burnley have not won there for 39 years and that goes back to the days of Ian Towers and Willie Irvine who scored three between them. Forest today raise and sell young quality players like we used to and seem to be recovering from their financial troubles of a year ago. It has been very much David Johnson's goals that have put them in the top six but he has only scored four since the New Year. Forest are without a win in the last four games and are now only two points ahead of Ipswich whose rise upwards has been steady and relentless since Joe Royle took over. It was this time last year of course that we ourselves were clinging to a play-off place with Gazza (now in an Arizona rehab centre) on our books. For the first time in four years we now have nothing to play for. It feels quite strange and there are those who suggest that the lack of stress and tension and nerves and nailbiting is actually quite pleasant for a change. Firmo's London Clarets website piece on the subject is well worth a read.

Ah well, it wasn't quite a walloping but it was another defeat.

NOTTINGHAM FOREST 2 BURNLEY 0

If you haven't won in four, scored only one in four, need a win, who yer gonna call?

Goalbusters… Burnley, who else?.. who yesterday gave away their eightieth league goal of the season. I begin to think this season that's why we exist. Norwich needed a win; we were conveniently there. Portsmouth needed a win; we were suitably on hand. Forest needed a win, yup there we were. It's a bugger. It's also a bugger when in all three games we could have got something from them. At Norwich, two gifted goals; at Portsmouth we are denied a penalty and off Portsmouth go, run up the field and they score. At Forest we gift them a goal from a nothing thirty-five yard speculative shot when they were just messing about and perambulating around in no man's land with nowhere to go. It's a beggar. No it's bigger than a beggar, it's a bugger.

"A massive stroke of luck for Forest," said Phil Bird on the commentary.

Why don't we ever get massive strokes of luck? Because we're Burnley that's why. And who was on hand at the end to wrap it up for Forest after a poor clearance fell straight to him. David Johnson in the final minutes, David bloody Johnson who has only scored four since Christmas. I give up.

Of greater importance perhaps is that the day, and the game, went off with no trouble between supporters. DC Mark Webster said:

The behaviour of both sets of fans was impeccable. There was no tension, no bad vibes and most Burnley fans travelled down in a reflective mood. I think a lot of fans stayed away because of what happened at the game here earlier in the season but we are delighted to say that there were no arrests before or after the game.

Before the game skipper Steve Davis presented a bouquet of flowers to his rival skipper Gareth Williams in memory of Nathan Shaw.

We now know we won't be playing Sheffield Wednesday next season or Grimsby. It looks reasonably certain Brighton will go down as well which saves us the long trek to that awful stadium where nobody is safe from the rocketman. As for the other two, it's a shame. Grimsby do a good plate of fish and chips and we were definitely due for a win there but now won't get the chance. Sheffield, it's just a tragedy and an easy game to get to. Sunderland and West Brom we know already will be at the Turf next season. Both bring massive away support, good for the coffers. West Ham won today and Leeds are only clear of the bottom three now by three points. The final relegation place must surely be taken by one of them. Wigan will certainly be coming up from Division Two. Will Paul Jewell make a bid for Robbie Blake (that's the whisper)? Accrington Stanley will certainly be in the Conference. Morecambe of all teams could win the play-offs and reach Division Three. Bugger Burnley, I'm now watching to see if Oldham make it to Division One, Morecambe reach Division Three, Stoke stay up, that's a nice game to get to, Leeds join us in Division One. Who says the season is ended?

Tuesday, April 22

Clubs in debt or facing debt could face Draconian new measures next season. Clubs who go into administration could face a points deduction, relegation, or even lose their place in the League if new proposals are accepted. To dissuade more clubs choosing to go into administration, the League want to introduce penalties that would persuade clubs not to choose that route. The 72 clubs meet soon and will discuss their proposals. A working party has come up with proposals and sanctions, which will be considered at the meeting, ironically in Leicester's Walkers Stadium. Mr. Neil Warnock, whose Sheffield side beat Leicester 2-1 yesterday, was scathing in his comments about clubs in administration i.e. Leicester, being able to go on and still win promotion to the Premiership.

The options to be considered are, a deduction of six points, a deduction of twelve points or relegation at the end of the season. The most hard-hitting proposal is that clubs entering administration for the second time in any three-year period should be removed from the Football League. It goes without saying that the implications for Burnley are obvious. It was alleged that the club was only two days away from administration earlier this season, and though the club's financial problems are stabilised they are far from rosy.

What is rosier however is the general view of Burnley's performances over the last few weeks since beating Preston. Claretsmad Tony Scholes writes for many of us in his post-Nottingham comments:

A year ago none of us cared how we played, the only thing that mattered was how many points we had won as we fought to win a place in the end of season play-offs. This time our season has been over for weeks and for the first time in ten years we were left with nothing to play for other than pride with weeks to go. To be honest we were failing miserably and pride was a word that in no way could be used for some of the performances. The weeks that saw us lose the cup tie at Watford and follow it up with defeats at Sheffield United and Walsall must have been one of the worst weeks for some time, three defeats and three performances, that were if we are being kind, appalling. Things got worse and culminated in us throwing one in big style against Watford in the most farcical of ways. Since then there have been a couple of home wins and more defeats away from home but today's defeat at Forest, as was the case at Portsmouth, was light years away from those in that most miserable of weeks...

...We lost it 2-0 but most left the City Ground more upbeat than anyone could have imagined after a performance that could easily have upset Forest's play-off hopes...

...A 0-0 half time scoreline was the least we deserved and from a Burnley line up that would have been impossible to predict just a short time ago...

... It is fair to say that the discussions on the coach journey home were all about the positives rather than the negatives - and that says much about our performance at a ground where we haven't picked up a single point since a draw in 1969 and where it is almost forty years since we won.

Wednesday, April 23

Leeds won 2-0 yesterday unfortunately and look safe+++ Glenn Roeder, Waddle's assistant manager whilst here at Burnley and now manager at West Ham, is in hospital with a suspected stroke+++ Man U go out of Champions League beating Real Madrid 4-3 at Old Trafford but losing on aggregate 6-5+++ Our former maestro Chris Waddle expresses an interest in the vacant managers post at Chesterfield+++ He was a very good vacant manager when he was here+++ reserve team striker Damian Hindle breaks jaw in three places in a sickening collision in this week's reserve game. A four-hour operation was necessary to repair the damage+++ Burnley announce the retirement of both Paul Cook and Andy Payton.

The messageboards fill up with tributes to both of them. Their time at Burnley coincides with all the good things that have happened over the last four years. Andy Payton is on record as saying that John Bond releasing him was the greatest disappointment in his football career. Payts once scored the winner for Celtic in an Auld Firm clash but to come back to Turf Moor was always his dream. Both players have been key factors in Burnley's resurgence since promotion in 2000. Andy Payton has scored 81 goals in his time here but sadly, for various reasons, has hardly featured this season. Both of them have played nearly 200 games. This cannot be said to be the end of an era for they have not been here long enough, but they have made their mark, left their imprint and are now members of that small fraternity whose names will be remembered for many years to come. They are part of Burnley folklore. Where we are now, established in Division One, is very much down to them.

Friday, April 25

Nationwide Chairmen and Chief Executives met yesterday to discuss various proposals with regard to restructuring the play-offs and penalising those clubs who go into administration. On the official club website Phil Bird has this to say:

Perhaps I should whisper this but I actually agree with Neil Warnock when he says that Leicester's promotion was unjust...

... The process of administration has allowed City to approach their creditors and agree a reduced settlement. So whilst other clubs including our own, have strived to balance the books, City can switch funds to their wage bill allowing them to reject bids for their better players. A level playing field, I don't think so.

Our board have worked miracles to agree deals with our creditors to defer debt and keep us out of administration whereas Leicester have worked the system. Leicester City should not have been allowed to achieve promotion whilst in administration. Grimsby Town shouldn't have been relegated whilst Bradford City, who underpaid creditors last summer, have survived. It's like playing poker, issuing an IOU and not having to honour it...

Administration: Is it a stigma to be avoided and an admission of poor management? Or just playing the system, a ruse and a ploy to avoid paying the bills?

At their meeting they did indeed announce proposals for some of the most radical changes in league history. The play-offs will now be extended to include clubs third to eighth thus involving six clubs instead of four. This means of course that Burnley will finish 9th next season. It is quite possible that a club just a few points away from relegation at the end of March could have a good late run and reach the new style play-offs. Division Three clubs will face a player salary cap of 60% of annual turnover and this scheme will be extended to Division One and Division One a year later if successful. Decisions on points deductions or even relegation for clubs going into administration were left for more discussion at the next July meeting.

The sign of the times is Coventry, £24million in debt, who have released fifteen players according to *The Express*.

Saturday, April 26

IT ONLY HAPPENS AT BURNLEY 2 SHEFFIELD WEDNESDAY 7

I bear it all with a patient shrug, for sufferance is the badge of all our tribe.
(Dassey, Claretsmad messageboard, and William Shakespeare)

It's happened again. It's just bloody ridiculous. It can't go on. We can't take any more. These scorelines are supposed to be the other way round. Will somebody please tell our players, our manager and his coaches?

Funny, I had a bad feeling when I saw the Commercial Manager walking away from the ground down Lebanon Street - and that was before the game. He must have known something we didn't. Our goals against column now reads 87, the worst in the Division. I've been writing about acts of selfless devotion to the Burnley cause. You think of things like flying over from New York, or divorcing the wife, or selling the last bits of furniture. Now just going to any home game is an act of selfless devotion. Sheffield Wednesday for God's sake are already relegated. Statistics, results, events prove conclusively they are crap. And they put seven in against us. Can we use the excuse that West, Drissa, Cox, Cook, Briscoe, Weller were all missing. Dare we mention the name Glen Little (who scored today)? That's seven regulars missing. Can we mention that our two goalkeepers are both having a nightmare time at the moment? No matter, today was bewildering and left Stan Ternent, Sam Ellis, Mick Docherty and Ronnie Jepson huddled in a touchline committee meeting without any answers.

Stan was blunt. "It's back to five years ago and I can't wait for the summer now so I can build a new team, because I have to. The end of the season can't come quick enough. I've known for some time who I want to keep and who I don't. Whether the ones I want accept what I can offer, I don't know though, so we'll see."

He spoke about Ian Moore who was sent off very early in the game. "He got what he deserved. The ref tells me he kicked the man and he deserved to be sent off so I'll be dealing with that matter internally."

Ternent was again pleased with his young players though. "They did very well again and a few of the other players can take a leaf out of their book."

What is there to report about this latest debacle, this banquet of goals, this feast of football, this harvest of clangers, unfortunately all at the wrong end? It began badly and then got worse. The first goal within minutes was a gift though it could be argued the long shot hit a pile of sand in a six yard box that looked like Pilling Beach and kicked up viciously, taking Niko by surprise. Whatever, Nik looked like he wanted the ground, or sand, to swallow him up there and then. From then on it was all downhill. Have we come back to win any league game this season after going a goal behind? From that point on Wednesday, big, strong, determined, but by no means brilliant, looked like they could score at will. They really could have had ten. Their 4,000 fans in carnival mood sang and sang and when towards the end they began to sing Always Look On The Bright Side of Life, more than just a few Claret fans sang along with them. Further calamity struck Niko when he was stretchered off with a neck injury. Marlon came on. Critics might point to more goalkeeping errors. All I can say is that without our two goalies we might have faced a massacre. Stan says five of their goals were gifts and they only scored one good one. The seventh seems to have gone missing somewhere. Roberto di Blakio scored our two, one from the penalty spot. The other was a result of yet another goalkeeping error this time by their custodian between the posts. Matt O'Neil was named man of the match and he and Chaplow were our two best players. They must wonder if it's like this all the time at Burnley.

London Clarets Vox Pop was hard hitting:

We made Sheffield Wednesday look like a top Premiership side, rather than one that'll be in Division Two next season... this is about lack of morale amongst the playing staff - we have some decent players, but for whatever reason they're not performing. (Pauline)

I think that when the Board loaned out our best player (Glen Little) four weeks ago, it sent a message to all the players that the season was over... in all the years I have been watching Burnley this is the most bizarre season I've witnessed. (Woody)

For the first time I'm seriously worried about getting relegated next season. If we carry on like this, we're one year behind Sheffield Wednesday... Radical change is needed or we'll go down next season. (Firmo)

It was a good view from the away end... the drains in the gents really need sorting out. (Paul, Sheffield Wed supporter).

What a way to end your career. In the programme Stan announced the departures of Payton, Cook and also Gordon Armstrong. Gordon can proudly tell his grandchildren that not only did he play in a Cup Final but that his last ever game was a 7-2 defeat. Not nice.

Andy Payton and Paul Cook took their bows and said farewell before the game as planned. The crowd rose in unison. The applause was long, loud and sustained. It was undeniably emotional. Payton had been offered the chance to play as Captain but declined saying he was disappointed not to. We can only assume he didn't feel himself fit enough. He made the right decision. My boyhood hero Ray Pointer came on at half time for the draw and must have wondered where he was.

Supporters, websites, messageboards, people leaving the ground, people in the pubs, people in town, feel shellshocked and numb. Burnley 4 Watford 7 had a certain amusing novelty value. But this, this was just a sad, sad way to end the season at Turf Moor. The suntanned referee Mr Clattenburg was the final addition to the collection of oddbods that have been here over this last season with his collection of decisions, some of which were just inexplicable.

To cap it all there's this on Planet Football Blue Is The Colour website:

LITTLE WANTS ROYALS MOVE

Glen Little has suggested that he will leave Burnley, should Reading make a decent offer for his services... "I was told I was going to Reading on loan so I said OK. But nobody has told me what happens at the end of that. I will just have to wait to find out, but if there is a chance of staying at Reading then of course I would have to be interested".

Tuesday, April 29

How can we cheer ourselves up? By gum we need to. There have been suggestions put forward for new shirt sponsors on the messageboard+++ POLO because there's a big hole in the centre+++ 7UP+++ Dog food maker WINALOT have turned us down+++ TAMPAX because we're going through a rough period+++

Or let's think about Coventry, just one win this year and £24million in debt?

Or how about Leeds, just three points from relegation and in bigger trouble than we are. The *Yorkshire Evening Post* carries the story that nobody is buying season tickets. Big surprise.

In the *Lancashire Evening Telegraph* however there's this today about Glen.

As far as I know the intention for me is to come back to Burnley at the end of the season... I'm under contract with Burnley and I've always been happy here... I haven't heard anything... I suppose it will be sorted out in the Summer.

Or how about the Awards Ceremony last night we went to for the first time. Research for this book is unceasing and there were pies to be sampled just to check they were up to standard. It took a second pie to confirm my views. They're OK but Pie E was better. Der Ceremoniesmeister was Mick Docherty with a nice line in understated pith. Mrs T couldn't believe that the now bespectacled and studious looking Mick was the same lad we used to watch in the Youth Team all those years ago. Gareth swept the board as expected but Deano picked up awards for goal of the season at Stoke. Maybe his Reading goal was even better but it came at the end of the 5-2 defeat and most people (including me) had left by then. Ain't life a bugger. Mrs T has now transferred her affections from Colin Firth's Mr D'Arcy in *Pride and Prejudice* (especially the wet shirt bit), to Big Gareth in his number

9 shirt. At photograph time she almost swooned in the radiance of his glow. I have banned all pictures of him in the house.

Our table would have made an award for the most indecipherable autograph but we couldn't read any of them. Most improved player of the year award went deservedly to Graham Branch, which must come as a big surprise when you're thirty-one. Worst shirt of the night award went to Brad Maylett who clearly shops not at Oxfam but in the bins behind. Best newcomer went to Drissa. Apparently he still thinks Burnley is Barnsley. Interesting that it was Deano, Gareth, Branchie, Marlon and Robbie Blake who stayed longest, to their credit. The younger lads stayed too but we suspect they may have been eyeing up the teenage totty.

The club too deserves an award every now and then. A while ago this season I heard a story about a dear little old lady somewhere in Burnley who'd had her small front lawn ruined by builders who had come to do some repairs. Upset and not knowing who to turn to she phoned BFC Towers. The problem was relayed to the groundsman who went up and sorted out the lawn. Nice.

'Fretters' put out a post on Claretsmad messageboard after Saturday's game:

> *Just thought I'd share some generosity with you. In January my mum was diagnosed with cancer (she's responding well to treatment) and we wanted to arrange it so she could go to the match today. She can't walk very far so we phoned the club to arrange a parking space and they said it was fine. But about half an hour later they phoned back and offered us free hospitality for the game and an after match meal in the James Hargreaves suite for up to four people. After all the season ticket price rantings and general having a go at our club's policies I thought this was quite heartwarming.*

I met Fretters' mum Mrs Fretwell at the Awards Ceremony when Tony Scholes introduced us. She was not only delighted with the gesture from the club (which was arranged by Alison Loftus), but also with the presentation to her of Graham Branch's shirt by the man himself who came to see her after the game. It takes a top man to do that when you've just lost 7-2.

Wednesday, April 30

Poor Shrewsbury are relegated to the Conference after losing last night to overjoyed Carlise who escape the dreaded drop+++ Impoverished Third Division clubs must be delighted at the prospect of the new trip to Yeovil+++ Leeds United, in danger of relegation and administration, are given a severe warning by the City to get their house in order and their act together. Peter Ridsdale it is revealed has received a £383,000 severance package. Chief Operating Officer Stephen Harrison who is also to leave will receive around £234,000+++ New Executive Chairman John McKenzie embarking on cost cutting is axing club cars. A staggering seventy-five employees have a club car+++ Leeds United just bleeds money.

A revolt of First Division clubs is threatening a split in the Football League over their demands for a bigger share of money available. My Lord, my Lord, the first division is revolting. Yes, I know, the second division isn't much better either. Millwall Chairman

Theo Paphitis is leading the moves, which include the First Division having their own Chief Executive. The proposals will be voted on at The League's general meeting in June. If prevented, then Paphitis warns that First Division clubs will go their own way. The First Division would like a knockout competition of its own and a TV deal to go with it to seek some compensation for the money problems that have resulted from ITV Digital, especially as penalties may be imposed in the future on clubs going into administration. This time they warn that they will go ahead with or without the co-operation of second and third division clubs.

From LancasterClaret on the Claretsmad MessageBoard:

Listening to Shrewsbury v Carlisle on the radio last night. Nice mention about the Orient game and then the phone-in after the game, they had a Shrewsbury director on. The poor bloke was close to tears and kept apologising to the fans as he regarded it as the Board's fault they had gone down. Must admit made me think about the Orient game and how lucky we are. I know it's been said before, but it puts things in perspective. Last night I realised the season could have been so much worse.

With supreme irony the Reserves won this afternoon. The score, 7-2: somebody up there, He who watches over all of us, has a nice sense of humour. Robbie Blake scored a hat trick. The Reserves now should not be relegated but it needs the final game to see them absolutely safe. No one wants them to be playing against really poor opposition, which is what relegation would mean.

It seems Blakey will not be going to Wigan. He can't go anywhere now he has lost his licence.

MAY

Thursday, May 1

Burnley you're a team that can tear me apart
But you're also the club lodged deep in my heart.
(Abigail Fawcett 2003)

"I told you I was ill"
(Epitaph Spike Milligan requested for his gravestone)

Following the Sheffield result we're almost in need of an epitaph here. We feel desperately ill and right now, the prognosis ain't good. We feel bushed, beat, down, battered and on our knees. But we're still in Division One for a fourth consecutive year. There is only the one futile game with the homeless ones of Wimbledon that remains. The fact that this of all games is the final match is another of those bizarre events of this wacky season and it is a fixture bordering on the meaningless except it would be nice to regain just a little pride and dignity after the humiliation of last Saturday. There's a definite melancholy to this one. This is no way to say goodbye to the season, at a ground which might be lucky to see 500 spectators with a club chaired by a man who wants to upstick them to Milton Dreadful. We'd like to say a farewell to our team, if not at our home ground, then at least at a proper football home. In one way, and only one, is it a shame that this game is not at Milton Concrete. At least it would have had a novelty value and we could all have seen what a horrible place it is.

Friday, May 2

One bright spot is the Reserves winning their final game 5-2 at Tranmere. A strong team mastered the mud and Blake was again magical. No relegation then. Well done Jeppo. Claretsmad Tony Scholes ended his report with:

> *And so the curtain came down on the end of a remarkable season for the reserves. At the turn of the year they looked doomed. But five wins in the last nine games have seen them come back in style. Mixed emotions greeted the final whistle as the players trooped off in the rain. Relief at survival and pleasure at witnessing a fine display, including a virtuoso performance from Robbie Blake; but sadness too as I've no doubt seen the last of Steve Davis, Marlon Beresford, Nik Michopoulos and Gordon Armstrong wearing the famous Claret and Blue. Also Andrew Waine, Andrew Leeson and Mark Rasmussen, all stalwarts of the youth and reserve teams. Whatever the current situation, all have served Burnley Football Club well and should go with our thanks and very best wishes. The sight of the sodden and mud spattered Steve Davis leaving the field with head bowed, receiving a firm handshake from Ronnie Jepson, will endure for a long, long time indeed...*

If we look back over the season what is there to be said that we have not said before. We can talk about the highs, the lows, the problems and the search not for champagne but for survival. We can mention the bad start of four defeats in August, the rumours of player unrest because of proposed wage and bonus restructuring. And then of course there is ITV Digital. I shall be accused no doubt of being one of those who bring up this subject yet again ad nauseum, but in truth it will not go away. It is a historical fact and history does not go away. It will be written about ten years from now. It created the whole tone of the season, it defined the objectives, it resulted in policy decisions, which the club would not otherwise have made, and it handcuffed Stan Ternent so that all plans to bring in new players were abandoned. The manager knew who he wanted to bring in and one of them was certainly David Johnson. Stan Ternent and Sam Ellis took wage reductions at the beginning of the season to ease the financial problems yet still the club sometime before October was only days away from administration.

Years from now, when the next of the definitive histories of the club is written, ITV Digital and its effect on this season will have a chapter of its own. This was never going to be a season of aiming for promotion and ITV Digital is the cause of that. We may be sick of hearing it but this single fact should not be forgotten. After August there was a flurry of good results and a run of unbeaten games and the bank of points accumulated during that period saved our Division One life. It was never going to be a platform for play-off success. Our stretched, depleted, and sometimes ravaged squad was simply not strong enough.

In any season that lasts from August to May there will undoubtedly be events that stick in the mind, there will be those games that can be seen as peaks, and there will be those games or even single events during a game that can be seen as turning points. These are the moments that change or make a season, from good to bad or from bad to good. The ball given away at Bradford in the final minute which lost us two points, the two goals given away at Brighton in the final minutes that lost us two points, referee's decisions at Millwall and Crystal Palace that each lost us two points. And then there was the Watford Cup game on that dreadful weekend when all our hopes and dreams were dashed.

On the other hand there were the great days at Derby in September, which brought a first win, the Boxing Day win against Wolves, the fabulous Tottenham game, the Fulham games and though we lost, the marvellous game against Man U. There were other memorable moments and excellent wins, Brentford, Norwich, Nottingham Forest and Preston. Then there were the games we lost undeservedly, especially those in April at Carrow Road, Fratton Park and The City Ground, but where we regained pride and optimism for the new season to come.

But March was the disaster. The month that could have been glorious turned into a month of utter dismay. If there have been defining moments then on the Claretsmad messageboard Babylon cited Watford as a key turning point, but prior to that conceding the goal at Millwall deprived Burnley of a fifth straight win and the boost of seventh place. ClaretTony says he knew it was all over when that first goal went in at Watford. Babylon adds the suggestion that deciding to share the winnings from this game gave out the wrong signals to the players. Claretrant suggests however that there is no such thing as any one turning point and that this season has hinged on player shortages and older players running out of legs and that it is the bigger, better squads that win out at the end of the day. LutonClaret lists Derby as a wonderful display, but then lists Grimsby away, Rotherham home and then Watford in the cup as the low points. Whooshy cites Watford and then Sheffield United after that. ClaretandTrue mentions Watford in the Cup and the inclusion of an unfit Steve Davis; Burnleybabe who has followed Burnley for thirty-five years, points to Watford in the cup and then followed by Sheffield United, two dreams gone in two matches. Claret59 too looks at the Watford cup game but argues that it was because whilst Watford rested their key players in the previous game, we didn't. ScouseClaret points to the whole month of March; 'March was an absolute nightmare, the worst month I can remember in my Burnley supporting history' - not just because we lost but because it ended any hopes of financial windfalls and increased season ticket sales and resulted in the off-loading of Glen Little. It was the beginning of a downward spiral both results-wise and financially, the latter with knock on effects for next season in terms of lost season ticket sales.

Who would have wanted to follow the Watford game with an away game at Sheffield? What worse game could there have been? The gods are cruel; they toy with us for their amusement. The droop in player's shoulders and their whole body language told its own story that night as they stepped out into that dreadful Star Wars cacophony. They may not care to admit it but you sensed they were beaten before they walked onto the field. And then Walsall, just days later, was even worse. For me, Watford left its legacy for weeks if not months. Financially it has left its mark not for months, but maybe years.

We grumble, we complain, we moan, but yet we soldier on dedicated to the Burnley cause. Do management, the administrators, the Board, the decision makers, really, really have any deep insight into the psyche of the football fan, or comprehend the magnitude of the loyalty, attachment and allegiance of the club supporters? Burnley Football Club is an entity; it is an extension of the town itself. Burnley FC is not just any one squad of players, or the people who manage them, during any one particular period. Players come and go, managers come and go, chairmen and directors come and go. The only thing that remains continuous and constant is supporter allegiance passed on from generation to generation. The club is part of the town. Our faithfulness may be tested to the extreme but it remains. Burnley FC is a notion, a concept, a history and an ideal that we follow. It is the bricks and mortar of Turf Moor. Of all the names of all the grounds in all the land, it is one of the best and most evocative of all.

It is dedication and devotion that takes people to Portsmouth, a seven-hour coach journey to a game we know we will lose, but still we go. Dedication is people like ClaretTony who will travel as far as Spurs or Cardiff for a youth team game or get the bus to Gawthorpe in the pouring rain. People like him braved the bad years of the '80s and the defeat at Crewe, before the final Orient game. Ask him any Burnley question and he will tell you the answer.

Dedication is the lad who lay in the boot of the supporter's coach on the way to Rotherham holding on to the accelerator cable so that the coach could lurch on and complete the journey. Dedication is Slats in South Australia who gets up at 1.30am in the morning to listen to an afternoon game or 4.15am to listen to an evening game. It is shinning up the pergola in a monsoon in the middle of the night with a torch in his mouth to re connect the wrecked phone line so that he could continue to listen to the win at Sheffield. While getting drenched and risking life and limb then he discovers he has missed two of the goals.

Devotion is SussexClaret making 600 mile round trips to visit exotic Grimsby or flying home a day early from New York to get to the Stoke game. He has been to sixty different grounds from his Sussex base.

It is Billyham and his mate painting his mate's mother's Fiat claret and blue while she was away on holiday for the Wembley game against Stockport.

Southwest Clarets begin their day at 8am for a game at Turf Moor and don't get back till after 10am and that's on a good day. London Clarets make the same sacrifices making journeys from all of the Home Counties.

BigKevClarke changed his holiday in Amsterdam so that he wouldn't miss a game, and for good measure once in Amsterdam abandoned his girlfriend for the afternoon to check up on the news of Ian Wright's signing. Before that he checked himself out of hospital just one day after his appendix operation so he could see Gazza's debut.

ClaretandTrue proclaimed his devotion to the ugliest girl in Burnley he says, so that he could cadge lifts in her brother's van. GBP discharged himself from hospital with the bone sticking out of a broken arm in agony as it rubbed against the cast, so that he could get to a game at Sheffield - which we lost of course. GBP's arm now has a metal plate.

Benbfc regularly made 500 mile round trips to Burnley. Ballbag was on a coach journey to Bristol that broke down at Worcester. What do you do? You spend a fortune and continue the journey by taxi. Burnleybabe got to the next game just a week after a hysterectomy.

For Claretextile devotion is finding where Billy Hamilton lives in Bangor whilst on a trip and seeking him out. Nobody comes to see me from QPR or Oxford, Billy told the motley crew who turned up on his doorstep. MJMClaret's wife Nicola went to matches in the first half of the Waddle season with her broken leg in a pot from foot to thigh. Bfcfan1881 has missed only three games this season and once spent £100 on an Easyjet flight only to find the game at Watford some time ago was postponed. He has his 510 programmes going back to 1958 logged perfectly.

Then there's the 161 Clarets who went to the night game at Millwall, returned at 3.30 in the morning, grabbed four hours sleep and then went to work. RossyClaret used his student overdraft not to study but to follow Burnley for a season, not missing one single game. He's done 68 different grounds following them, got married on a Friday so as not to miss the opening game of the season, called his first dog Kindon, and today his kids' goldfish are called Sam and Stan.

CJL some years ago drove up from Maidenhead to see the Port Vale game - the one that was abandoned in the monsoon. ClaretTony remembers giving the Chelsea Chairman an earbashing when a Chelsea game was abandoned - the Chairman was Sir Richard Attenborough.

W-white cancelled a weekend in Paris so he could watch the Watford Cup game. The weekend was to celebrate his seventh anniversary. He sweetened the news by taking the Mrs out for a curry. LeedsClaret was in Southampton with friends for the Portsmouth game one year. He sacrificed a night of rampant passion with a newly-met stunning bird so he wouldn't risk missing the game next day.

And how's this for cool from 'ballbag':

I was heading south on the M1 driving to the FA Cup game in at Derby in 1999 when my wife rings to tell me she has gone into labour. I managed to convince her there was no rush, continued to the game, took in the superb performance and celebrations. Dashed back up the M1, arrived Burnley General 8.30, wife gives birth at 9pm. Just in time to watch Match Of The Day at 10.30.

Now that, my friends, is style.

And then there's Dave Burnley with his daughter Clarette. Dave has not missed a first team game for thirty years or a Saturday game for thirty-five. He doesn't even live in Burnley but miles away near Keele. He used to cycle to Burnley. Now he only works if it fits in with Burnley games. He once carried a nun's case for three miles hoping for a blessing to help Burnley avoid relegation. And if I remember rightly he was featured in a Sunday supplement years ago.

Is such devotion and commitment selfless, or mindless, or is it noble and altruistic? There are elements of stubbornness, even masochism and certainly blind, unadulterated, unthinking loyalty. Whatever it is, there are countless examples of the sacrifices that people make, the money they spend, and the efforts they go to for Burnley Football Club. The one fundamental thing is the camaraderie, the helpfulness, togetherness and the common identity, which binds any collection of supporters, large or small, into one single group. You have to be there to feel it and to understand it. Going to away games for the first time in years it is something I have learned this season.

What we earnestly hope is that the growing business oriented, commercial, corporateness of modern football doesn't entirely destroy what we can only describe as the Burnleyness of Burnley.

****

The Friday before WimbledonFranchise I managed to speak to Andrew Watson who outlined his thoughts on the season. His office is on the floor above the club shop. From the tiny cramped reception area on the ground floor, a dark narrow stairway, where two people would find it impossible to pass, leads up to a larger wider landing with rooms and offices on all sides. The media and programme boys are in a room immediately at the top of the stairs and sit surrounded by computers and printers producing the award winning matchday programme. Creativity and energy hits you when you walk in. It's full of the heaps of working organised chaos that only a hectic office can produce, half-eaten sandwiches, programmes, shirts, paperwork, and a box of pies when I went in one day. Kept casually in a bottom drawer is a file of this season's photographs taken by Phill Heywood. It's a stunning collection. Next to the media room is another moderately sized room that serves as a mini boardroom filled with a huge polished table and chairs. On the walls are Burnley pictures, photographs and memorabilia. Much of the life history, documents and material of BFC was lost, given away, or just thrown away when the Bob Lord Stand was built and the old buildings demolished. Where is it now? Priceless material gone forever.

Beyond this, around the landing area, are all the other offices. In one of them Stan is meeting people. I've no idea who. Andrew Watson's office is neat, tidy, organised, the desk free of clutter. Pictures of his family fill another tabletop. It's unpretentious up here. There's none of the Marble Halls of Highbury.

His day usually begins with the forty-minute drive across from Huddersfield where he lives with his wife and two daughters. His father was Chief Sports Photographer for the

Huddersfield Examiner for forty-nine years. For three seasons Andrew Watson played for Huddersfield Town but never got beyond the reserves. At that time the manager was Mick Buxton and his assistant was Jimmy Robson both ex-Burnley players, the latter now back here at Burnley. From Huddersfield he went to Exeter City and played fifty games for them over two years, seasons 86/87 and then 87/88. Yes, you read it right, 86/87, our Orient Season, the season Burnley nearly died. At Exeter we lost 3-0, here we scraped a 0-0 draw. It's a bizarre surprise to learn that the Chief Executive, who now works to keep us solvent, was once instrumental in the club's near demise. Life works in mysterious ways. The following season we beat them twice. At Exeter however he realised that the bigtime would not be beckoning him and he turned down the chance to join Wrexham preferring to leave football and start a business studies course. Steve Kindon, commercial manager at Huddersfield at the time, with whom he is a still great friend, was his mentor giving him encouragement and support. His only worry now he says is that he will be called upon to play next season if Stan hasn't enough players. There is no record of the look on Jimmy Robson's face when Andrew Watson walked through the door on his first morning as Chief Executive.

A typical day if there is such a thing revolves round departmental meetings; endless phone calls, meeting people, and the 101 things and decisions involved in running a football club. He is a Director of the English Sports Association for People with Learning Difficulties, Chairman of the Burnley Community Scheme, and is a Director of Burnley College. He has served on different Football League panels and committees; last week in Leicester, this week in Newcastle, the job is endless.

"I've been here at Burnley four years now," he said, "and before that I was commercial manager at Everton for four years, preceded by four years at Leeds Rugby League Club again for four years. My brief when I arrived in 1999 quite simply was to maximise revenue, reflect on the club's history, provide a superb community department for the good of the town and to open communication with supporters. I'd like to think we have made a difference here and though it's sometimes difficult for supporters to think of a football club as a business, these days that's what it is. If people look back to 1997/98 I think they will accept that most things have changed for the better and we have achieved the objectives I have set out. Certainly when I came here supporters were saying that they wanted those things. I still have lists of suggestions from supporters attending meetings and suggestions made in letters and verbally. Supporters wanted to see a shop in town, a credit card, lotteries, a good website and matchday programme. Now the criticism is that we are too commercial. Our answer is, if you don't want to join the commercial activities, simply say no, there is nothing more to it. 11,000 Burnley supporters want to buy a shirt, 1,000 want a credit card, there are 2,300 in the Clarets Foundation and 9,000 in the Claret and Blue Bond. Unfortunately it's hardheaded business decisions that fund the emotional football side of things. The money that comes into the club through the turnstiles only partly funds the club and for that reason we have to have all the other ongoing commercial ventures of which we are accused of having too many. The survival of this club depends on them and on us thinking what to do next. All of us here are conscious of the feelings amongst some fans that we see them as a bottomless well of money but in all honesty that is not the truth. We literally wrack our brains, particularly in the Commercial section to find ways to raise money other than making yet more demands on supporters. We appreciate too that supporters can only spend what they can afford. The person who can only attend the game and spend maybe £2.50 on a programme is just as important as the businessman who sponsors the matchball or the man of the match award and we are certainly conscious of the amounts of money people spend for example to travel to Ipswich or Portsmouth."

I mentioned to him that whilst most people reluctantly agree that season ticket prices must rise, there are grumbles and certainly one of them is the early cut-off date for discounted season tickets. It comes up repeatedly on messageboards and in conversations.

"What we want here," he replied, "is to provide a winning football team. We want to provide the funds to enable the manager to attract the players he wants and to give him an approximate budget as early as possible. It's for that reason that there is the early cut off date. The manager needs his budget to know roughly what kind of salary he can offer. He can't do this without some indication of what money he has to play around with. You cannot achieve this by having a cut-off period in June, players will have gone elsewhere by then."

"Did the club receive any financial support or help from the FA this season? There were reports that all clubs would get financial packages but were they ever actually received?"

"We lost almost £5million of TV revenue over two years and have received £300,000 so far, but a large chunk of it is a loan and therefore has to be paid back."

"So has Stan Ternent already made approaches to certain players he'd like to bring in?"

"That is for the Gaffer to answer, we have a great relationship with the Boss and we leave him to run his department which he has done extraordinarily well, particularly as he came here after the club had had almost three decades of misery."

"Is there a new realism here at Turf Moor?" I asked. "Are players aware that the pot of gold is just about empty?"

"Truth is we don't quite know until contract negotiations begin, obviously at some clubs players are aware. In some cases we do pay high wages. If we don't do this we are accused of having no ambition. The club wage bill has doubled in recent years and gone up faster than ticket sales but prices have not doubled. Gate money is down £300,000 on last year. We have stabilised, consolidated and managed to avoid redundancies. The consequences of relegation at places like Sunderland, Grimsby and Sheffield Wednesday are just enormous. None of us want to see that here."

"Is there anything on the horizon that could be a big problem?"

"Yes, there are new proposals that could hit clubs going into administration hard. There could be points deductions, relegation or even expulsion from the league. These aren't worrying they are frightening. This club was on the brink of administration."

"Do you ever feel you have a thankless job then?"

"No, I love it. I'm sometimes accused of being uncaring and unapproachable, that I don't have Claret and Blue blood. I care deeply about what this club does. I rarely miss a match home or away and there is something special about this place. It can be argued that being objective and slightly divorced from the passions of football is a necessary requisite for a Chief Executive. If this club fails financially or administratively the Board carry the can. I don't want it to fail. In all honesty the survival of this club this season both financially and playing wise has been extraordinary."

"How are season ticket sales going?" I asked and mentioned that the timing of the price information and Glen Little's loan couldn't have been more damaging.

"It is looking like by the end of April we will be approaching 8,000 sales by our magnificent supporters and we always have 1,000 purchases in July with that figure expected to be higher this summer. We had 11,500 season holders this last season. As for Glen the furore seems to have died down and it's interesting that his absence, along with others caused by injury, has given Matt O'Neil and Richard Chaplow their chance. They've done so well and got supporters really talking."

"If advance season ticket sales are below what you expect have you set a minimum weekly attendance figure which you must have in order to survive? Would a figure of below 10,000 be disastrous?"

"No we haven't set any figure."

With time running out Andrew Watson added one more thing. "We really do have some first class people working here and they work their socks off to generate income for the club and provide the base from which we can move up."

"Just one more question then?" I asked. "If there was one message you'd like to get across to people what would it be?"

Andrew Watson thought for a minute. "That this club will be back in business next season, I know Stan too well. I wouldn't get off the bus just yet."

I made my decision there and then. If there is a chance of seeing Andrew Watson play at centre half next season, I'm staying for the ride.

****

The game at Wimbledon, or Selhurst Park, marked the final game for Steve Davis. On principle a number of Burnley supporters refused to attend the game and congregated instead on Wimbledon Common with Wimbledon supporters in a show of solidarity to protest against the planned move to Milton Keynes. Koppel is adamant that crowds will turn up at MK in the 9,300 capacity stadium and already 1,000 season tickets have been sold. But a healthy 478 Burnley supporters were part of a crowd of 1,972 at Selhurst, which I must admit is 1,000 more than I thought would be there.

Firmo of London Clarets wrote a long piece about the move, the gist of it being...

There is an important principle at stake here. You can't just 'move' a football club to a completely different town. You can't just take a club away from its supporters, without the consent of those supporters. Imagine if Burnley were 'moved' to Stoke. It makes about as much sense as Wimbledon 'moving' to Milton Keynes. If the 'move' is successful a precedent will have been set. Any unscrupulous businessman could seize on a struggling club, uproot it from its community, and plonk it down in a distant town. Any town looking for a lucrative stadium (plus of course attached shops and leisure development) could buy a ready-made league place. This is what franchising means, and if Milton Keynes succeeds, the concept will have been introduced to English football...

The score for the record and the sake of tidiness was

WIMBLEDON 2 BURNLEY 1

Burnley took the lead with Gareth's eighteenth goal of the season and held it well into the second half but then as ever conceded a sloppy goal. The Wimbledon second was at least the result of class play on their part rather than yet another mess up by us. Steve Davis received a prolonged ovation when he came off. O'Neill by all accounts had a cracking game and Branchie too. And overall this was yet another game that had chances been tucked away could have been a win for us.

It hardly matters now save for one happy ending. On the Claretsmad messageboard Big Kevin Clarke posted a request for help. On the same messageboard the mysterious Morgan is a regular contributor and Morgan, guess what, says he knows big Gareth. Kevin in September will be doing the Great North Run in aid of a charity that supports sufferers of Retts Syndrome. A family friend, Jenna, is seventeen and has suffered all her life. Kev did some internet research and decided to try and raise £500. Can you help me Morgan, says BigKev on the messageboard, and if you really do know him can you ask Gareth for his shirt for me to run in? Now here's a test. Does the mysterious Morgan really exist? Does Morgan really know Gareth? Who is Morgan? Will Kev get his wish? E-mail addresses are exchanged. Sunday comes. And yes. Morgan comes up trumps. Gareth meets Big Kev before the game at Selhurst. And not only does Kev get the prized shirt but also four tickets for the game. Thanks to Morgan and Gareth, Kev now thinks he will raise more than his hoped for £500 target. Magic does exist if you look for it.

For us, the fans, this long, unusual and sometimes shattering season is over at last. We end in sixteenth place with 55 points and surely all of us at the beginning of the season those long months ago would have happily settled for that. Survival.

Stoke City with a 1-0 win today stay up at the expense of Brighton who go down along with Grimsby and Wednesday. At least we are spared the long journey to the South Coast, and Stoke is an easy journey. West Ham won yesterday against Chelsea, with a single goal by Paolo di Canio, returning from a long absence. The script was made for him. He wept with joy. Bolton or West Ham will join us in Division 1 with Sunderland and West Brom. How Leeds got into a position so close to relegation beggars belief but today in a major shock they won at Arsenal leaving Arsene Wenger distraught and Manchester United champions. Not even the most blinkered Leeds fan could have predicted such a 3-2 victory. All we need to know now is who joins Wigan and Crewe coming up from Division Two. Neither of these two will set the cash tills ringing in the away end at Turf Moor.

For the players at Burnley who will not be retained it is now a time of disappointment, anxiety and worry if they have dreams of continuing their careers. We say what seems an inadequate thankyou to all of them. It sounds like Cook and Payton will go to Accrington Stanley. The list of thirteen players released stunned us all a few days ago. Everyone knew that some must go but to see Beresford, Michopoulos, Cox, Davis and Briscoe go, in addition to Cook, Payton and Armstrong whom we knew about on Saturday, staggered us all. Few if any supporters will quarrel with Stan's draconian measures. Neither goalkeeper in recent games has reached anything like their standards of old. On occasions I can well remember they have won us games single-handed. Both at their best were stunning. Cox has been a wonderful player for us with his timing and pace. He has been a rock and in some games unbeatable. This season injuries have set him back and those awful words 'injury-prone' rear their ugly heads. Briscoe too has been a stalwart member of Burnley sides for a long time now; another player who at his best can be excellent, hard working and dependable but maybe his best is gone too. I'll remember his two cracking goals against Walsall two years ago.

And Davis. Steve Davis. What can one say? There is a sadness writing these words about him. In fact what can you write to adequately express his value and worth over the years? He was one of the first players Stan brought back to Burnley. He has been our legend, our skipper, the lynchpin and pivot of Burnley teams for so long. Cool under pressure, skilful, elegant, a giant amongst players, only his lack of pace has kept him from Premiership glory and possibly even an England place. This season we have seen injuries hold him back and play havoc with his ability. The levels that he once attained have faded. Age and a battered body have taken their toll. Time has caught up with him. We want to remember him in his pomp and glory. I looked into his distant eyes in the lounge at Norwich airport and I think I saw then that he knew that his standards were slipping, that his time was nearly up and maybe even that this was his last season at Burnley. I want to remember how he snuffed van Nistelrooy out of the Man U Cup game: not struggling next season as he surely would if he remained. I want to remember that glorious headed goal against Tottenham and his marvellous, wonderful, ecstatic celebration, which surely produced one of sport's great photographs. I think all of us knew in our hearts that Stan should let him go but it is still a hard thing to accept. Farewell Steve, you were a class act, and a prince amongst footballers.

Stan Ternent wants to retain Drissa Diallo and Graham Branch. We shall see later if they wish to stay. The messageboards and websites hum and buzz with rumour and gossip of who is coming in from here or there, of who we want and who we don't. Now it's Coyne from Grimsby to play in goal, now it's three young lads from Man U on long loan, now it's somebody who knows somebody who works at the petrol station down the road where someone fills up with petrol who has heard it's Beckham who might be on his way. Now it's that bloke with the foreign name who's a pal of Drissa.

At the Awards Evening I managed to speak briefly to Stan Ternent. For him, the next few weeks are a time of wheeling, dealing, negotiating and bringing in the players he wants. Some of them he knows now, other names will emerge as clubs release unwanted players. There is rebuilding to do and he knows it. He said so;

> *I have already spoken to quite a few different players but at the moment they are still employed by other clubs, and we won't be taking their wages on now, until they are out of contract. I would prefer to get top quality First Division Players in but whether finances will allow that remains to be seen.*

Everything depends on player's demands when there is only limited money to build a team. That money has to go a long way. He has already spoken to several players he is interested in and says he has irons in the fire. He thinks this last season has been like no other before. Things have happened, crazy games and scores he has never experienced in his time as a manager anywhere. He has never known a season of such incredible contrasts. Sometimes he has been left baffled, just shaking his head. He has been stunned by the manner of some of the defeats, yet incredibly elated at others, especially the Cup games. He has one year remaining on his contract and no one can say whether he will extend it or not. The bad start of August in hindsight he thinks may well have been linked to bonus wranglings and players being made available for sale, lock stock and barrel. He faces huge challenges at a club where the word crisis might not go amiss following the run of results and events since March. Not the least of these is replacing the thirteen non-retained players with precious little money in the pot, and having done that, integrating so many new faces all at once into the Turf Moor scene. He has said quite categorically that the squad last summer needed changing but he wasn't able to do it. David Johnson was certainly on his wanted list. This summer there will be enormous changes with the unexpectedly big turn around of players. He thinks it will be a massive job. The players he brings in will be good players he insists, younger players and there will be a radical restructuring of the club. He still dreams of being a Premiership manager - with Burnley. He'll take a holiday in Portugal and recharge his batteries. Pre-season training will begin in early July. The Isle of Man tournament begins on July 20.

And the cycle begins all over again.

POSTSCRIPT

Eight Seats For The BNP, screamed the *Burnley Express* headline on Friday May 2nd. The night before that, the national spotlight had focussed on the town fiercely as results were announced in the Turf Moor Leisure Centre of all places. And now over to Turf Moor, said TV commentators more than once through the evening. The BNP polled 8,543 votes and took over from the Liberal Democrats as the main opposition to Labour. Nick Griffin, leader of the BNP, declared it would aim to take over Burnley Council in 2004 and was committed to becoming the main party in the town. He claimed it was disillusionment with Burnley Council that had aided the BNP.

Does this have anything to do with football? Does this have a place in a football diary? It does in this one. In no other town is there a council with eight BNP seats. This took place in Burnley and people in many areas outside of the town now associate the name Burnley not just with the Football Club but also with those three letters, BNP. My friend from Ormskirk who occasionally comes to a game rang to say he would no longer come to Turf Moor, he felt so ashamed. I asked him why. Because Burnley is obviously a racist town he answered and I spent a long while telling him it is not and that there are other issues involved. My friend is an educated man. It made me wonder just how many people there are out there who think the same.

A colleague of my wife rang her from his school to ask about it. He knows we are Burnley fans.

"What on earth happened in Burnley?" he asked, expecting us to know. Why should he expect us to know? We have no special knowledge of Burnley the town or Burnley politics. It's because we are Burnley FC supporters, that's why he expected us to know. He saw BNP and in his misguided way immediately thought of Burnley FC.

"And what's the football club doing about it?" he asked, as if it were any fault of a club that endorses anti-racism campaigns and runs active community programmes.

"You support Burnley so why have you voted BNP?," more than one supporter has been asked; the sad assumption being in their minds that the two go together.

'It really is distressing to consider what the rest of the country must think of our town - and therefore our club', wrote Barnsey on the messageboard. And there it is in a nutshell. The town and our club, the two go together, and the association of the BNP vote tarnishes the club, for our club is situated in the BNP capital of the country.

BNP policy is the promotion of an all-white Britain. The BNP vote in Burnley is not unanimously for that. Burnley as a town is not racist. The vote is a call for help in other areas that are easy to recognize. MP Peter Pike has already identified them - secondary education, better care for the elderly, renewing the town's appalling housing position, anti-social behaviour and bad landlords. The vote is a demand that Government Grants and funding are better and more fairly spent. The vote is a statement that the current Labour council is failing in these areas. It puts the question to Peter Pike, if you know what the problems are, why aren't you solving them? The vote isn't saying we are racist, it is saying that you who are in power are inadequate in a range of needs.

It is a fair assumption that some of those who voted BNP will not understand, or if they do they will disregard it, that an all-white Britain is the central plank of their message. More important to them is that the BNP provides an alternative when the Liberal Democrats and Tories are so anonymous and ineffective. A dynamic Lib Dem or even Tory party would have done better. There are claims and accusations that in some areas where BNP did well, the other parties did not even distribute leaflets. And then there is apathy. Only 42% of eligible people voted overall and therein lies the disillusionment that Nick Griffin talks about, as well as disinterest. There is complacency among the main parties themselves, certainly Labour, who think they have safe seats and don't need to canvass. They have been taught a lesson. It is for them to sit up and take notice.

I'm forty miles away and make no judgements. I can't. But I read through twenty pages of the Claretsmad messageboard with over eighty comments and views. They talk of the economic decline of the area, the lack of opportunity to make progress within the current political framework, and the national perception of Burnley. They talk of the BNP votes being the result of fed-up people wanting to be heard, that it's not a racist vote but a huge dollop of protest against general problems. There are arguments about how money is spent in Burnley. Where is it spent and on what projects? Is it spent in ways the Government says it must be spent, which are sometimes inappropriate, or is it the Council themselves who make inappropriate choices? Is it appropriate to pour money into ethnic areas at the expense of others just as deprived?

One particular contributor who did vote BNP said this:

We all know the reason the BNP are doing so well in Burnley, it's because Labour has let the town decay. Take a good look round any part of the town and you will see what I mean. People have had enough... A lot of us who live here have voted for a change...

There is a comment from someone who did not vote BNP but says:

Basically speaking let the BNP have as many seats as they want, makes a change from that shambles called Labour

'Change' is perhaps the key word. People (and not just those who vote BNP) are fed up of continuing decline. People can change their lives by leaving the town to get better jobs. Many do. That's why you find Clarets all over the country in such huge numbers. But those who stay find work hard to come by. A contributor points out that Burnley jobs where they do exist pay less than a comparable job elsewhere.

The word 'ashamed' appears several times with the retort that it is the politicians who should be ashamed for it is they who have allowed the decline to happen. But it's a decline that began long ago with the demise of the cotton and coalmining industries. The roots of all this go back decades but they can only be solved now with regeneration of housing, job creation and more reliable transport links to places like Manchester and Leeds. It isn't any one council responsible; it's a whole procession of them.

The point is made that a prosperous Burnley might mean a prosperous and better Burnley FC. In the very first pages of this book we said that the decline of the club since the '60s has accompanied the decline of the town. The financial sacrifices that people make to support this club have already been mentioned. Because Burnley is not a wealthy town and has a whole raft of problems, some supporters have to think twice about the number of games they can afford to attend. Attendances are affected. The club's revenue stream diminishes. The point is made that players might think twice about joining a club in a town that has the smear of being racist. Didn't Stan in his book point to one player turning down a move to Burnley after the riots, because his wife felt uncomfortable at the idea? The club currently seeks a shirt sponsor. It may now be harder to find. Who is to say that a company based outside of Burnley wouldn't be wary of any connection with the town?

No link between politics and football? None of us want there to be but what about this from a Leicester website after we beat them 1-0 at Leicester, when there was disgraceful chanting and behaviour from a hard core of Burnley followers:

Some Burnley fans would be more at home at a BNP rally than a football match.

I live in Leeds and see a prosperous, thriving and regenerated city. Wherever you look you see new buildings, conversions, reclamation of derelict land and cranes dominating the skyline. The transformation of South Leeds over the last ten years has been staggering. Of course the city has its bleak areas and no-go districts. What city doesn't these days? But change can be created. If there is good leadership, vision and energy, then work and prosperity can be achieved. Burnley Labour Council and MP Peter Pike have to listen to what the voters and indeed the non-voters said. The electorate who didn't vote have to wake up. It was not the people who did vote that created BNP success, it was just as much the 58% who didn't.

What happened on Thursday was a cry for help from ALL the people of Burnley... we have a town that is dieing around us... backed into a corner the people are desperate for change... Burnley is in dire need of assistance... We are a town in decay...

The messages go on. How can I end? With this one maybe from Slats in Australia:

I've read the whole thread and can't make sense of what's going on.

The politicians, be they local or in Westminster, be they Peter Pike in Burnley or Tony Blair in Downing Street, need to make sense of it... and soon.

****

Season 2002/2003, the strangest for years, sometimes thrilled us, but at other times kept us all shaking our heads, made us apprehensive, frequently had us wondering what would happen next, and after some games left us just open-mouthed.

At this moment in time we have not the faintest idea of what even half our team might be in August. Blake might have gone to Wigan. Taylor might have gone to... Norwich, Wolves, Crystal Palace... who knows? But gone somewhere... Little might or might not be back from Reading... Diallo and Branch have not as yet accepted the terms offered to them... The rest of our heroes and management meanwhile are sunning themselves in Portugal, with a final record of

PLAYED 46 WON 15 DRAWN 10 LOST 21 SCORED 65 AGAINST 89 PTS 55

Just one short of the magic 90. Hard luck lads.

For the record, not one club went out of business this season in spite of doom and gloom and administration... the great British muddle is alive and well and works with superb efficiency.

We did a little Christmas Quiz didn't we? Remember? The answers are:

1. Scarbourgh (Christmas cracker spelling, not mine).
2. Burnley sold Billy Ingham to Bradford City.
3. Freddie Smith was born in West Sleekburn.
4. Colin Harvey was assistant to Adrian Heath after John Ward.
5. Who were the last non-league team to play on Turf Moor in an FA Cup-tie? Accrington v Scunthorpe. Ho ho tricked yer.

This book is finished. The cut-off point is reached. The Wimbledon game has ended and the season is over. Not even if Ronaldo signs for us tomorrow will I open the page again. For me, there's a void to fill until the new season, start a new book maybe, catch up on jobs around the house, paint the garden chairs, the rusty fencing, give that pesky dog a few more walks down to our favourite quiet places where we can watch the herons, kingfishers and foxes. It's looking at me now with begging eyes. Maybe it's time to get out into the sun with him and sit by the canal watching the brightly decorated barges chug their way along on their timeless journey up to Skipton. He can have my full attention now - until that is, the boat leaves for the Isles de Manne ...

REFERENCE MATERIAL

Burnley A Complete Record 1882-1991. Edward Lee and Ray Simpson.
(pub by Breedon Books 1991)

The Clarets Collection 1947/8-1996. Ray Simpson.
(pub by Ray Simpson 1996)

The Pride and Glory. Edward Lee and Phil Walley.
(pub by Burnley FC 2002)

Forever and Ever. The Rock and Roll Years Diary of Burnley FC. Tim Quelch.

My Fight For Football. Bob Lord.
(pub 1963 Stanley Paul)

Right Inside Soccer. Jimmy McIlroy.
(pub Nicholas Kaye Ltd 1960)

One Night At the Palace - A Referee's Story. Alan Wilkie.
(pub by Parrs Wood 2002)

Football Grounds of Britain. Simon Inglis.
(pub by Collins Willow, various editions)

Something To Write Home About.
London Clarets Fanzine.

When The Ball Moves.
Burnley fanzine produced by Martin Barnes.

Don't Call Me Happy. John Hendrie.
(pub by Middlesbrough FC 1997)

The Real McCall. Stuart McCall.
(pub by Mainstream Publishing 1998)

Stan The Man. Stan Ternent and Tony Livesey.
(pub by John Blake 2002)

Left Foot Forward. Garry Nelson.
(pub by Headline 1995)

Left Foot In The Grave. Garry Nelson.
(pub by Collins Willow 1997)

Fathers, Sons and Football. Colin Schindler.
(pub by Headline 2001)

The Glory Game. Hunter Davies.
(pub by Mainstream reissued 2001)

Burnley Were Back. Stephen Cummings.
(pub by Janus 1996)

The Soccer Tribe. Desmond Morris.
(pub by Jonathan Cape 1981)

A Season To Remember. Burnley 1959/60. Bill Evans.
(pub by Tempus 2002)

Up The Clarets. David Wiseman.
(Pub by Robert Hale 1973)

Burnley Football Club 1882 - 1968. Ray Simpson.
(pub by Tempus 1999)

Life Sentence. Mark Hodkinson.
(pub by Parrs Wood Press 2001)

Blue Moon. Mark Hodkinson.
(pub by Mainstream 1999)

AND SPECIAL THANKS to Mrs T who comes to every game, and knows all about Microsoft, PDF Files, which plug goes in which socket, and is always there to rescue me when there is a computer problem.

To Claire
with Best Wishes
Joe Brown

Lots of love
to Claire
Steve [illegible]

To Claire
[illegible] Holland

To Claire
[illegible]

To, Claire
Best Wishes
[illegible]